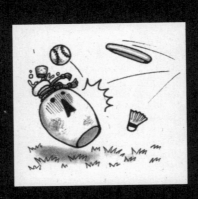

Kazunari Kakei

In order to get more exercise, I took a break from work and walked to the park. But I quit after a short while and proceeded to drink, eat and fall asleep. Old habits die hard. I'll try to get some exercise next time...

NORA: The Last Chronicle of Devildom is Kazunari Kakei's first manga series. It debuted in the April 2004 issue of *Monthly Shonen Jump* and eventually spawned a second series, *SUREBREC: NORA the 2nd*, which premiered in *Monthly Shonen Jump*'s March 2007 issue.

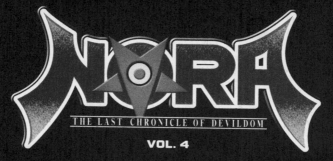

VOL. 4

STORY AND ART BY
KAZUNARI KAKEI

English Adaptation/Park Cooper & Barb Lien-Cooper
Translation/Nori Minami
Touch-up Art & Lettering/Annaliese Christman
Design/Sam Elzway
Editor/Shaenon K. Garrity

Editor in Chief, Books/Alvin Lu
Editor in Chief, Magazines/Marc Weidenbaum
VP, Publishing Licensing/Rika Inouye
VP, Sales & Product Marketing/Gonzalo Ferreyra
VP, Creative/Linda Espinosa
Publisher/Hyoe Narita

Printed in the U.S.A.

Published by VIZ Media, LLC
P.O. Box 77010
San Francisco, CA 94107

10 9 8 7 6 5 4 3 2 1
First printing, April 2009

www.viz.com

www.shonenjump.com

SHONEN JUMP ADVANCED
Manga Edition

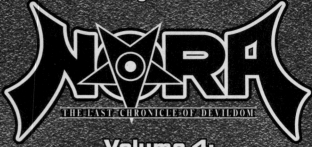

NORA
THE LAST CHRONICLE OF DEVILDOM

Volume 4:
The Truth About Cerberus

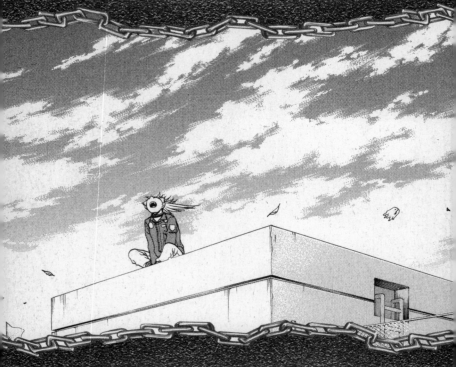

Kazunari Kakei

OUR FIENDIS

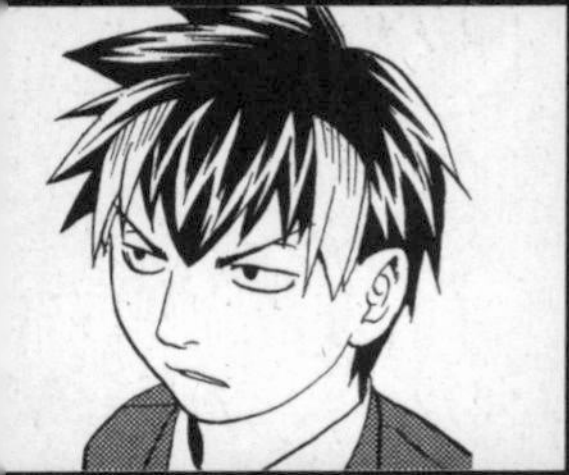

KAZUMA

KAZUMA SEEMS TO HAVE IT ALL. HE'S THE PRESIDENT OF THE STUDENT COUNCIL, AS WELL AS A CLEVER GUY WHO'S GOOD AT SPORTS. HE'S ALSO NORA'S MASTER. DESPITE SEEMING CALM AND COMPOSED, KAZUMA'S GOT QUITE A TEMPER. AS A RESULT, OTHER STUDENTS FEAR HIM. VERDICT: HE'S MORE DEVILISH THAN ANY DEMON.

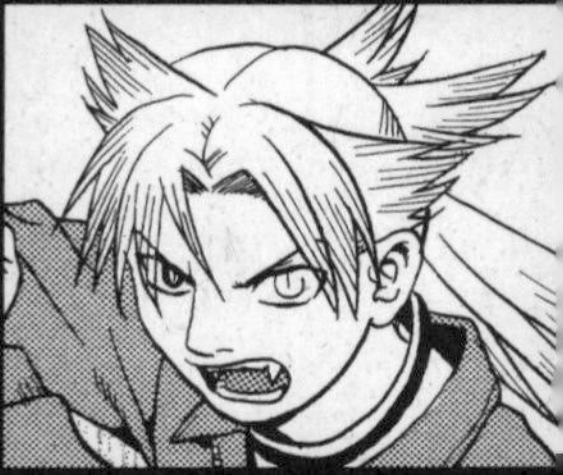

NORA

THE DEMON WORLD'S PROBLEM CHILD, NORA'S FOUL TEMPER IS SURPASSED ONLY BY HIS STUPIDITY NORA IS BETTER KNOWN AS THE VICIOUS DOG OF DISASTER, THE LEGENDARY DEMON CERBERUS. HI POWER IS SAID TO SURPASS THAT OF THE DARK LIEGE HERSELF.

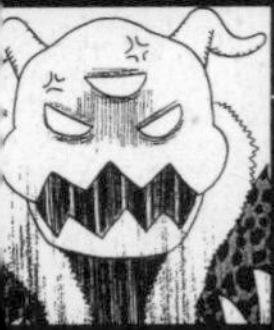

HER INFERNAL MAJESTY, THE DARK LIEGE

THE COMMANDER-IN-CHIEF OF THE DARK LIEGE ARMY, AND THE ONE WHO EXILED NORA TO THE HUMAN WORLD. WHEN SHE WEARS HER GLAMOUR SPELL, SHE'S ONE SMOKIN' HOTTIE.

DARK LIEG

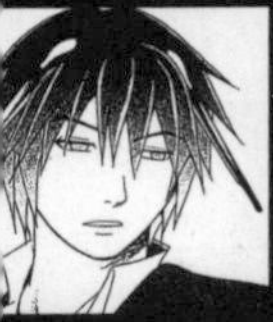

NAVAL FLEET GENERAL

RIVAN

LAID BACK AND SEEMINGLY LAZY, ONCE RIVAN SNAPS, NOBODY CAN HOLD HIM DOWN. HE'S INTO FISHING.

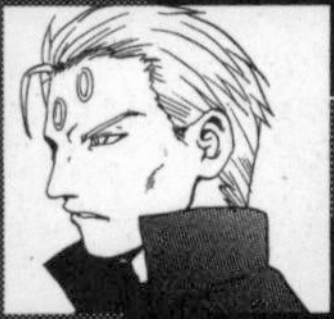

LAND CORPS GENERAL

LEONARD

THE DEMON WORL NUMBER ONE GO- DEDICATED AND S LEONARD IS ALWA WORRYING, LEADIN STRESS-RELATED MALADIES.

TENRYO ACADEMY MIDDLE SCHOOL STUDENT COUNCIL

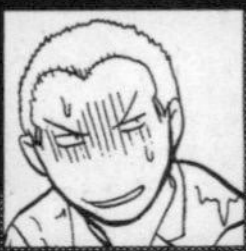

FUJIMOTO

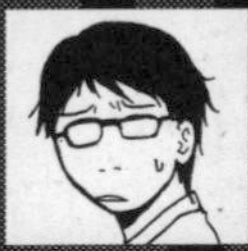

YANO

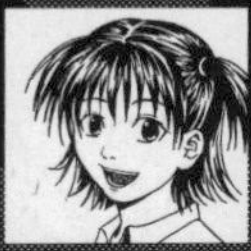

KOYUKI HIRASAKA

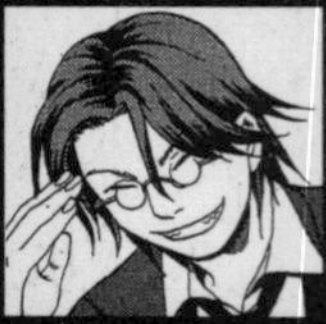

KNELL

A MEMBER OF THE DEMON RESISTANCE WHO MAY HAVE HIS OWN SECRET AGENDA. OR MAYBE HE'D JUST RATHER PICK UP GIRLS. IGUNISU MAGIA HAS NO EFFECT ON HIM—INSTEAD, THE *LADIES* SEEM TO BE HIS WEAKNESS.

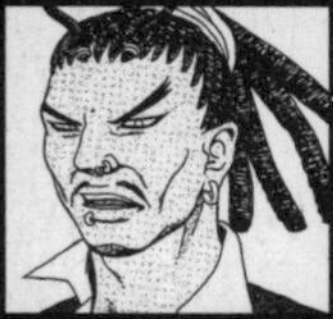

TYRON

A POWERFUL FOE, HE CAN CAUSE EARTHQUAKES AND SLICE THROUGH HIS OPPONENTS' SPELLS WITH A MERE SWORD.

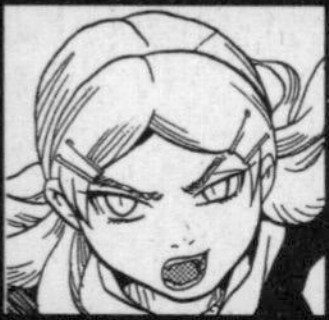

KEINI

ALTHOUGH SHE SELDOM LEAPS INTO THE FRAY, KEINI'S A TERROR WHEN SHE'S MIFFED. SHE ALSO SEEMS TO HAVE A THING FOR HER BOSS.

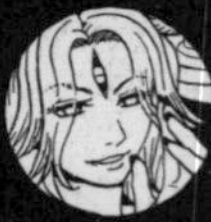

LISTEN TO TEACHER! ♥

THE DARK LIEGE EXPLAINS IT ALL

HELLO, SWEETUMS, DARK LIEGE HERE! MISS ME? ♥

FOR THOSE WHO'VE JUST ARRIVED...GOSH, MY LITTLE DEMON PUP NORA HAS BEEN A BOTHER! DON'T I HAVE ENOUGH TROUBLE WITH THE RESISTANCE AND OUTLAW DEMONS REBELLING AGAINST MY DARK LIEGE ARMY WITHOUT NORA CAUSING ME PROBLEMS?

THAT'S WHY I SENT MY STRAY DOGGIE TO THE HUMAN WORLD, TELLING HIM HE SIMPLY MUST LEARN TO BEHAVE. IF HE ALSO HELPS BY BATTLING THE OUTLAW DEMONS THAT HAVE TRESPASSED INTO THE HUMAN WORLD, SO MUCH THE BETTER. ♥

OH, I'M SO WICKED! THE HUMAN I CHOSE TO HOUSEBREAK MY LITTLE CUR IS KAZUMA MAGARI.

BY ENTERING INTO A MASTER AND SERVANT CONTRACT WITH KAZUMA, NORA BECAME KAZUMA'S "FAMILIAR SPIRIT." AS SUCH, NORA CAN'T USE HIS MAGIC OR RELEASE HIS SEAL SPELL TO RETURN TO HIS DEMON DOG FORM WITHOUT HIS NEW MASTER'S "APPROVAL."

THOSE TWO ALWAYS SEEM TO BE SNARLING AT EACH OTHER. BUT THAT OH-SO-HOT TENSION MAKES NORA'S MAGIC STRONGER. AREN'T I *CLEVER?* SEE, I'M MORE THAN JUST A PRETTY FACE. ♥

BUT I MADE ONE LITTLE BOO-BOO. I HID FRAGMENTS OF MY SOUL, DISGUISED AS JEWELS, IN THE HUMAN WORLD FOR SAFEKEEPING. NOW THE RESISTANCE IS AFTER THEM! WHAT'S MORE, NORA IS LOOKING FOR THEM TOO SO HE CAN FORCE ME TO BREAK HIS CONTRACT WITH KAZUMA!! OOPS! ENOUGH EXPOSITION! I'M LATE FOR MY SPA TREATMENT!

NORA

THE LAST CHRONICLE OF DEVILDOM

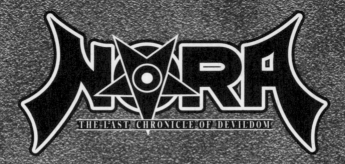

CONTENTS

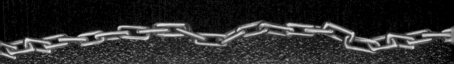

Volume 4: The Truth About Cerberus

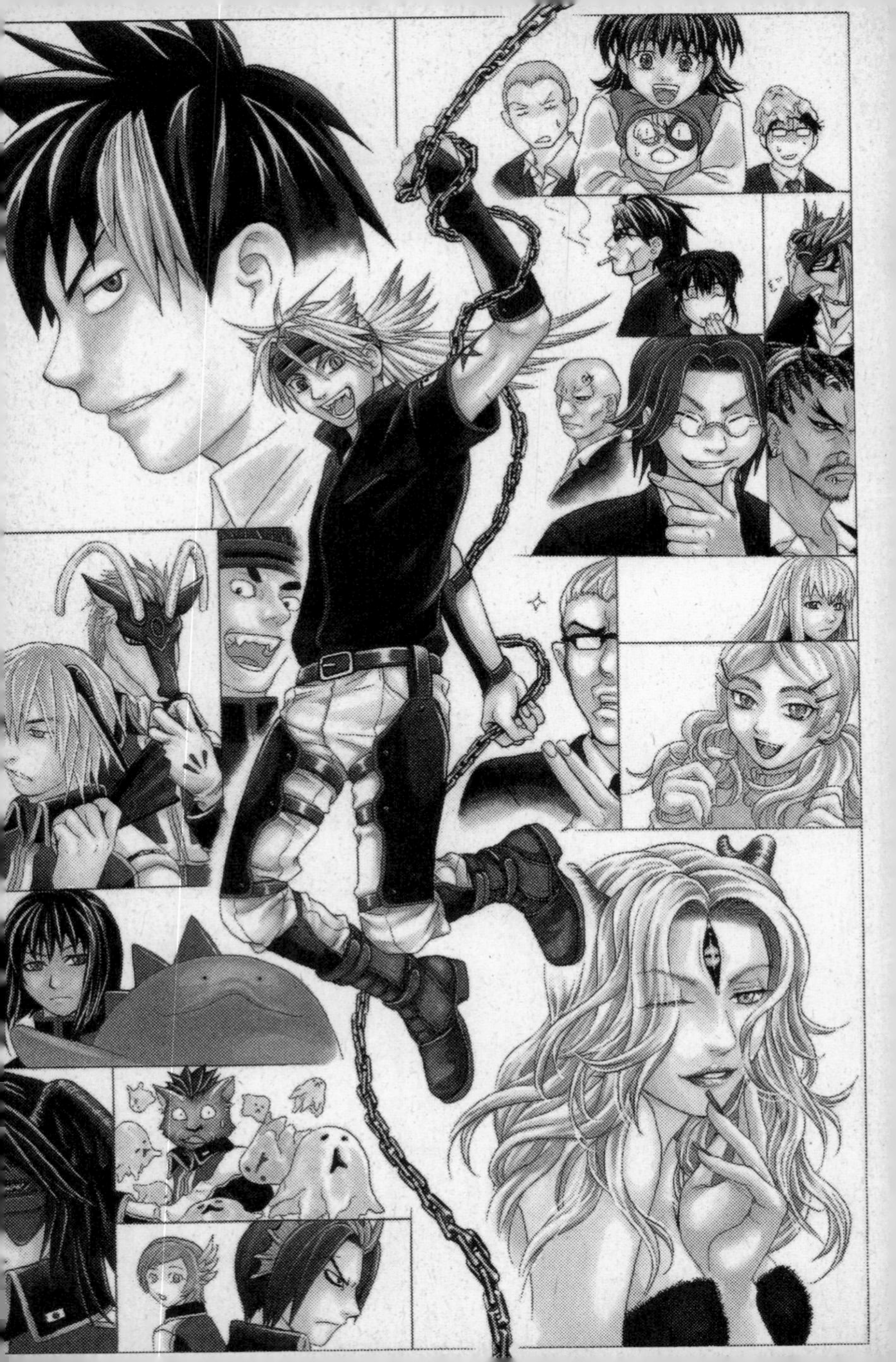

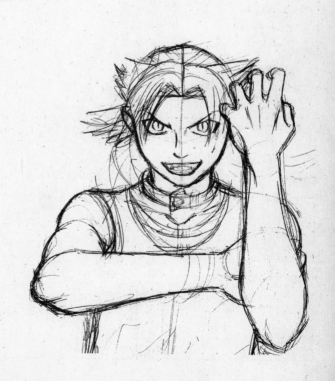

Story 13: Face to Face

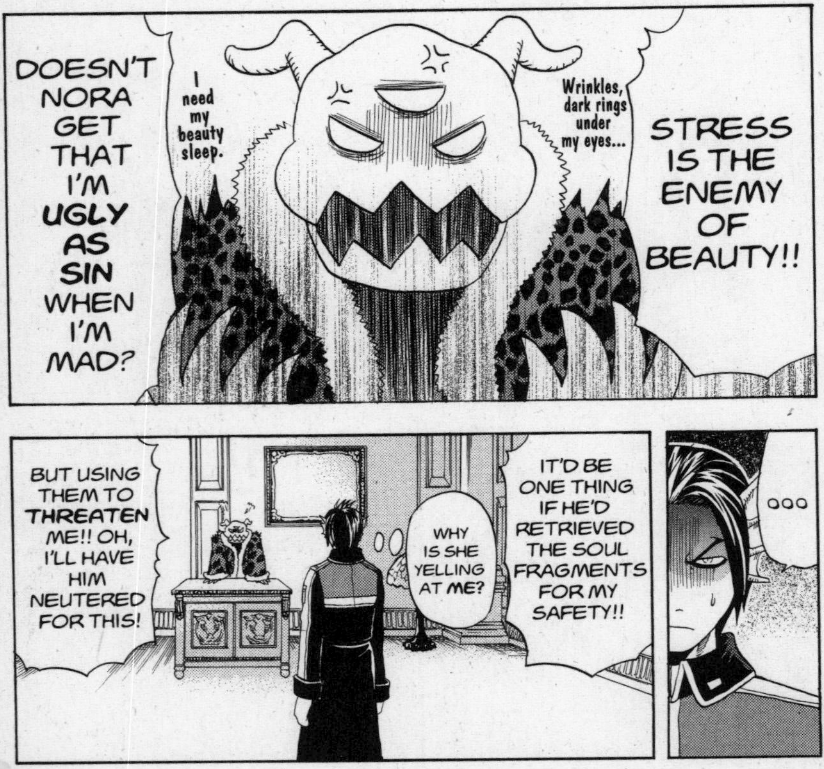
STRESS IS THE ENEMY OF BEAUTY!!
Wrinkles, dark rings under my eyes...
I need my beauty sleep.
DOESN'T NORA GET THAT I'M UGLY AS SIN WHEN I'M MAD?
ooo
IT'D BE ONE THING IF HE'D RETRIEVED THE SOUL FRAGMENTS FOR MY SAFETY!!
WHY IS SHE YELLING AT ME?
BUT USING THEM TO THREATEN ME!! OH, I'LL HAVE HIM NEUTERED FOR THIS!

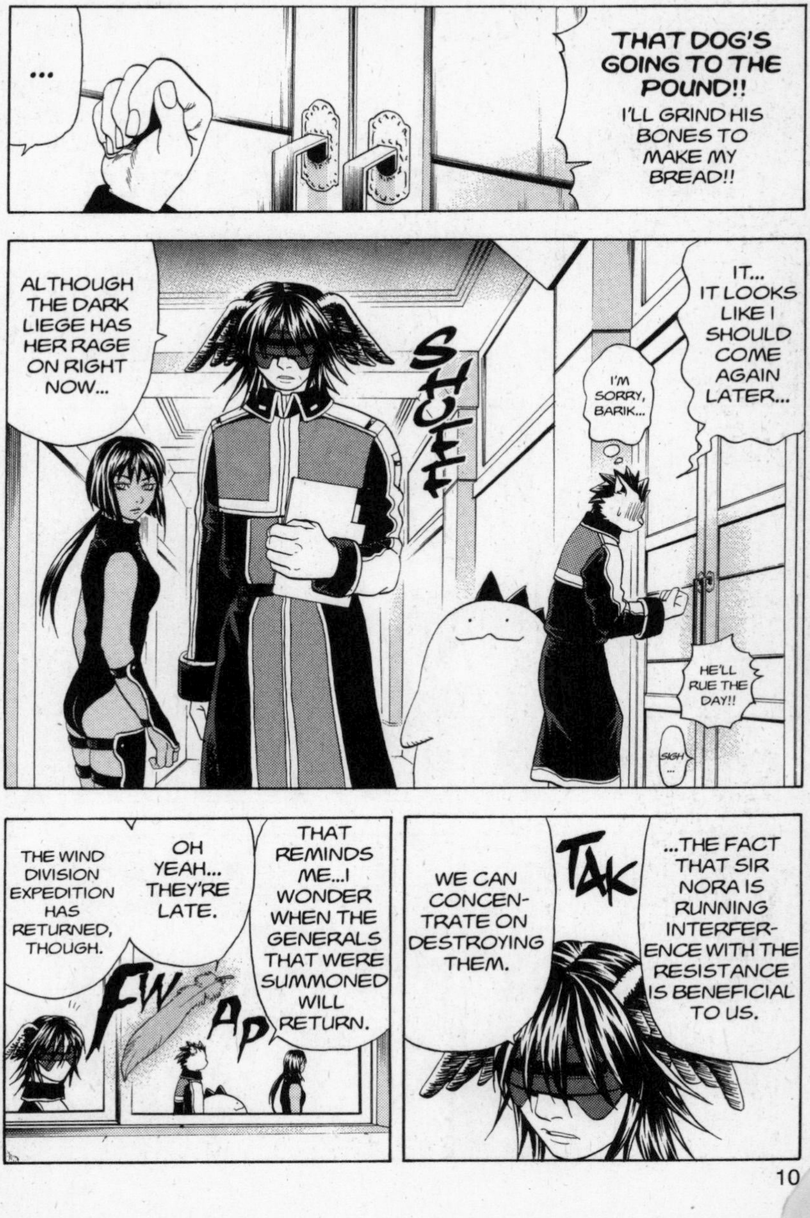
THAT DOG'S GOING TO THE POUND!!
I'LL GRIND HIS BONES TO MAKE MY BREAD!!
...
IT... IT LOOKS LIKE I SHOULD COME AGAIN LATER...
I'M SORRY, BARIK...
SHOFF
HE'LL RUE THE DAY!!
SIGH...
ALTHOUGH THE DARK LIEGE HAS HER RAGE ON RIGHT NOW...
...THE FACT THAT SIR NORA IS RUNNING INTERFERENCE WITH THE RESISTANCE IS BENEFICIAL TO US.
TAK
WE CAN CONCENTRATE ON DESTROYING THEM.
THAT REMINDS ME...I WONDER WHEN THE GENERALS THAT WERE SUMMONED WILL RETURN.
OH YEAH... THEY'RE LATE.
THE WIND DIVISION EXPEDITION HAS RETURNED, THOUGH.
FWAP

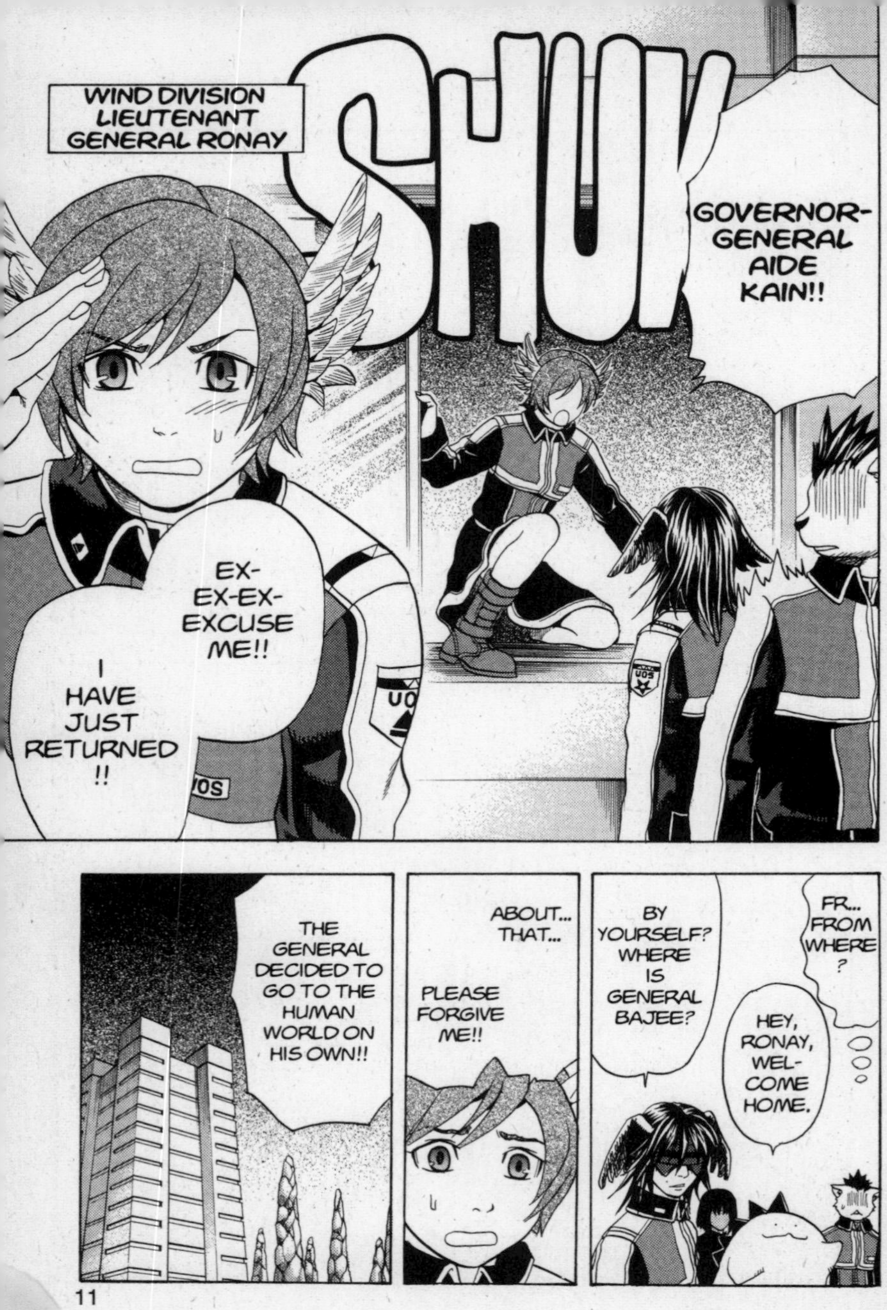

SHUK
GOVERNOR-GENERAL AIDE KAIN!!
WIND DIVISION LIEUTENANT GENERAL RONAY
EX-EX-EX-EXCUSE ME!!
I HAVE JUST RETURNED!!
FR... FROM WHERE?
HEY, RONAY, WEL-COME HOME.
BY YOURSELF? WHERE IS GENERAL BAJEE?
ABOUT... THAT...
PLEASE FORGIVE ME!!
THE GENERAL DECIDED TO GO TO THE HUMAN WORLD ON HIS OWN!!

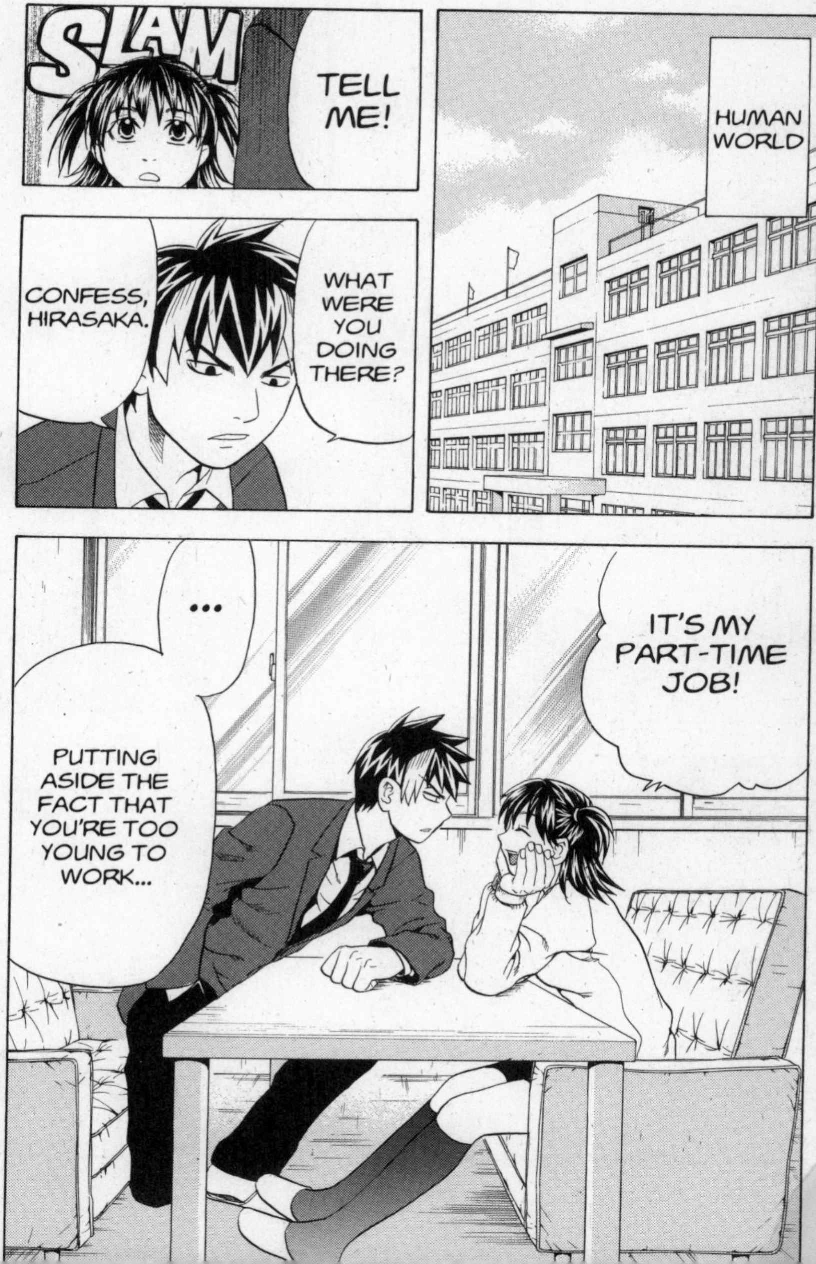
HUMAN WORLD
SLAM
TELL ME!
WHAT WERE YOU DOING THERE?
CONFESS, HIRASAKA.
IT'S MY PART-TIME JOB!
...
PUTTING ASIDE THE FACT THAT YOU'RE TOO YOUNG TO WORK...

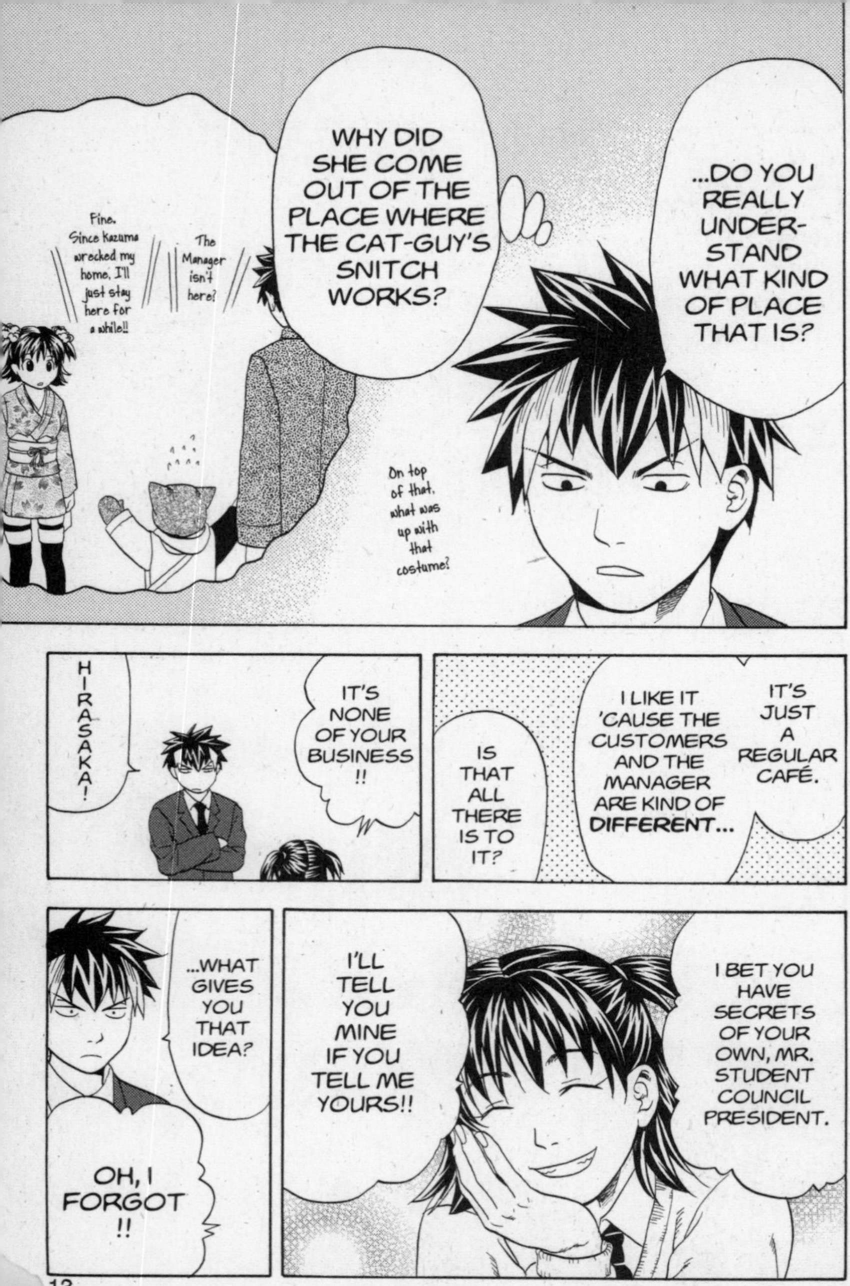
...DO YOU REALLY UNDER-STAND WHAT KIND OF PLACE THAT IS?
WHY DID SHE COME OUT OF THE PLACE WHERE THE CAT-GUY'S SNITCH WORKS?
The Manager isn't here?
Fine. Since Kazuma wrecked my home, I'll just stay here for a while!!
On top of that, what was up with that costume?
IT'S JUST A REGULAR CAFÉ.
I LIKE IT 'CAUSE THE CUSTOMERS AND THE MANAGER ARE KIND OF **DIFFERENT...**
IS THAT ALL THERE IS TO IT?
IT'S NONE OF YOUR BUSINESS!!
HIRASAKA!
I BET YOU HAVE SECRETS OF YOUR OWN, MR. STUDENT COUNCIL PRESIDENT.
I'LL TELL YOU MINE IF YOU TELL ME YOURS!!
...WHAT GIVES YOU THAT IDEA?
OH, I FORGOT!!

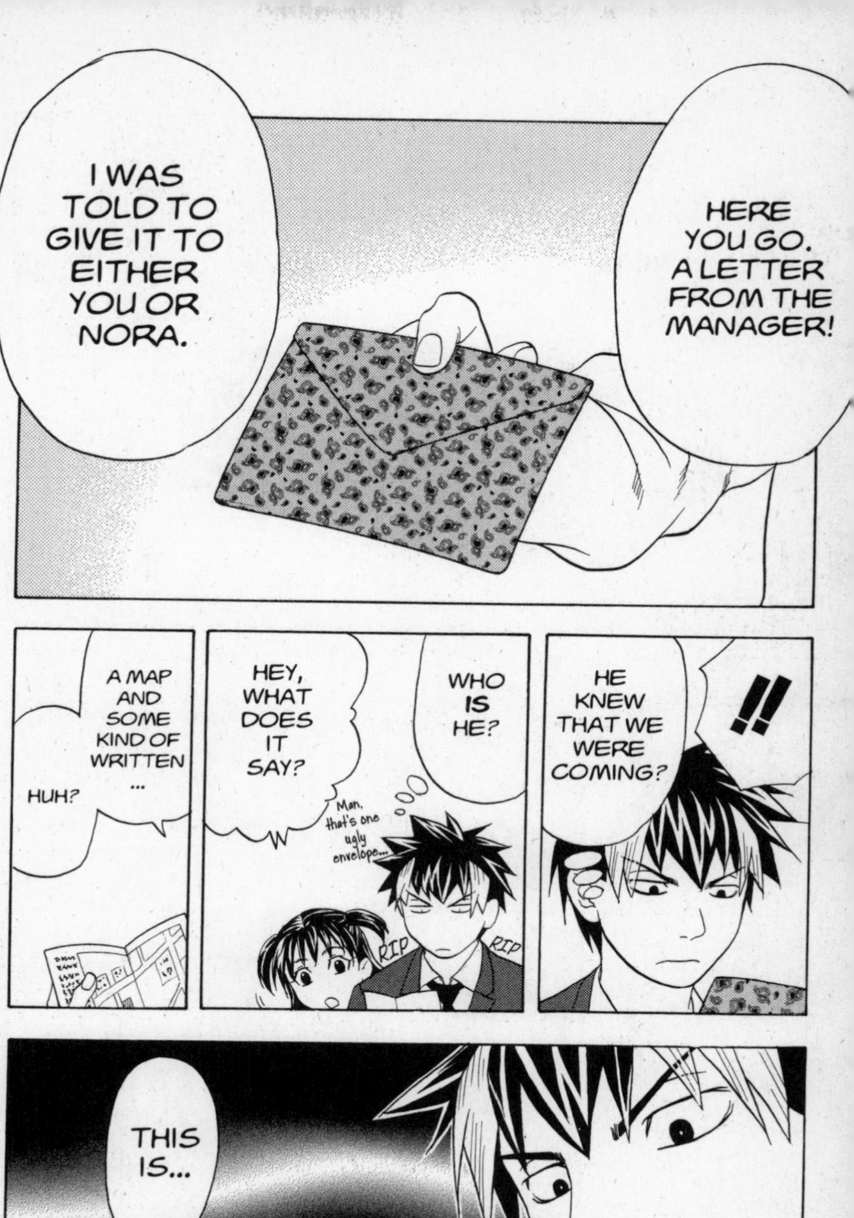
HERE YOU GO. A LETTER FROM THE MANAGER!
I WAS TOLD TO GIVE IT TO EITHER YOU OR NORA.
!!
HE KNEW THAT WE WERE COMING?
WHO IS HE?
HEY, WHAT DOES IT SAY?
Man, that's one ugly envelope...
RIP
RIP
A MAP AND SOME KIND OF WRITTEN ...
HUH?
THIS IS...

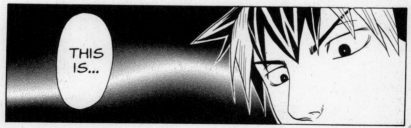

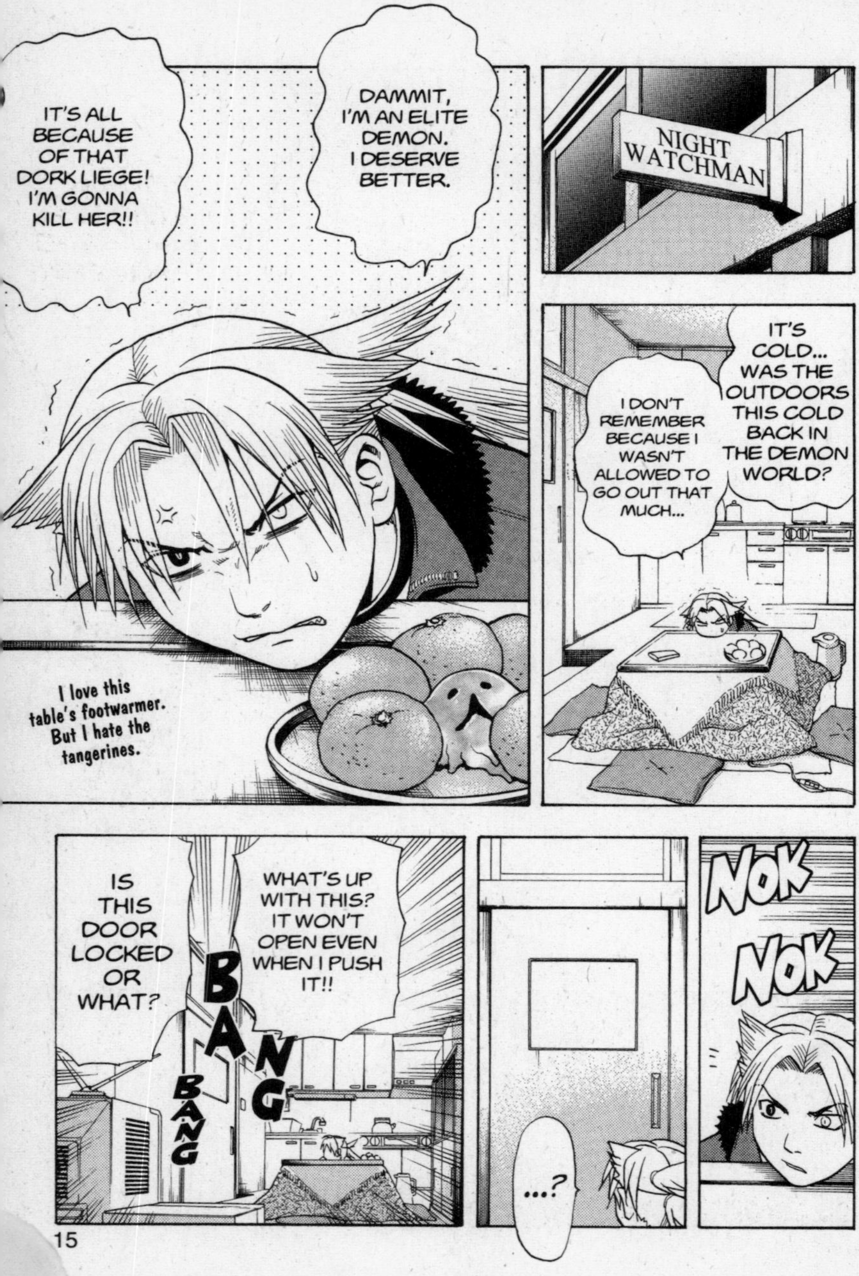
NIGHT WATCHMAN
IT'S COLD... WAS THE OUTDOORS THIS COLD BACK IN THE DEMON WORLD?
I DON'T REMEMBER BECAUSE I WASN'T ALLOWED TO GO OUT THAT MUCH...
DAMMIT, I'M AN ELITE DEMON. I DESERVE BETTER.
IT'S ALL BECAUSE OF THAT DORK LIEGE! I'M GONNA KILL HER!!
I love this table's footwarmer. But I hate the tangerines.
NOK
NOK
...?
WHAT'S UP WITH THIS? IT WON'T OPEN EVEN WHEN I PUSH IT!!
IS THIS DOOR LOCKED OR WHAT?
BANG
BANG
BANG

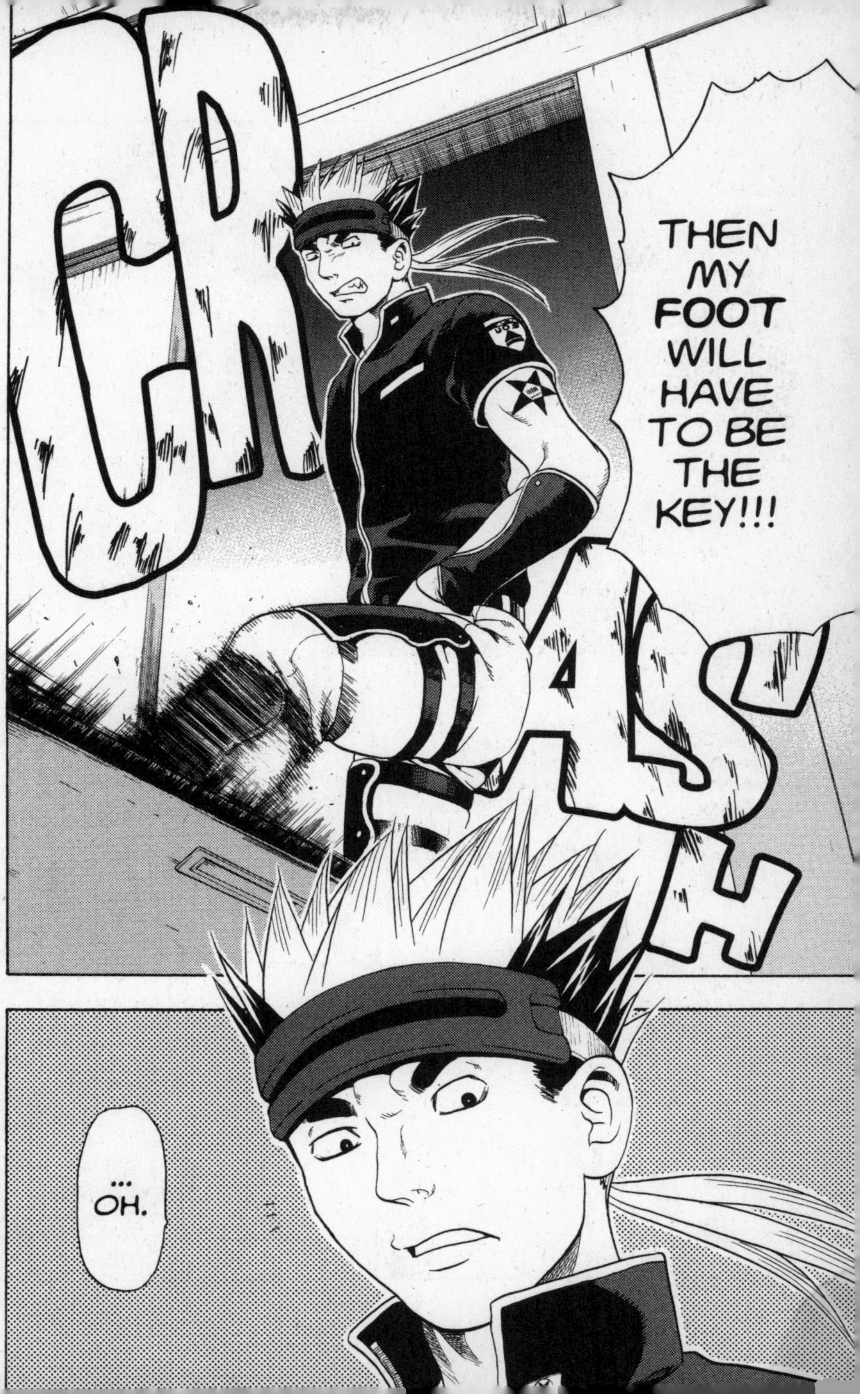
THEN MY FOOT WILL HAVE TO BE THE KEY!!!
CRASH
...OH.

READ THIS WAY

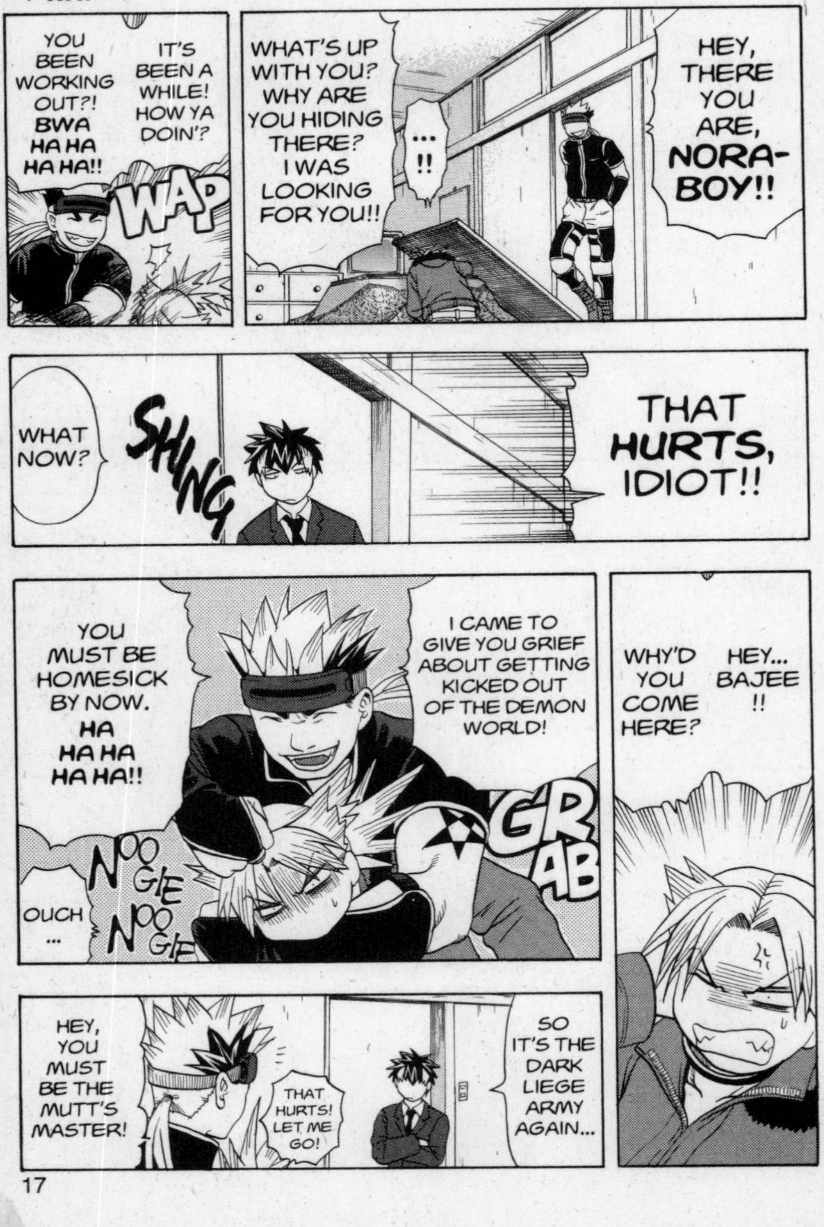

HEY, THERE YOU ARE, NORA-BOY!!
...!!
WHAT'S UP WITH YOU? WHY ARE YOU HIDING THERE? I WAS LOOKING FOR YOU!!
IT'S BEEN A WHILE! HOW YA DOIN'?
YOU BEEN WORKING OUT?! BWA HA HA HA HA!!
WAP
THAT HURTS, IDIOT!!
SHING
WHAT NOW?
HEY... BAJEE!!
WHY'D YOU COME HERE?
I CAME TO GIVE YOU GRIEF ABOUT GETTING KICKED OUT OF THE DEMON WORLD!
YOU MUST BE HOMESICK BY NOW. HA HA HA HA HA HA!!
GRAB
NOOGIE NOOGIE
OUCH...
SO IT'S THE DARK LIEGE ARMY AGAIN...
THAT HURTS! LET ME GO!
HEY, YOU MUST BE THE MUTT'S MASTER!

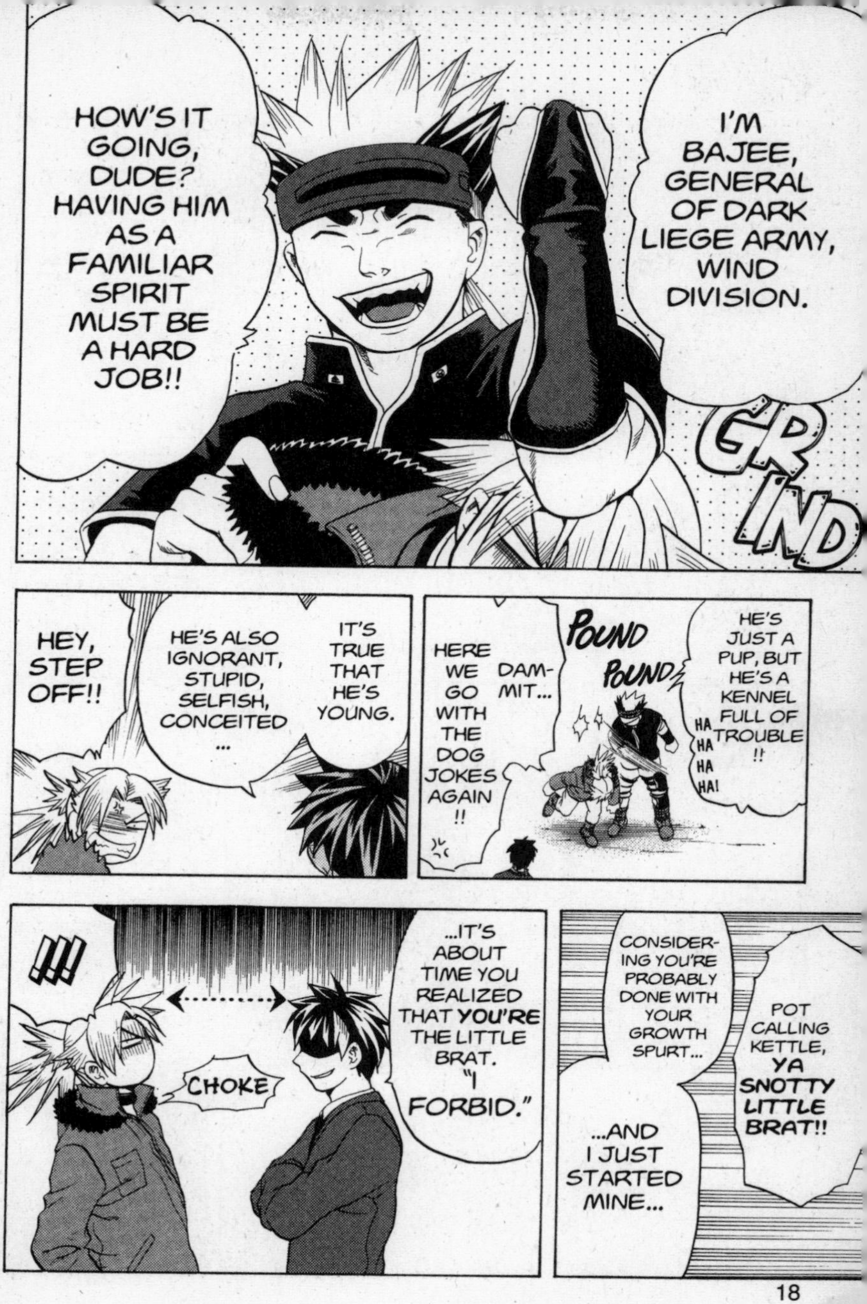
I'M BAJEE, GENERAL OF DARK LIEGE ARMY, WIND DIVISION.
GRIND
HOW'S IT GOING, DUDE? HAVING HIM AS A FAMILIAR SPIRIT MUST BE A HARD JOB!!
HE'S JUST A PUP, BUT HE'S A KENNEL FULL OF TROUBLE!!
HA HA HA HA HA!
POUND POUND
DAM-MIT...
HERE WE GO WITH THE DOG JOKES AGAIN!!
IT'S TRUE THAT HE'S YOUNG.
HE'S ALSO IGNORANT, STUPID, SELFISH, CONCEITED...
HEY, STEP OFF!!
POT CALLING KETTLE, **YA SNOTTY LITTLE BRAT!!**
CONSIDER-ING YOU'RE PROBABLY DONE WITH YOUR GROWTH SPURT...
...AND I JUST STARTED MINE...
...IT'S ABOUT TIME YOU REALIZED THAT **YOU'RE** THE LITTLE BRAT. "I FORBID."
!!!
CHOKE

READ THIS WAY

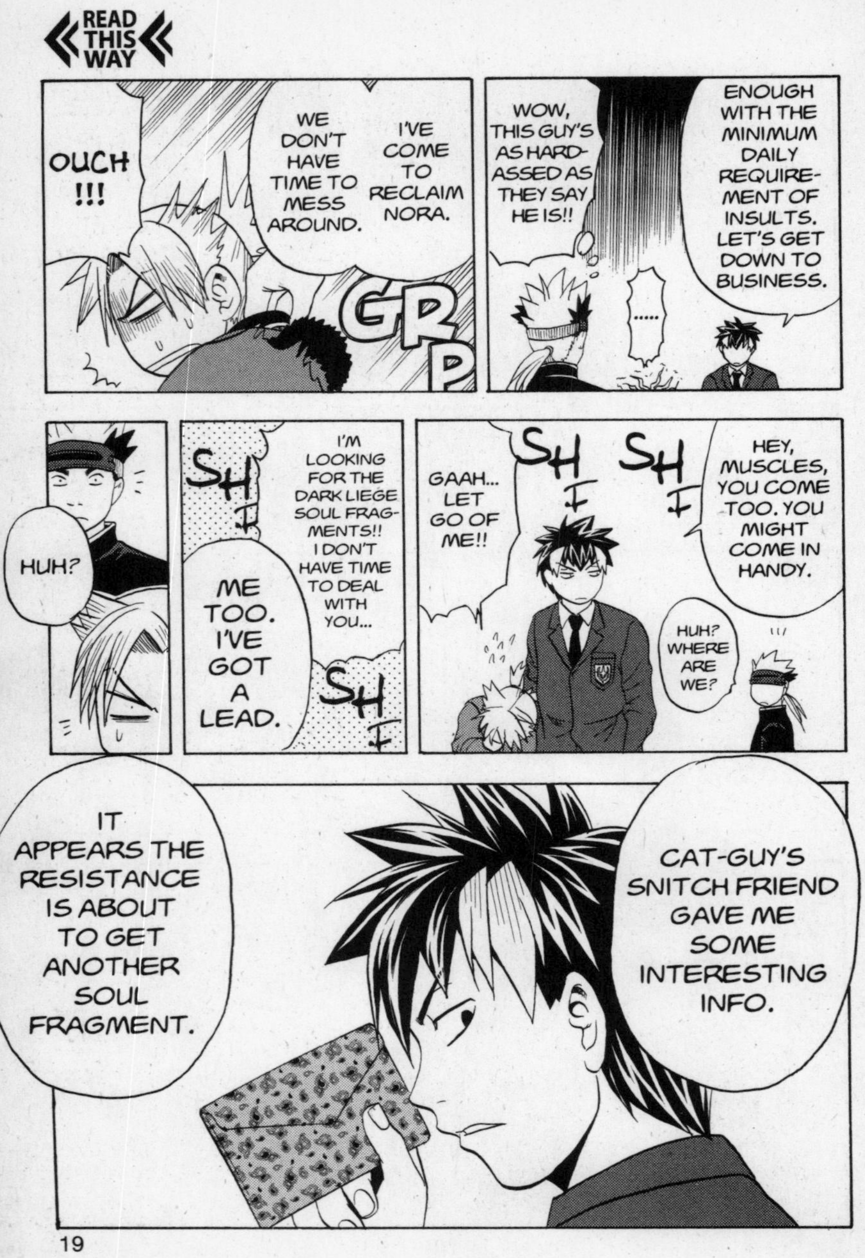

ENOUGH WITH THE MINIMUM DAILY REQUIREMENT OF INSULTS. LET'S GET DOWN TO BUSINESS.
WOW, THIS GUY'S AS HARD-ASSED AS THEY SAY HE IS!!
......
I'VE COME TO RECLAIM NORA.
WE DON'T HAVE TIME TO MESS AROUND.
GRP
OUCH !!!
HEY, MUSCLES, YOU COME TOO. YOU MIGHT COME IN HANDY.
SHF
SHF
GAAH... LET GO OF ME!!
HUH? WHERE ARE WE?
I'M LOOKING FOR THE DARK LIEGE SOUL FRAGMENTS!! I DON'T HAVE TIME TO DEAL WITH YOU...
SHF
ME TOO. I'VE GOT A LEAD.
SHF
HUH?
CAT-GUY'S SNITCH FRIEND GAVE ME SOME INTERESTING INFO.
IT APPEARS THE RESISTANCE IS ABOUT TO GET ANOTHER SOUL FRAGMENT.

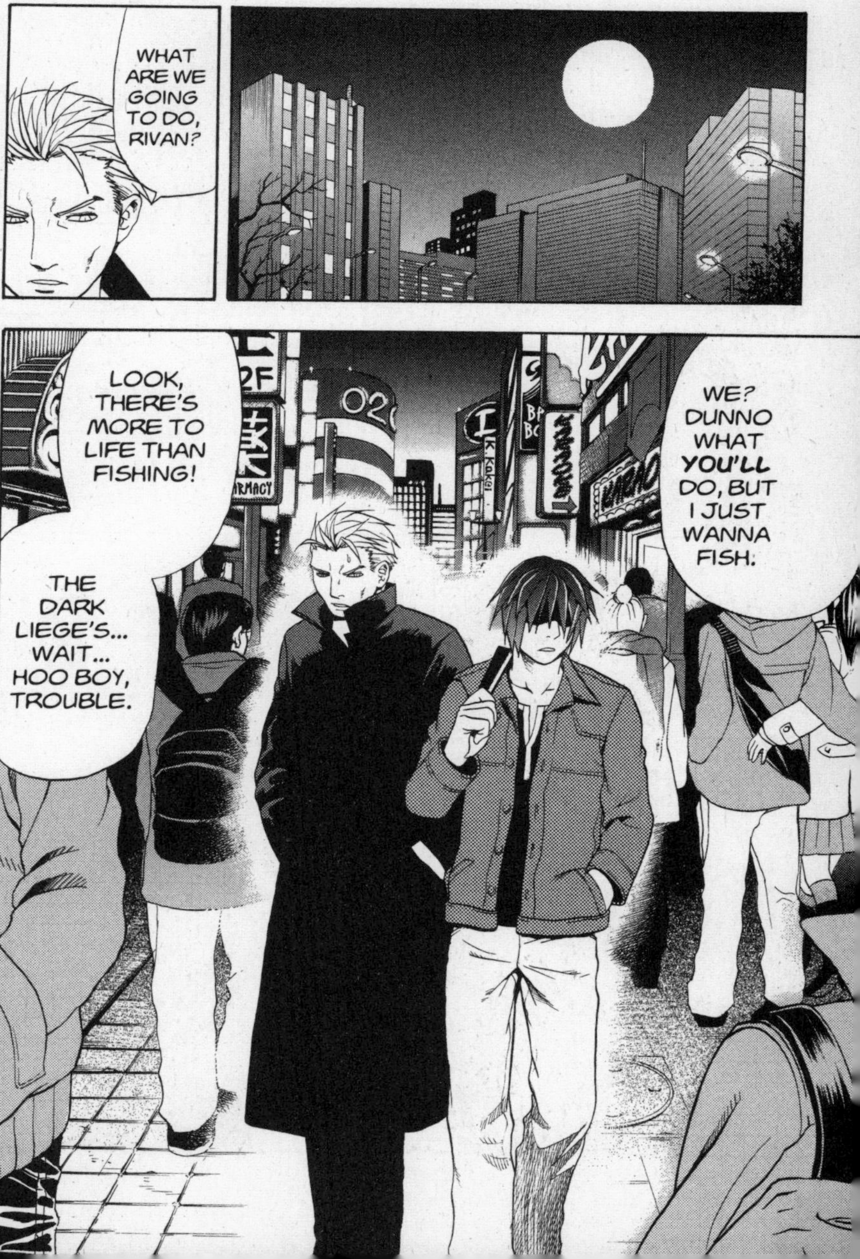
WHAT ARE WE GOING TO DO, RIVAN?
WE? DUNNO WHAT YOU'LL DO, BUT I JUST WANNA FISH.
LOOK, THERE'S MORE TO LIFE THAN FISHING!
THE DARK LIEGE'S... WAIT... HOO BOY, TROUBLE.

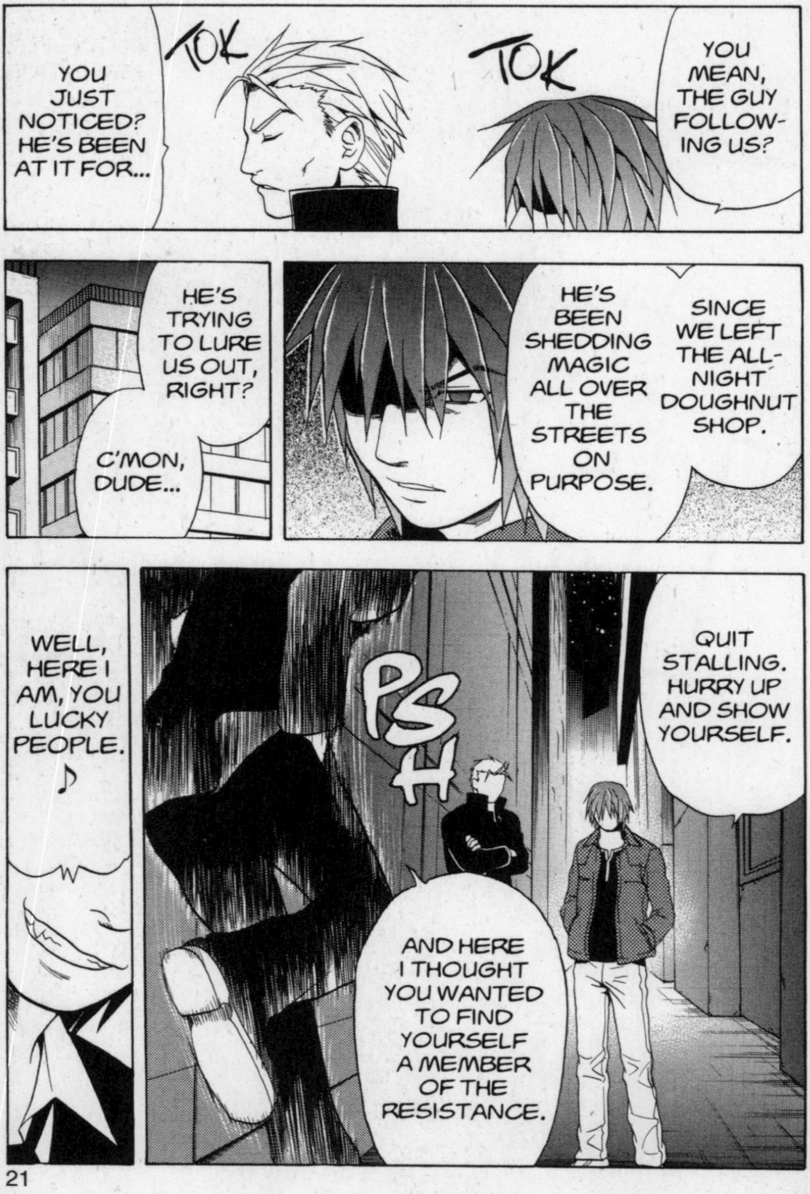
YOU MEAN, THE GUY FOLLOW-ING US?
TOK
TOK
YOU JUST NOTICED? HE'S BEEN AT IT FOR...
SINCE WE LEFT THE ALL-NIGHT DOUGHNUT SHOP.
HE'S BEEN SHEDDING MAGIC ALL OVER THE STREETS ON PURPOSE.
HE'S TRYING TO LURE US OUT, RIGHT?
C'MON, DUDE...
QUIT STALLING. HURRY UP AND SHOW YOURSELF.
PSH
AND HERE I THOUGHT YOU WANTED TO FIND YOURSELF A MEMBER OF THE RESISTANCE.
WELL, HERE I AM, YOU LUCKY PEOPLE. ♪

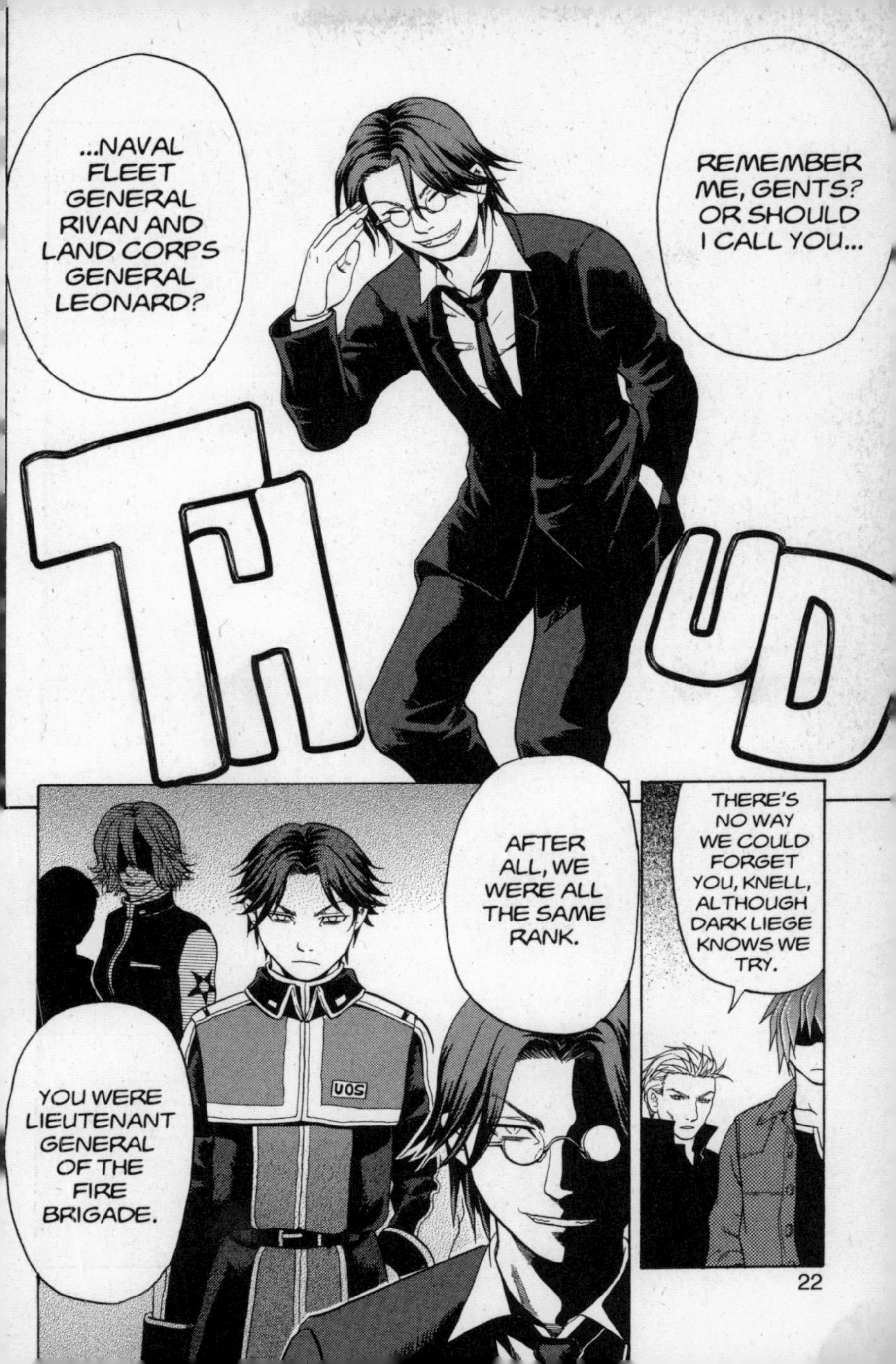
REMEMBER ME, GENTS? OR SHOULD I CALL YOU...
...NAVAL FLEET GENERAL RIVAN AND LAND CORPS GENERAL LEONARD?
THUD
THERE'S NO WAY WE COULD FORGET YOU, KNELL, ALTHOUGH DARK LIEGE KNOWS WE TRY.
AFTER ALL, WE WERE ALL THE SAME RANK.
UOS
YOU WERE LIEUTENANT GENERAL OF THE FIRE BRIGADE.

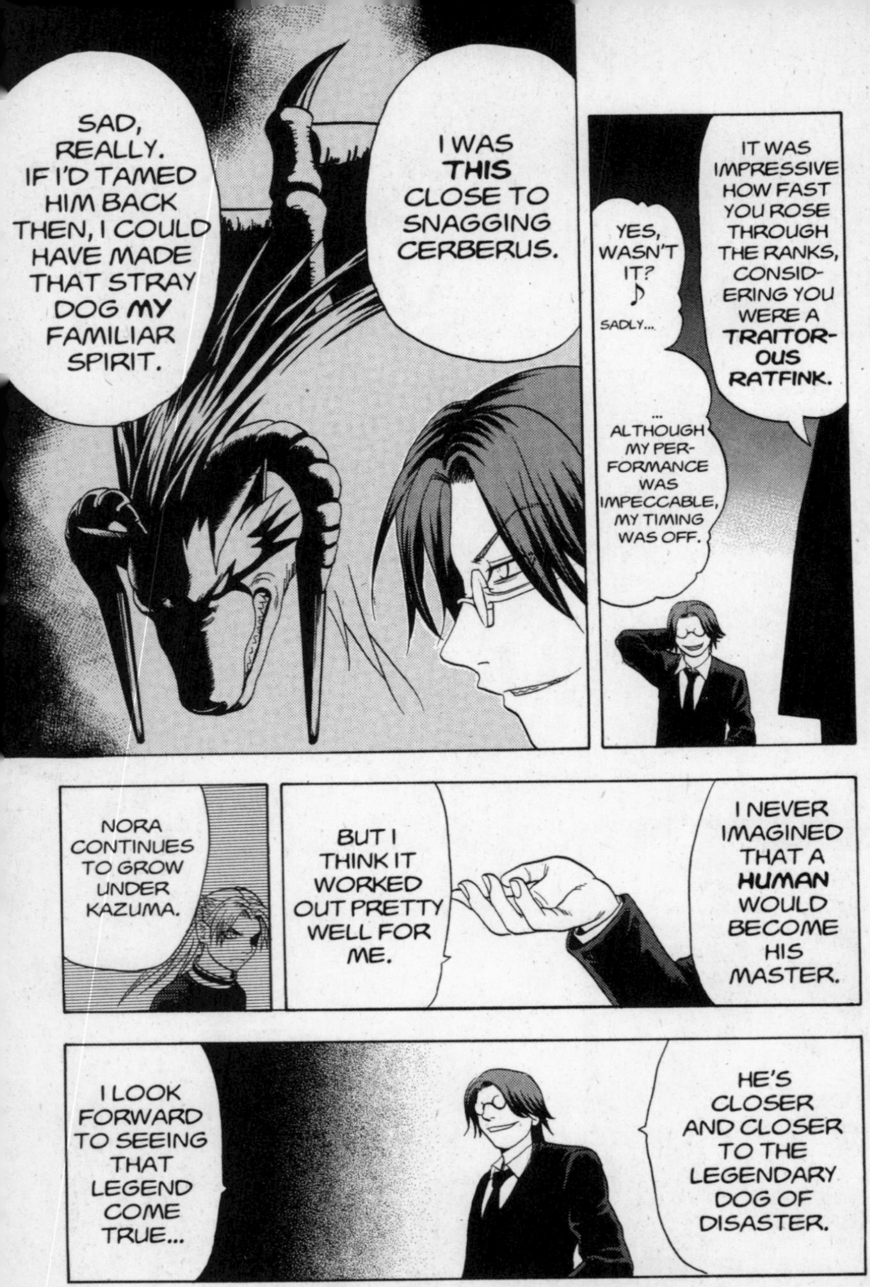
IT WAS IMPRESSIVE HOW FAST YOU ROSE THROUGH THE RANKS, CONSIDERING YOU WERE A TRAITOROUS RATFINK.
YES, WASN'T IT? ♪
SADLY...
...ALTHOUGH MY PERFORMANCE WAS IMPECCABLE, MY TIMING WAS OFF.
I WAS THIS CLOSE TO SNAGGING CERBERUS.
SAD, REALLY. IF I'D TAMED HIM BACK THEN, I COULD HAVE MADE THAT STRAY DOG MY FAMILIAR SPIRIT.
I NEVER IMAGINED THAT A HUMAN WOULD BECOME HIS MASTER.
BUT I THINK IT WORKED OUT PRETTY WELL FOR ME.
NORA CONTINUES TO GROW UNDER KAZUMA.
HE'S CLOSER AND CLOSER TO THE LEGENDARY DOG OF DISASTER.
I LOOK FORWARD TO SEEING THAT LEGEND COME TRUE...

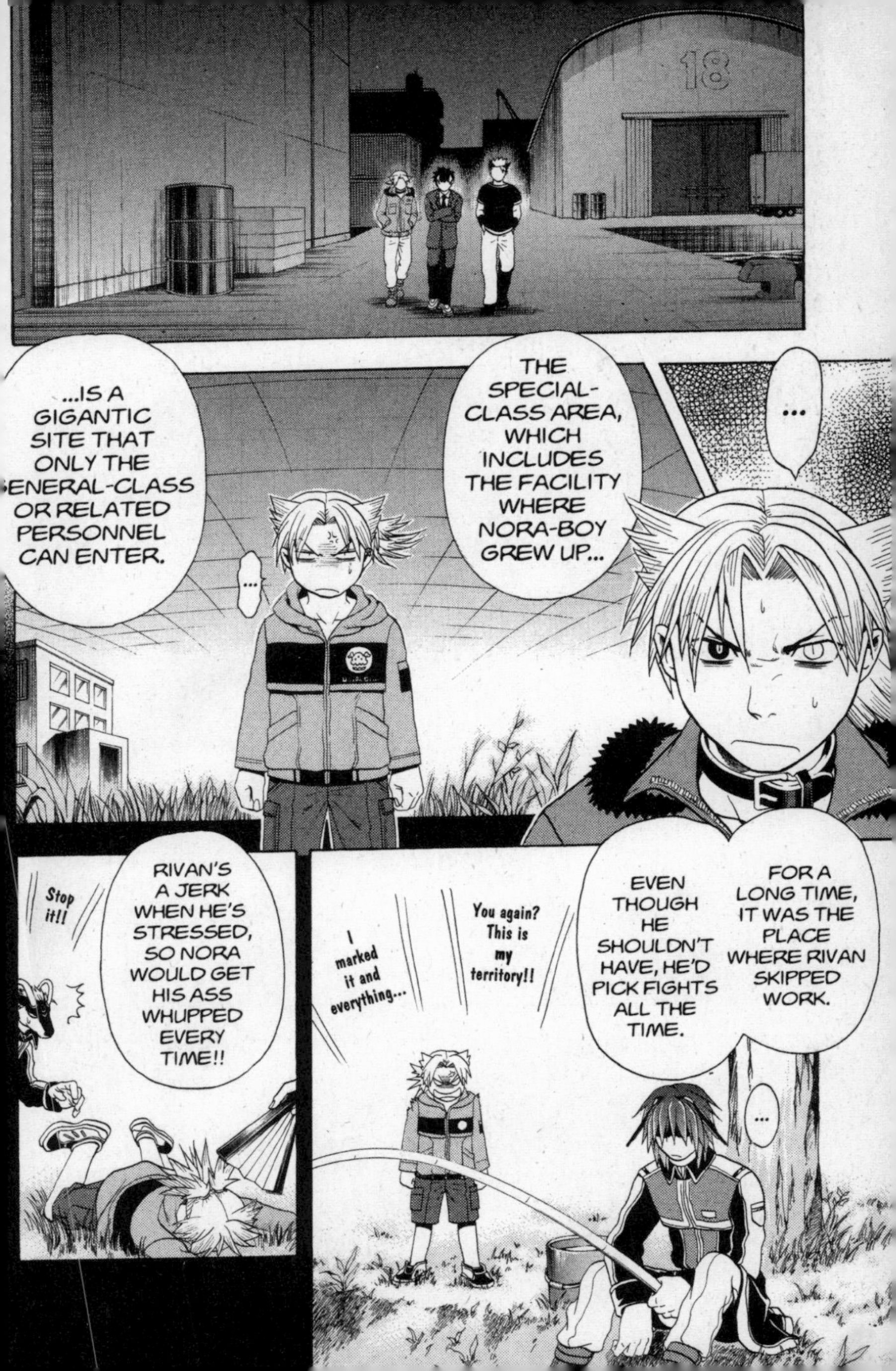
...
THE SPECIAL-CLASS AREA, WHICH INCLUDES THE FACILITY WHERE NORA-BOY GREW UP...
...IS A GIGANTIC SITE THAT ONLY THE ENERAL-CLASS OR RELATED PERSONNEL CAN ENTER.
...
FOR A LONG TIME, IT WAS THE PLACE WHERE RIVAN SKIPPED WORK.
EVEN THOUGH HE SHOULDN'T HAVE, HE'D PICK FIGHTS ALL THE TIME.
You again? This is my territory!!
I marked it and everything...
...
RIVAN'S A JERK WHEN HE'S STRESSED, SO NORA WOULD GET HIS ASS WHUPPED EVERY TIME!!
Stop it!!

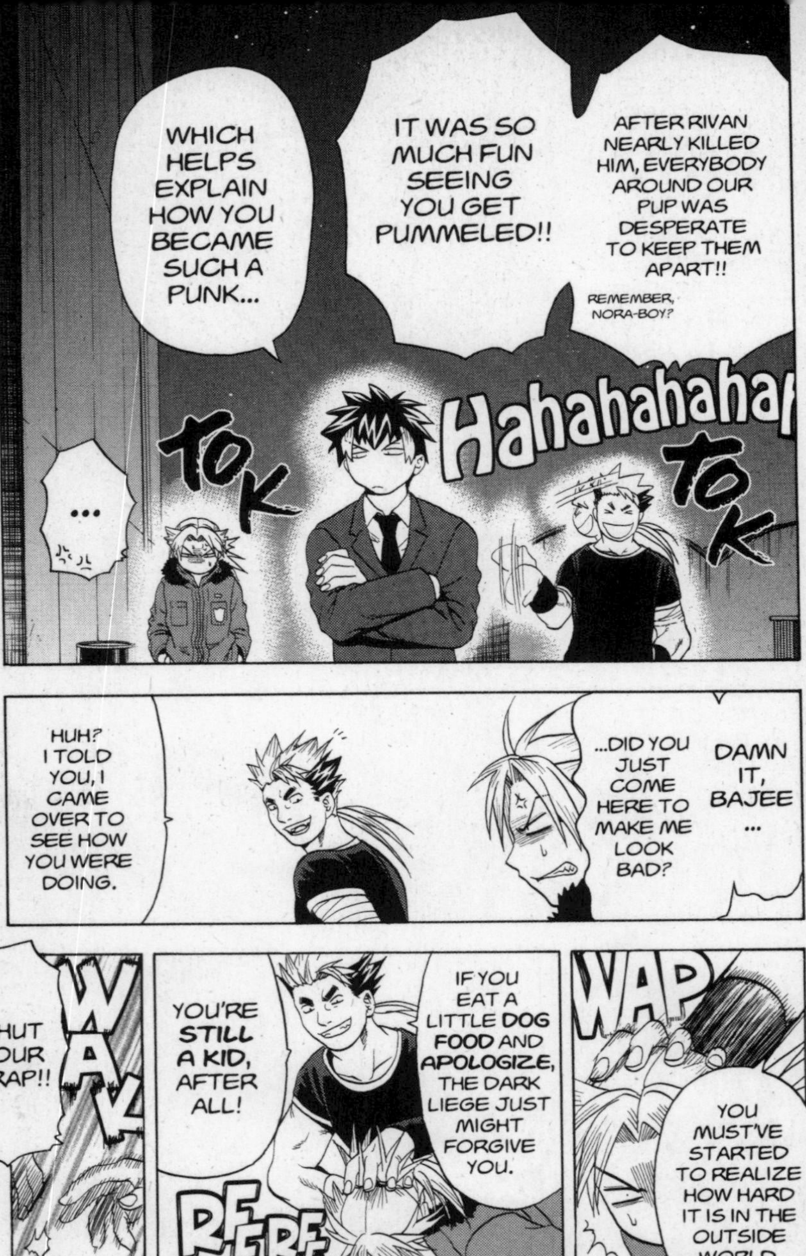
AFTER RIVAN NEARLY KILLED HIM, EVERYBODY AROUND OUR PUP WAS DESPERATE TO KEEP THEM APART!!
REMEMBER, NORA-BOY?
IT WAS SO MUCH FUN SEEING YOU GET PUMMELED!!
WHICH HELPS EXPLAIN HOW YOU BECAME SUCH A PUNK...
Hahahahahah
TOK
TOK
...
DAMN IT, BAJEE ...
...DID YOU JUST COME HERE TO MAKE ME LOOK BAD?
HUH? I TOLD YOU, I CAME OVER TO SEE HOW YOU WERE DOING.
WAP
YOU MUST'VE STARTED TO REALIZE HOW HARD IT IS IN THE OUTSIDE WORLD.
IF YOU EAT A LITTLE DOG FOOD AND APOLOGIZE, THE DARK LIEGE JUST MIGHT FORGIVE YOU.
YOU'RE STILL A KID, AFTER ALL!
RFFRFF
WAK
SHUT YOUR TRAP!!

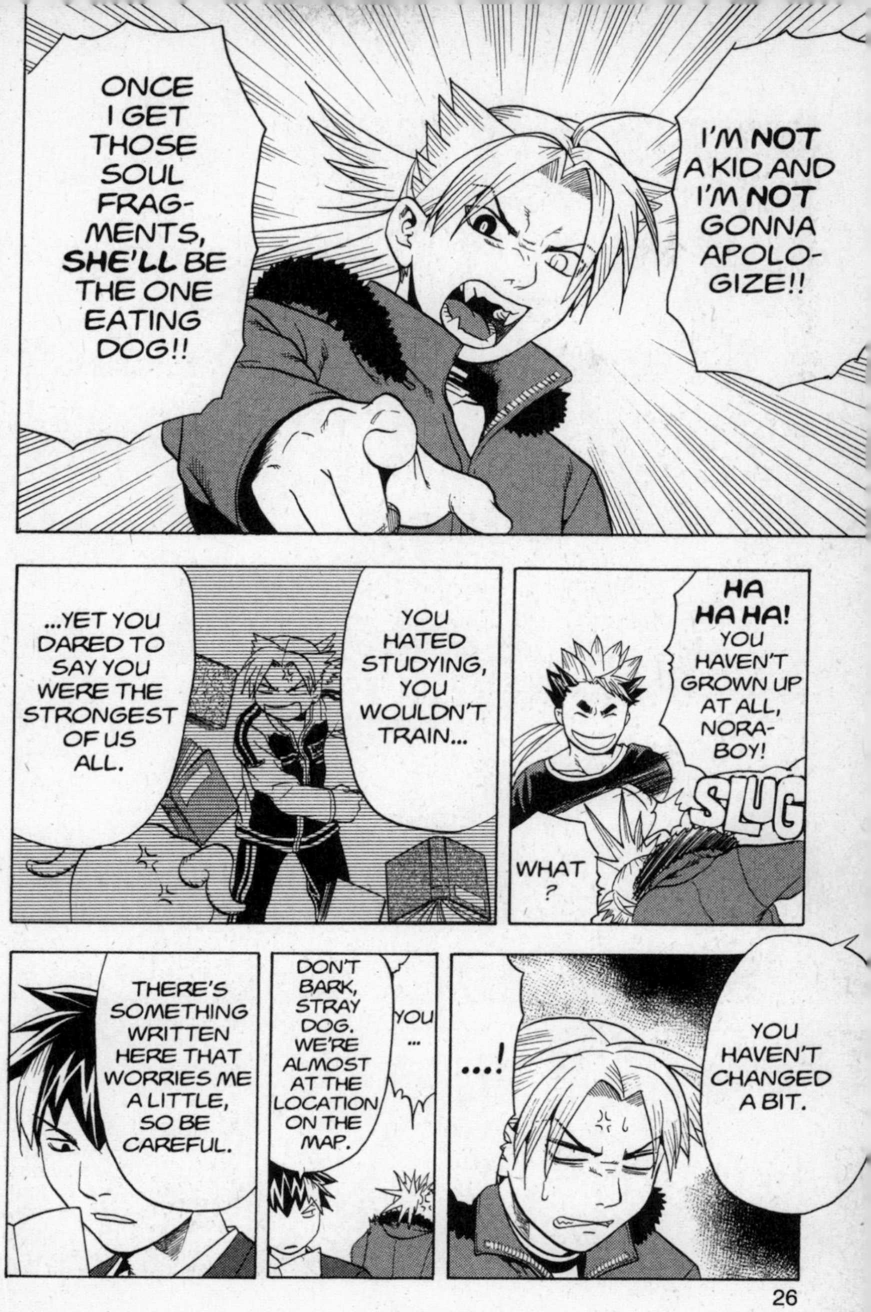
I'M NOT A KID AND I'M NOT GONNA APOLOGIZE!!
ONCE I GET THOSE SOUL FRAGMENTS, SHE'LL BE THE ONE EATING DOG!!
HA HA HA! YOU HAVEN'T GROWN UP AT ALL, NORA-BOY!
SLUG
WHAT ?
YOU HATED STUDYING, YOU WOULDN'T TRAIN...
...YET YOU DARED TO SAY YOU WERE THE STRONGEST OF US ALL.
YOU HAVEN'T CHANGED A BIT.
...!
YOU ...
DON'T BARK, STRAY DOG. WE'RE ALMOST AT THE LOCATION ON THE MAP.
THERE'S SOMETHING WRITTEN HERE THAT WORRIES ME A LITTLE, SO BE CAREFUL.

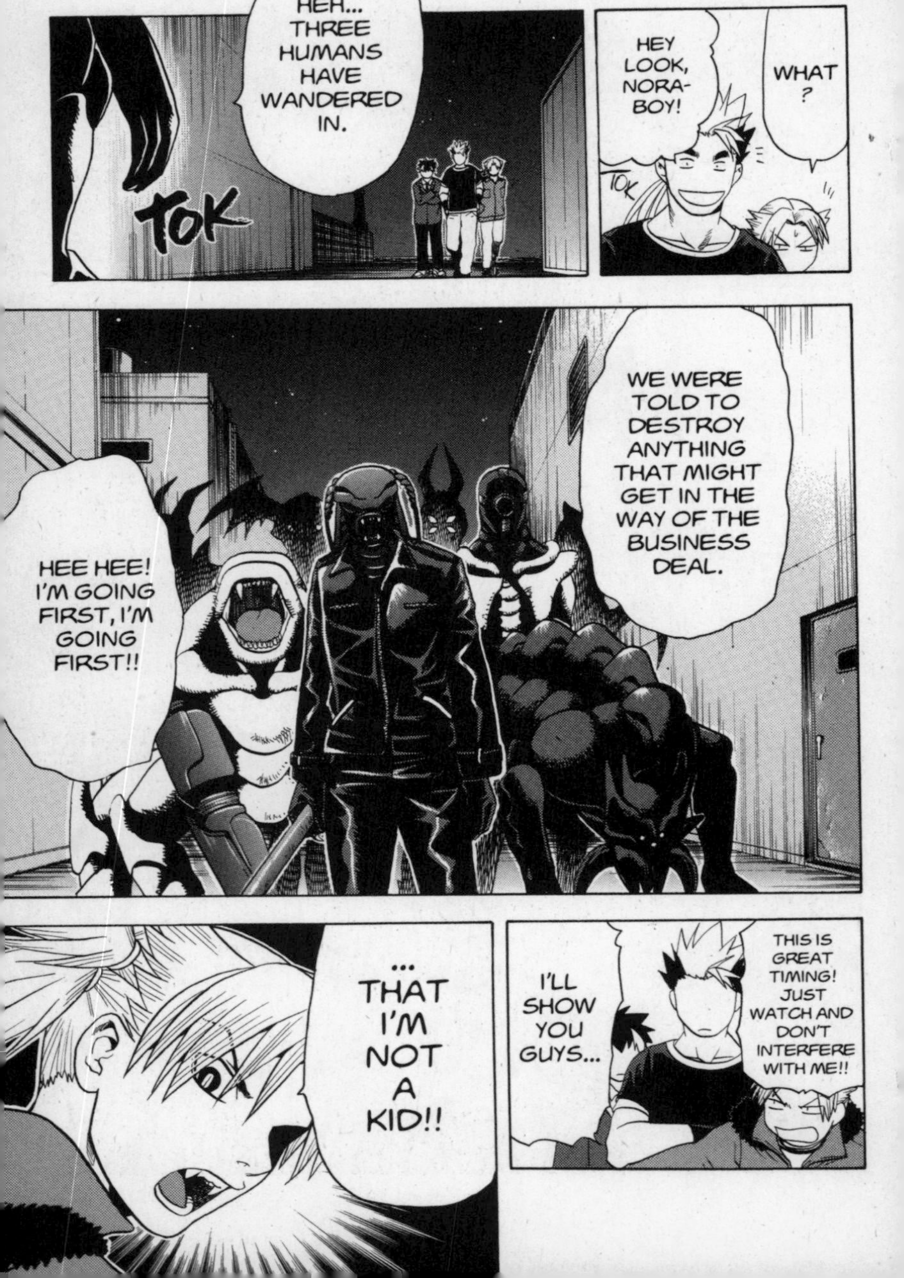
HEY LOOK, NORA-BOY!
WHAT?
TOK
HEH... THREE HUMANS HAVE WANDERED IN.
TOK
WE WERE TOLD TO DESTROY ANYTHING THAT MIGHT GET IN THE WAY OF THE BUSINESS DEAL.
HEE HEE! I'M GOING FIRST, I'M GOING FIRST!!
THIS IS GREAT TIMING! JUST WATCH AND DON'T INTERFERE WITH ME!!
I'LL SHOW YOU GUYS...
... THAT I'M NOT A KID!!

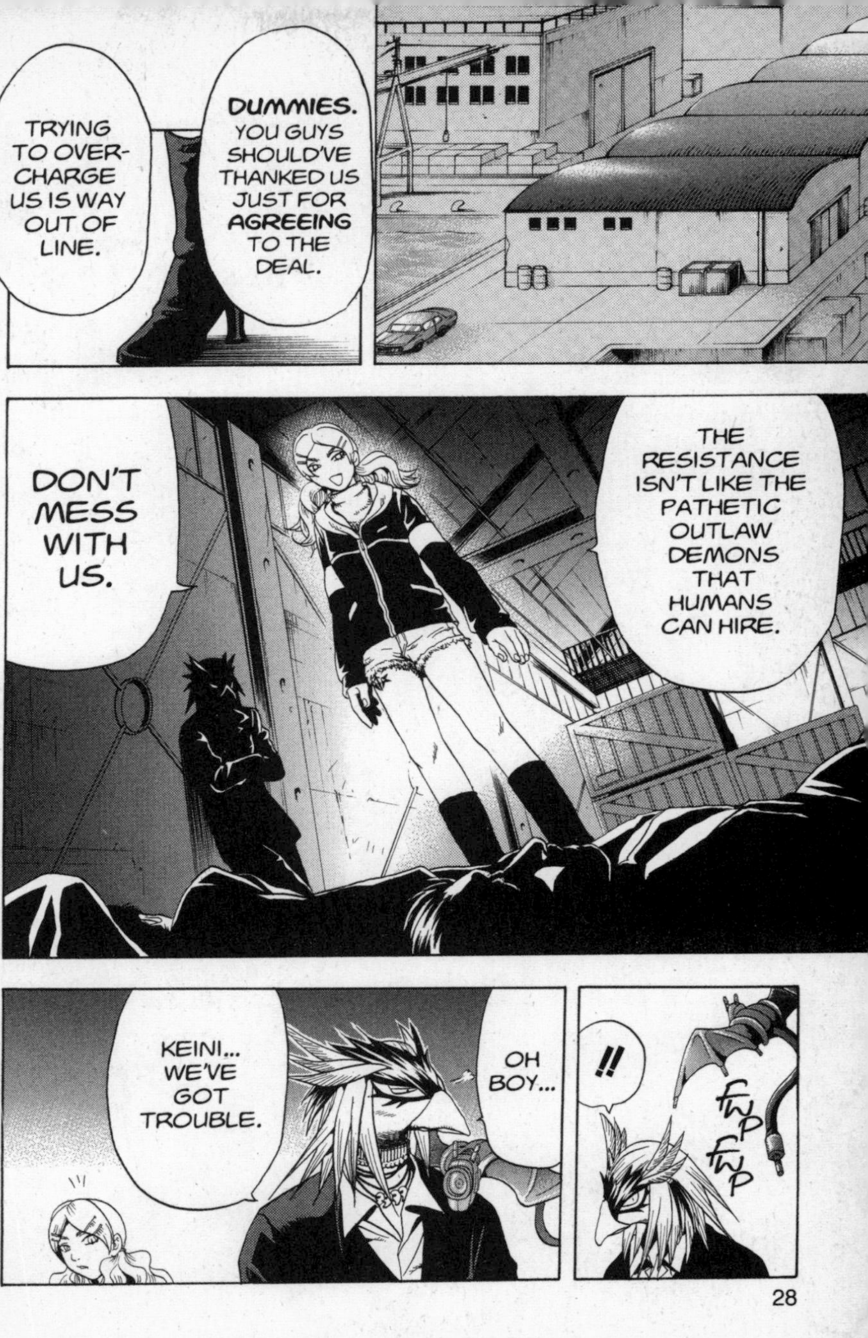
DUMMIES. YOU GUYS SHOULD'VE THANKED US JUST FOR AGREEING TO THE DEAL.
TRYING TO OVER-CHARGE US IS WAY OUT OF LINE.
THE RESISTANCE ISN'T LIKE THE PATHETIC OUTLAW DEMONS THAT HUMANS CAN HIRE.
DON'T MESS WITH US.
!!
FWP FWP
OH BOY...
KEINI... WE'VE GOT TROUBLE.

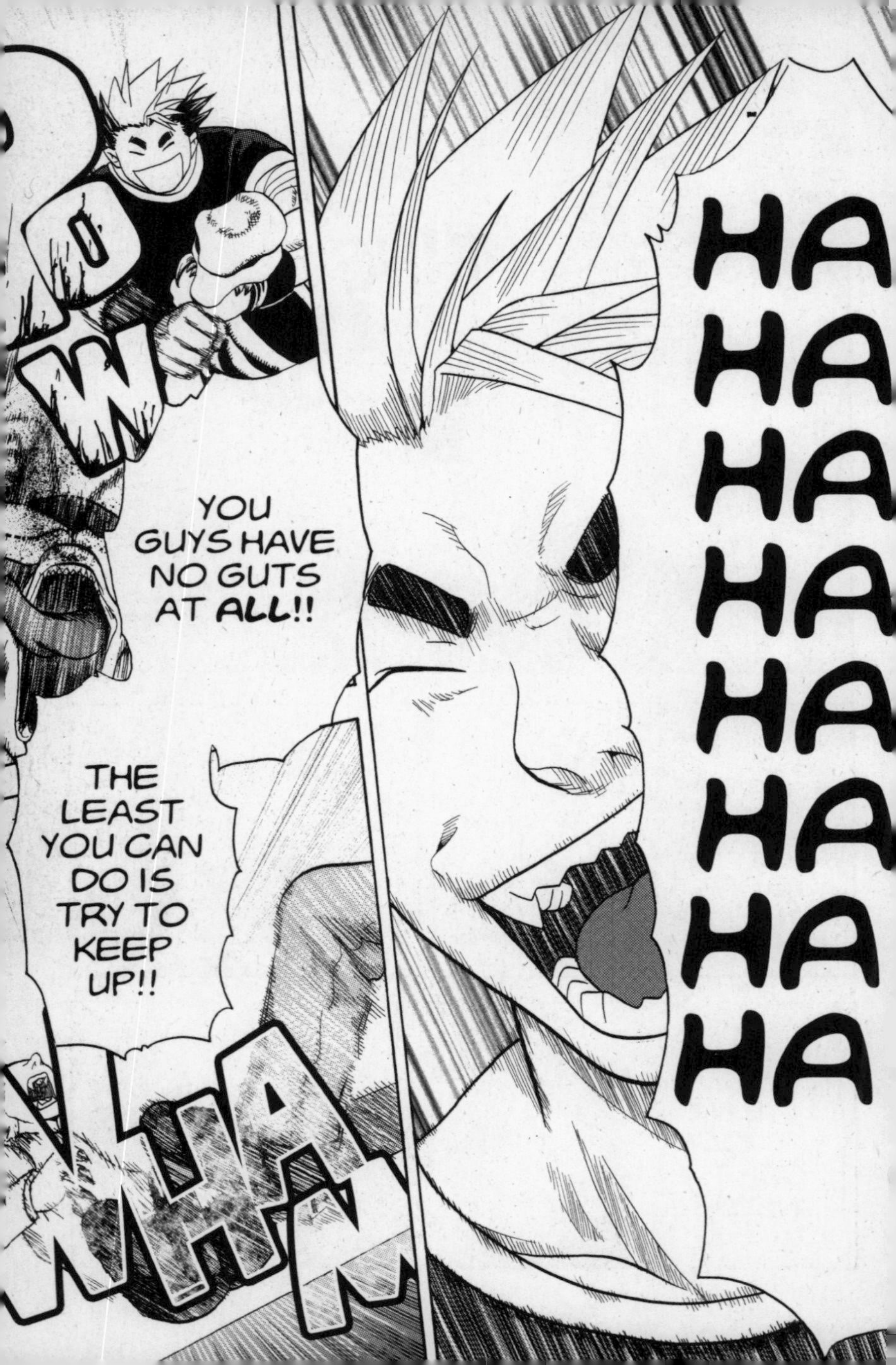

HA HA HA HA HA HA HA HA HA
YOU GUYS HAVE NO GUTS AT **ALL**!!
THE LEAST YOU CAN DO IS TRY TO KEEP UP!!

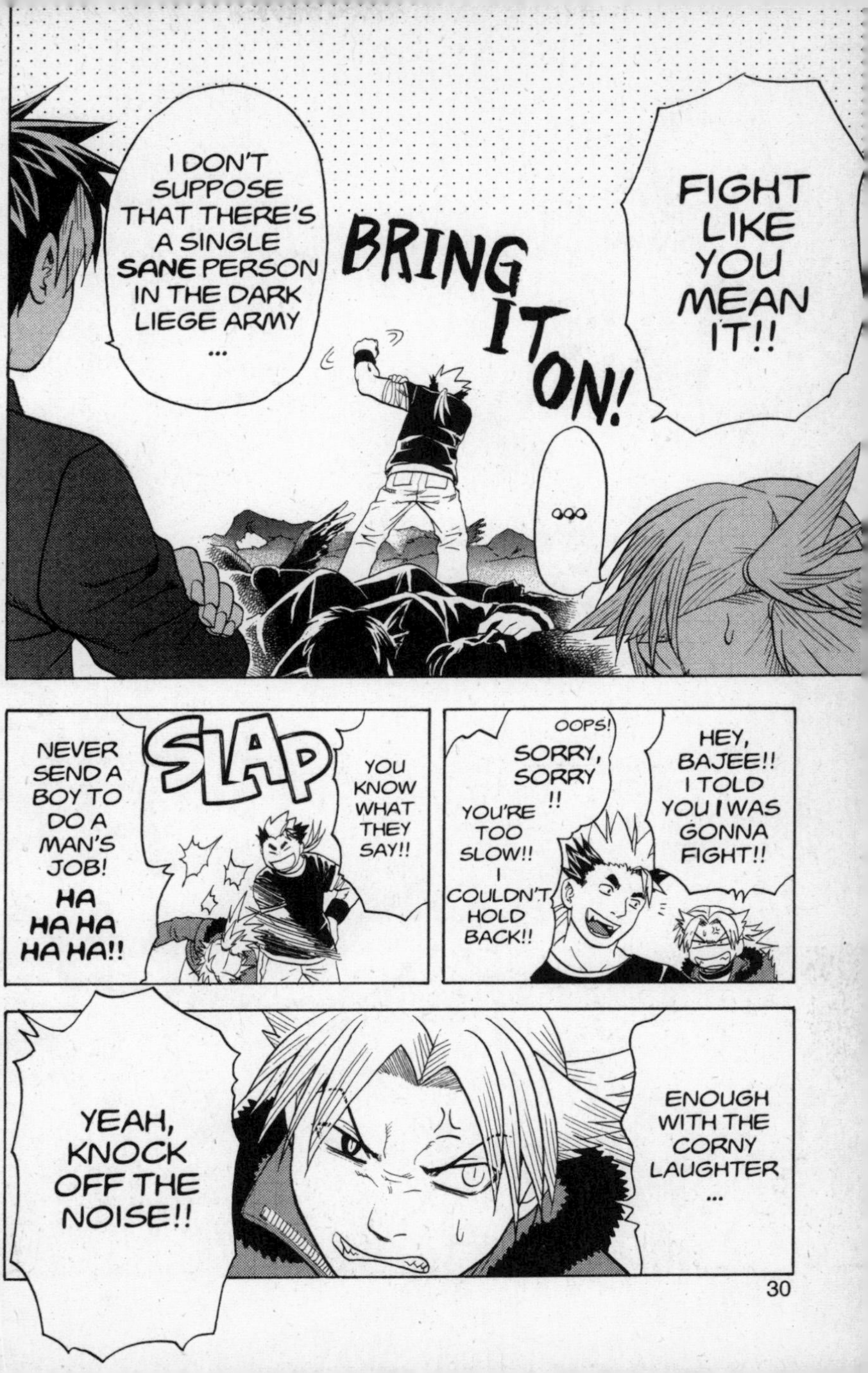
FIGHT LIKE YOU MEAN IT!!
BRING IT ON!
I DON'T SUPPOSE THAT THERE'S A SINGLE SANE PERSON IN THE DARK LIEGE ARMY ...
...
HEY, BAJEE!! I TOLD YOU I WAS GONNA FIGHT!!
OOPS!
SORRY, SORRY !!
YOU'RE TOO SLOW!! I COULDN'T HOLD BACK!!
YOU KNOW WHAT THEY SAY!!
SLAP
NEVER SEND A BOY TO DO A MAN'S JOB!
HA HA HA HA HA!!
ENOUGH WITH THE CORNY LAUGHTER ...
YEAH, KNOCK OFF THE NOISE!!

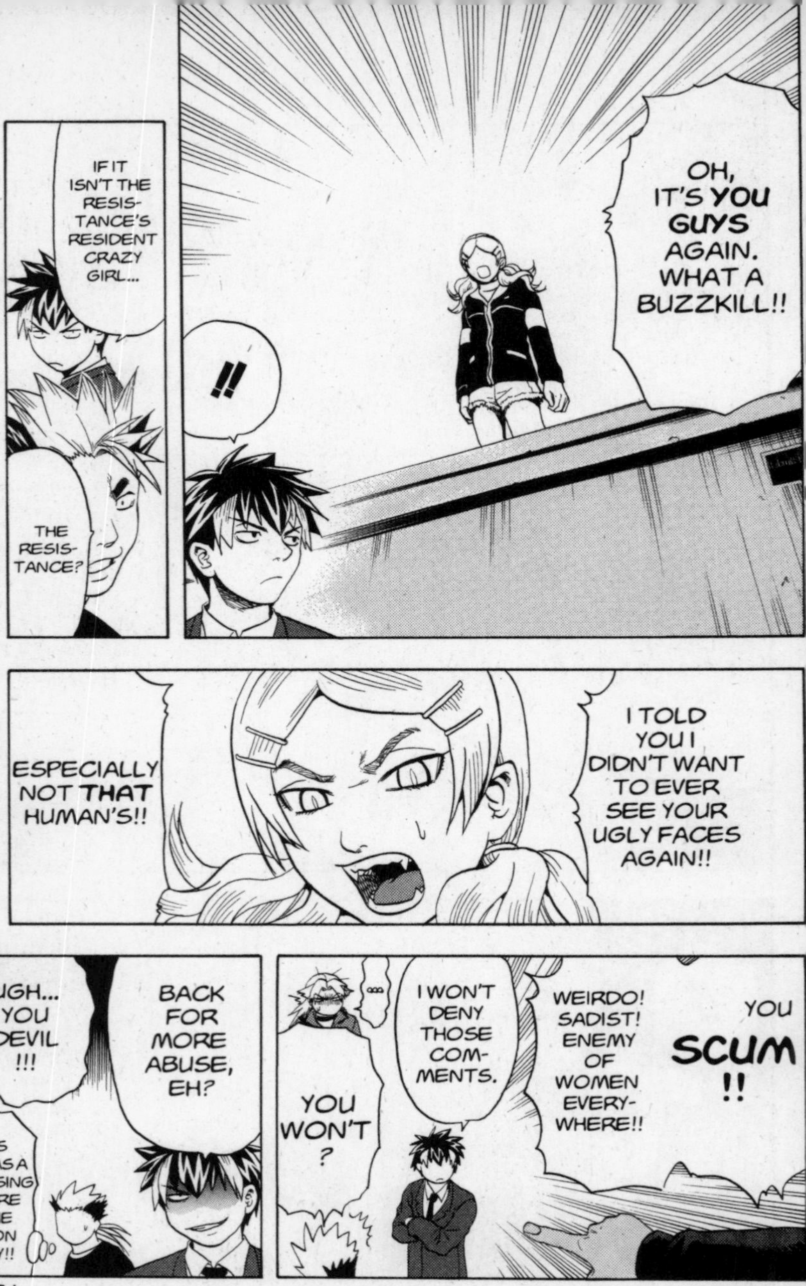
OH, IT'S YOU GUYS AGAIN. WHAT A BUZZKILL!!
!!
IF IT ISN'T THE RESIS-TANCE'S RESIDENT CRAZY GIRL...
THE RESIS-TANCE?
I TOLD YOU I DIDN'T WANT TO EVER SEE YOUR UGLY FACES AGAIN!!
ESPECIALLY NOT THAT HUMAN'S!!
YOU SCUM!!
WEIRDO! SADIST! ENEMY OF WOMEN EVERY-WHERE!!
I WON'T DENY THOSE COM-MENTS.
...
YOU WON'T?
BACK FOR MORE ABUSE, EH?
UGH... YOU DEVIL!!!
THIS GUY HAS A PROMISING FUTURE IN THE DEMON ARMY!!

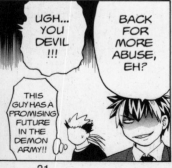

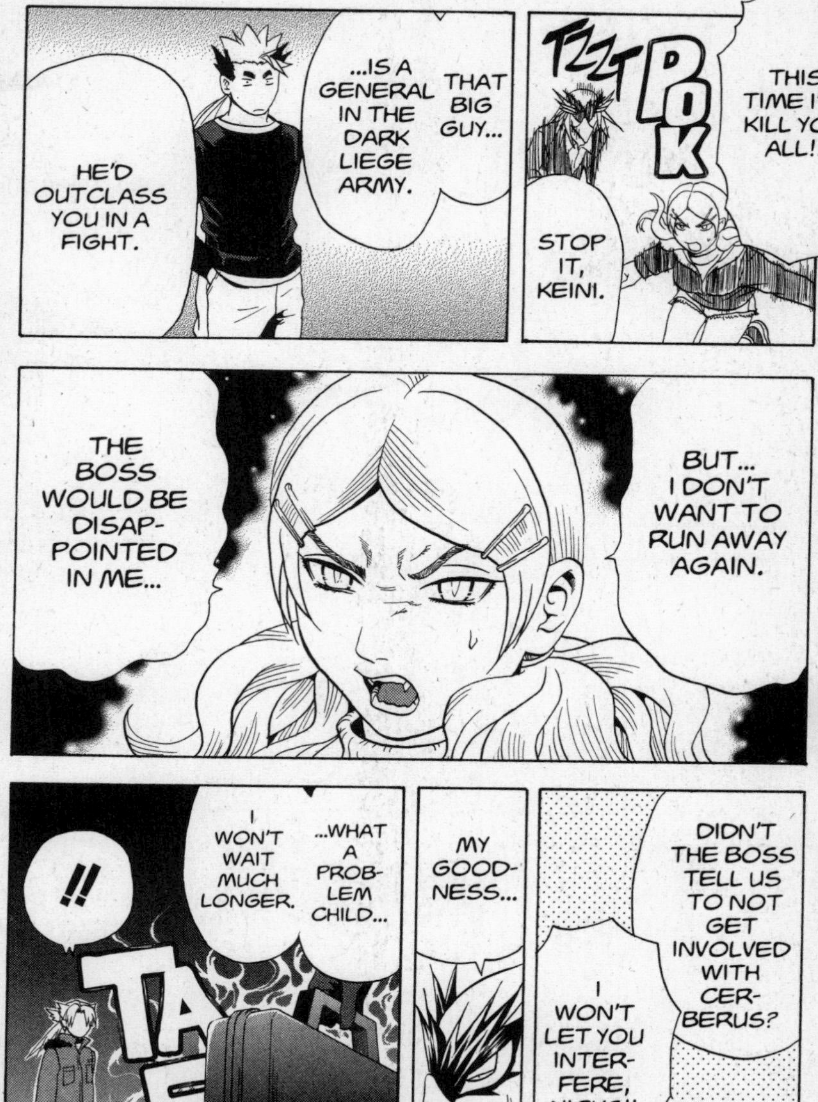
TZZT
POK
THIS TIME I'LL KILL YOU ALL!!
STOP IT, KEINI.
THAT BIG GUY...
...IS A GENERAL IN THE DARK LIEGE ARMY.
HE'D OUTCLASS YOU IN A FIGHT.
BUT... I DON'T WANT TO RUN AWAY AGAIN.
THE BOSS WOULD BE DISAP- POINTED IN ME...
DIDN'T THE BOSS TELL US TO NOT GET INVOLVED WITH CER- BERUS?
I WON'T LET YOU INTER- FERE, NICKS!!
MY GOOD- NESS...
...WHAT A PROB- LEM CHILD...
I WON'T WAIT MUCH LONGER.
!!

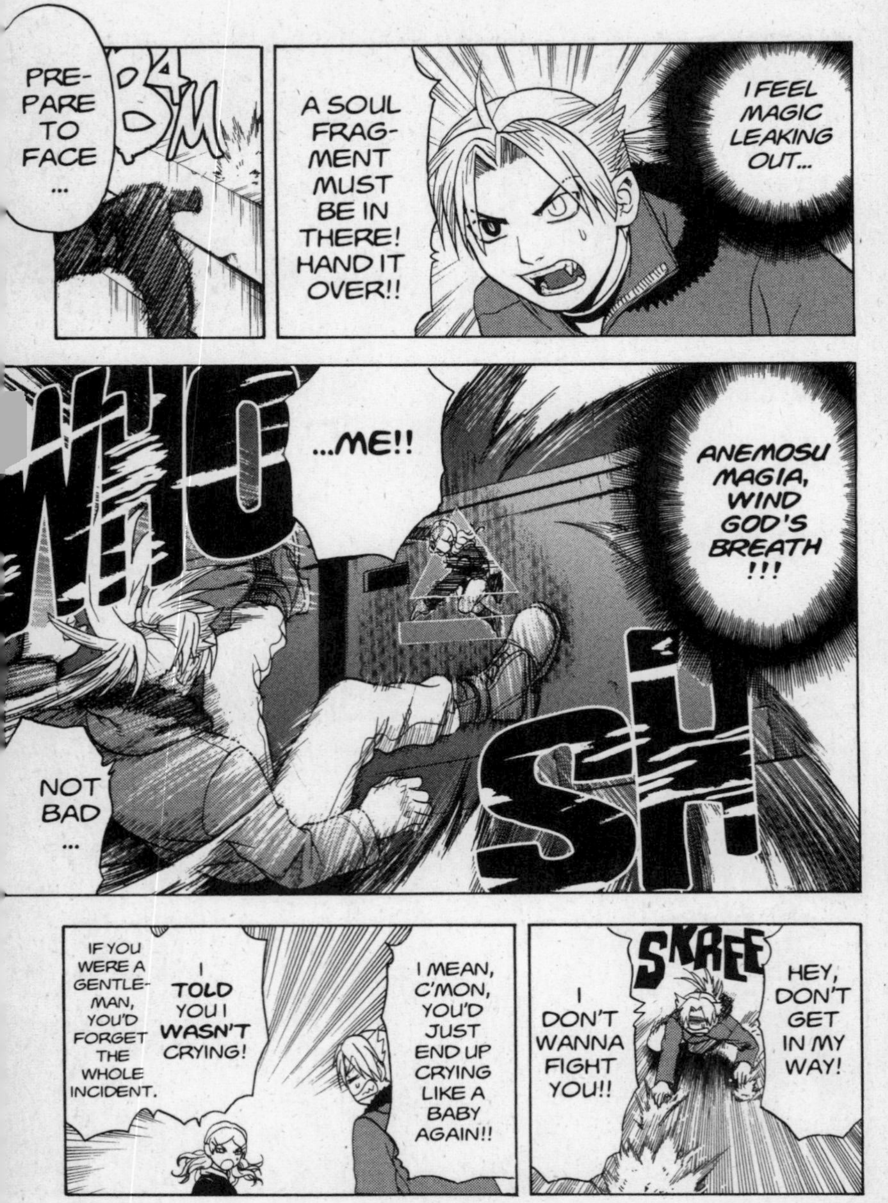
I FEEL MAGIC LEAKING OUT...
A SOUL FRAGMENT MUST BE IN THERE! HAND IT OVER!!
PREPARE TO FACE ...
ANEMOSU MAGIA, WIND GOD'S BREATH!!!
...ME!!
NOT BAD ...
HEY, DON'T GET IN MY WAY!
SKREE
I DON'T WANNA FIGHT YOU!!
I MEAN, C'MON, YOU'D JUST END UP CRYING LIKE A BABY AGAIN!!
I **TOLD** YOU I **WASN'T** CRYING!
IF YOU WERE A GENTLEMAN, YOU'D FORGET THE WHOLE INCIDENT.

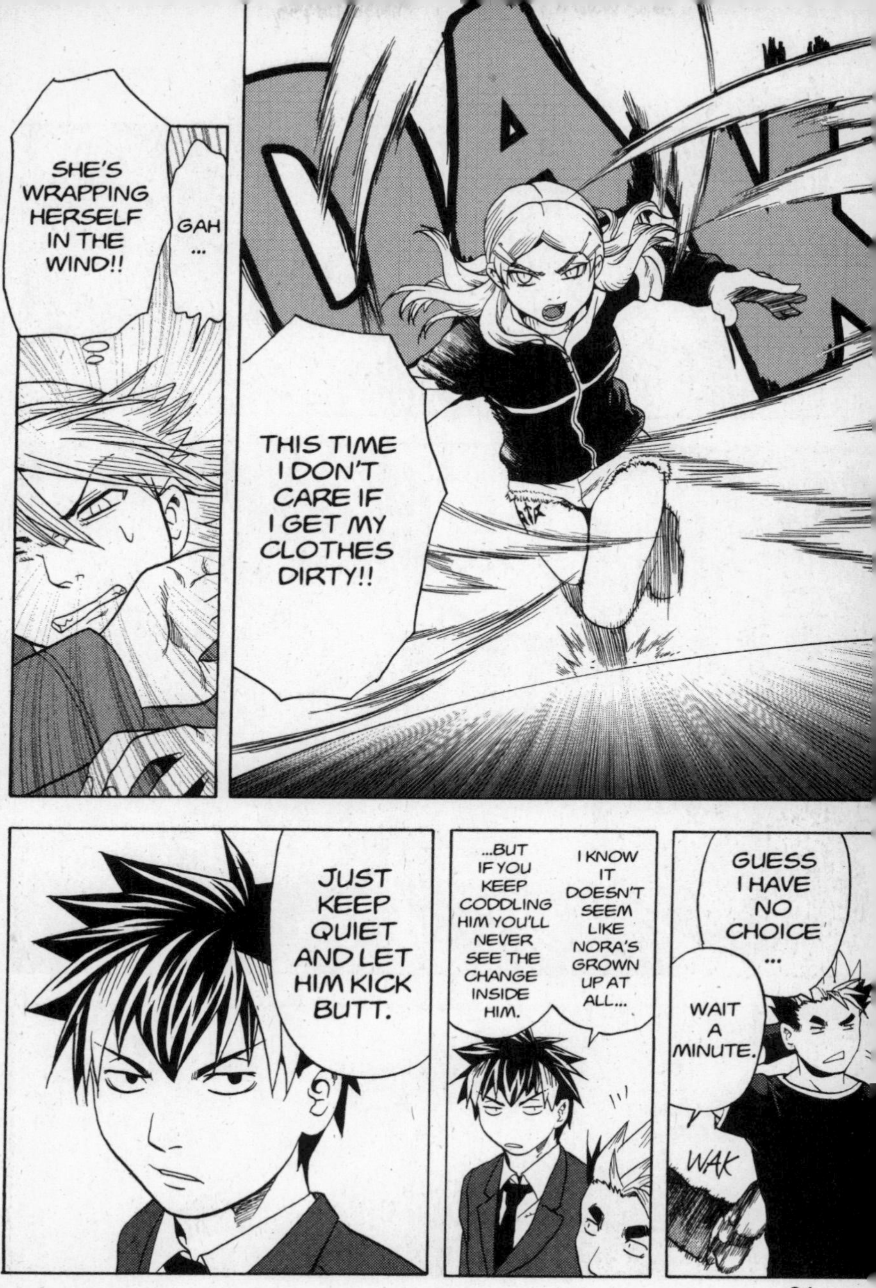
THIS TIME I DON'T CARE IF I GET MY CLOTHES DIRTY!!
GAH ...
SHE'S WRAPPING HERSELF IN THE WIND!!
GUESS I HAVE NO CHOICE ...
WAIT A MINUTE.
WAK
I KNOW IT DOESN'T SEEM LIKE NORA'S GROWN UP AT ALL...
...BUT IF YOU KEEP CODDLING HIM YOU'LL NEVER SEE THE CHANGE INSIDE HIM.
JUST KEEP QUIET AND LET HIM KICK BUTT.

READ THIS WAY

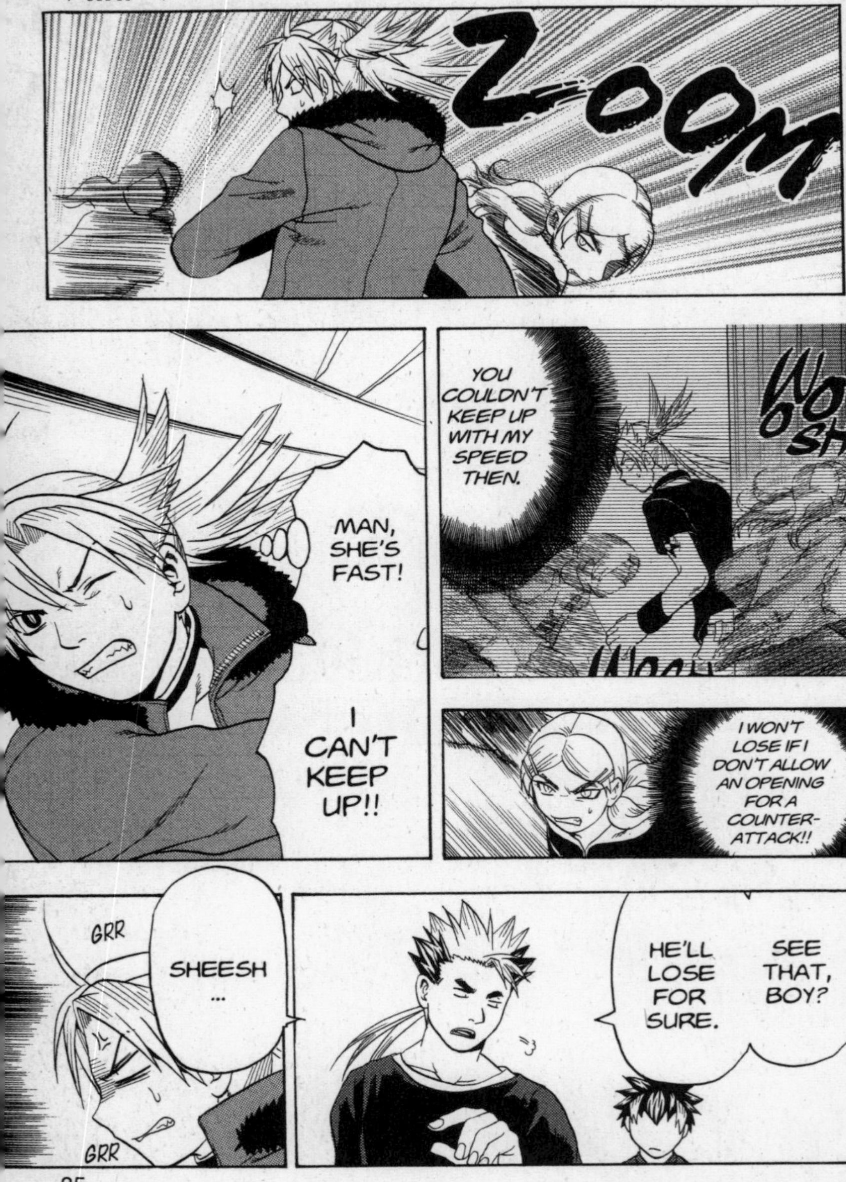
ZOOM
YOU COULDN'T KEEP UP WITH MY SPEED THEN.
I WON'T LOSE IF I DON'T ALLOW AN OPENING FOR A COUNTER-ATTACK!!
MAN, SHE'S FAST!
I CAN'T KEEP UP!!
SEE THAT, BOY?
HE'LL LOSE FOR SURE.
SHEESH ...
GRR
GRR

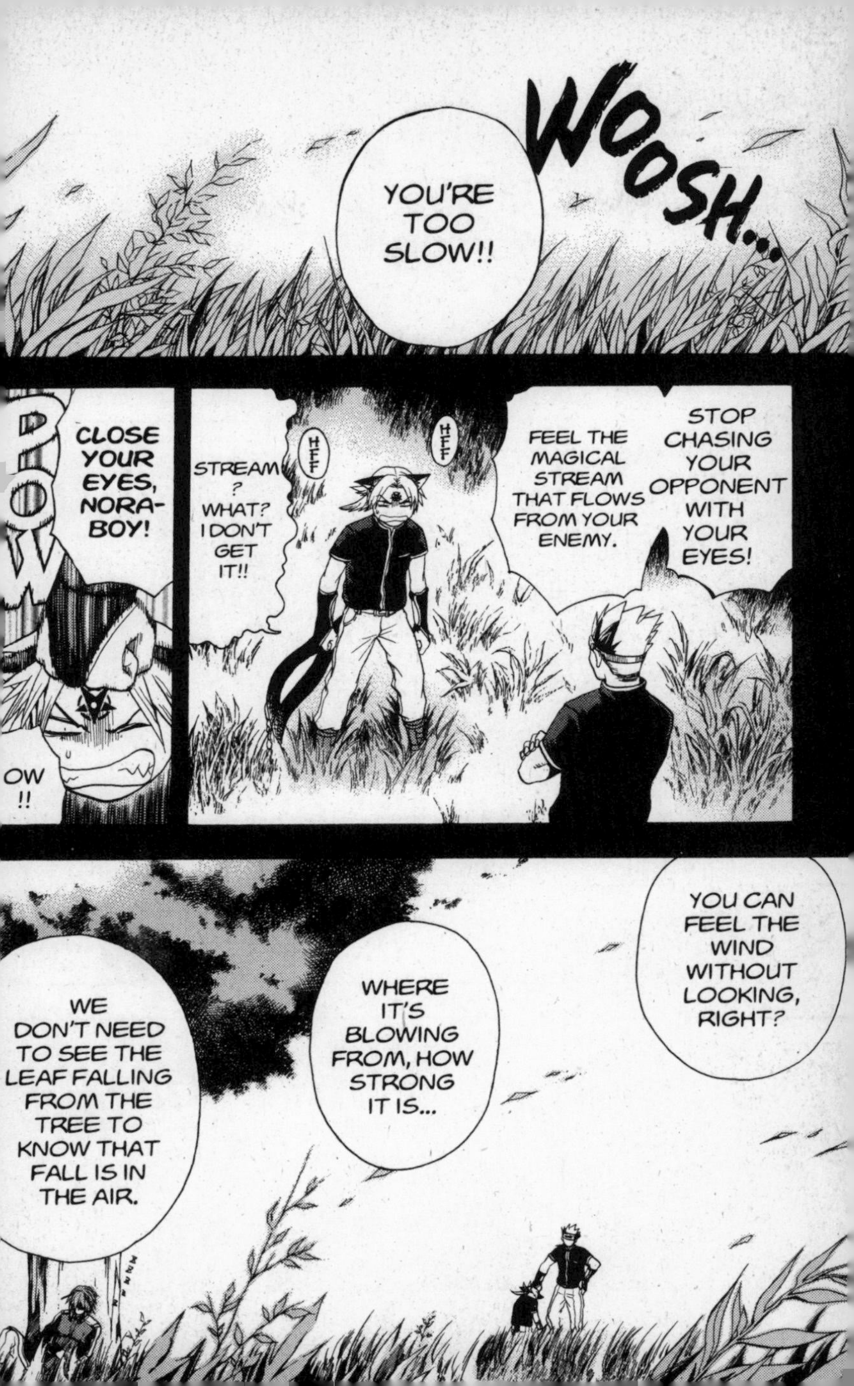
WOOSH...
YOU'RE TOO SLOW!!
STOP CHASING YOUR OPPONENT WITH YOUR EYES!
FEEL THE MAGICAL STREAM THAT FLOWS FROM YOUR ENEMY.
HFF
HFF
STREAM? WHAT? I DON'T GET IT!!
CLOSE YOUR EYES, NORA-BOY!
OW!!
YOU CAN FEEL THE WIND WITHOUT LOOKING, RIGHT?
WHERE IT'S BLOWING FROM, HOW STRONG IT IS...
WE DON'T NEED TO SEE THE LEAF FALLING FROM THE TREE TO KNOW THAT FALL IS IN THE AIR.

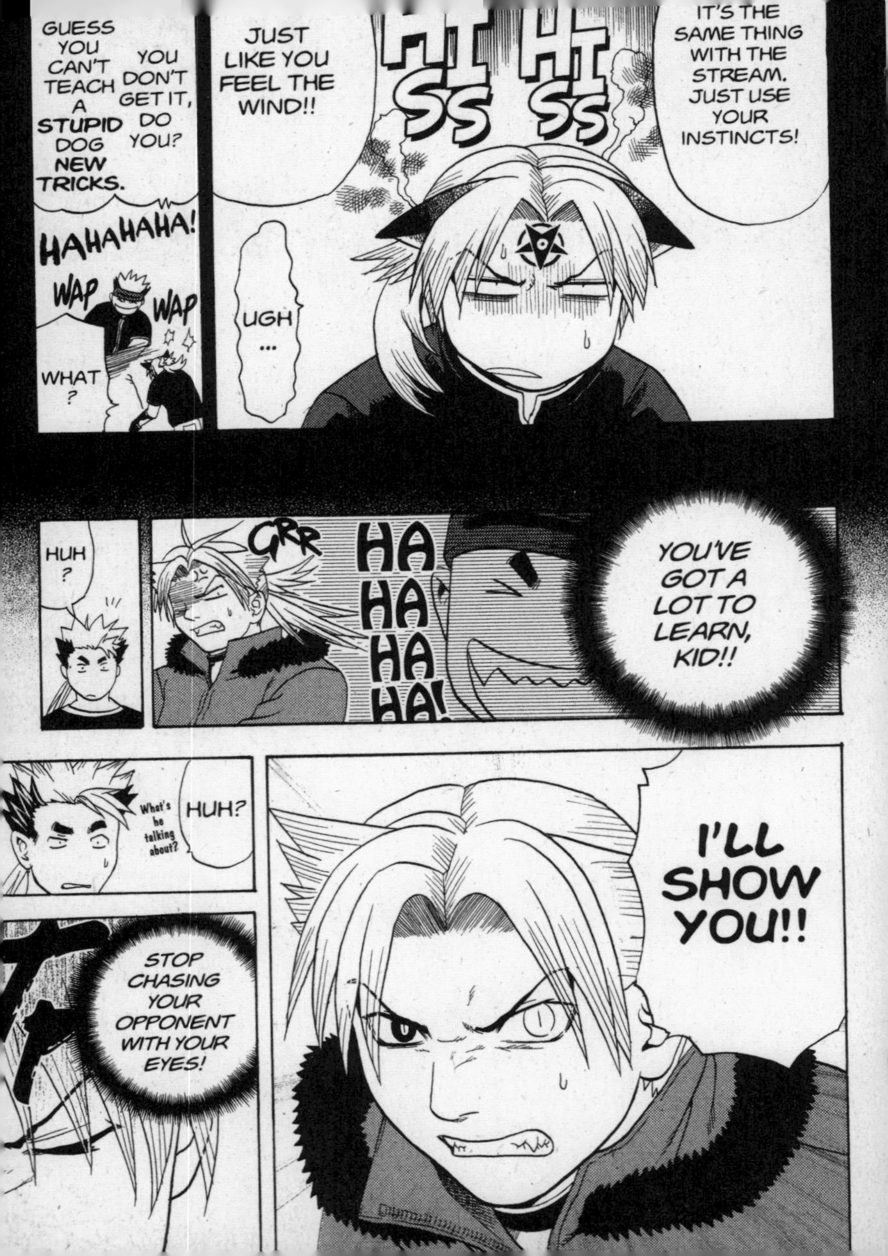
IT'S THE SAME THING WITH THE STREAM. JUST USE YOUR INSTINCTS!
HISS HISS
JUST LIKE YOU FEEL THE WIND!!
UGH ...
YOU DON'T GET IT, DO YOU?
GUESS YOU CAN'T TEACH A STUPID DOG NEW TRICKS.
HAHAHAHA!
WAP WAP
WHAT ?
YOU'VE GOT A LOT TO LEARN, KID!!
HA HA HA HA HA!
GRR
HUH ?
I'LL SHOW YOU!!
HUH?
What's he talking about?
STOP CHASING YOUR OPPONENT WITH YOUR EYES!

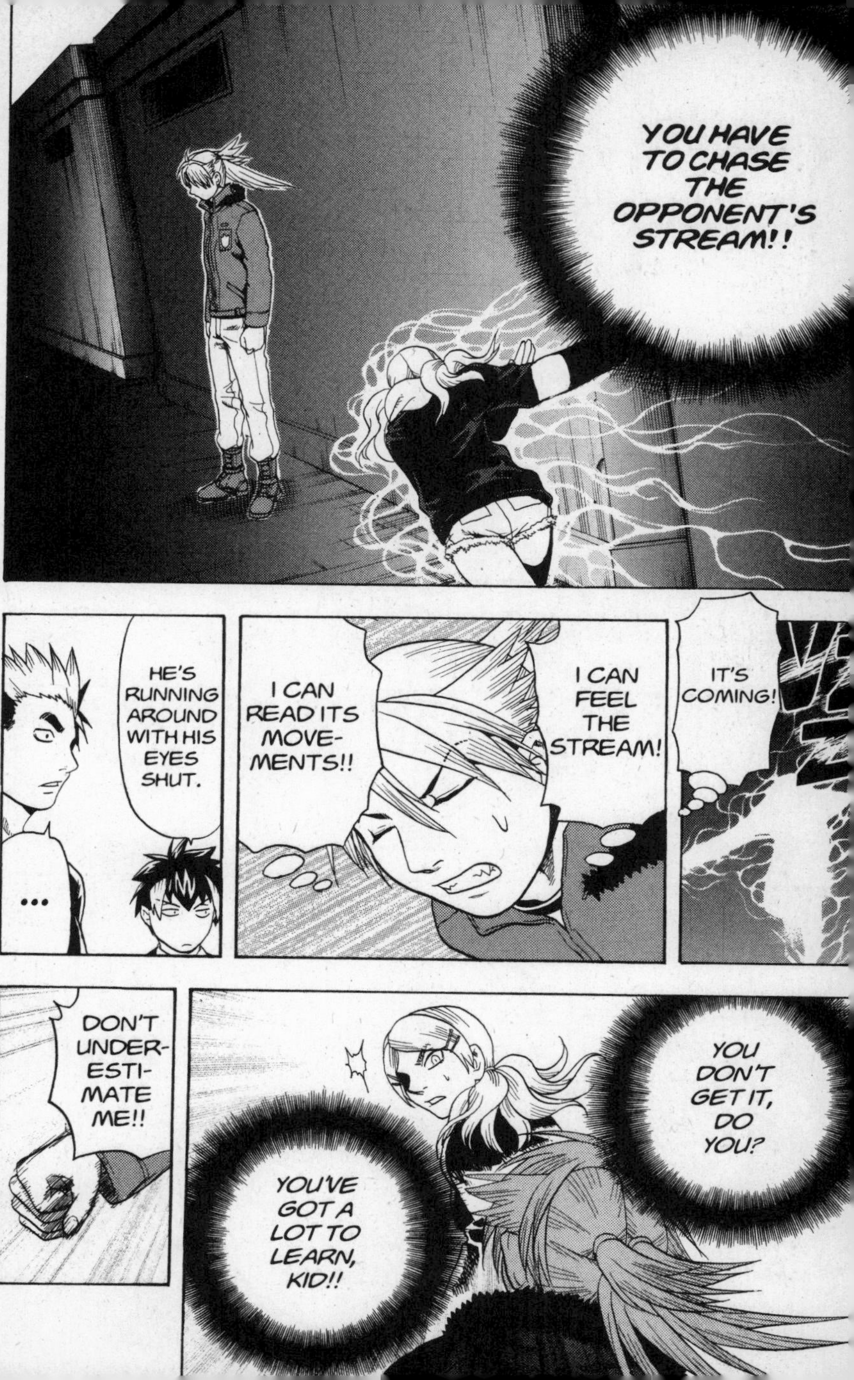
YOU HAVE TO CHASE THE OPPONENT'S STREAM!!
IT'S COMING!
I CAN FEEL THE STREAM!
I CAN READ ITS MOVE-MENTS!!
HE'S RUNNING AROUND WITH HIS EYES SHUT.
...
YOU DON'T GET IT, DO YOU?
YOU'VE GOT A LOT TO LEARN, KID!!
DON'T UNDER-ESTI-MATE ME!!

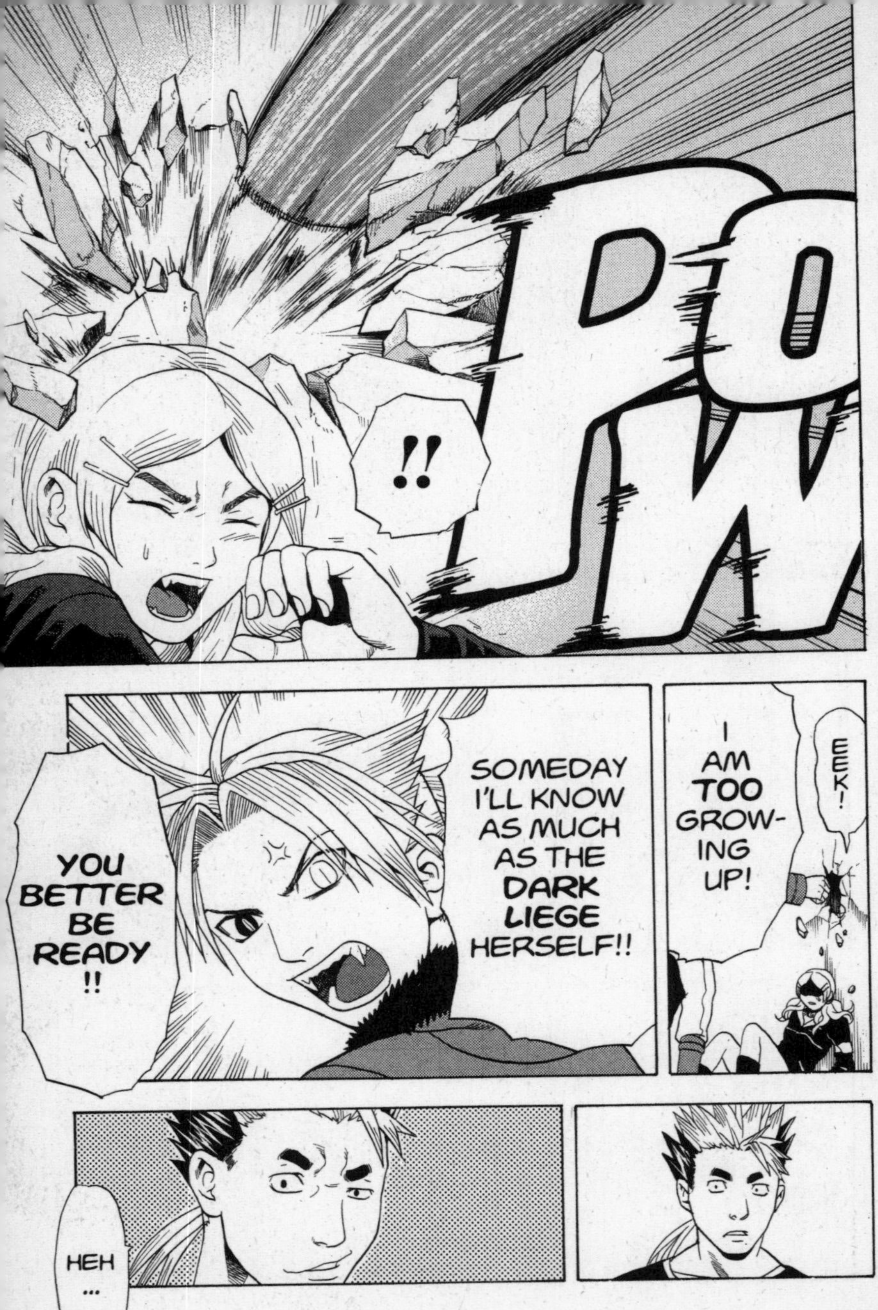
!!
EEK!
I AM TOO GROWING UP!
SOMEDAY I'LL KNOW AS MUCH AS THE DARK LIEGE HERSELF!!
YOU BETTER BE READY!!
HEH ...

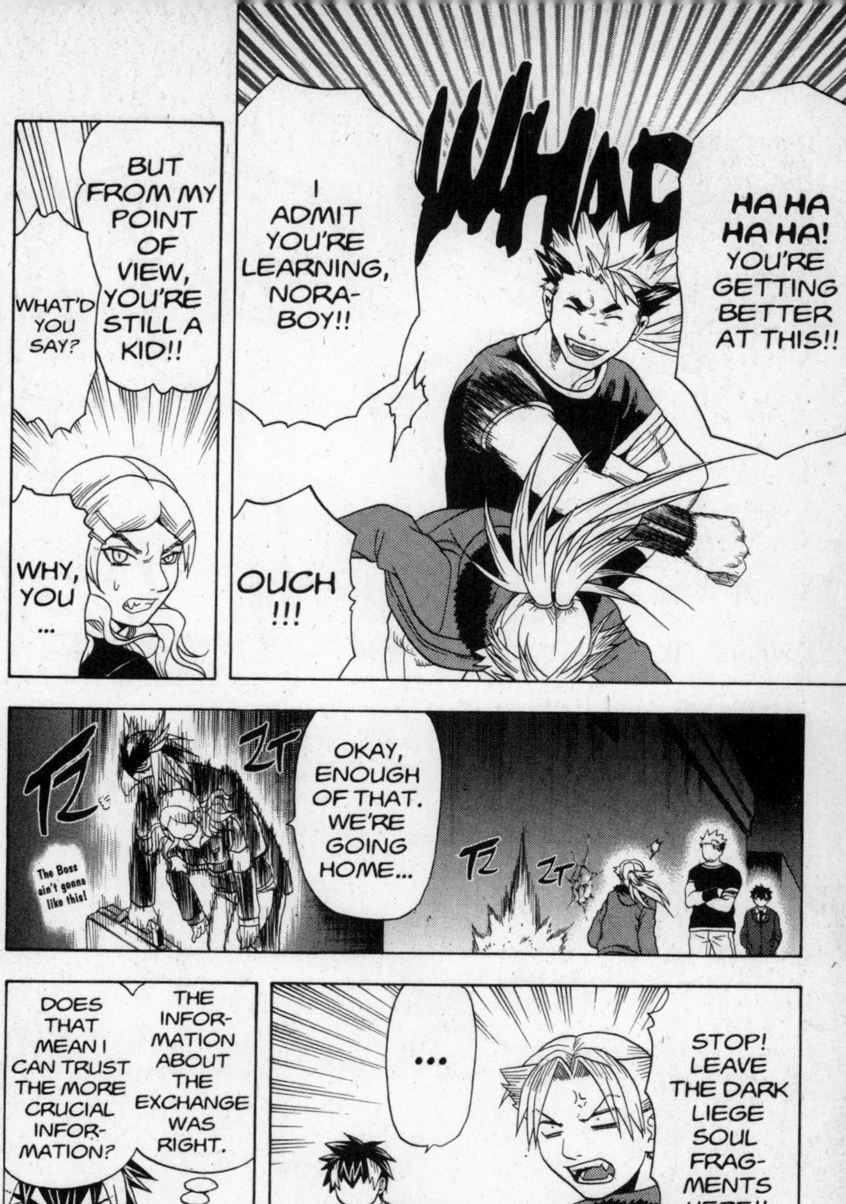
WHAP
HA HA HA HA! YOU'RE GETTING BETTER AT THIS!!
I ADMIT YOU'RE LEARNING, NORA-BOY!!
OUCH!!!
BUT FROM MY POINT OF VIEW, YOU'RE STILL A KID!!
WHAT'D YOU SAY?
WHY, YOU ...
TZ
ZT
OKAY, ENOUGH OF THAT. WE'RE GOING HOME...
ZT
TZ
The Boss ain't gonna like this!
STOP! LEAVE THE DARK LIEGE SOUL FRAGMENTS HERE!!
...
THE INFORMATION ABOUT THE EXCHANGE WAS RIGHT.
DOES THAT MEAN I CAN TRUST THE MORE CRUCIAL INFORMATION?

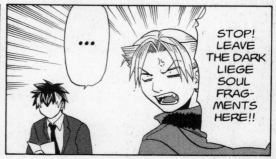

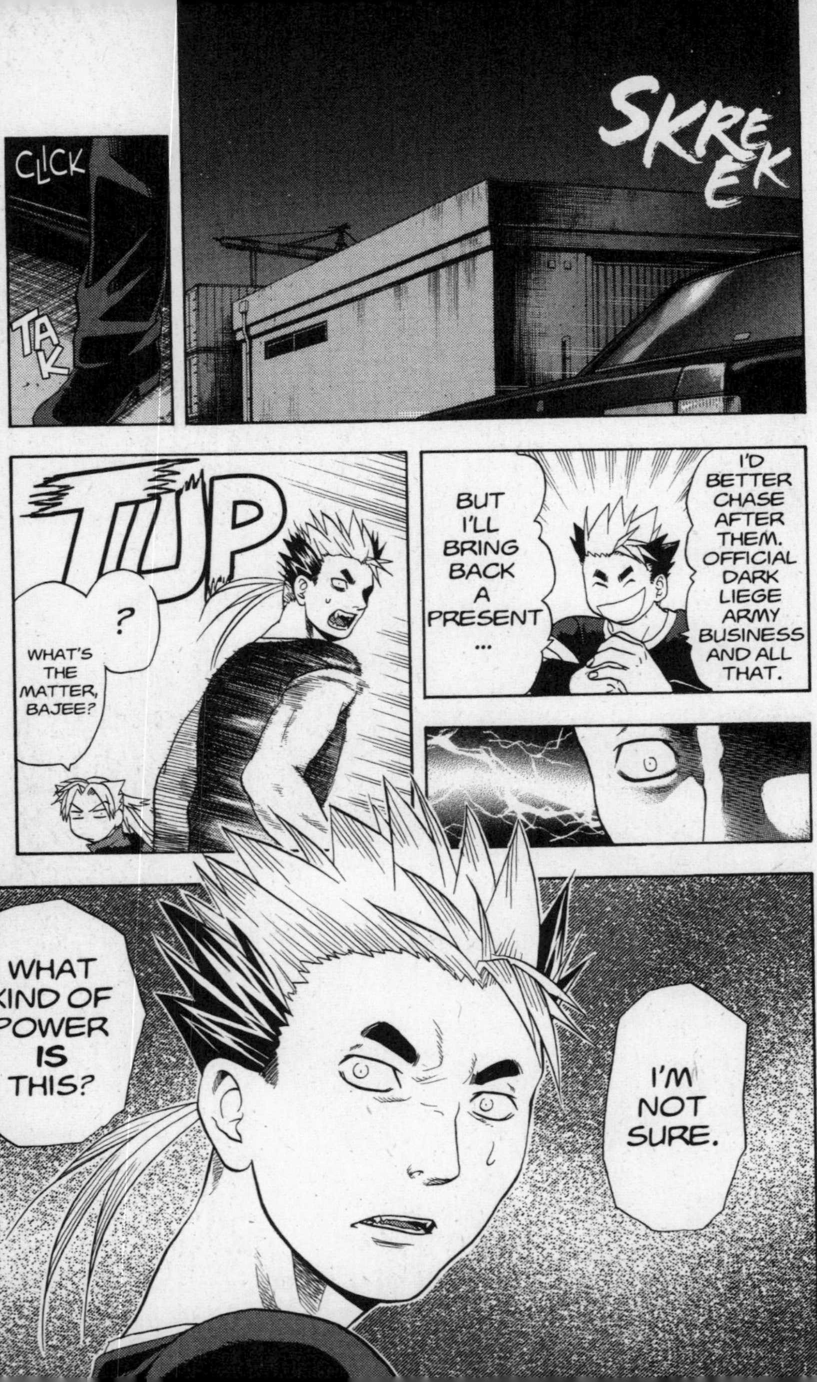
SKREEK
CLICK
TAK
I'D BETTER CHASE AFTER THEM. OFFICIAL DARK LIEGE ARMY BUSINESS AND ALL THAT.
BUT I'LL BRING BACK A PRESENT...
TUP
?
WHAT'S THE MATTER, BAJEE?
WHAT KIND OF POWER IS THIS?
I'M NOT SURE.

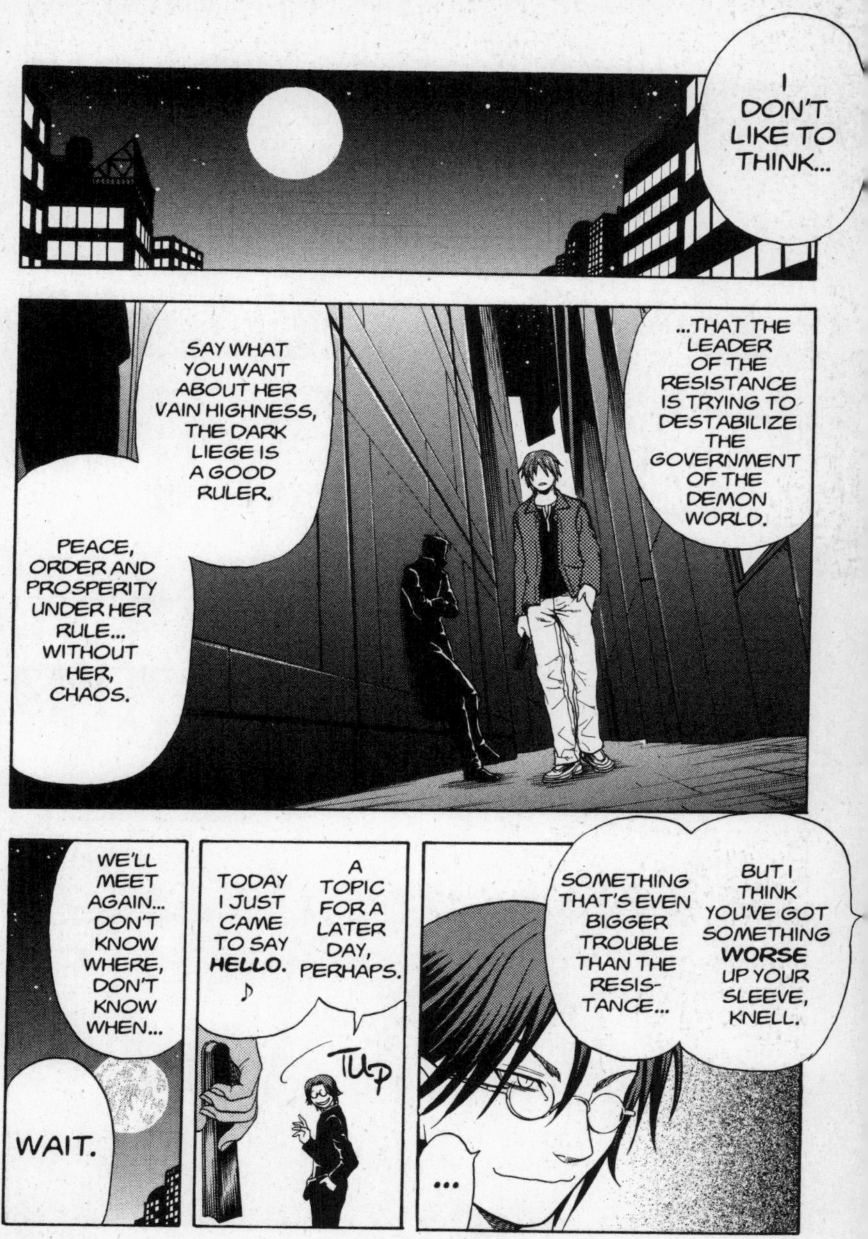
I DON'T LIKE TO THINK...
...THAT THE LEADER OF THE RESISTANCE IS TRYING TO DESTABILIZE THE GOVERNMENT OF THE DEMON WORLD.
SAY WHAT YOU WANT ABOUT HER VAIN HIGHNESS, THE DARK LIEGE IS A GOOD RULER.
PEACE, ORDER AND PROSPERITY UNDER HER RULE... WITHOUT HER, CHAOS.
BUT I THINK YOU'VE GOT SOMETHING **WORSE** UP YOUR SLEEVE, KNELL.
SOMETHING THAT'S EVEN BIGGER TROUBLE THAN THE RESIS-TANCE...
...
A TOPIC FOR A LATER DAY, PERHAPS.
TODAY I JUST CAME TO SAY **HELLO.** ♪
TUP
WE'LL MEET AGAIN... DON'T KNOW WHERE, DON'T KNOW WHEN...
WAIT.

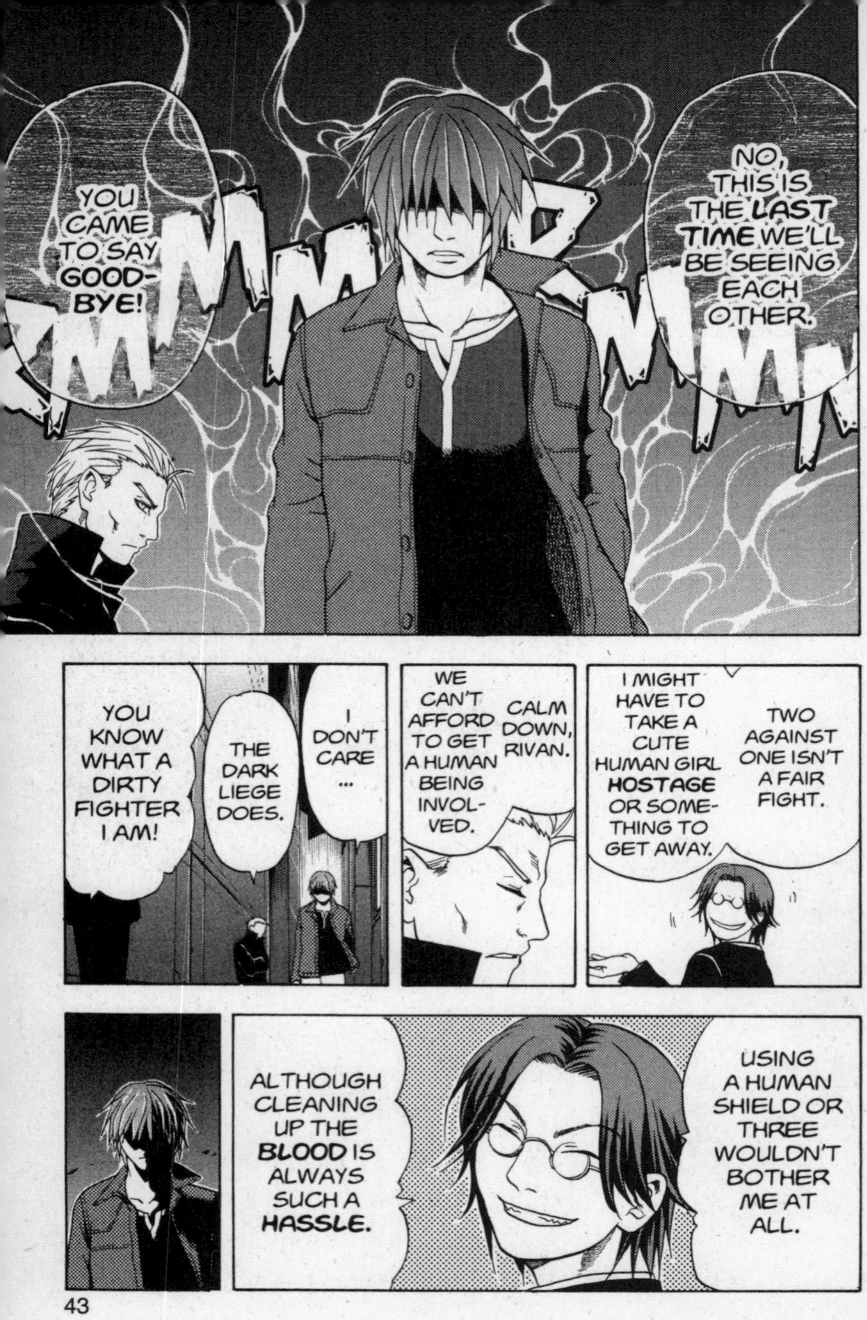
NO, THIS IS THE LAST TIME WE'LL BE SEEING EACH OTHER.
YOU CAME TO SAY GOOD-BYE!
TWO AGAINST ONE ISN'T A FAIR FIGHT.
I MIGHT HAVE TO TAKE A CUTE HUMAN GIRL HOSTAGE OR SOME-THING TO GET AWAY.
CALM DOWN, RIVAN.
WE CAN'T AFFORD TO GET A HUMAN BEING INVOL-VED.
I DON'T CARE ...
THE DARK LIEGE DOES.
YOU KNOW WHAT A DIRTY FIGHTER I AM!
USING A HUMAN SHIELD OR THREE WOULDN'T BOTHER ME AT ALL.
ALTHOUGH CLEANING UP THE BLOOD IS ALWAYS SUCH A HASSLE.

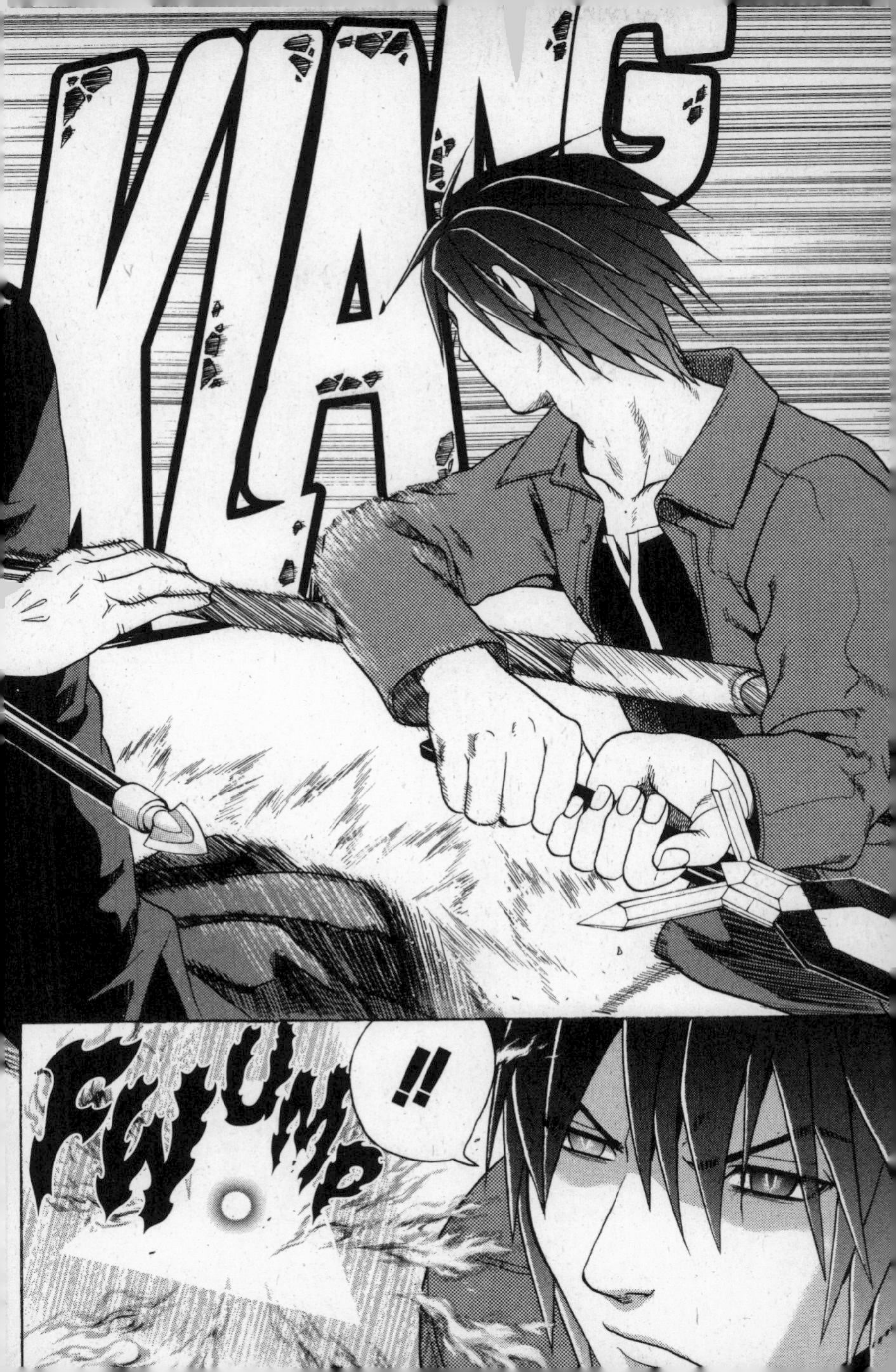
WANG
!!
FWUMP

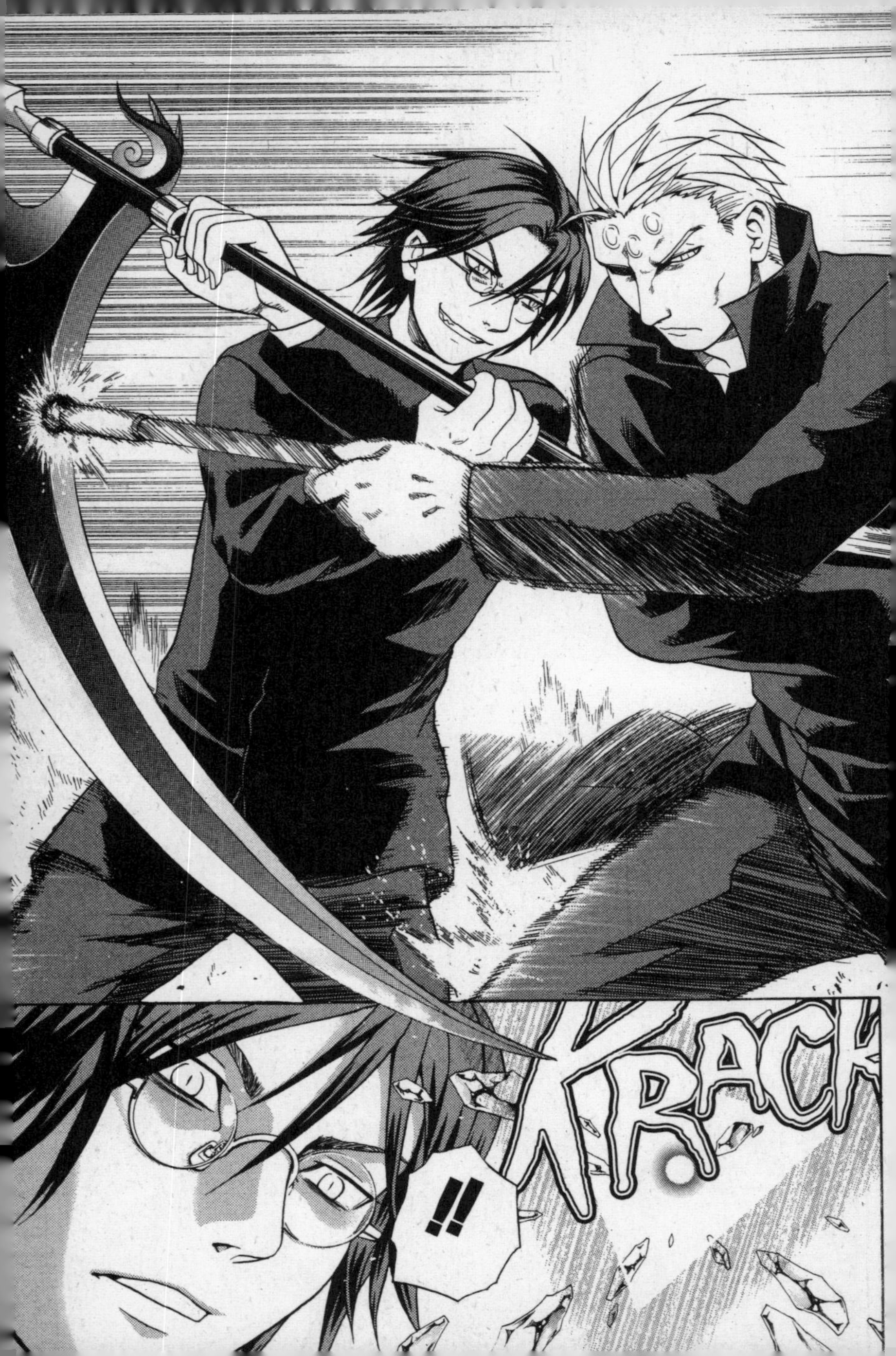
KRACK
!!

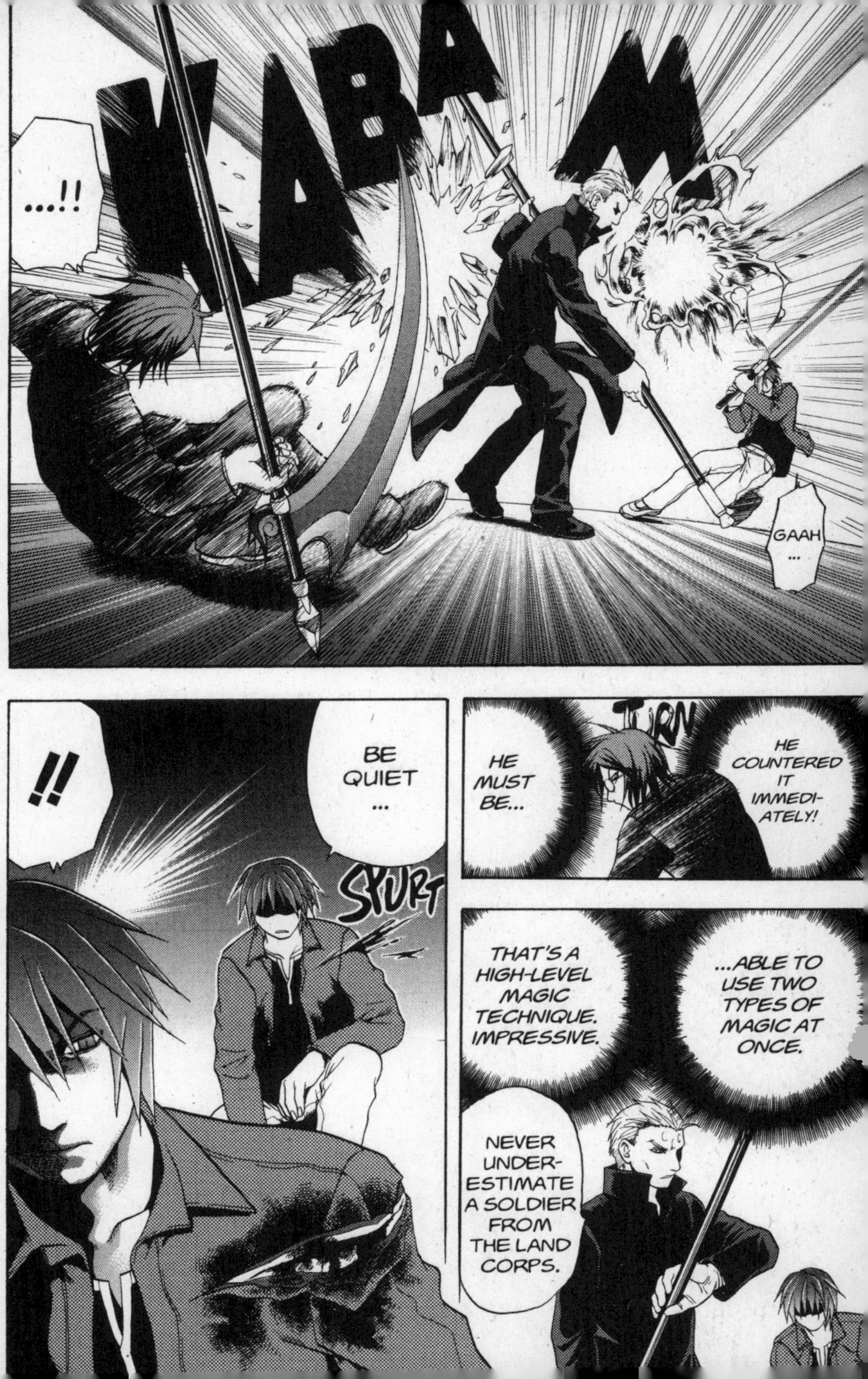
WABAM
GAAH ...
...!!
HE COUNTERED IT IMMEDI-ATELY!
TURN
HE MUST BE...
...ABLE TO USE TWO TYPES OF MAGIC AT ONCE.
THAT'S A HIGH-LEVEL MAGIC TECHNIQUE. IMPRESSIVE.
NEVER UNDER-ESTIMATE A SOLDIER FROM THE LAND CORPS.
BE QUIET ...
SPURT
!!

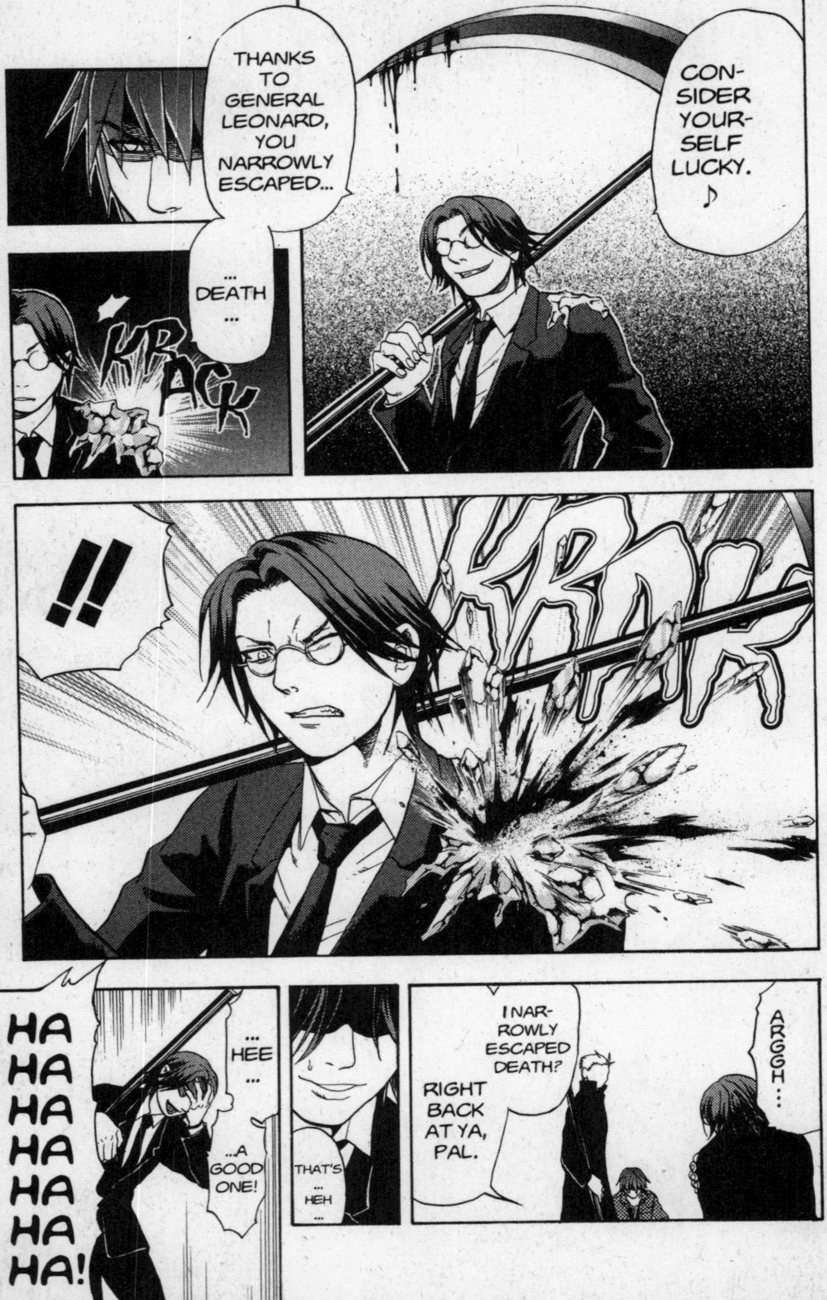
CON-SIDER YOUR-SELF LUCKY. ♪
THANKS TO GENERAL LEONARD, YOU NARROWLY ESCAPED...
...DEATH...
KRACK
!!
KRAK
ARGGH...
I NAR-ROWLY ESCAPED DEATH?
RIGHT BACK AT YA, PAL.
THAT'S... HEH...
...HEE...
...A GOOD ONE!
HA HA HA HA HA HA HA HA HA!

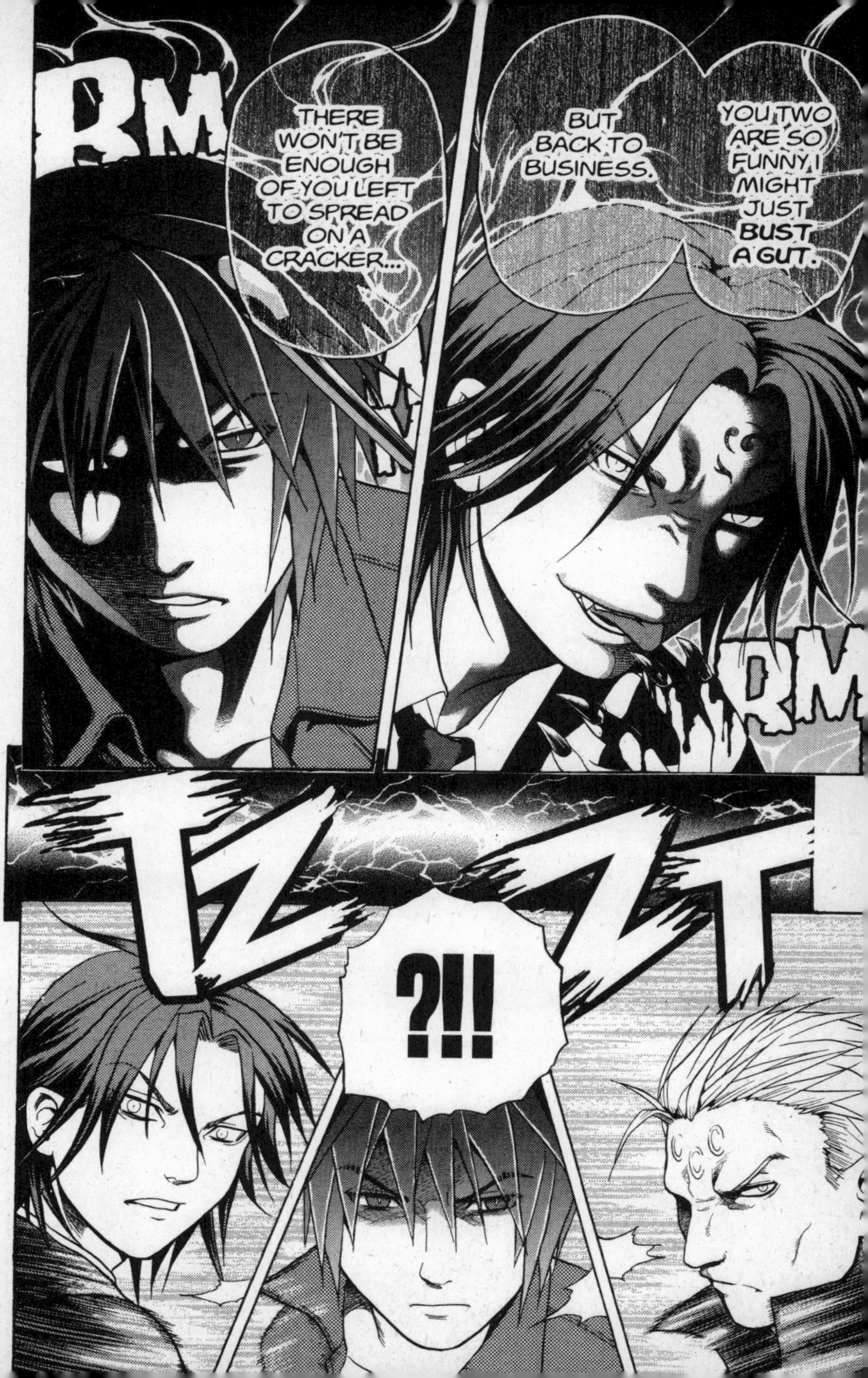
YOU TWO ARE SO FUNNY I MIGHT JUST **BUST** A GUT.
BUT BACK TO BUSINESS.
RM
RM
THERE WON'T BE ENOUGH OF YOU LEFT TO SPREAD ON A CRACKER...
TZZT
?!!

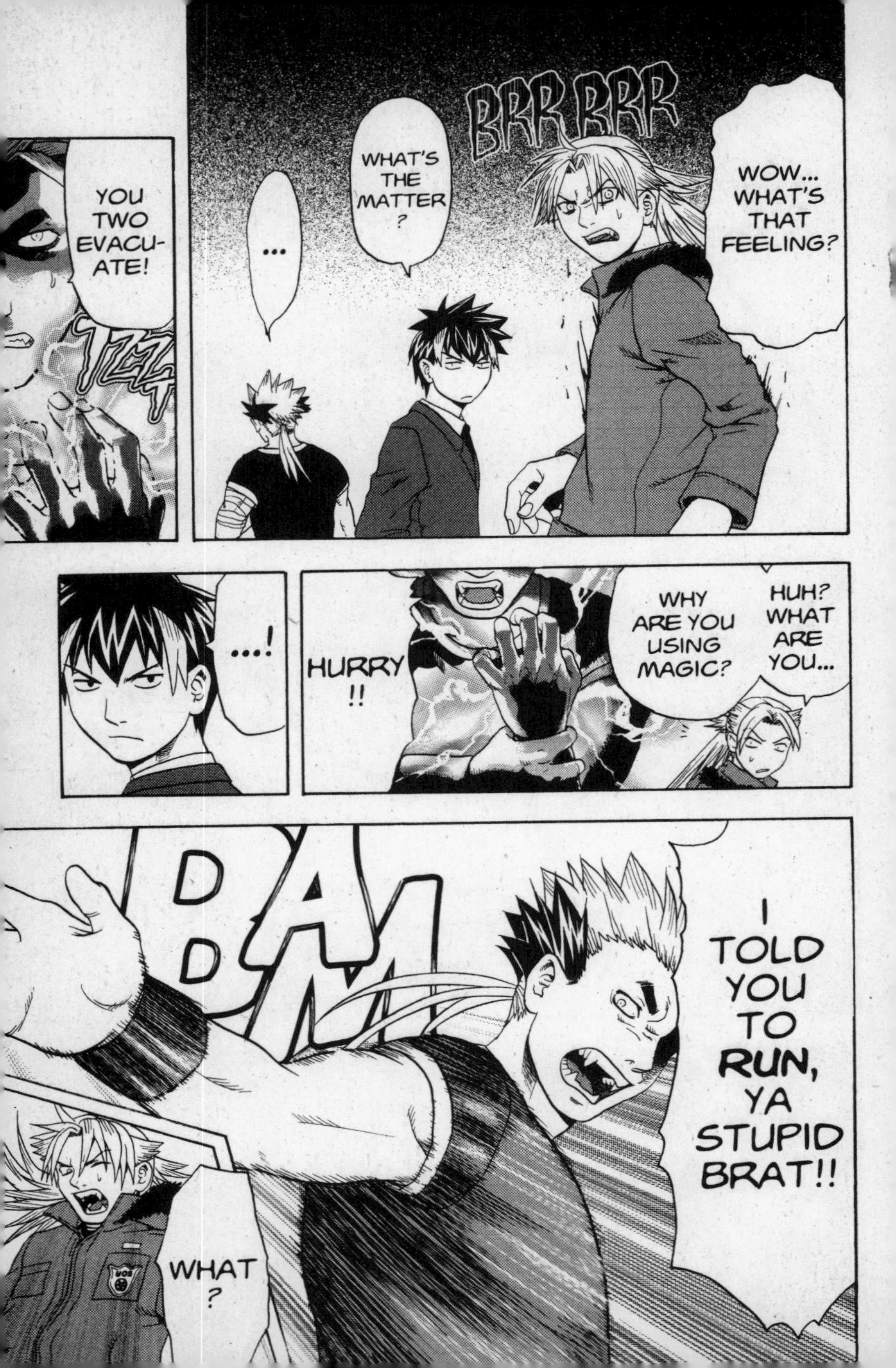
BRRRRR
WOW... WHAT'S THAT FEELING?
WHAT'S THE MATTER?
...
YOU TWO EVACUATE!
HUH? WHAT ARE YOU...
WHY ARE YOU USING MAGIC?
HURRY!!
...!
I TOLD YOU TO RUN, YA STUPID BRAT!!
WHAT?

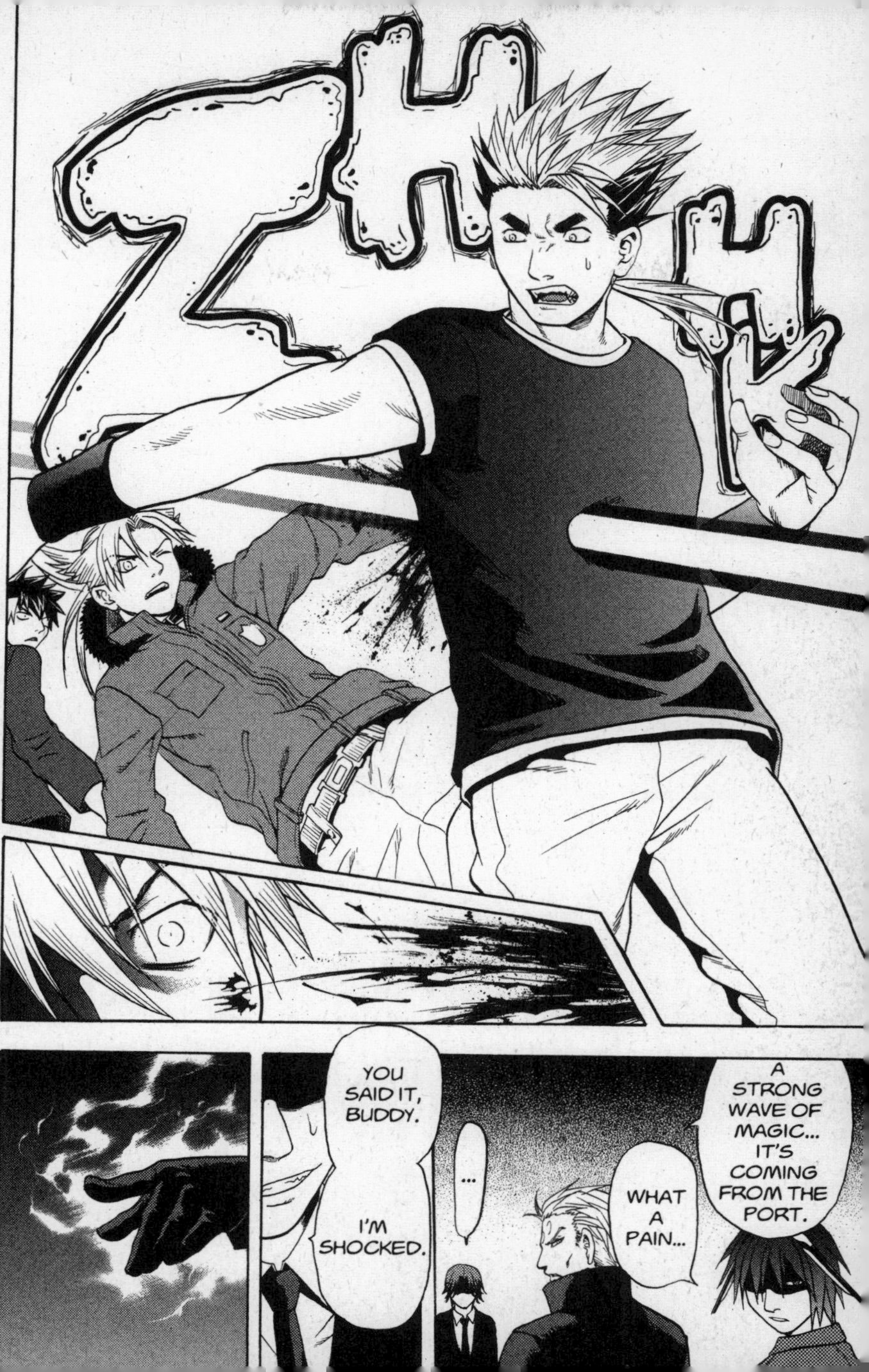
A STRONG WAVE OF MAGIC... IT'S COMING FROM THE PORT.
WHAT A PAIN...
...
YOU SAID IT, BUDDY.
I'M SHOCKED.

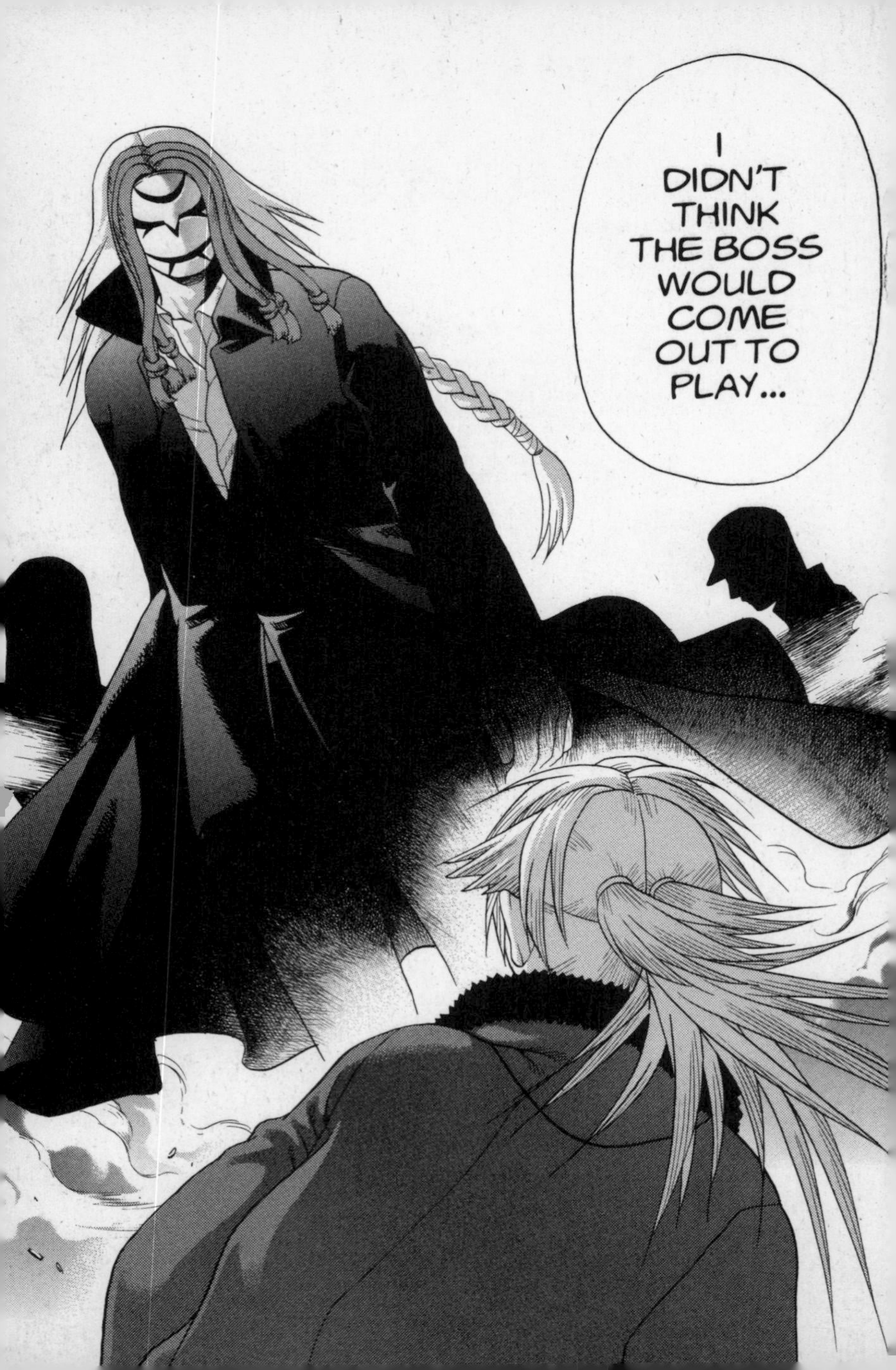
I DIDN'T THINK THE BOSS WOULD COME OUT TO PLAY...

CHARACTER DATA

BAJEE

HEIGHT: 193 CM
FAVORITE FOOD: JAPANESE SAKE
LEAST FAVORITE FOOD: CUCUMBERS
INTERESTS AND
SPECIAL TALENTS: WEIGHT TRAINING WITH
DUMBBELLS, RUNNING
NOTES: THE GENERAL OF THE DARK
LIEGE ARMY, WIND DIVISION.
IN OTHER WORDS, HE'S A BAG
OF HOT AIR, BUT HIS HEART'S IN
THE RIGHT PLACE. NORA'S LIKE
A KID BROTHER TO HIM, WHICH IS
PROBABLY WHY BAJEE TEASES
THE POOR KID MERCILESSLY.

KOYUKI HIRASAKA

HEIGHT: 151 CM
FAVORITE FOOD: CHOCOLATE CHIP COOKIES
LEAST FAVORITE FOOD: COUGH DROPS
INTERESTS AND
SPECIAL TALENTS: MAKING COOKIES (FOR HERSELF,
NATURALLY)
NOTES: KAZUMA'S CLASSMATE AND THE
VICE-PRESIDENT OF THE STUDENT
COUNCIL. MAYBE SHE'S ON THE COUNCIL
BECAUSE SHE'S NUTS ABOUT PRESIDENT
KAZUMA, OR MAYBE SHE'S JUST PLAIN
SCREWY. HER FAMILY RUNS A CAFÉ. SHE
HAS TWO YOUNGER BROTHERS (WHICH
MIGHT BE ENOUGH TO DRIVE ANY GIRL
CRAZY).

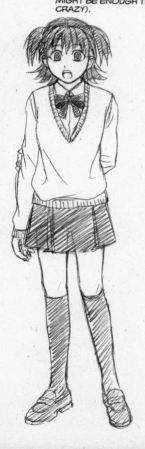

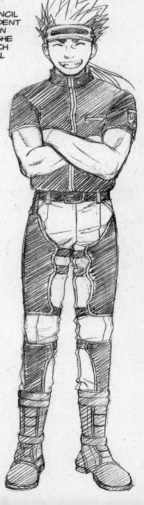

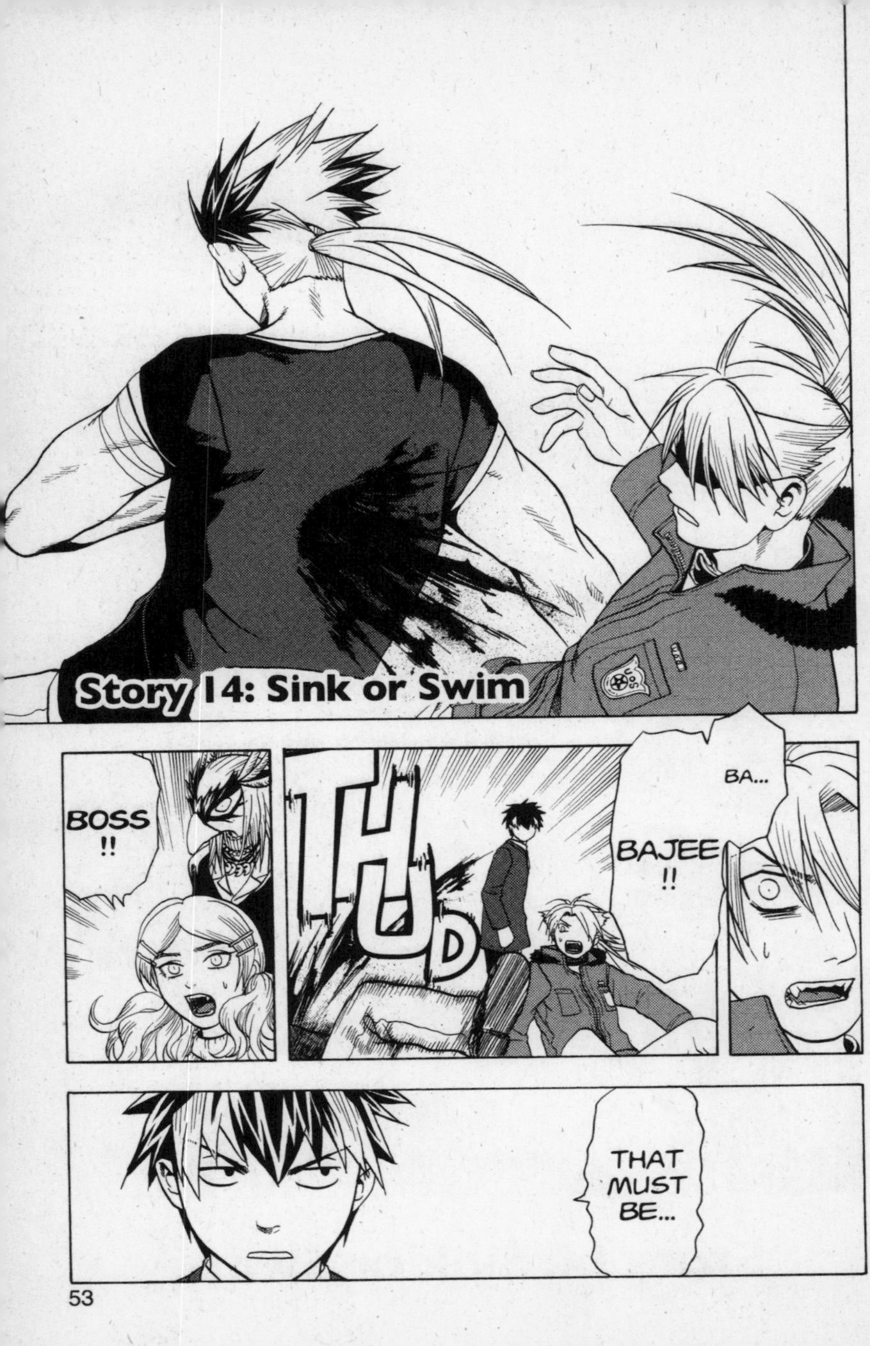
Story 14: Sink or Swim
BA...
BAJEE !!
THUD
BOSS !!
THAT MUST BE...

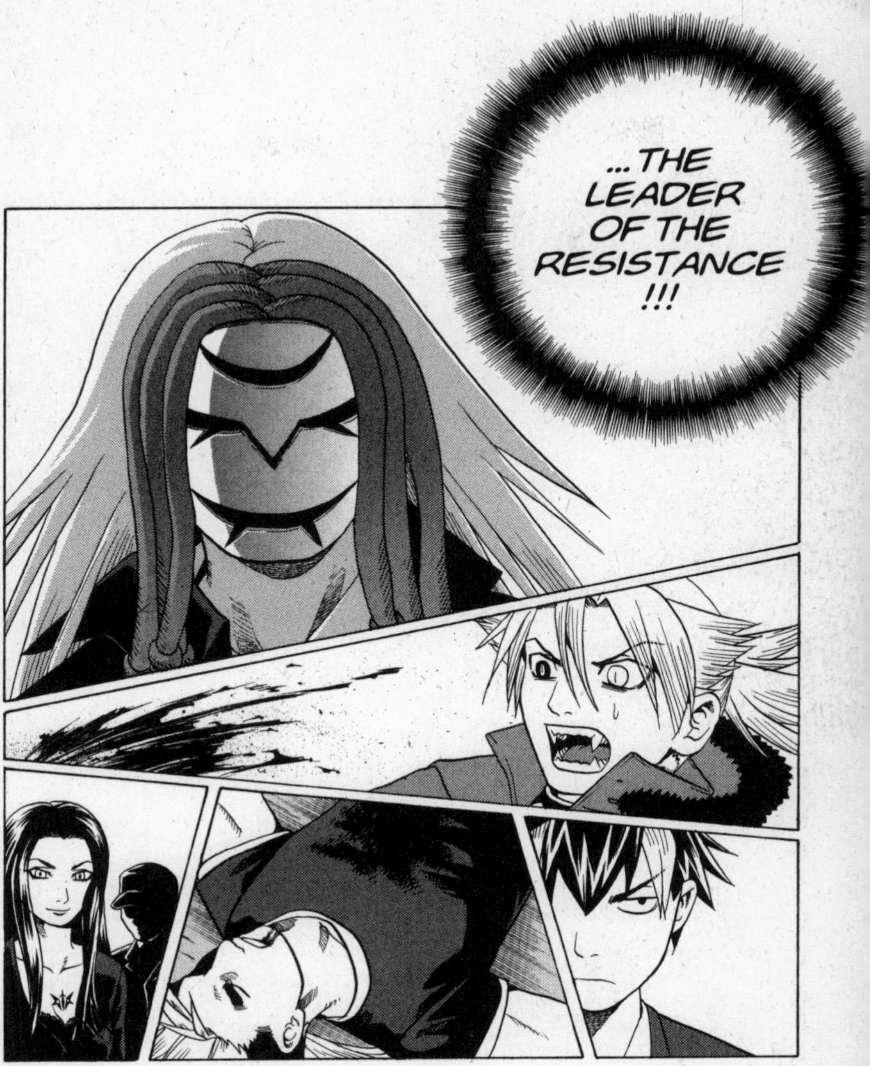
...THE LEADER OF THE RESISTANCE !!!

Story 14: Sink or Swim

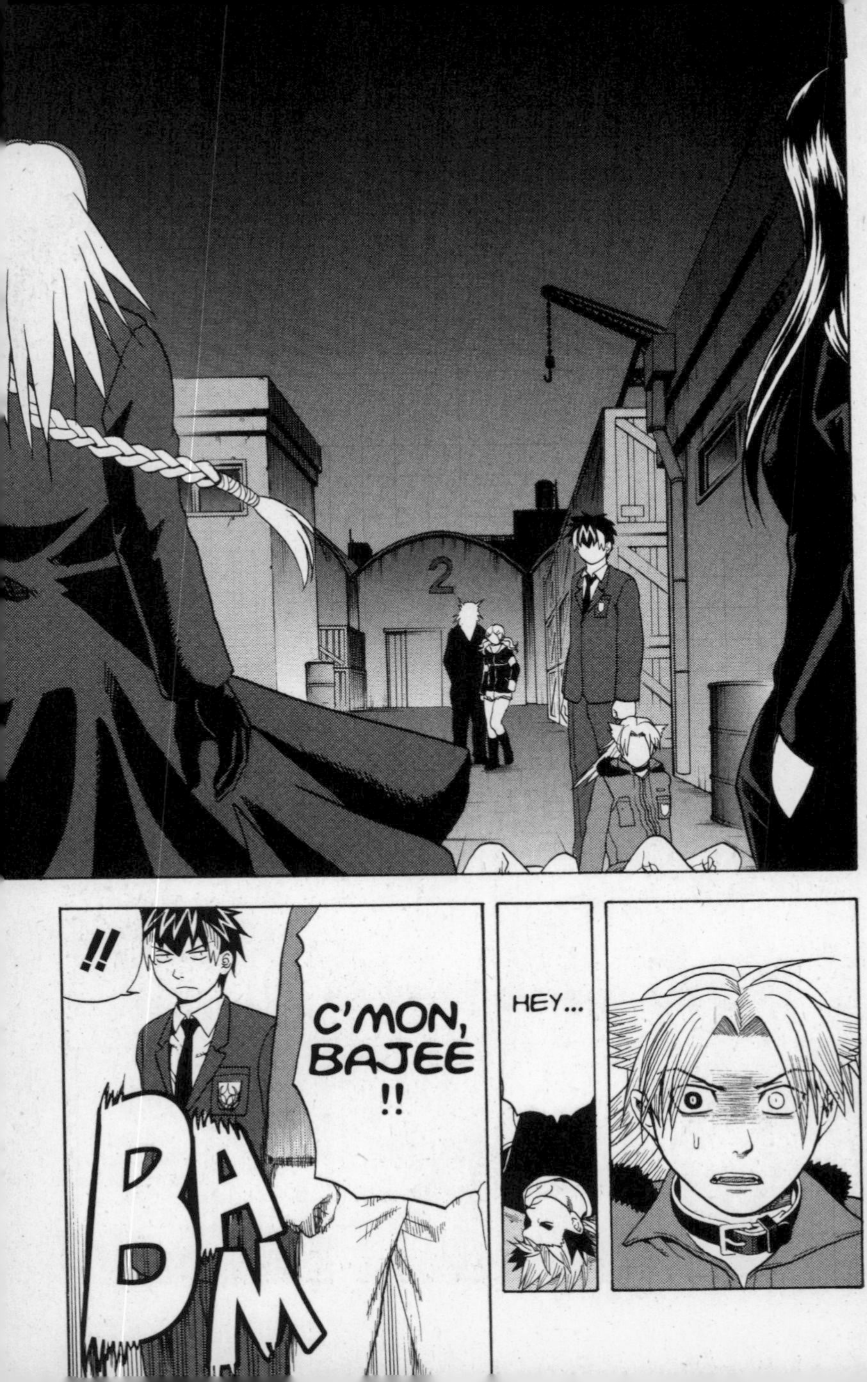
HEY...
C'MON, BAJEE !!
!!
BAM

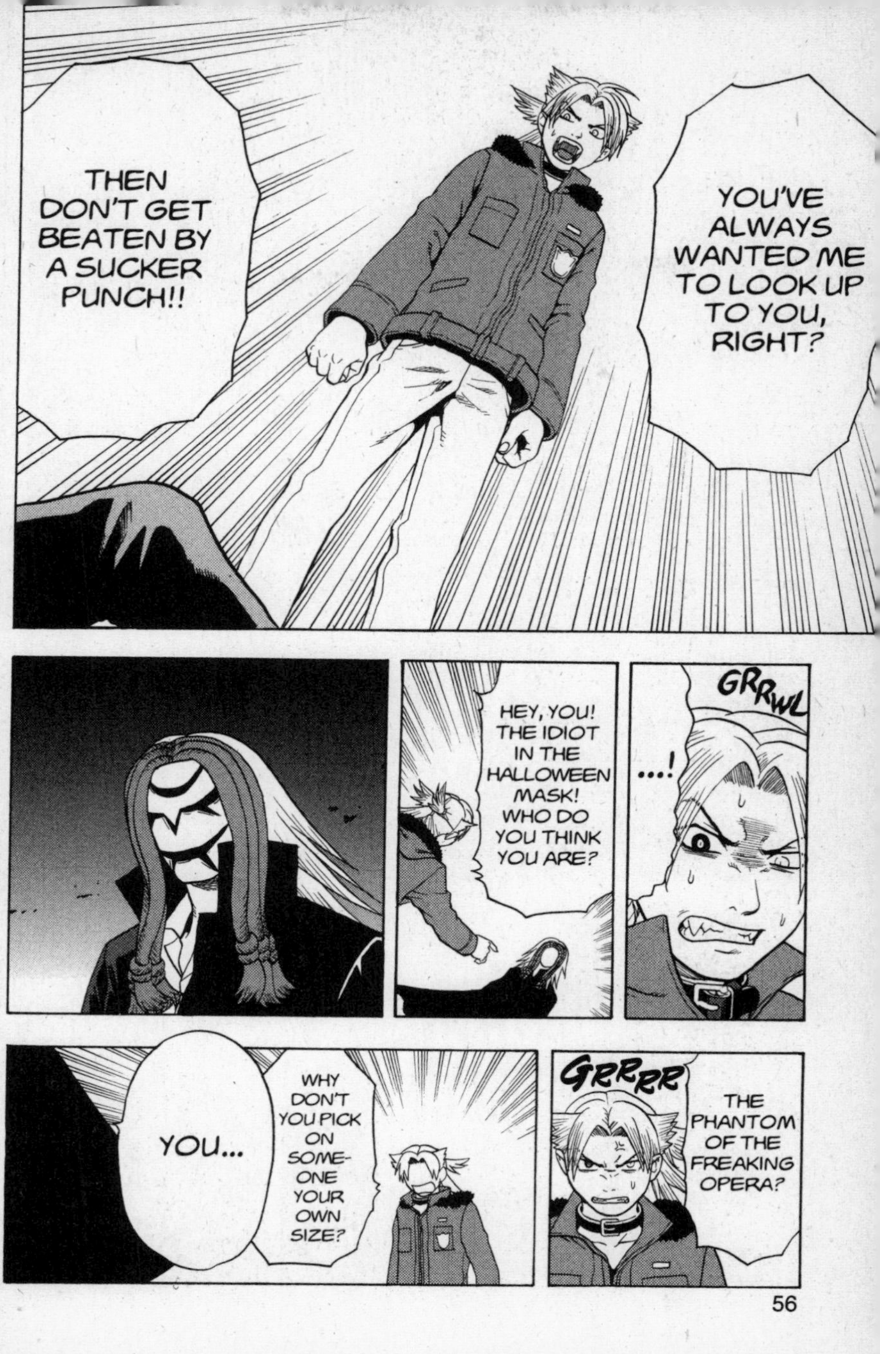
YOU'VE ALWAYS WANTED ME TO LOOK UP TO YOU, RIGHT?
THEN DON'T GET BEATEN BY A SUCKER PUNCH!!
GRRWL
...!
HEY, YOU! THE IDIOT IN THE HALLOWEEN MASK! WHO DO YOU THINK YOU ARE?
GRRRR
THE PHANTOM OF THE FREAKING OPERA?
WHY DON'T YOU PICK ON SOME-ONE YOUR OWN SIZE?
YOU...

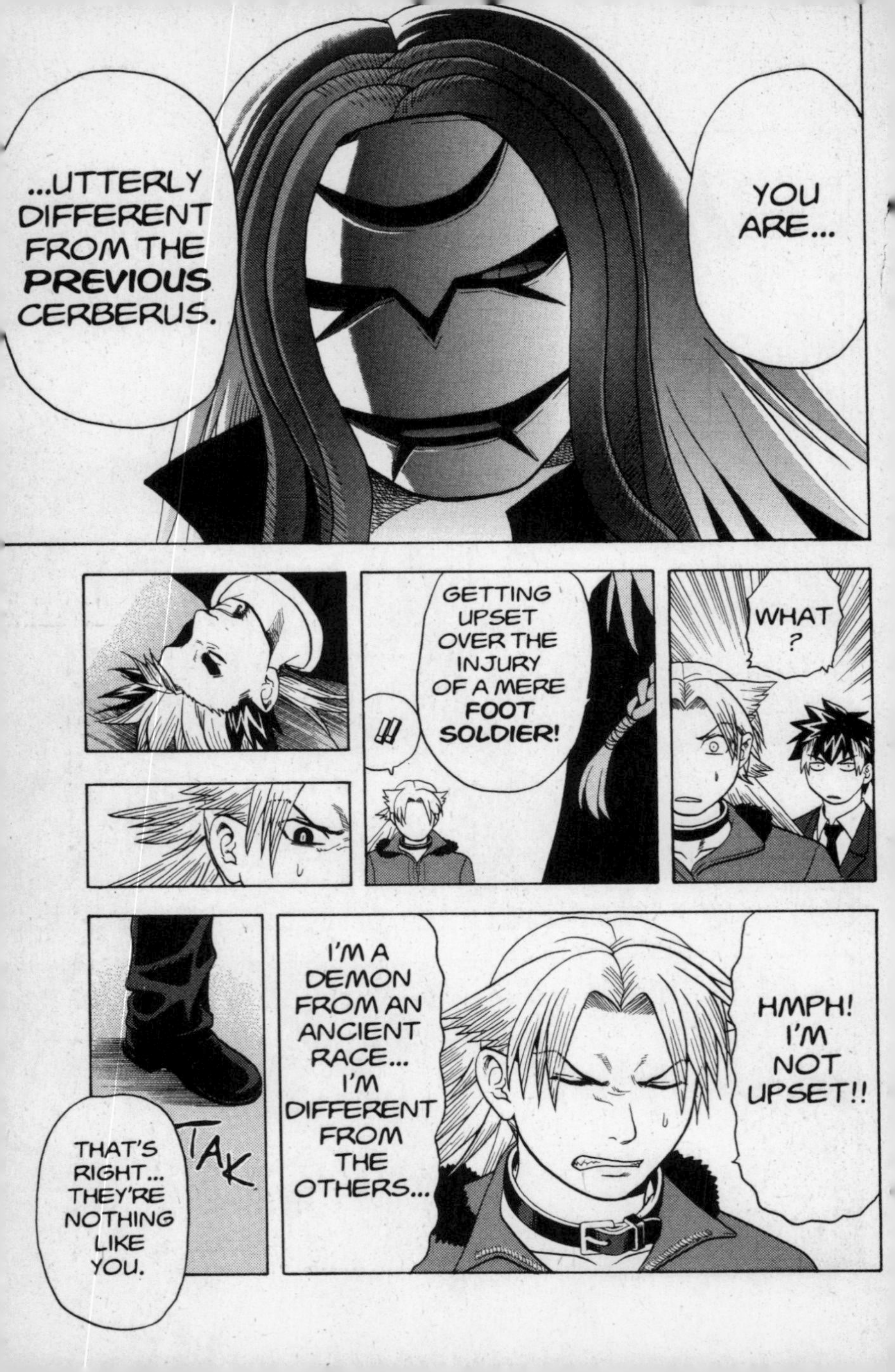
YOU ARE...
...UTTERLY DIFFERENT FROM THE **PREVIOUS** CERBERUS.
WHAT?
GETTING UPSET OVER THE INJURY OF A MERE **FOOT SOLDIER!**
!!
HMPH! I'M NOT UPSET!!
I'M A DEMON FROM AN ANCIENT RACE... I'M DIFFERENT FROM THE OTHERS...
TAK
THAT'S RIGHT... THEY'RE NOTHING LIKE YOU.

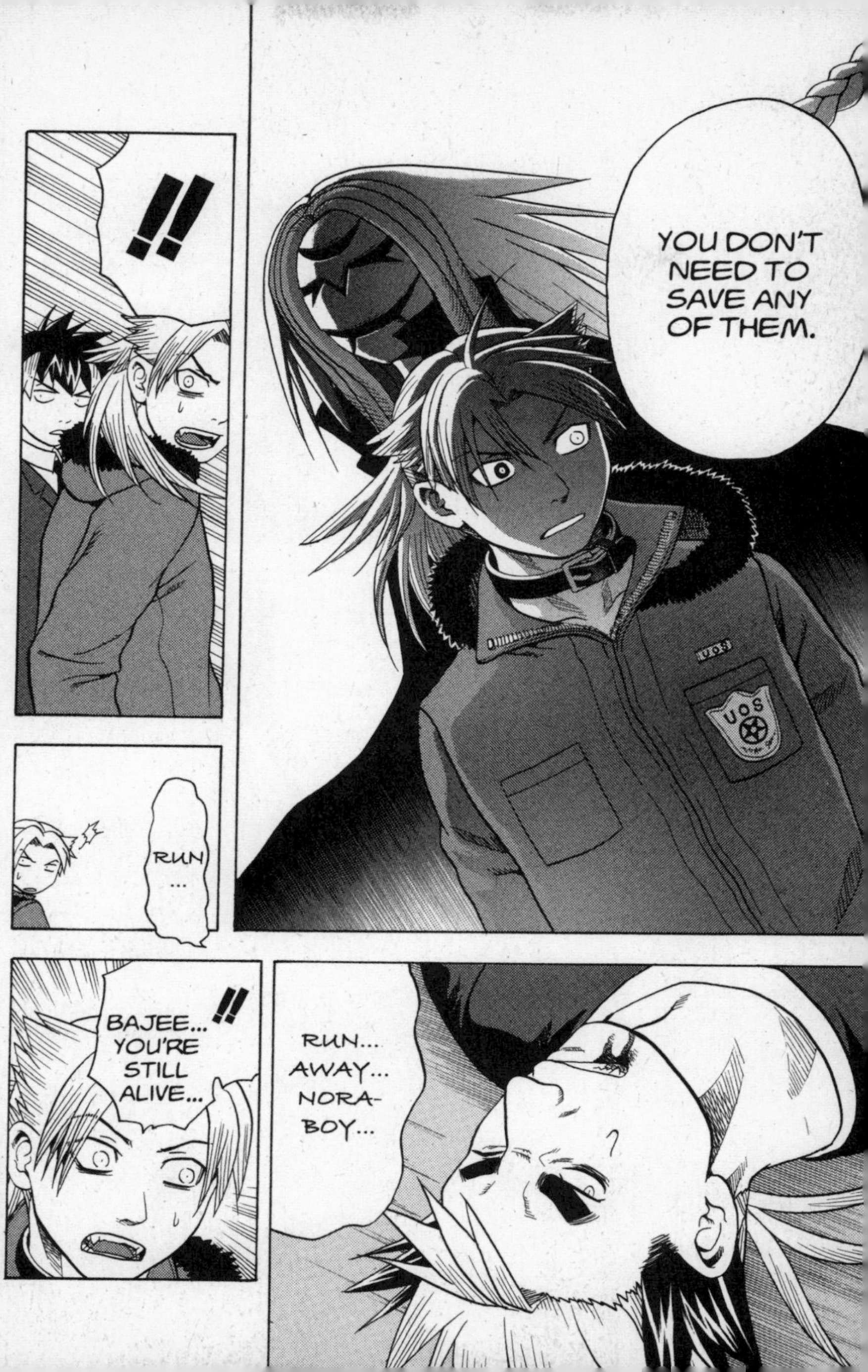
YOU DON'T NEED TO SAVE ANY OF THEM.
!!
RUN ...
RUN... AWAY... NORA-BOY...
!!
BAJEE... YOU'RE STILL ALIVE...

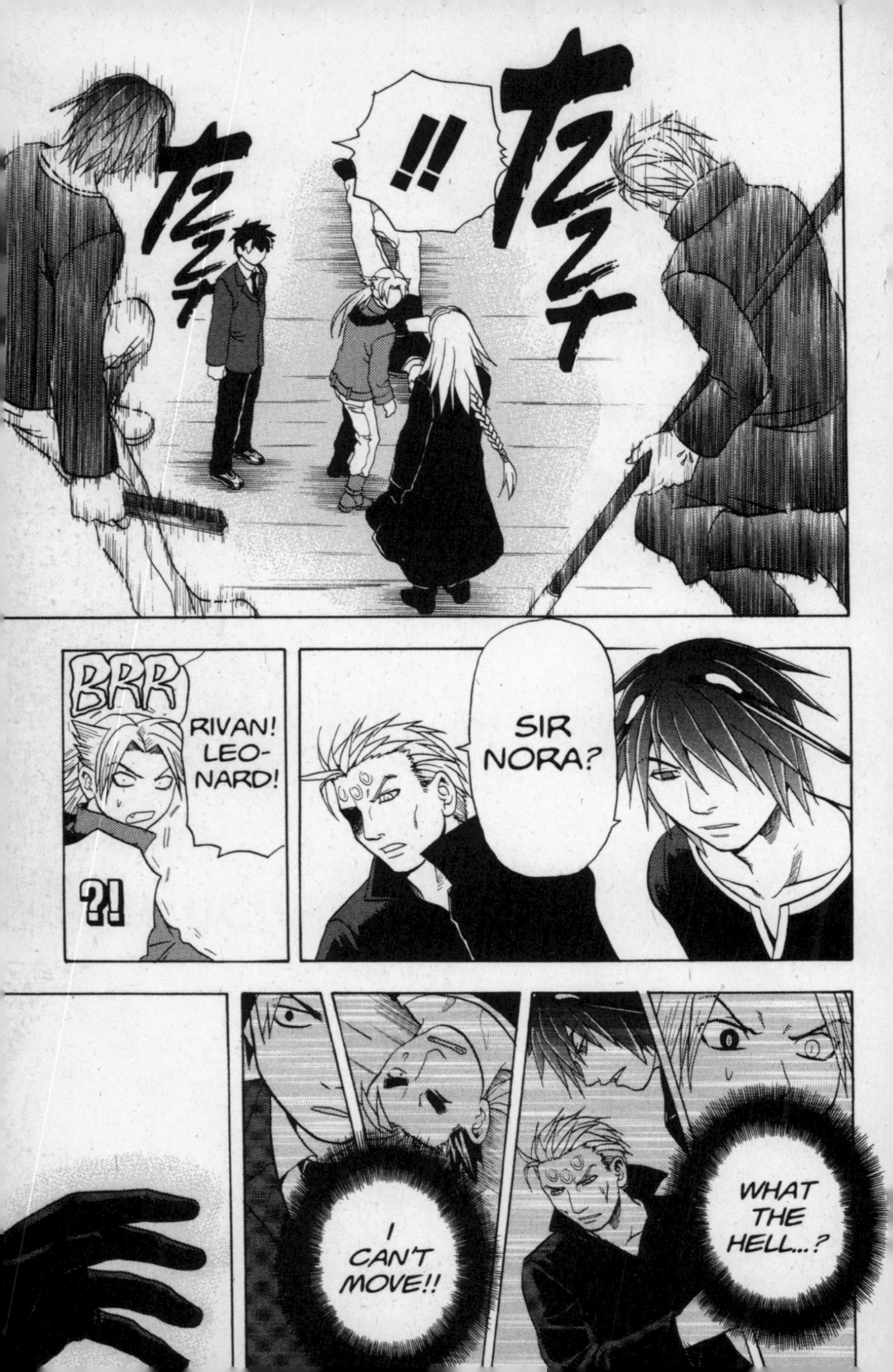
!!
SIR NORA?
BRR
RIVAN! LEO-NARD!
?!
WHAT THE HELL...?
I CAN'T MOVE!!

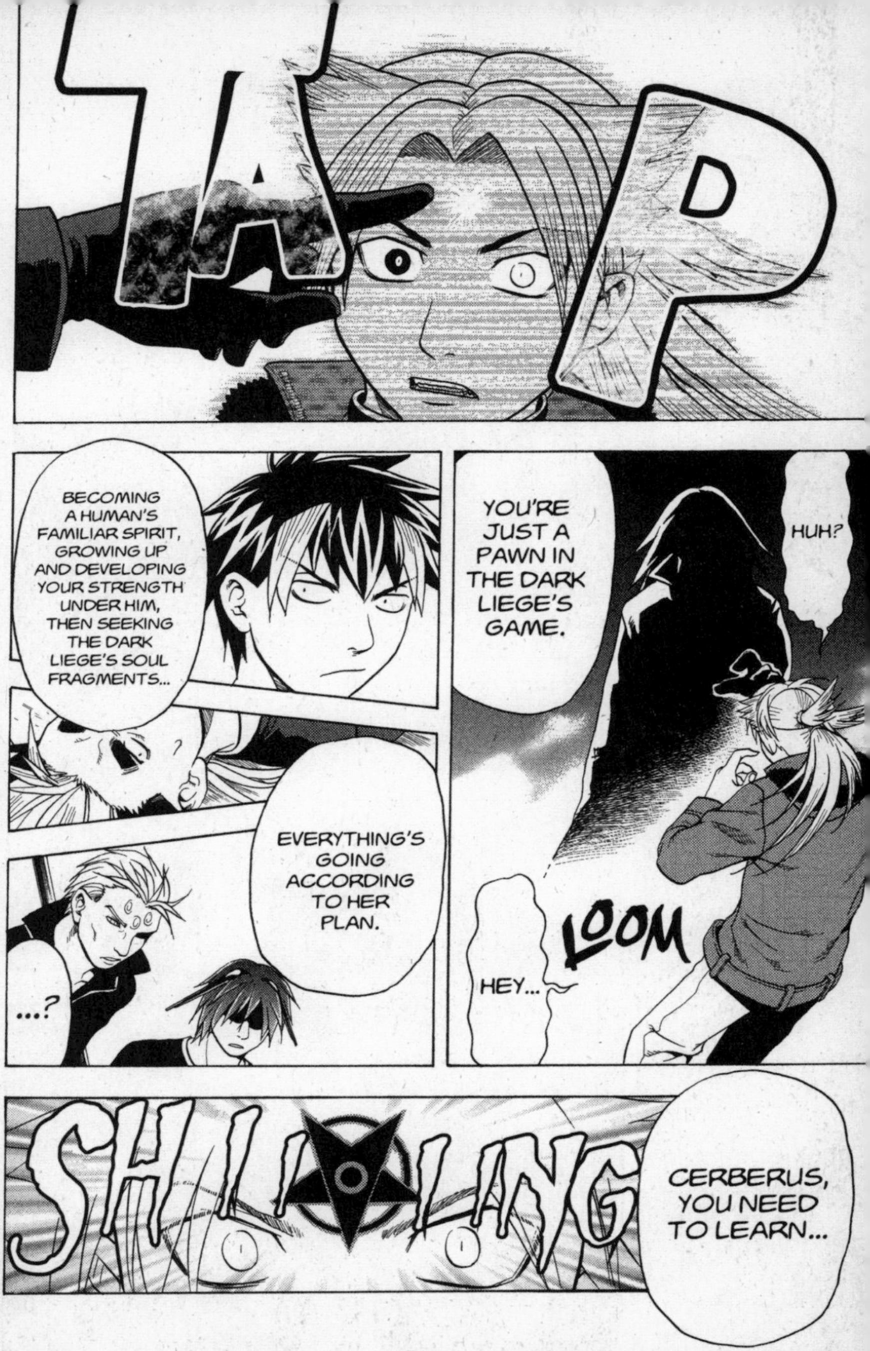
SLAP
HUH?
YOU'RE JUST A PAWN IN THE DARK LIEGE'S GAME.
LOOM
HEY...
BECOMING A HUMAN'S FAMILIAR SPIRIT, GROWING UP AND DEVELOPING YOUR STRENGTH UNDER HIM, THEN SEEKING THE DARK LIEGE'S SOUL FRAGMENTS...
?
EVERYTHING'S GOING ACCORDING TO HER PLAN.
...?
CERBERUS, YOU NEED TO LEARN...
SHIIING

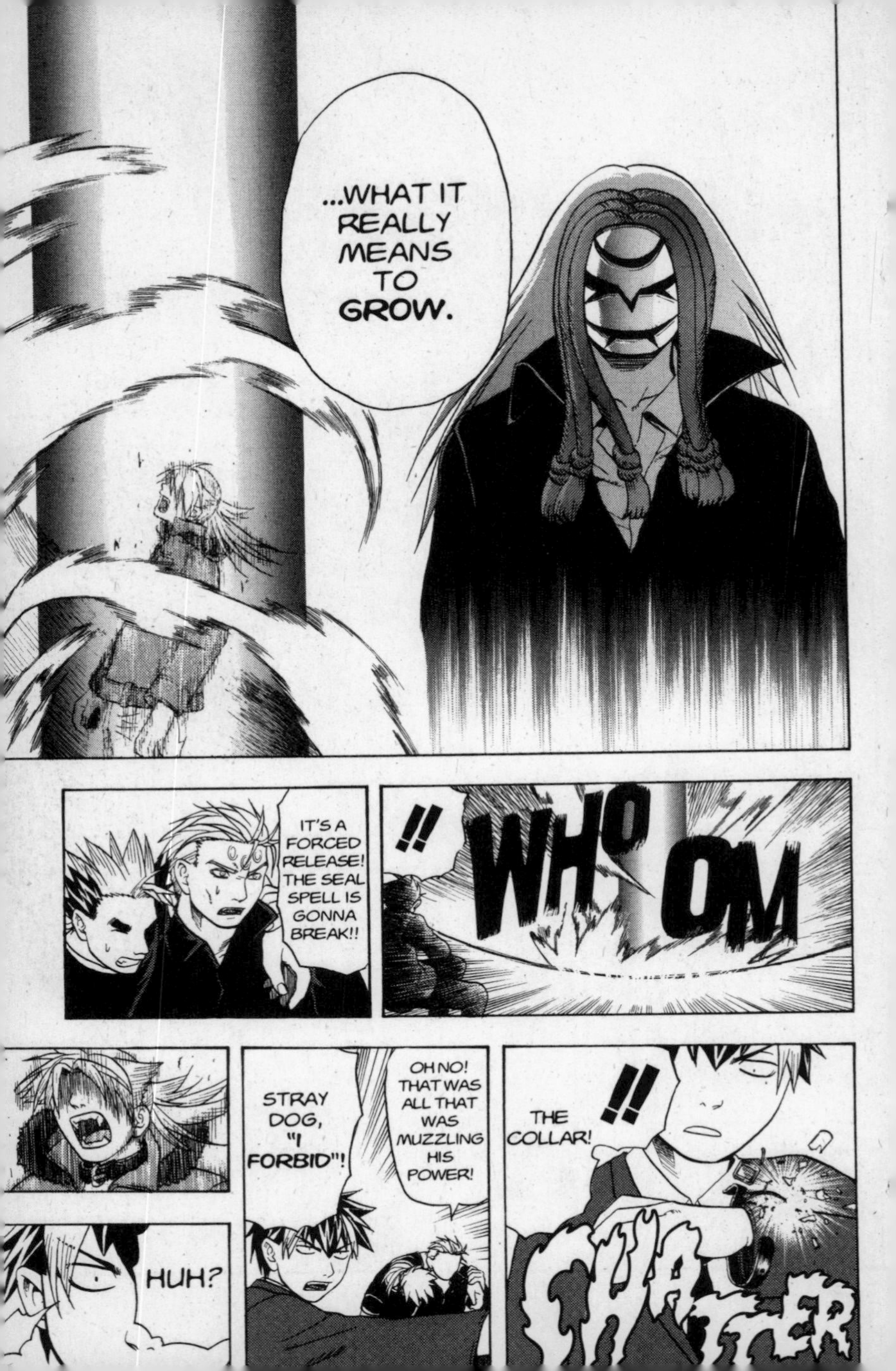
...WHAT IT REALLY MEANS TO GROW.
!!
WHOOM
IT'S A FORCED RELEASE! THE SEAL SPELL IS GONNA BREAK!!
!!
THE COLLAR!
CHATTER
OH NO! THAT WAS ALL THAT WAS MUZZLING HIS POWER!
STRAY DOG, "I FORBID"!
HUH?

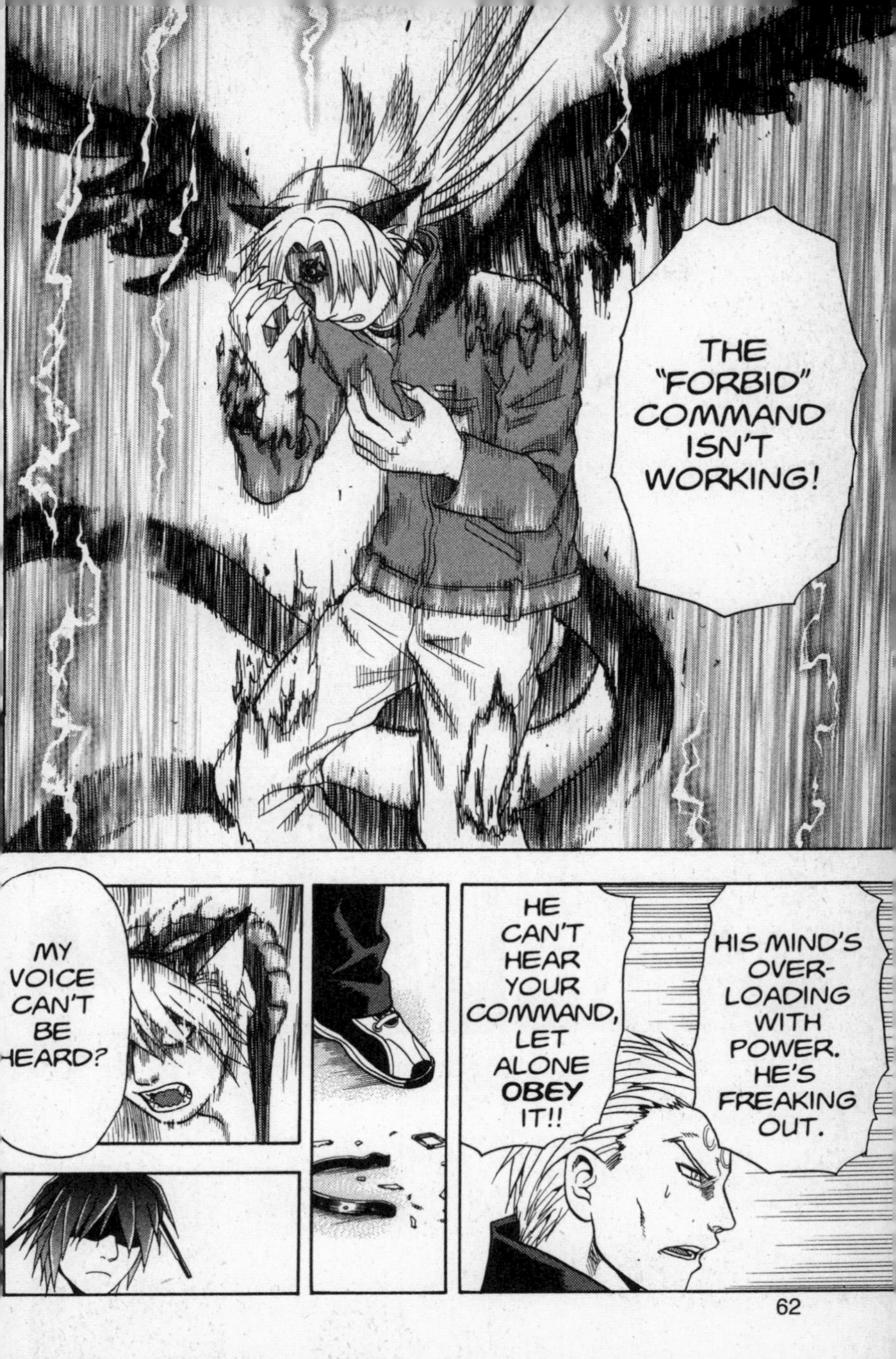
THE "FORBID" COMMAND ISN'T WORKING!
HIS MIND'S OVER-LOADING WITH POWER. HE'S FREAKING OUT.
HE CAN'T HEAR YOUR COMMAND, LET ALONE OBEY IT!!
MY VOICE CAN'T BE HEARD?

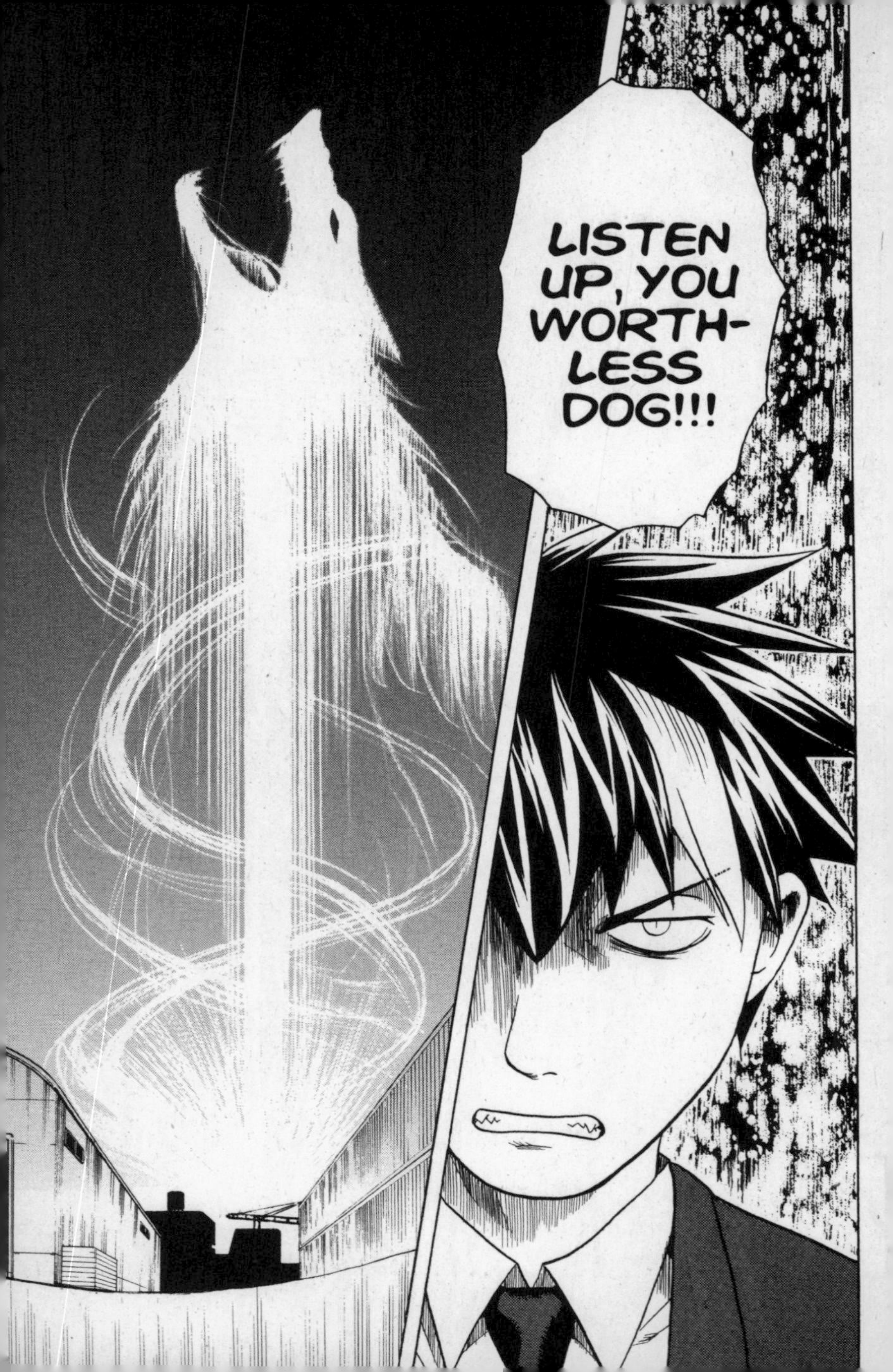
LISTEN UP, YOU WORTH-LESS DOG!!!

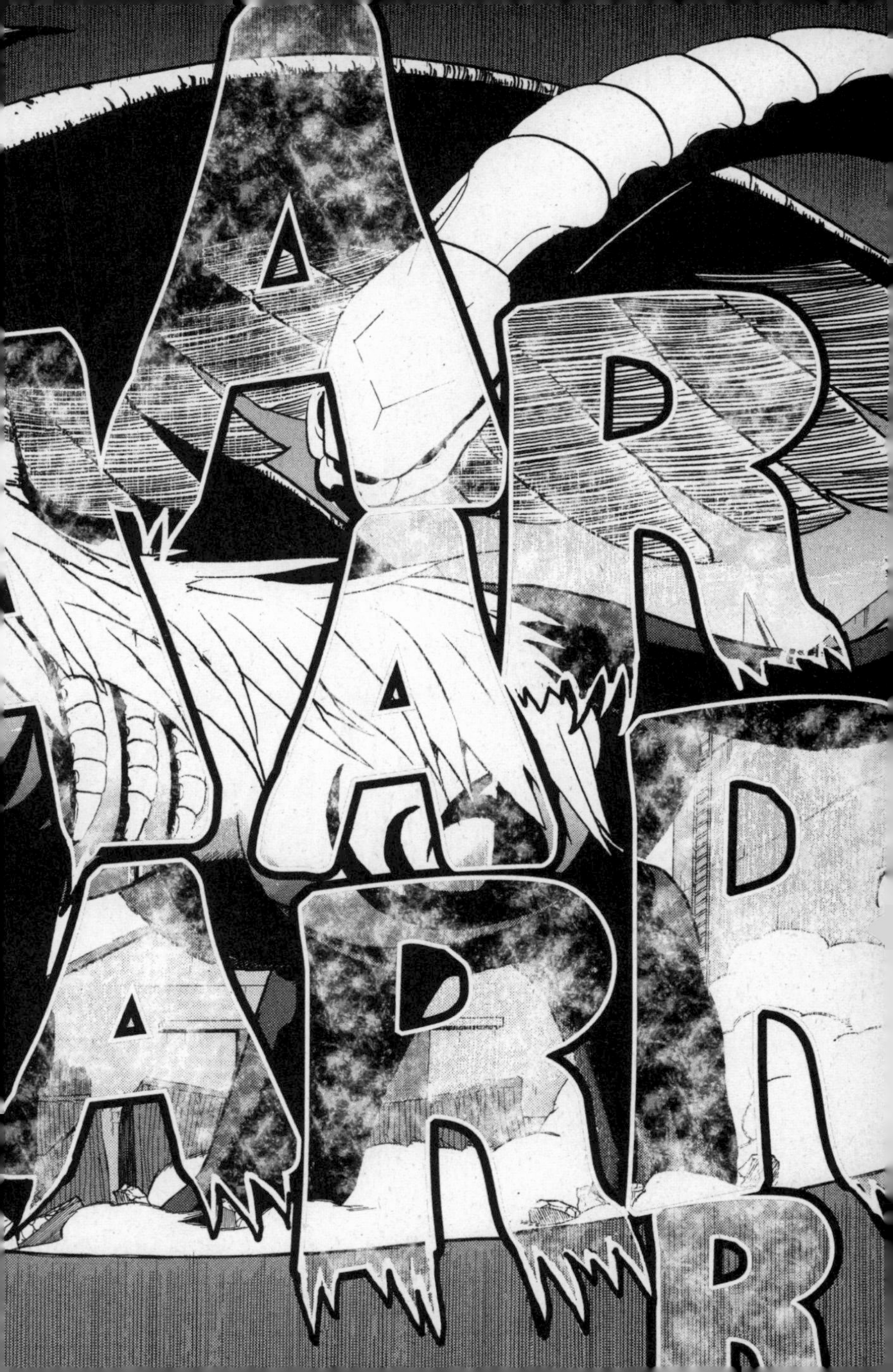
AR
AR
ARR

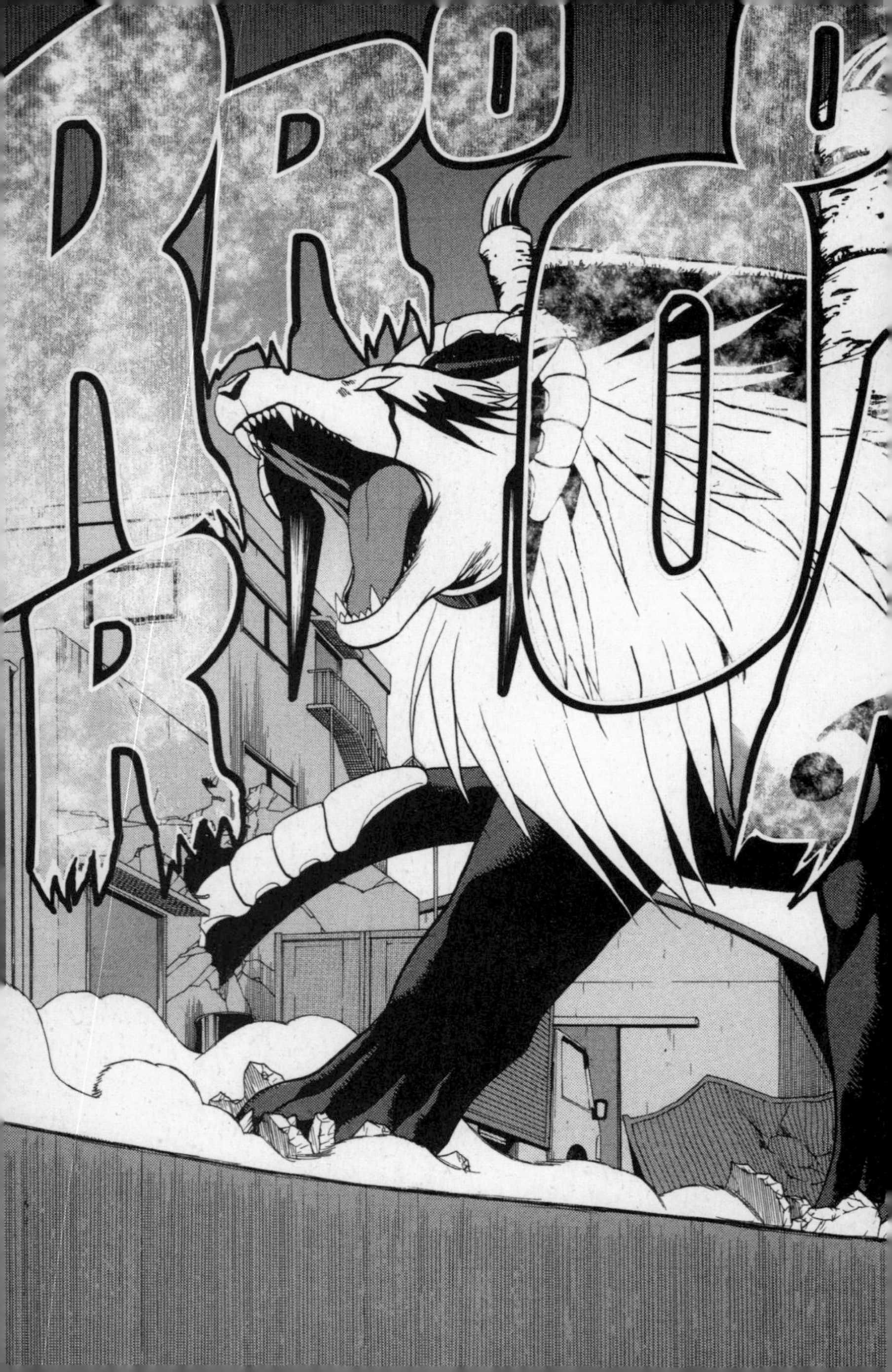

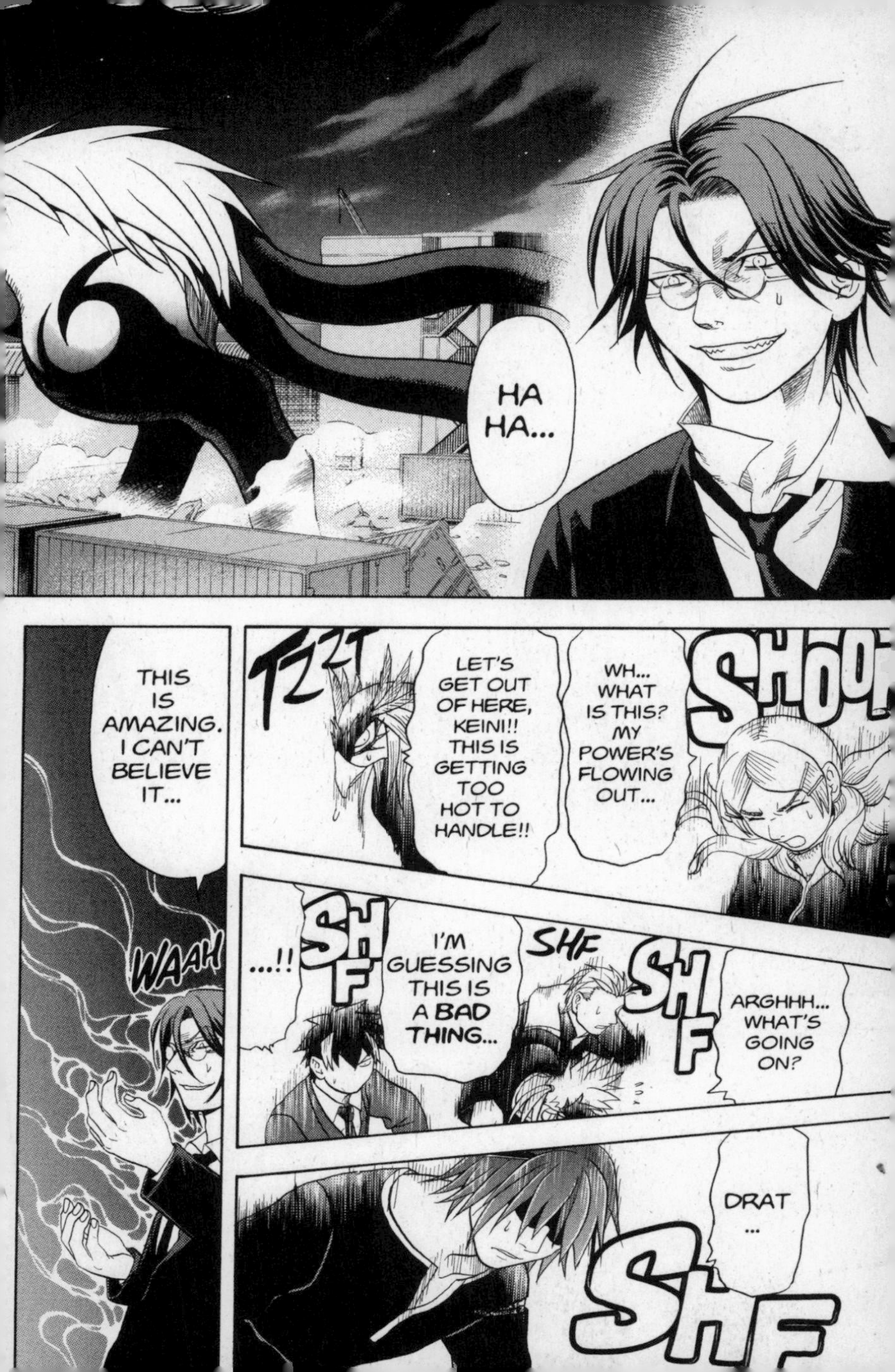
HA HA...
SHOOO
WH... WHAT IS THIS? MY POWER'S FLOWING OUT...
LET'S GET OUT OF HERE, KEINI!! THIS IS GETTING TOO HOT TO HANDLE!!
TZZT
ARGHHH... WHAT'S GOING ON?
SHF
SHF
I'M GUESSING THIS IS A BAD THING...
SHF
...!!
DRAT...
SHF
THIS IS AMAZING. I CAN'T BELIEVE IT...
WAAH

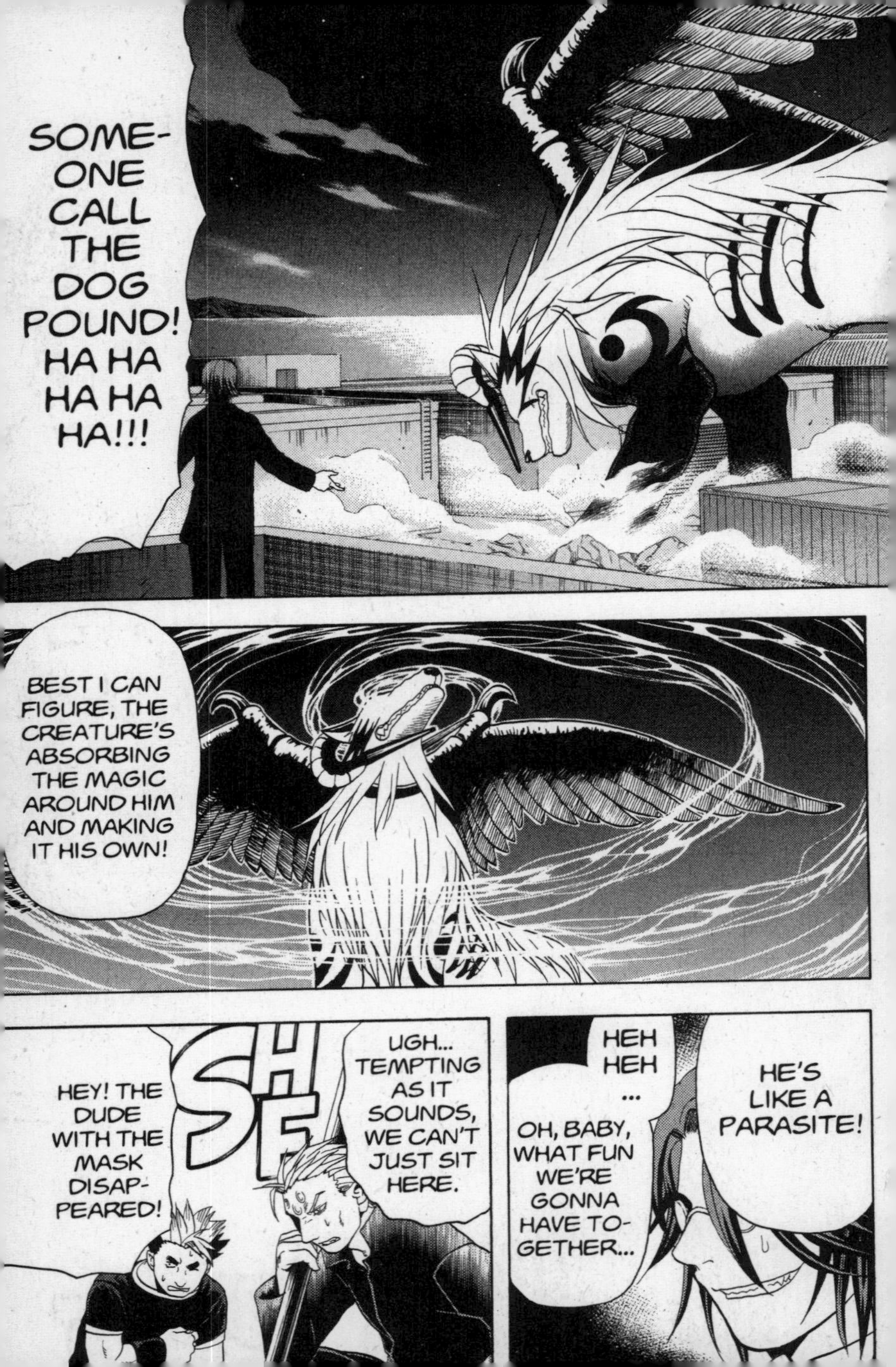
SOME-ONE CALL THE DOG POUND! HA HA HA HA HA!!!
BEST I CAN FIGURE, THE CREATURE'S ABSORBING THE MAGIC AROUND HIM AND MAKING IT HIS OWN!
HE'S LIKE A PARASITE!
HEH HEH ...
OH, BABY, WHAT FUN WE'RE GONNA HAVE TO-GETHER...
UGH... TEMPTING AS IT SOUNDS, WE CAN'T JUST SIT HERE.
SHF
HEY! THE DUDE WITH THE MASK DISAP-PEARED!

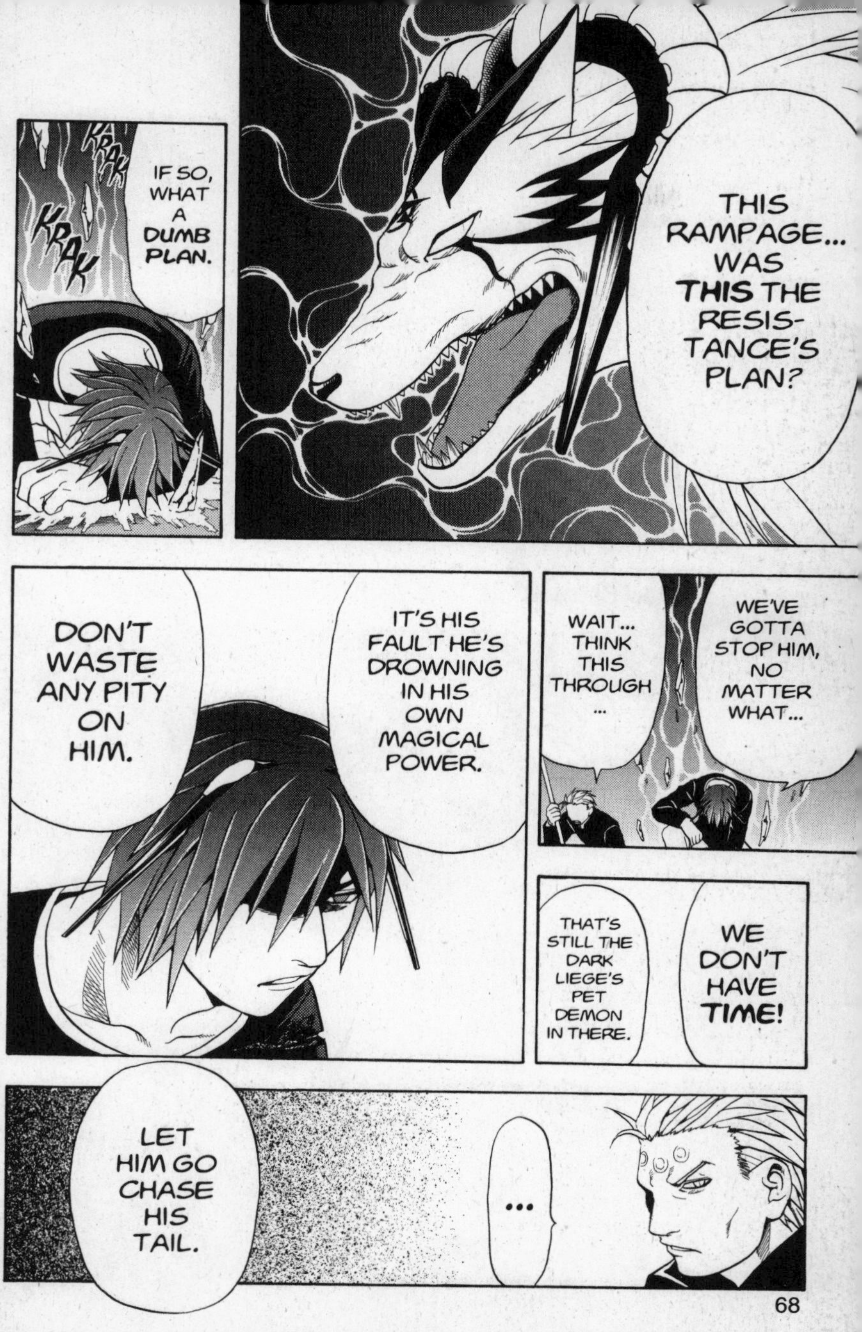
THIS RAMPAGE... WAS THIS THE RESISTANCE'S PLAN?
KRAK
KRAK
IF SO, WHAT A DUMB PLAN.
WE'VE GOTTA STOP HIM, NO MATTER WHAT...
WAIT... THINK THIS THROUGH...
WE DON'T HAVE TIME!
THAT'S STILL THE DARK LIEGE'S PET DEMON IN THERE.
IT'S HIS FAULT HE'S DROWNING IN HIS OWN MAGICAL POWER.
DON'T WASTE ANY PITY ON HIM.
...
LET HIM GO CHASE HIS TAIL.

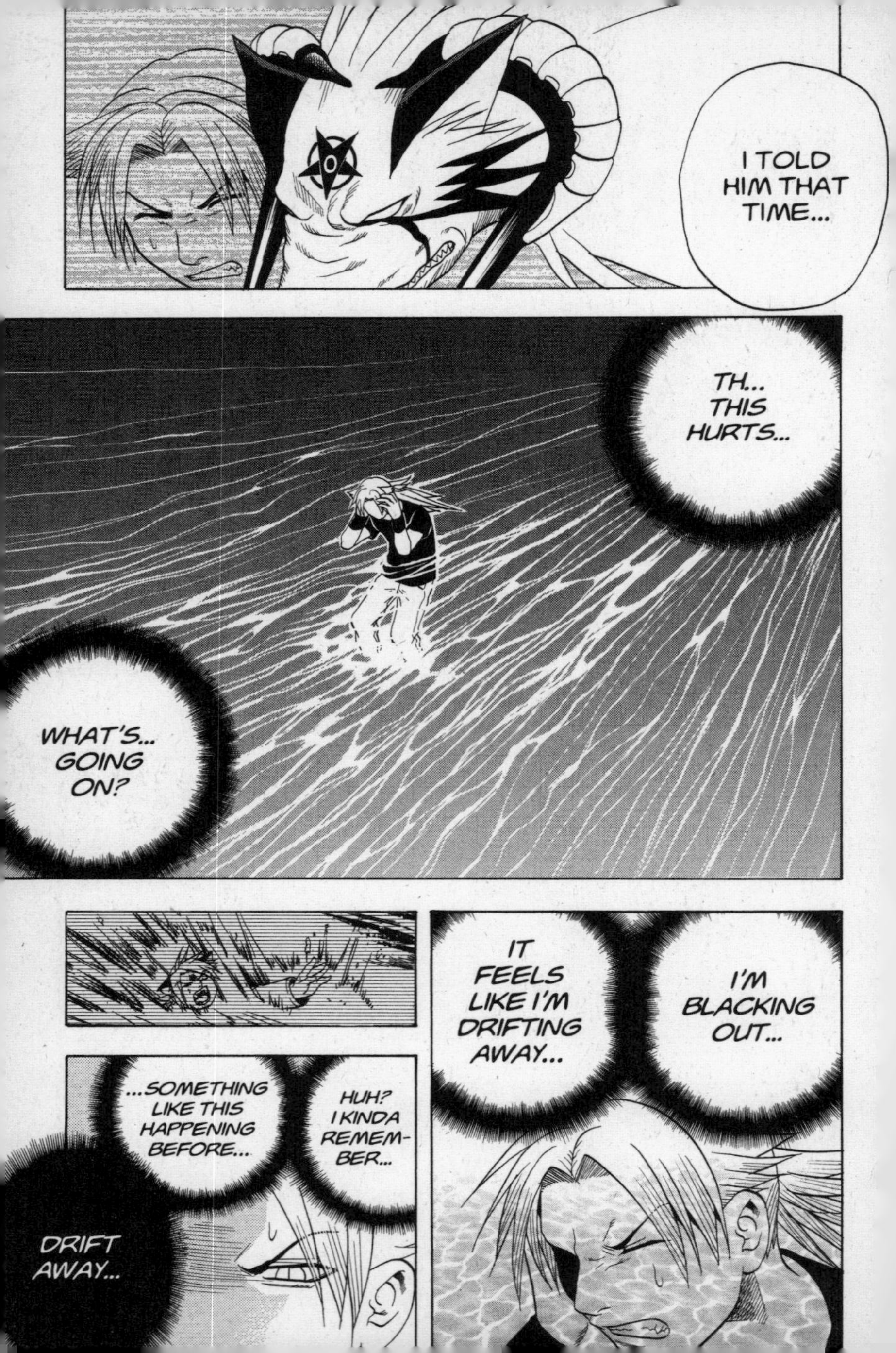
I TOLD HIM THAT TIME...
TH... THIS HURTS...
WHAT'S... GOING ON?
I'M BLACKING OUT...
IT FEELS LIKE I'M DRIFTING AWAY...
HUH? I KINDA REMEM-BER...
...SOMETHING LIKE THIS HAPPENING BEFORE...
DRIFT AWAY...

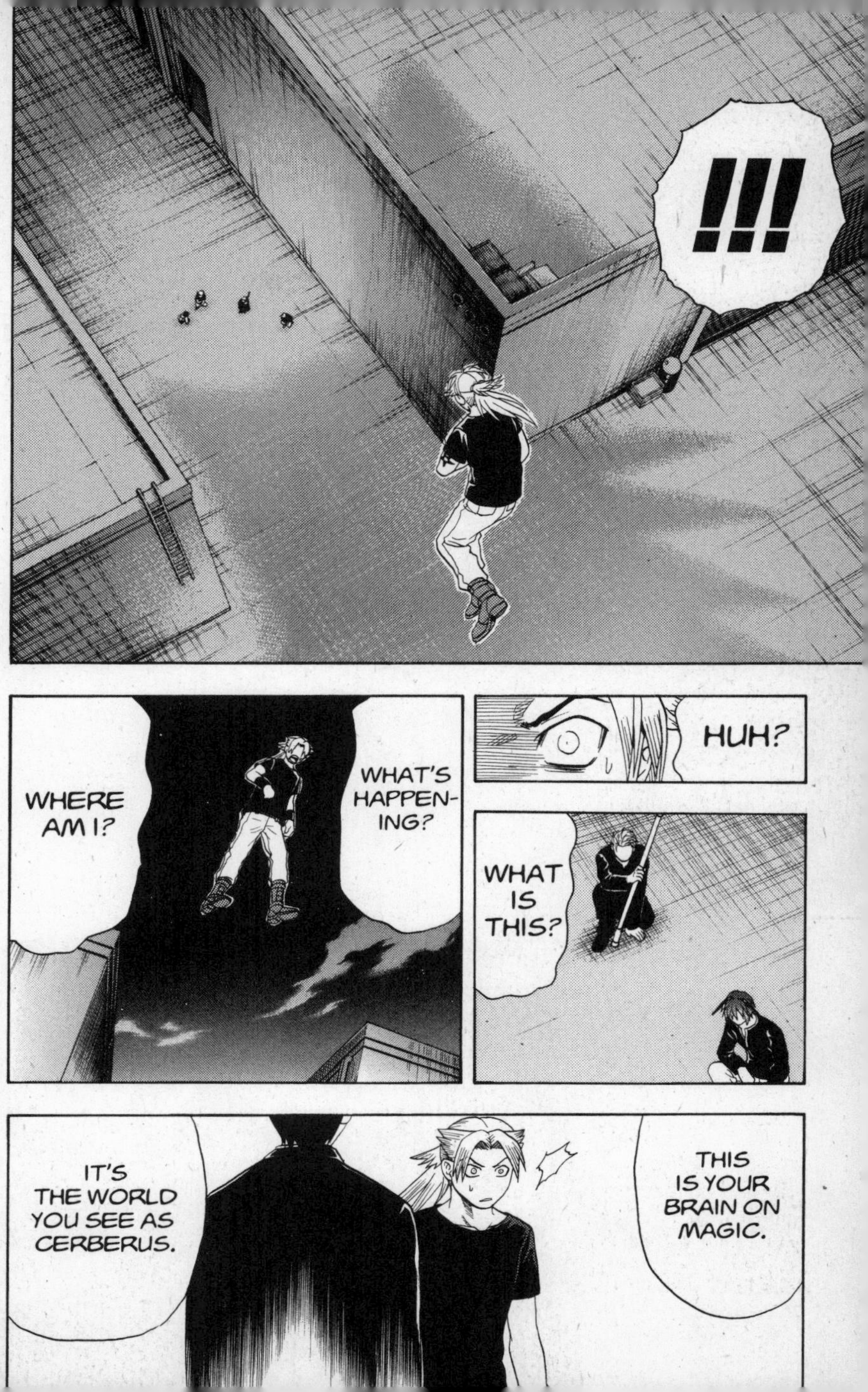
!!!
HUH?
WHAT IS THIS?
WHAT'S HAPPEN-ING?
WHERE AM I?
THIS IS YOUR BRAIN ON MAGIC.
IT'S THE WORLD YOU SEE AS CERBERUS.

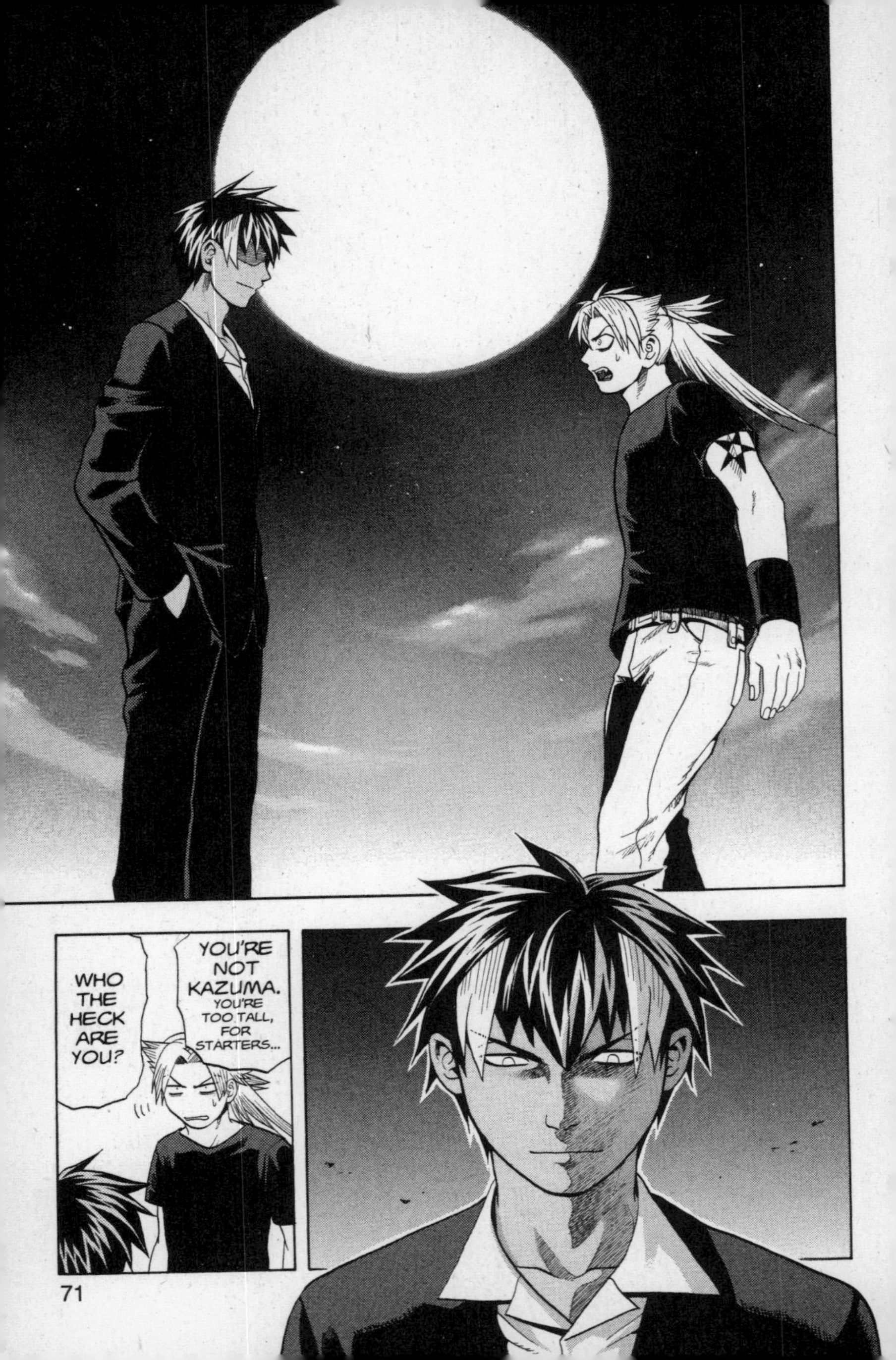
YOU'RE NOT KAZUMA. YOU'RE TOO TALL, FOR STARTERS...
WHO THE HECK ARE YOU?

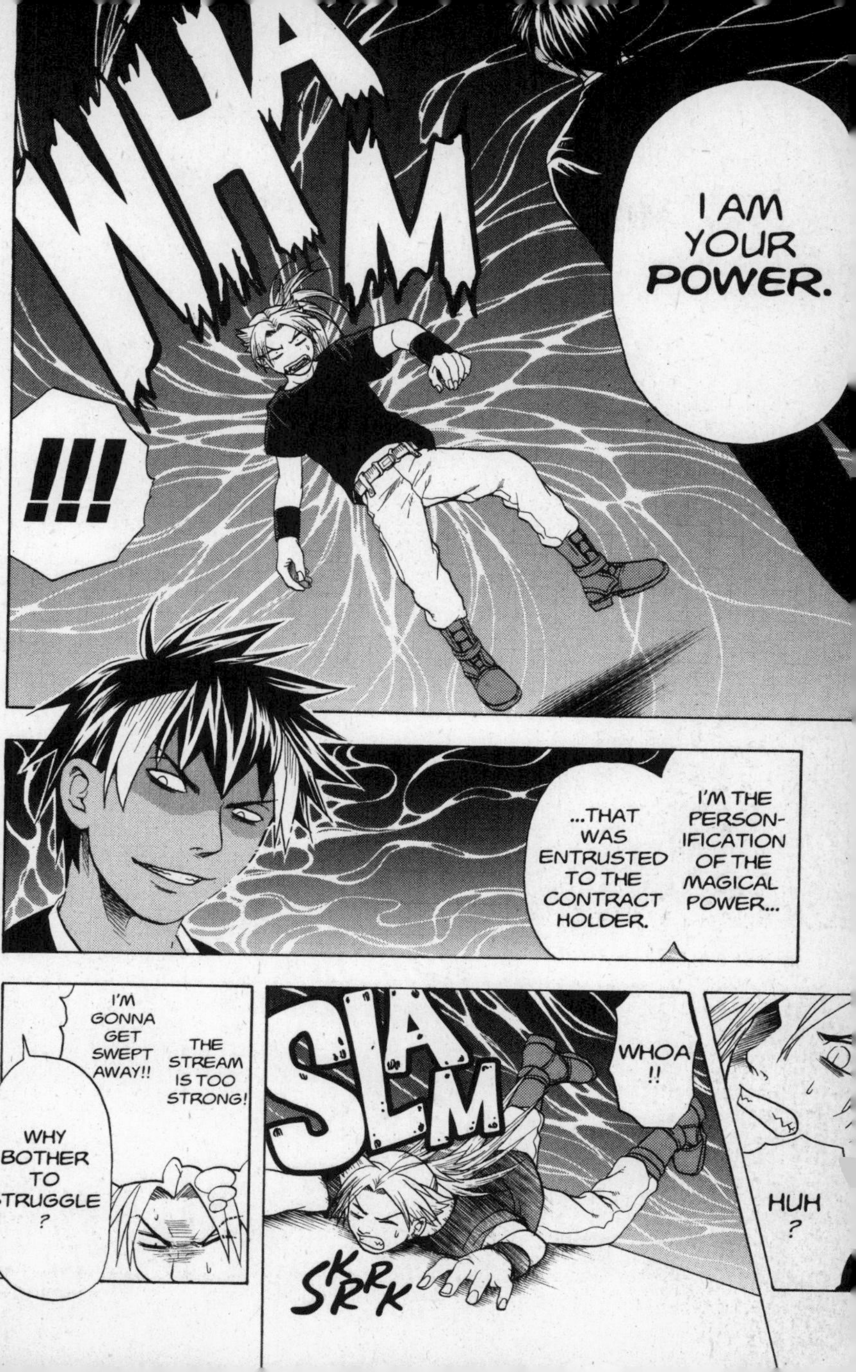
I AM YOUR POWER.
WHAM
!!!
I'M THE PERSON-IFICATION OF THE MAGICAL POWER...
...THAT WAS ENTRUSTED TO THE CONTRACT HOLDER.
HUH ?
WHOA !!
SLAM
SKRRK
THE STREAM IS TOO STRONG!
I'M GONNA GET SWEPT AWAY!!
WHY BOTHER TO STRUGGLE ?

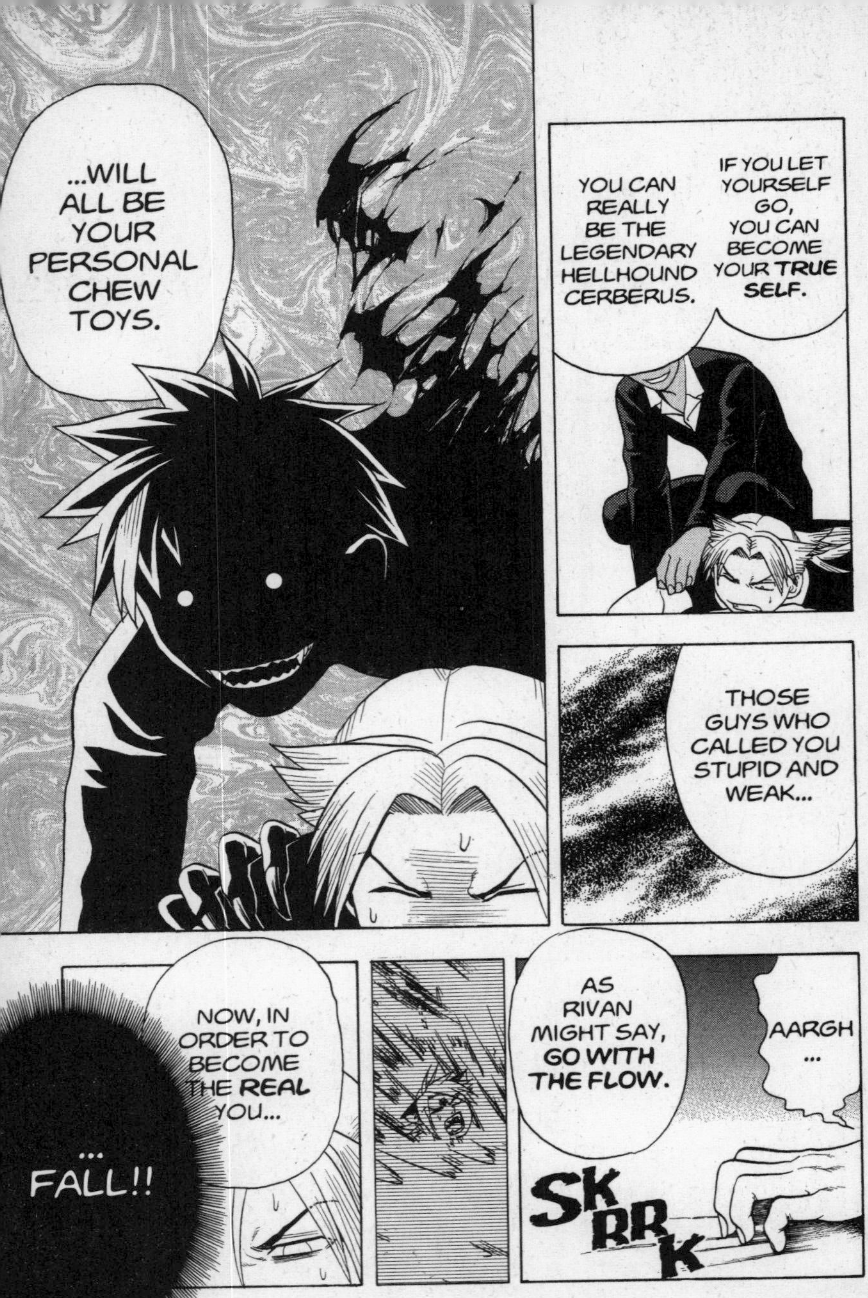
IF YOU LET YOURSELF GO, YOU CAN BECOME YOUR **TRUE SELF.**
YOU CAN REALLY BE THE LEGENDARY HELLHOUND CERBERUS.
THOSE GUYS WHO CALLED YOU STUPID AND WEAK...
...WILL ALL BE YOUR PERSONAL CHEW TOYS.
AARGH ...
AS RIVAN MIGHT SAY, **GO WITH THE FLOW.**
SKRRK
NOW, IN ORDER TO BECOME THE **REAL** YOU...
... FALL!!

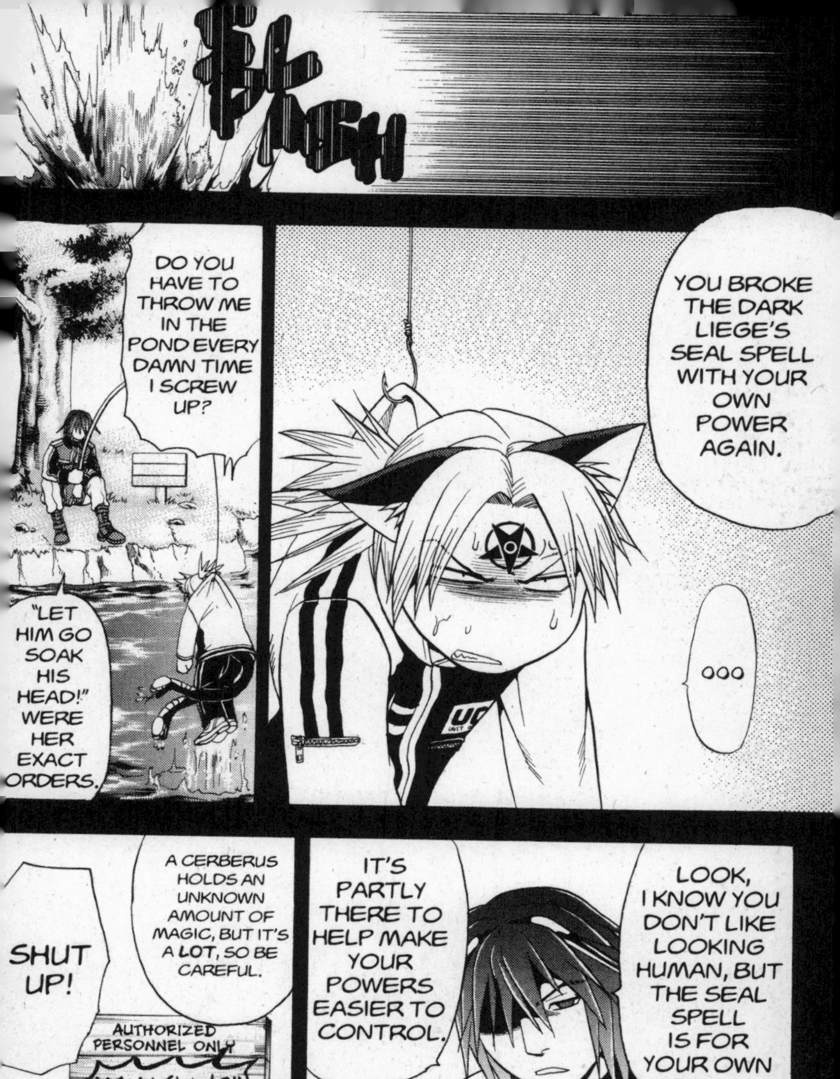
YOU BROKE THE DARK LIEGE'S SEAL SPELL WITH YOUR OWN POWER AGAIN.
...
DO YOU HAVE TO THROW ME IN THE POND EVERY DAMN TIME I SCREW UP?
"LET HIM GO SOAK HIS HEAD!" WERE HER EXACT ORDERS.
LOOK, I KNOW YOU DON'T LIKE LOOKING HUMAN, BUT THE SEAL SPELL IS FOR YOUR OWN GOOD.
IT'S PARTLY THERE TO HELP MAKE YOUR POWERS EASIER TO CONTROL.
A CERBERUS HOLDS AN UNKNOWN AMOUNT OF MAGIC, BUT IT'S A **LOT**, SO BE CAREFUL.
SHUT UP!
AUTHORIZED PERSONNEL ONLY
NO FISHING!!

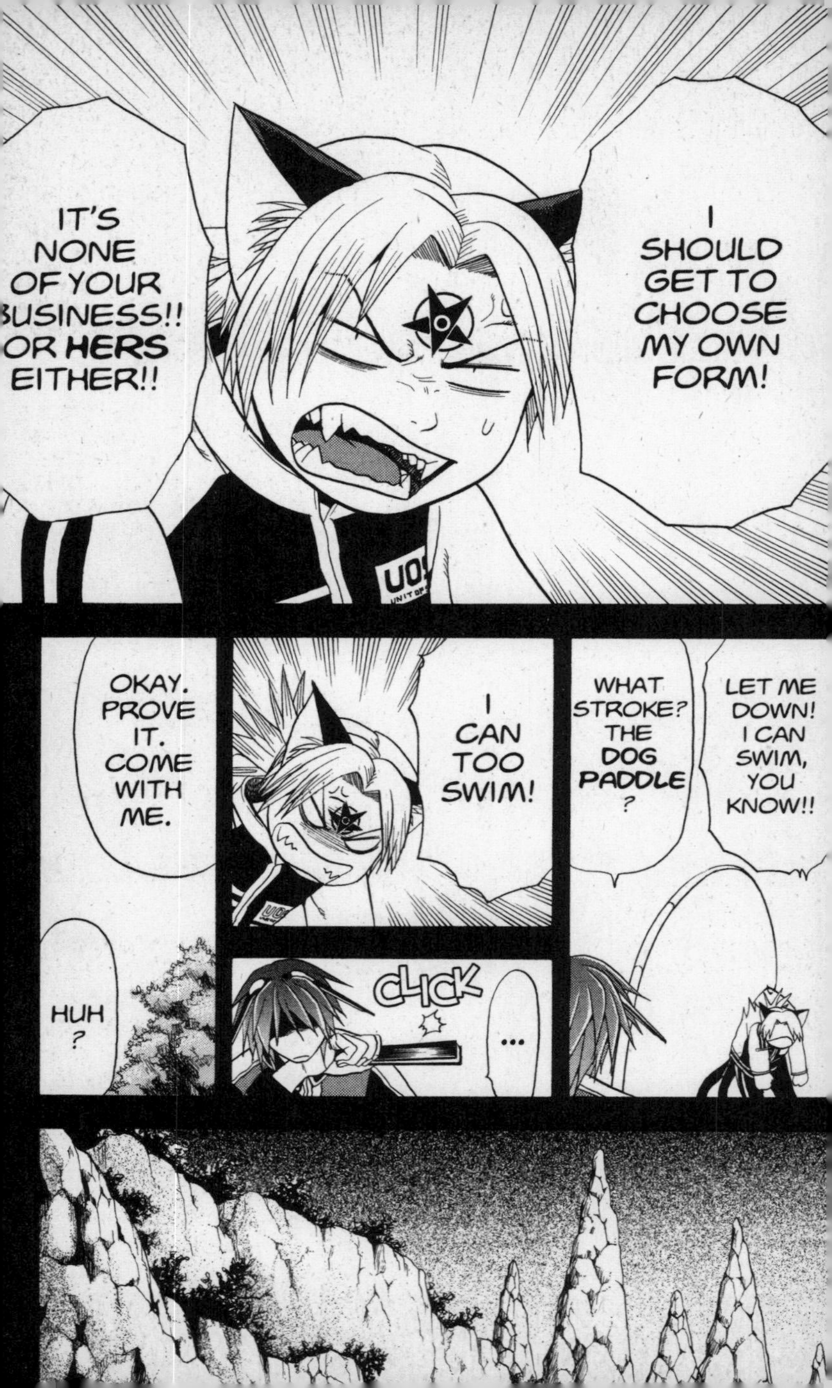
I SHOULD GET TO CHOOSE MY OWN FORM!
IT'S NONE OF YOUR BUSINESS!! OR **HERS** EITHER!!
LET ME DOWN! I CAN SWIM, YOU KNOW!!
WHAT STROKE? THE **DOG PADDLE**?
I CAN TOO SWIM!
OKAY. PROVE IT. COME WITH ME.
CLICK
...
HUH?

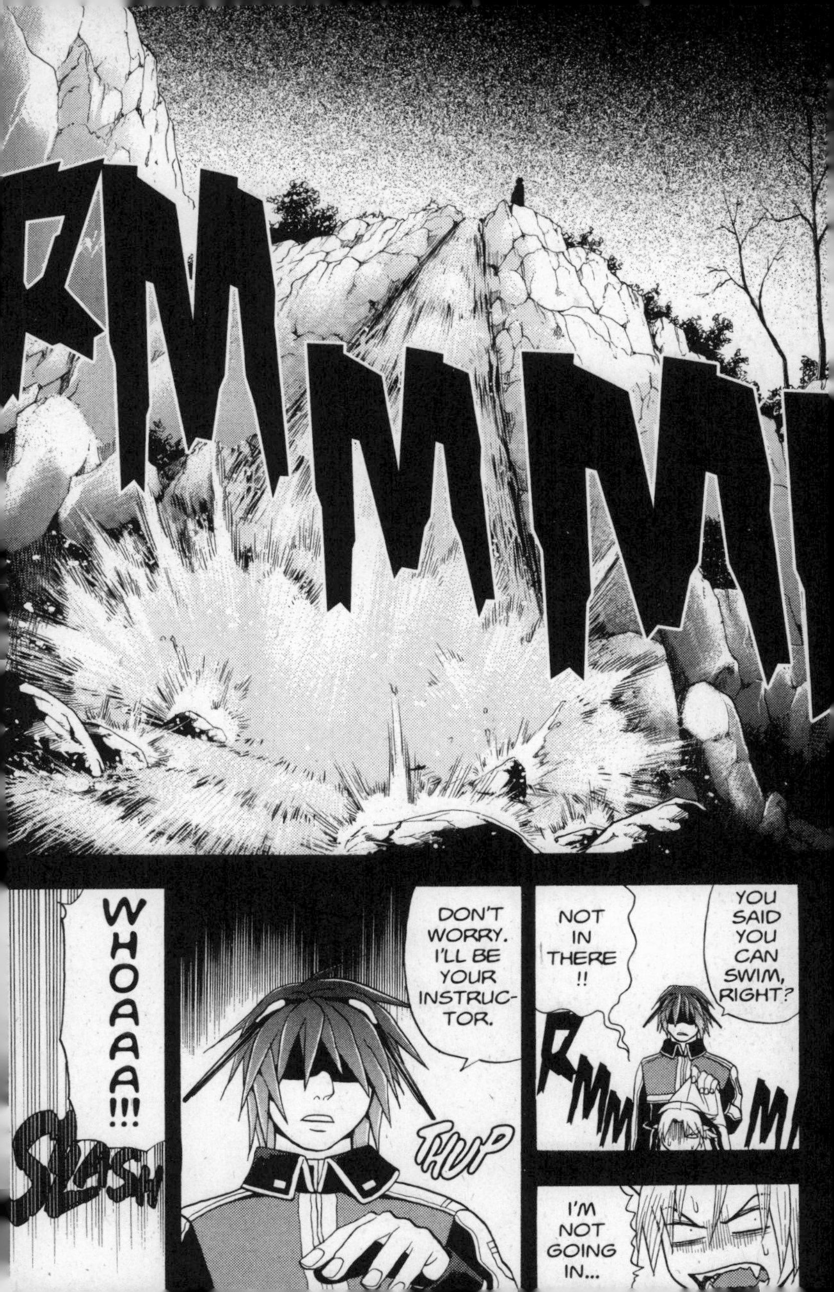
RMMMM
YOU SAID YOU CAN SWIM, RIGHT?
NOT IN THERE!!
RMMMM
I'M NOT GOING IN...
DON'T WORRY. I'LL BE YOUR INSTRUCTOR.
THUP
WHOAAAA!!!
SPLASH

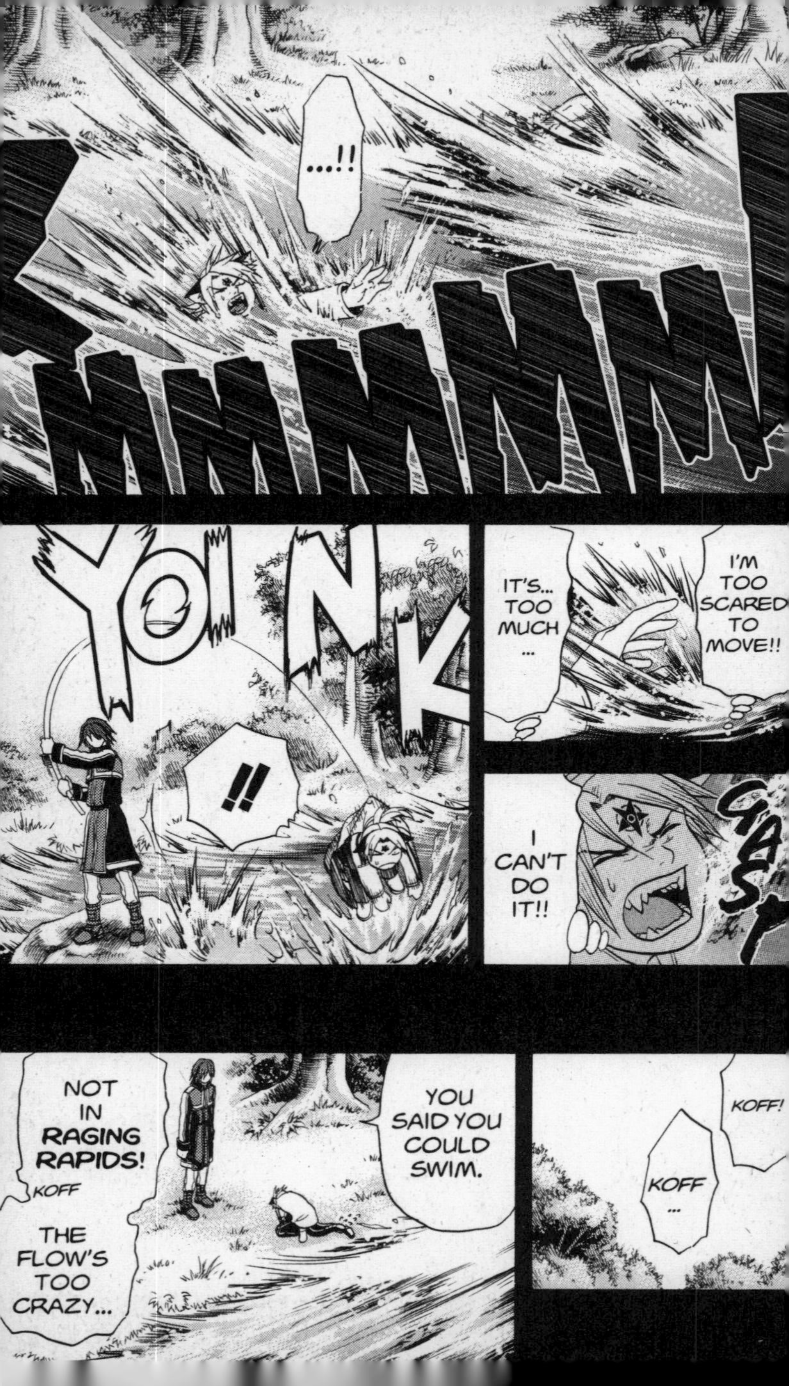
...!!
I'M TOO SCARED TO MOVE!!
IT'S... TOO MUCH ...
I CAN'T DO IT!!
YOINK
!!
KOFF!
KOFF ...
YOU SAID YOU COULD SWIM.
NOT IN RAGING RAPIDS!
KOFF
THE FLOW'S TOO CRAZY...

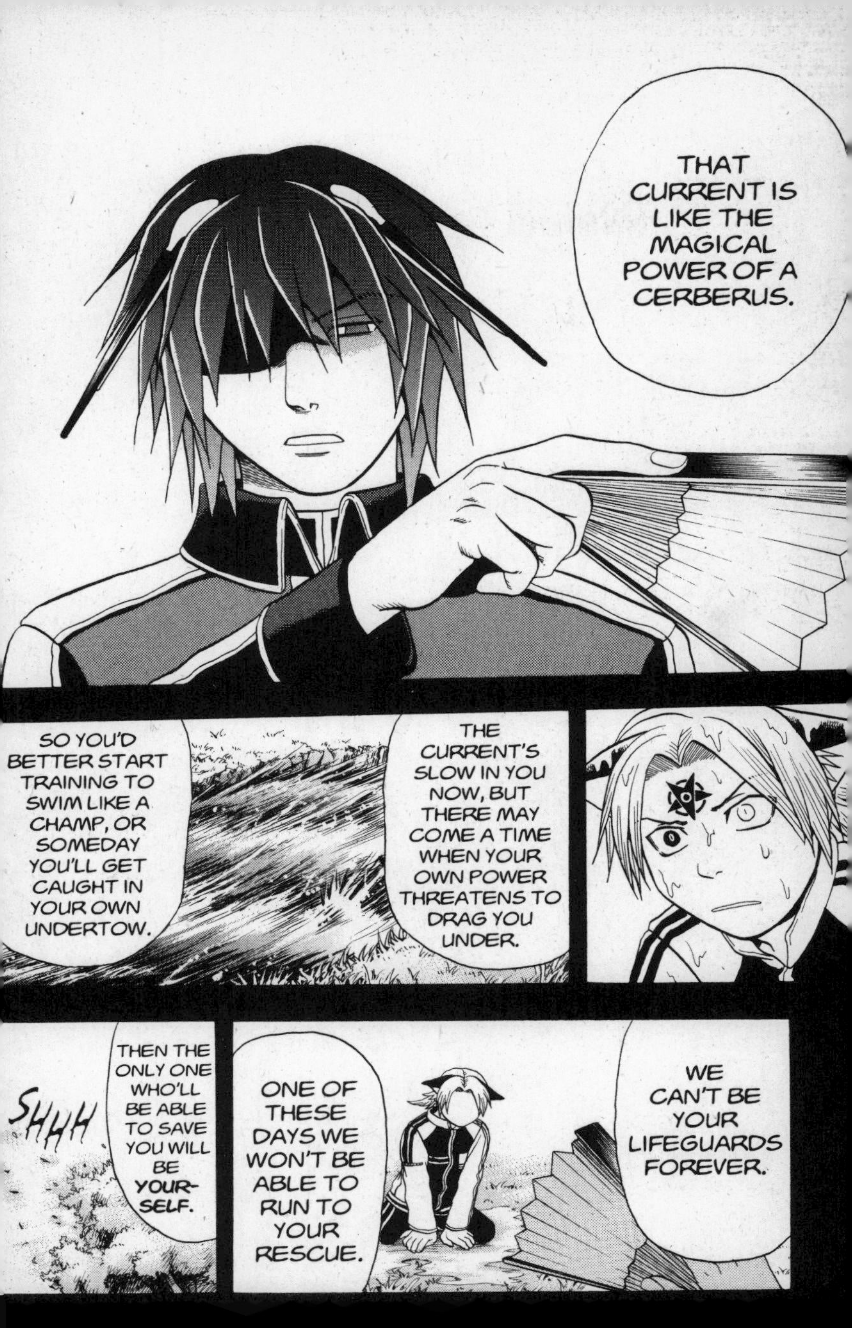
THAT CURRENT IS LIKE THE MAGICAL POWER OF A CERBERUS.
THE CURRENT'S SLOW IN YOU NOW, BUT THERE MAY COME A TIME WHEN YOUR OWN POWER THREATENS TO DRAG YOU UNDER.
SO YOU'D BETTER START TRAINING TO SWIM LIKE A CHAMP, OR SOMEDAY YOU'LL GET CAUGHT IN YOUR OWN UNDERTOW.
WE CAN'T BE YOUR LIFEGUARDS FOREVER.
ONE OF THESE DAYS WE WON'T BE ABLE TO RUN TO YOUR RESCUE.
THEN THE ONLY ONE WHO'LL BE ABLE TO SAVE YOU WILL BE **YOURSELF**.
SHHH

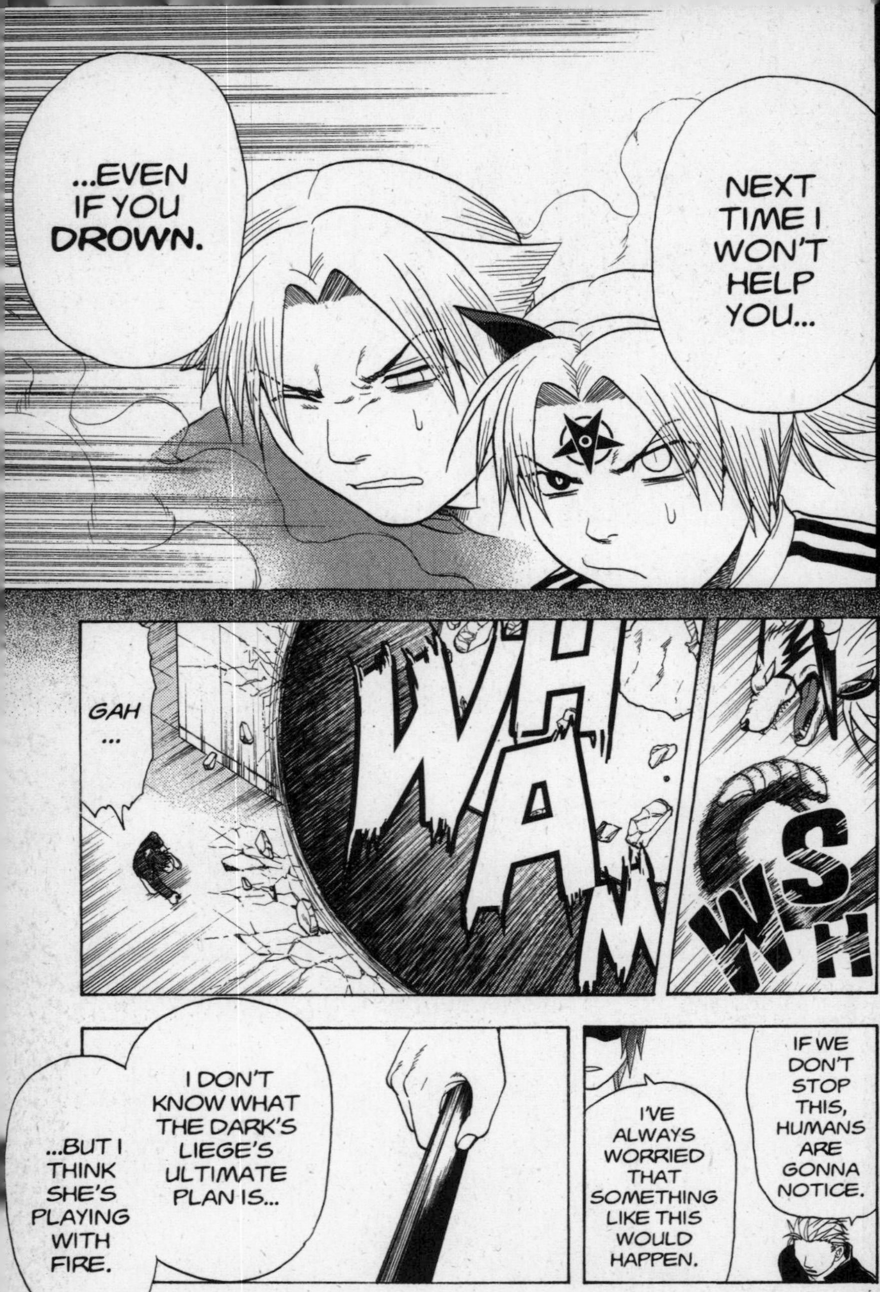
NEXT TIME I WON'T HELP YOU...
...EVEN IF YOU DROWN.
WSH
WHAM
GAH ...
IF WE DON'T STOP THIS, HUMANS ARE GONNA NOTICE.
I'VE ALWAYS WORRIED THAT SOMETHING LIKE THIS WOULD HAPPEN.
I DON'T KNOW WHAT THE DARK'S LIEGE'S ULTIMATE PLAN IS...
...BUT I THINK SHE'S PLAYING WITH FIRE.

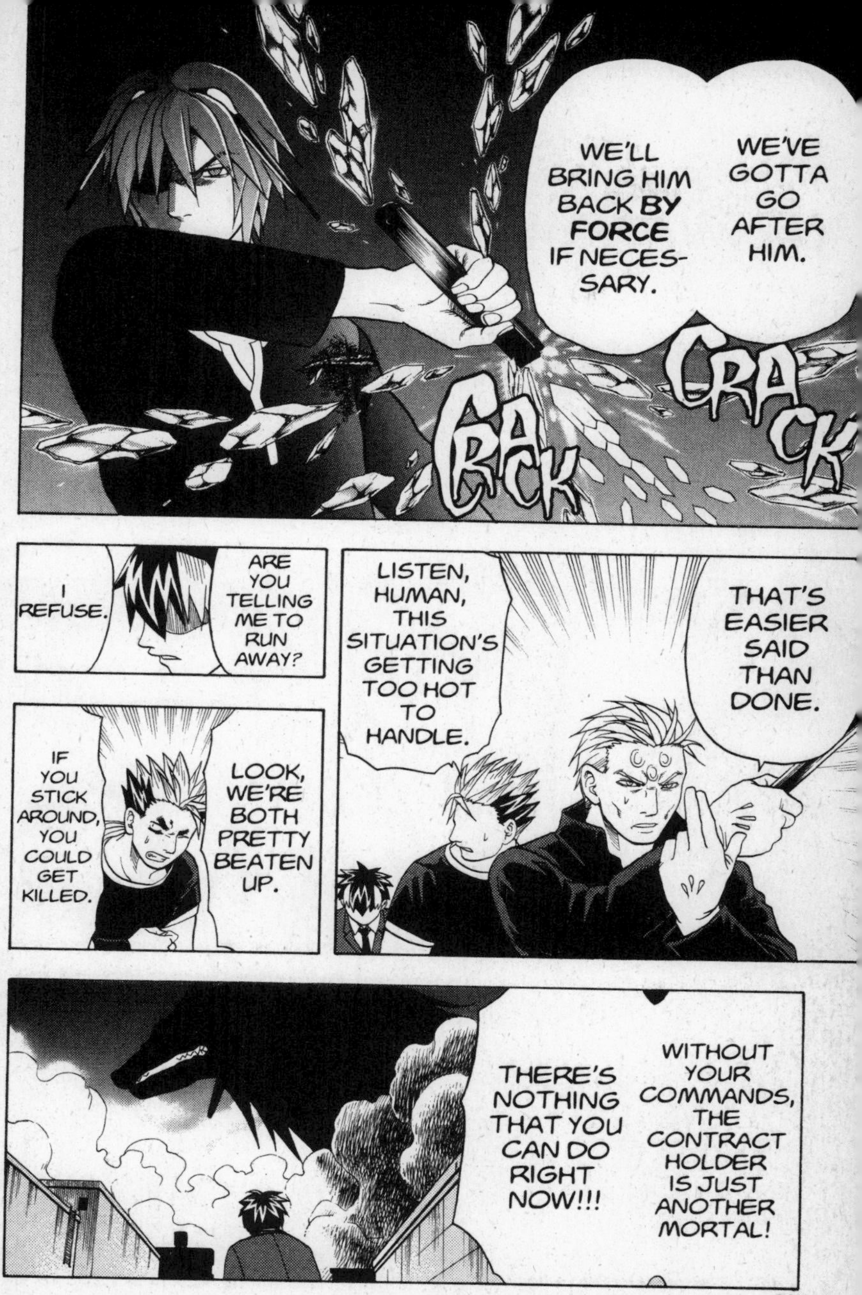
WE'VE GOTTA GO AFTER HIM.
WE'LL BRING HIM BACK BY FORCE IF NECES-SARY.
CRACK
CRACK
THAT'S EASIER SAID THAN DONE.
LISTEN, HUMAN, THIS SITUATION'S GETTING TOO HOT TO HANDLE.
ARE YOU TELLING ME TO RUN AWAY?
I REFUSE.
LOOK, WE'RE BOTH PRETTY BEATEN UP.
IF YOU STICK AROUND, YOU COULD GET KILLED.
WITHOUT YOUR COMMANDS, THE CONTRACT HOLDER IS JUST ANOTHER MORTAL!
THERE'S NOTHING THAT YOU CAN DO RIGHT NOW!!!

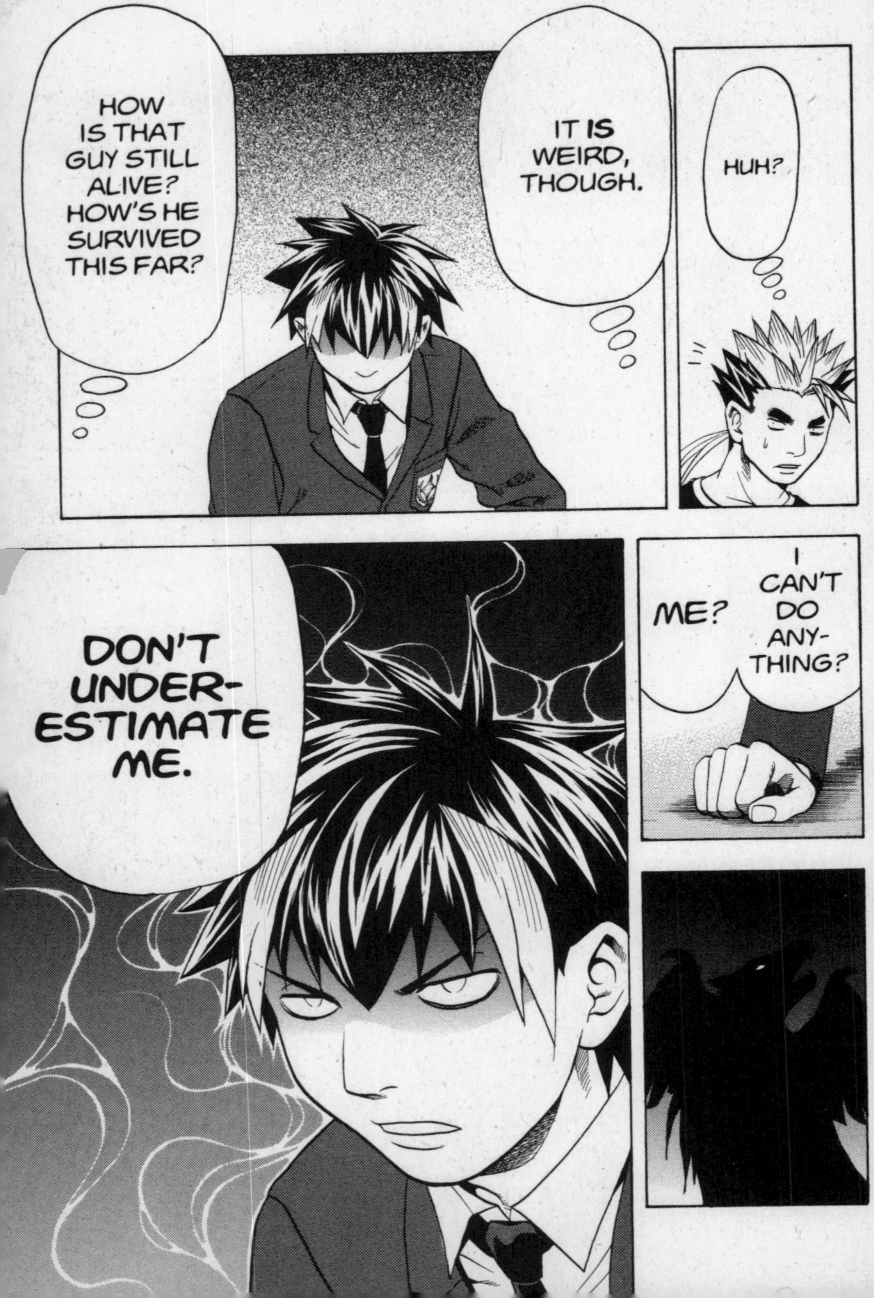
HUH?
IT IS WEIRD, THOUGH.
HOW IS THAT GUY STILL ALIVE? HOW'S HE SURVIVED THIS FAR?
ME? I CAN'T DO ANY-THING?
DON'T UNDER-ESTIMATE ME.

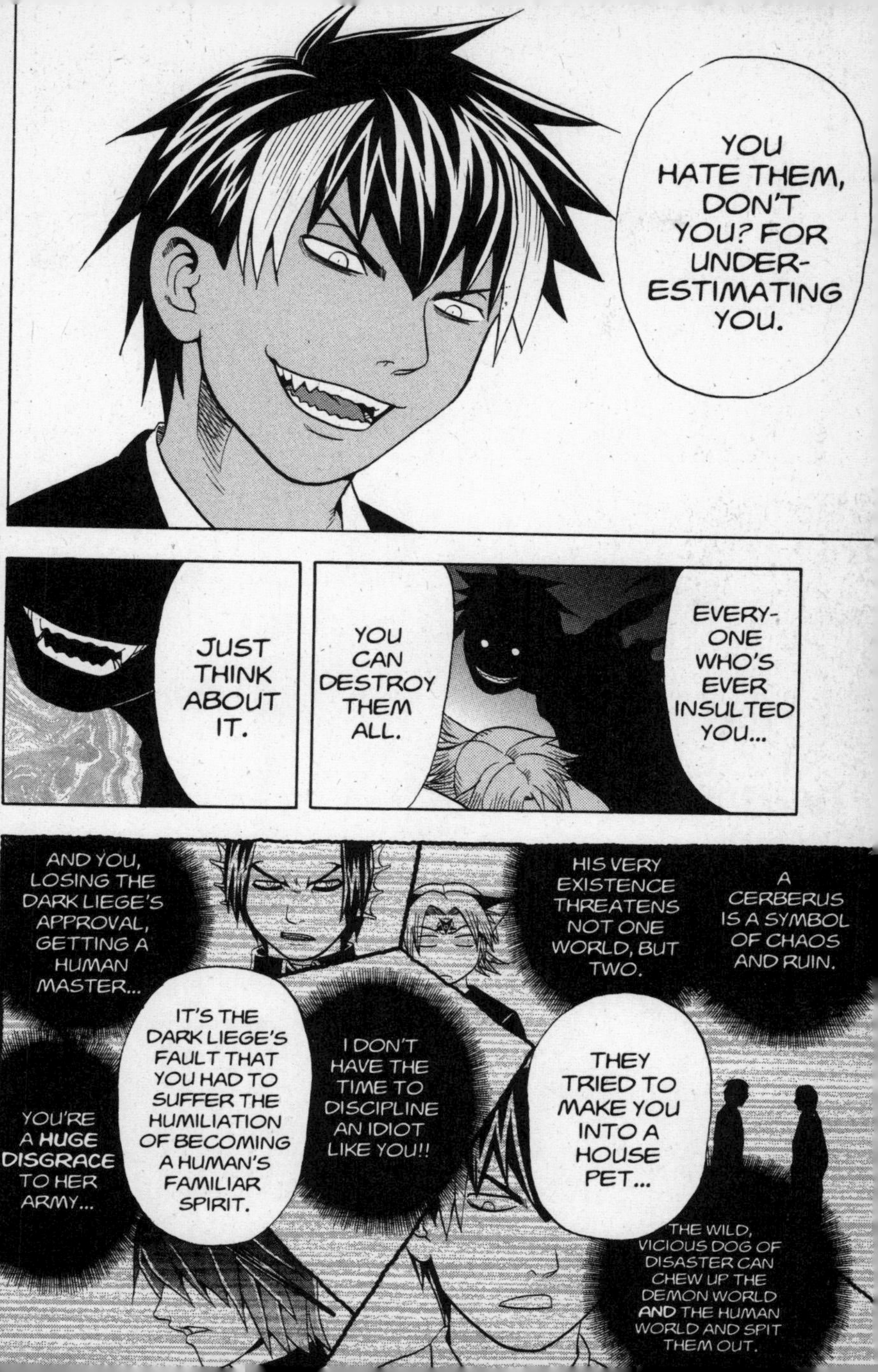
YOU HATE THEM, DON'T YOU? FOR UNDER-ESTIMATING YOU.
EVERY-ONE WHO'S EVER INSULTED YOU...
YOU CAN DESTROY THEM ALL.
JUST THINK ABOUT IT.
A CERBERUS IS A SYMBOL OF CHAOS AND RUIN.
HIS VERY EXISTENCE THREATENS NOT ONE WORLD, BUT TWO.
THEY TRIED TO MAKE YOU INTO A HOUSE PET...
THE WILD, VICIOUS DOG OF DISASTER CAN CHEW UP THE DEMON WORLD **AND** THE HUMAN WORLD AND SPIT THEM OUT.
AND YOU, LOSING THE DARK LIEGE'S APPROVAL, GETTING A HUMAN MASTER...
I DON'T HAVE THE TIME TO DISCIPLINE AN IDIOT LIKE YOU!!
IT'S THE DARK LIEGE'S FAULT THAT YOU HAD TO SUFFER THE HUMILIATION OF BECOMING A HUMAN'S FAMILIAR SPIRIT.
YOU'RE A **HUGE DISGRACE** TO HER ARMY...

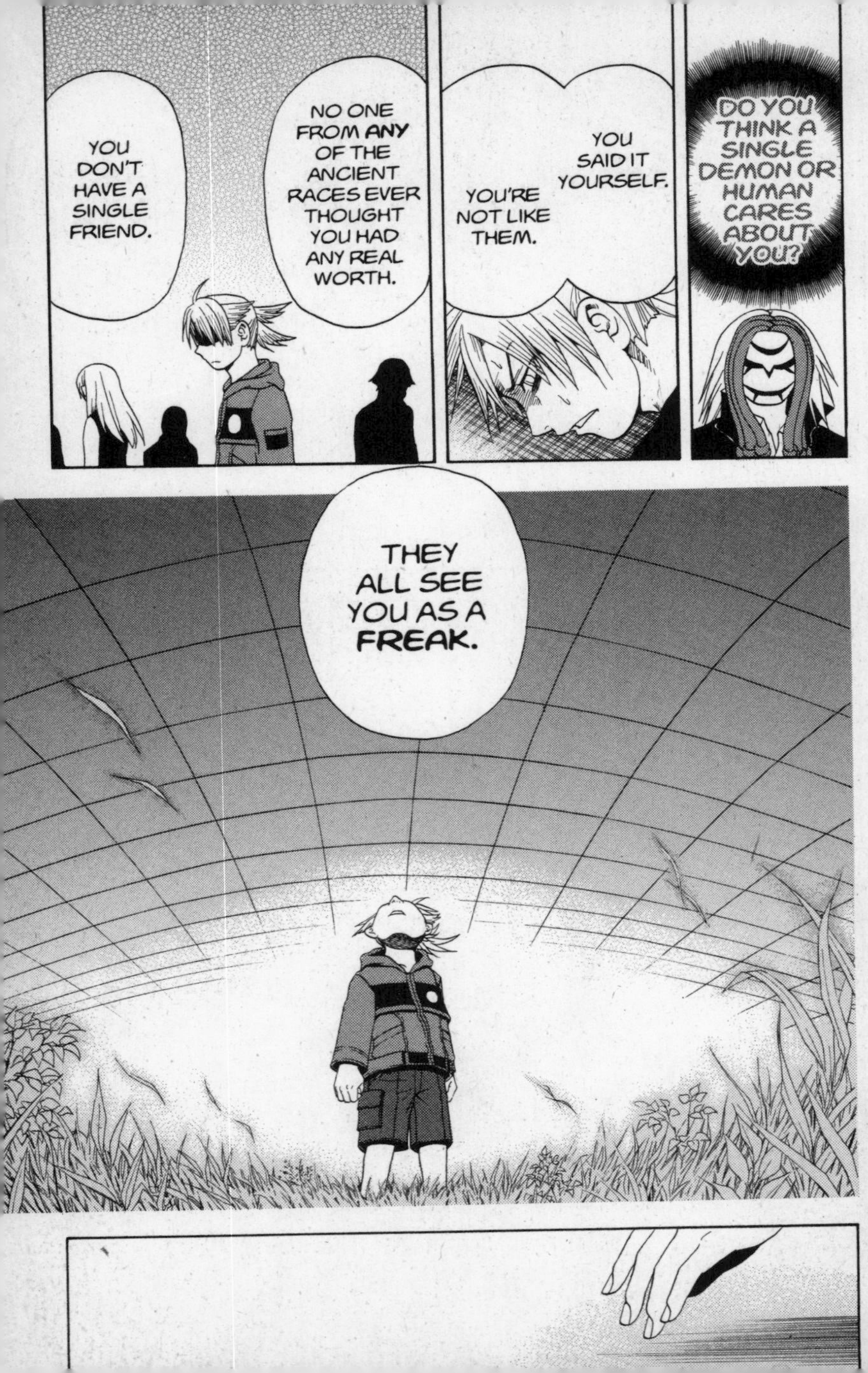
DO YOU THINK A SINGLE DEMON OR HUMAN CARES ABOUT YOU?
YOU SAID IT YOURSELF.
YOU'RE NOT LIKE THEM.
NO ONE FROM **ANY** OF THE ANCIENT RACES EVER THOUGHT YOU HAD ANY REAL WORTH.
YOU DON'T HAVE A SINGLE FRIEND.
THEY ALL SEE YOU AS A **FREAK.**

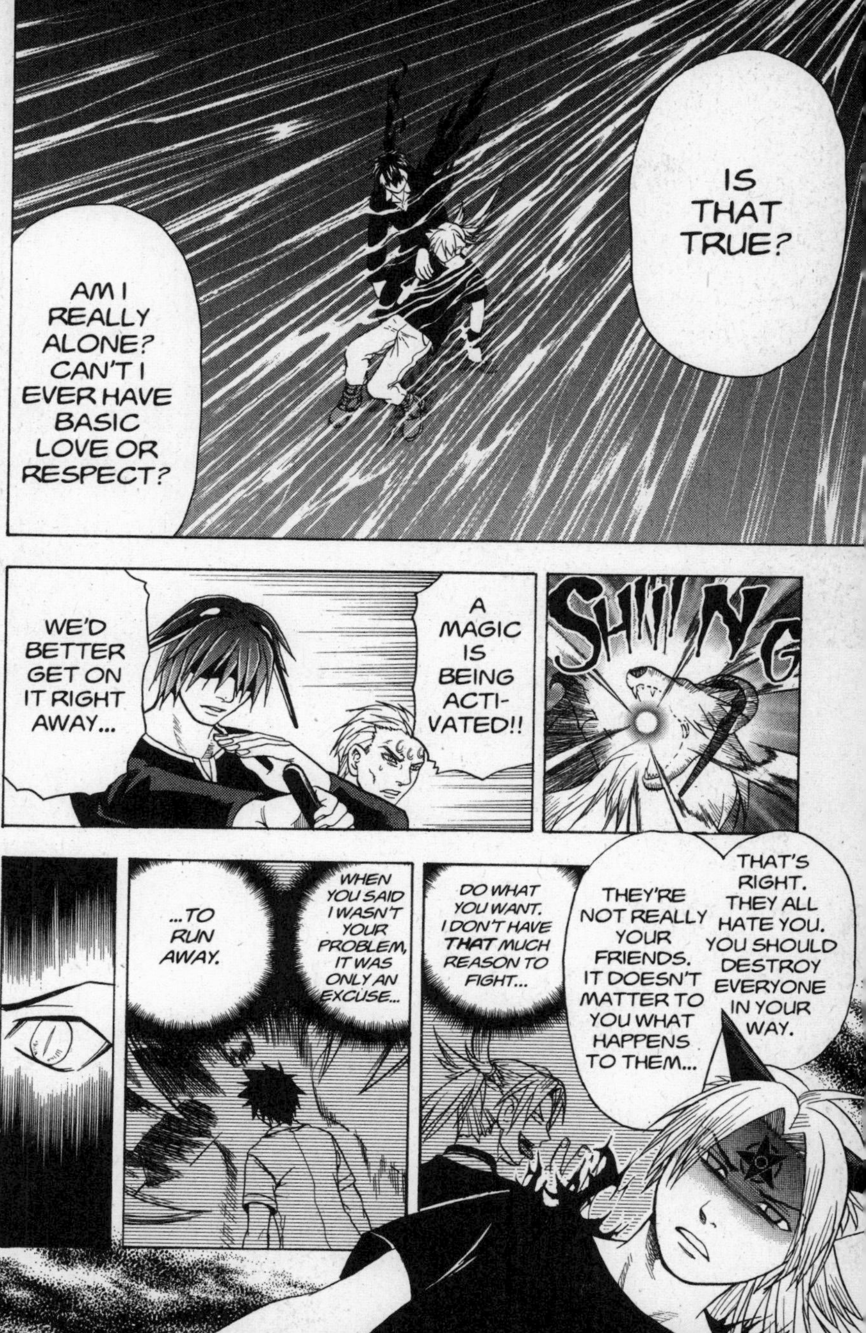
IS THAT TRUE?
AM I REALLY ALONE? CAN'T I EVER HAVE BASIC LOVE OR RESPECT?
SHIIING
A MAGIC IS BEING ACTI-VATED!!
WE'D BETTER GET ON IT RIGHT AWAY...
THAT'S RIGHT. THEY ALL HATE YOU. YOU SHOULD DESTROY EVERYONE IN YOUR WAY.
THEY'RE NOT REALLY YOUR FRIENDS. IT DOESN'T MATTER TO YOU WHAT HAPPENS TO THEM...
DO WHAT YOU WANT. I DON'T HAVE *THAT* MUCH REASON TO FIGHT...
WHEN YOU SAID I WASN'T YOUR PROBLEM, IT WAS ONLY AN EXCUSE...
...TO RUN AWAY.

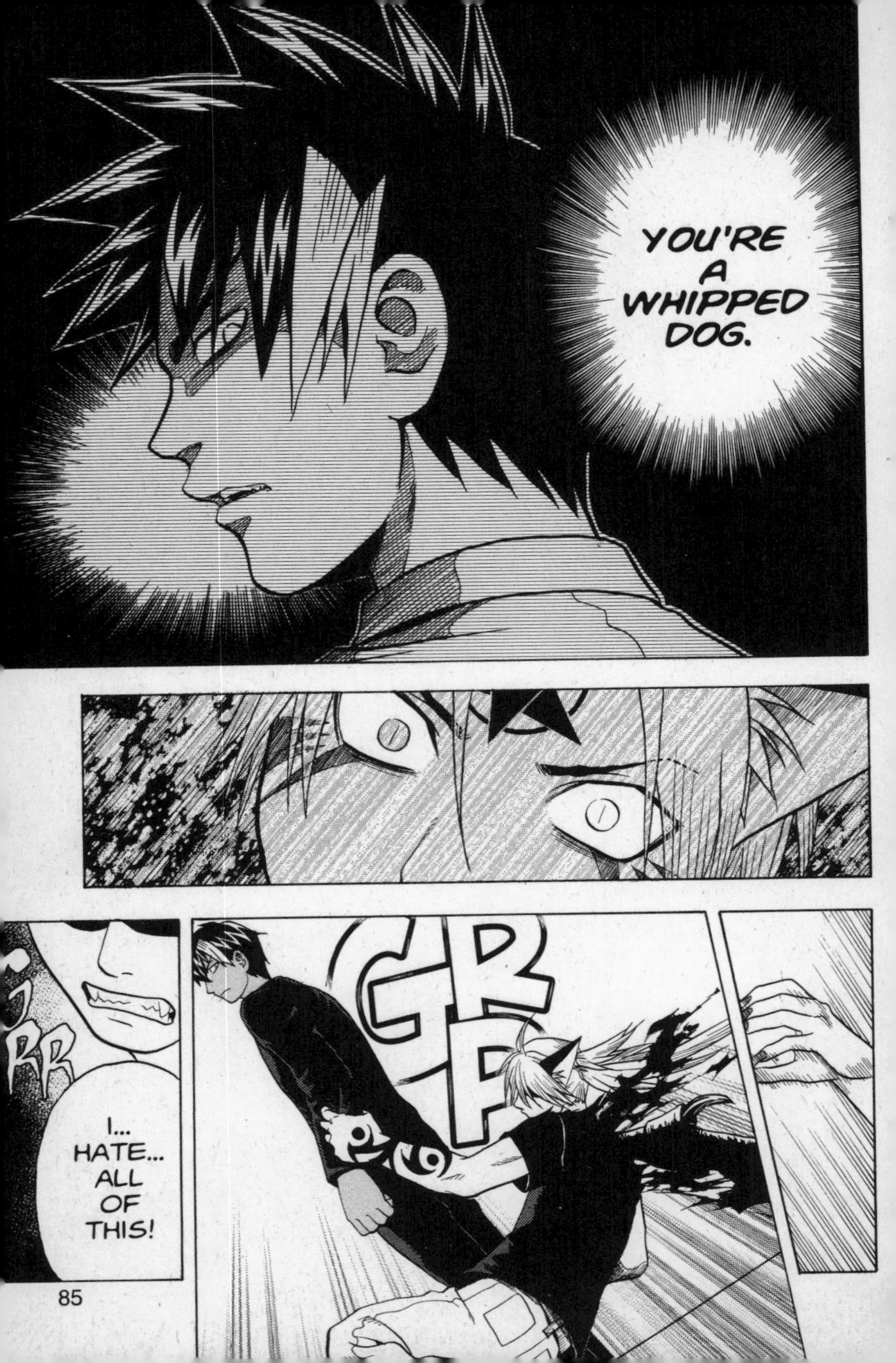
YOU'RE A WHIPPED DOG.
GRP
I... HATE... ALL OF THIS!

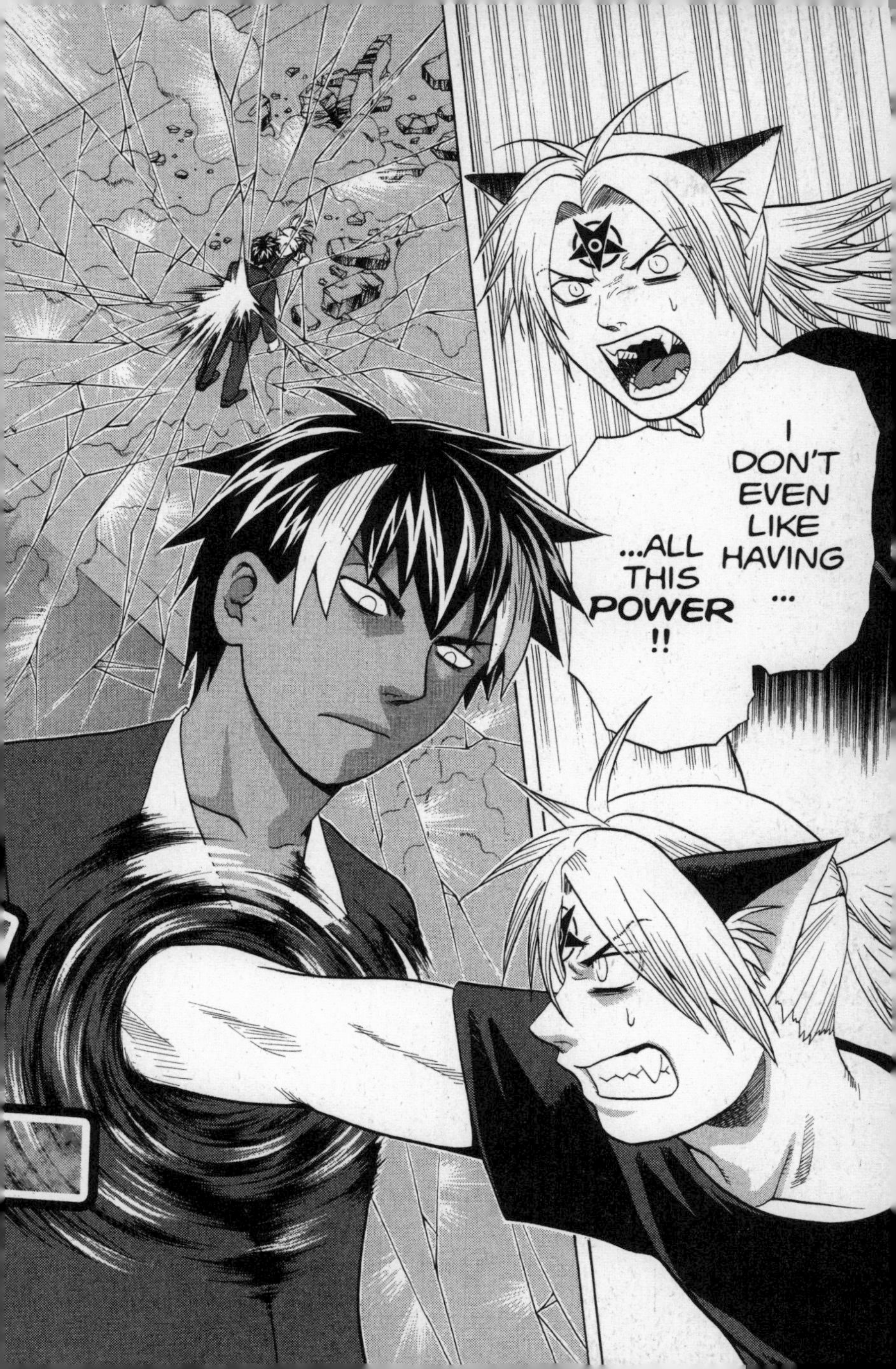
I DON'T EVEN LIKE HAVING ...
...ALL THIS POWER !!

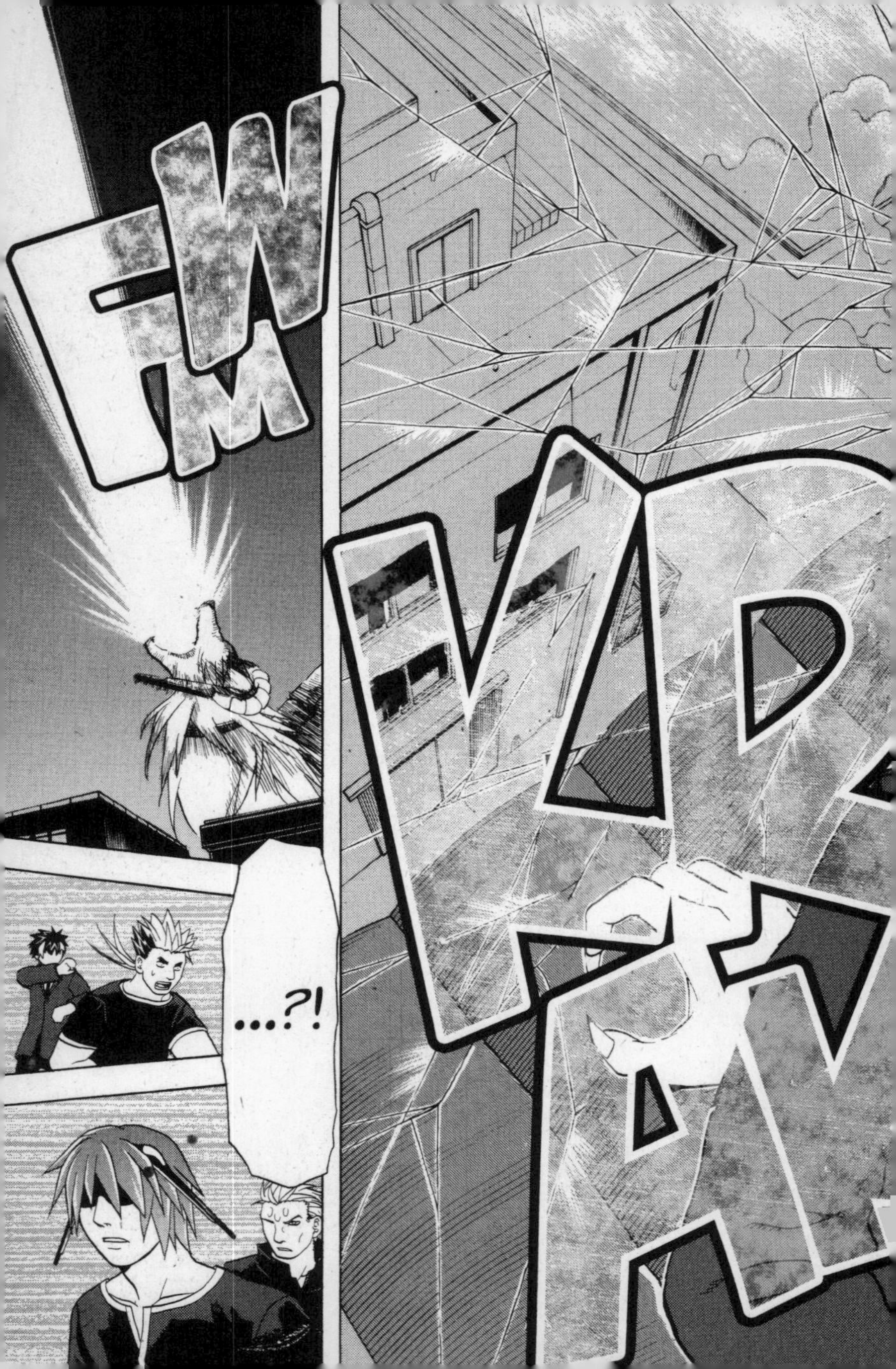
VR
FWM
...?!

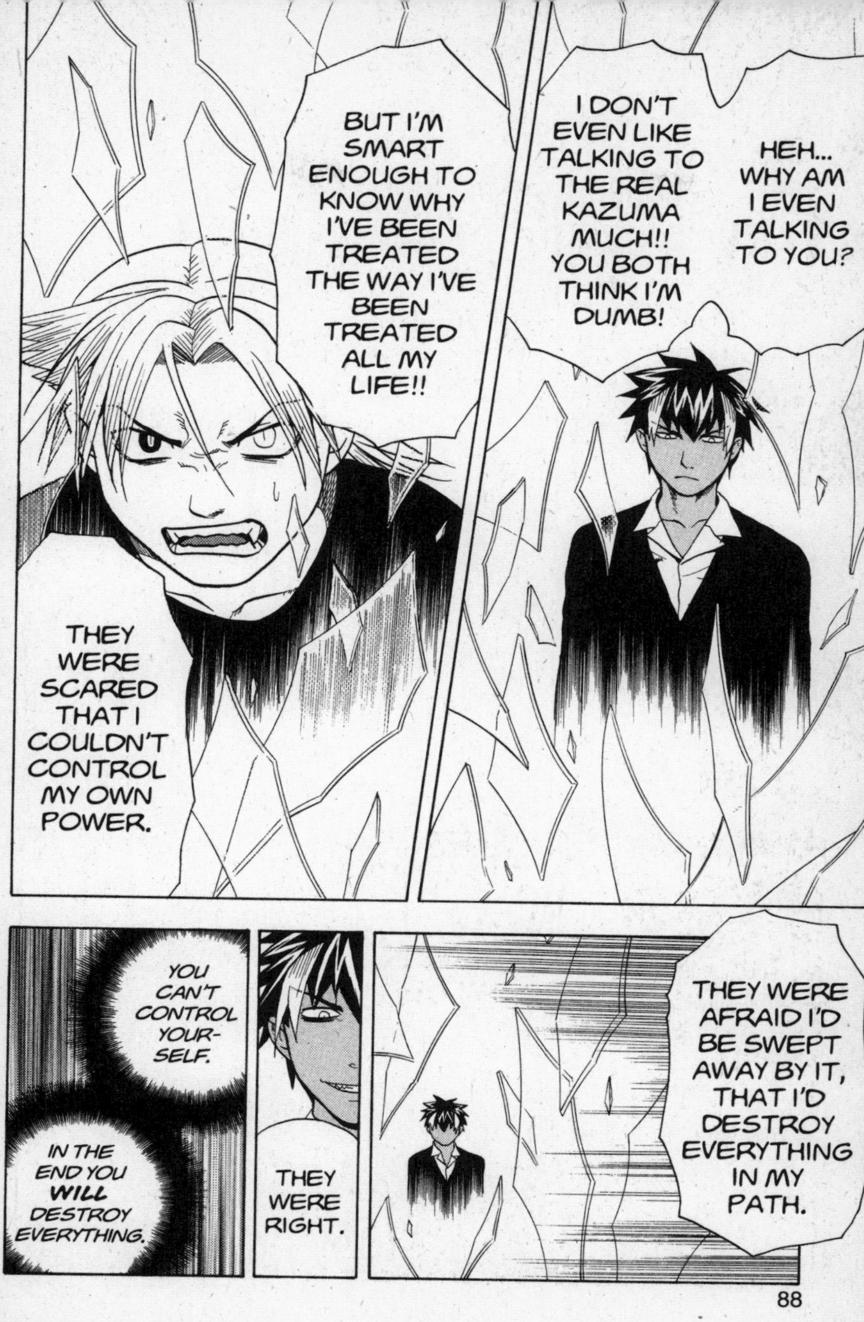
HEH... WHY AM I EVEN TALKING TO YOU?
I DON'T EVEN LIKE TALKING TO THE REAL KAZUMA MUCH!! YOU BOTH THINK I'M DUMB!
BUT I'M SMART ENOUGH TO KNOW WHY I'VE BEEN TREATED THE WAY I'VE BEEN TREATED ALL MY LIFE!!
THEY WERE SCARED THAT I COULDN'T CONTROL MY OWN POWER.
THEY WERE AFRAID I'D BE SWEPT AWAY BY IT, THAT I'D DESTROY EVERYTHING IN MY PATH.
THEY WERE RIGHT.
YOU CAN'T CONTROL YOUR-SELF.
IN THE END YOU **WILL** DESTROY EVERYTHING.

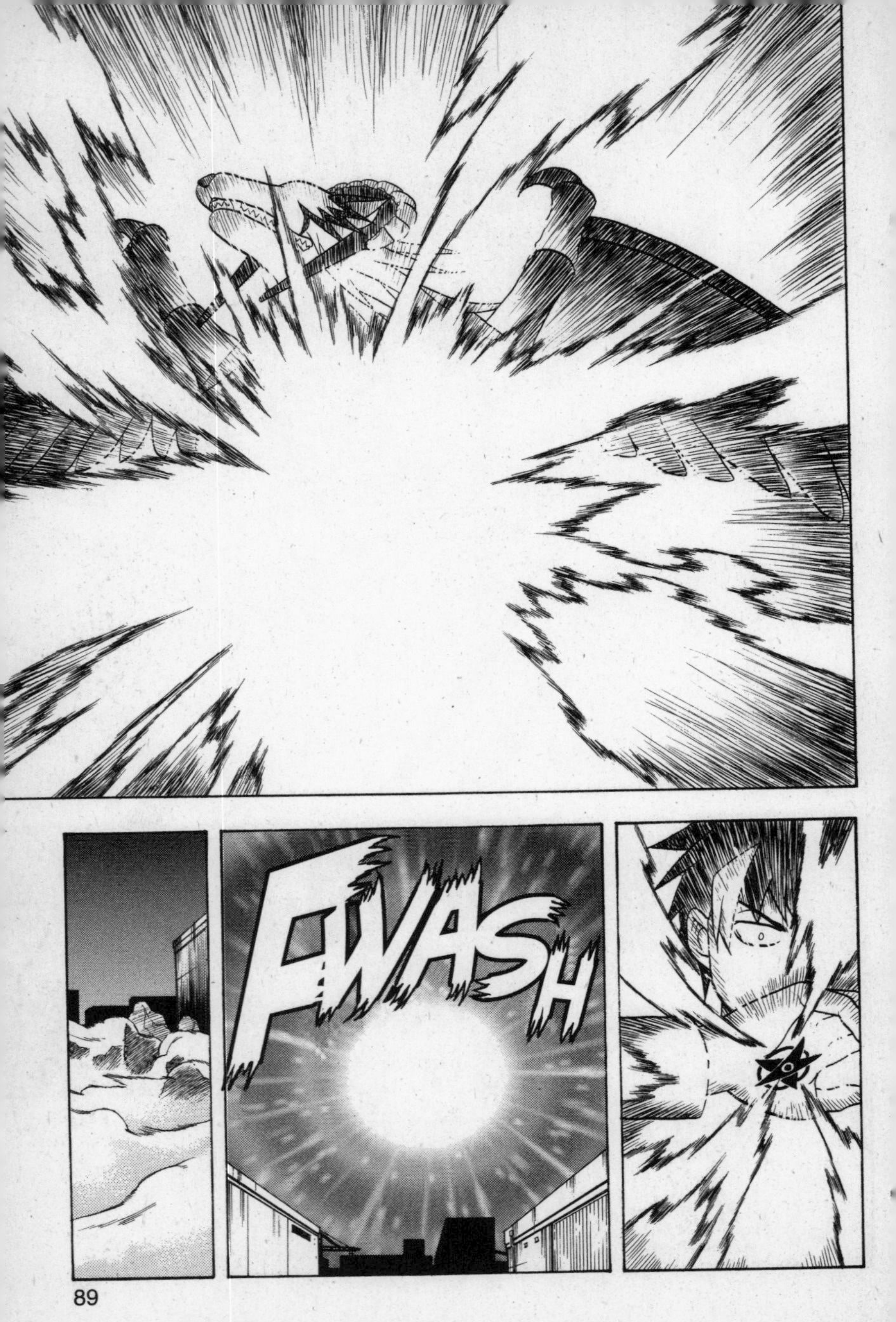
FWASH

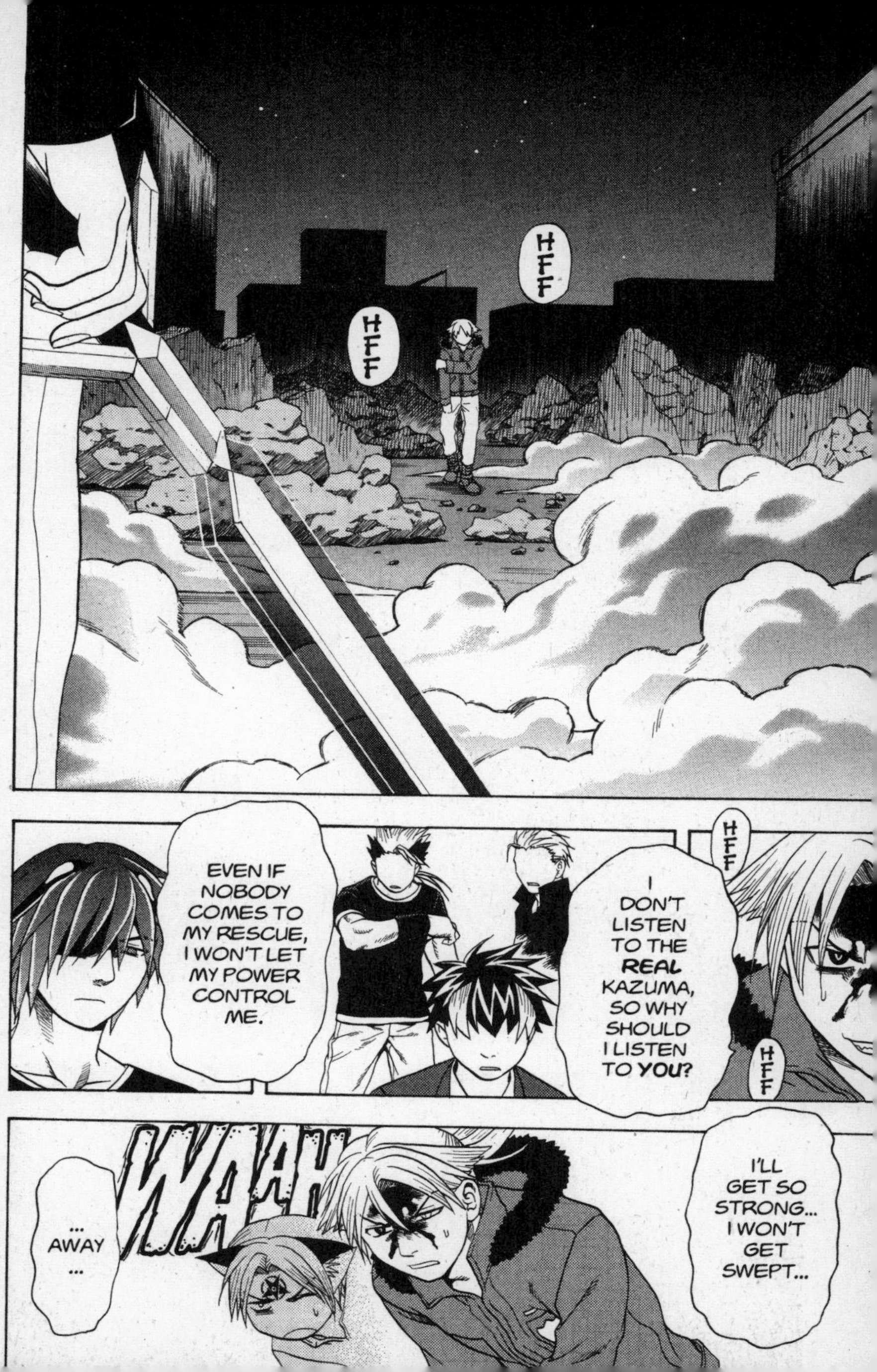

HFF
HFF
HFF
HFF
I DON'T LISTEN TO THE REAL KAZUMA, SO WHY SHOULD I LISTEN TO YOU?
EVEN IF NOBODY COMES TO MY RESCUE, I WON'T LET MY POWER CONTROL ME.
I'LL GET SO STRONG... I WON'T GET SWEPT...
WAAH
... AWAY ...

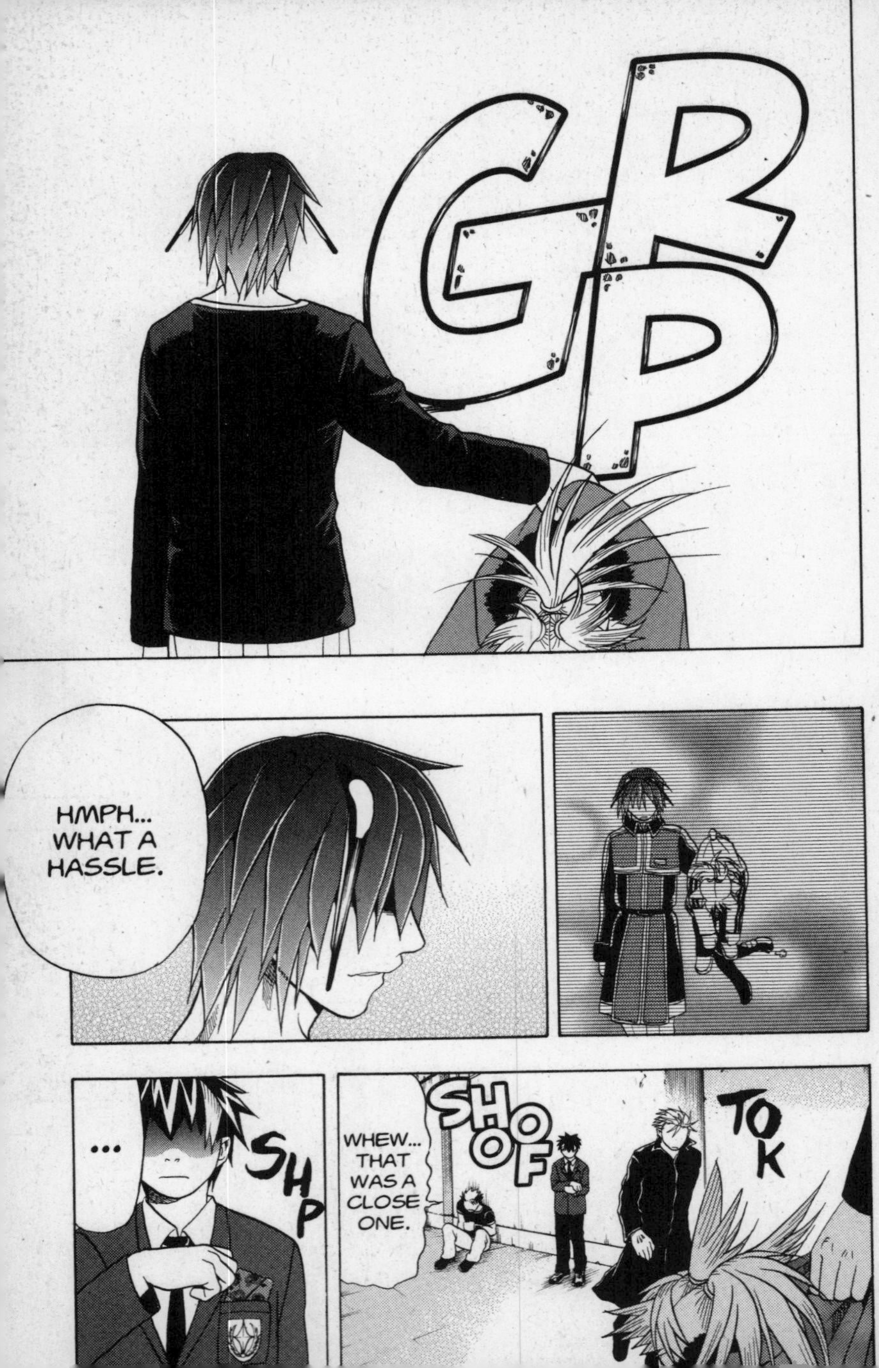
GBP
HMPH... WHAT A HASSLE.
TOK
SHOOF
WHEW... THAT WAS A CLOSE ONE.
SHP
...

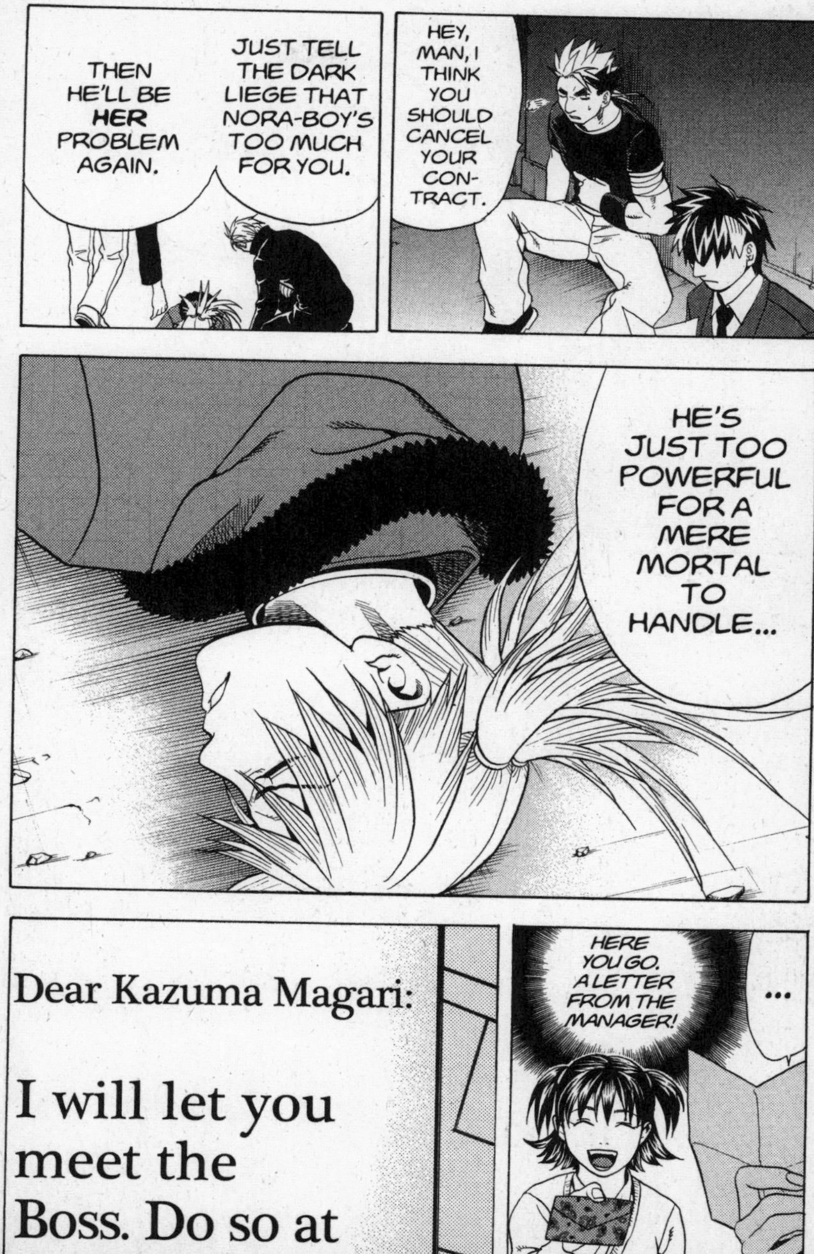
HEY, MAN, I THINK YOU SHOULD CANCEL YOUR CONTRACT.
JUST TELL THE DARK LIEGE THAT NORA-BOY'S TOO MUCH FOR YOU.
THEN HE'LL BE **HER** PROBLEM AGAIN.
HE'S JUST TOO POWERFUL FOR A MERE MORTAL TO HANDLE...
...
HERE YOU GO. A LETTER FROM THE MANAGER!
Dear Kazuma Magari:
I will let you meet the Boss. Do so at

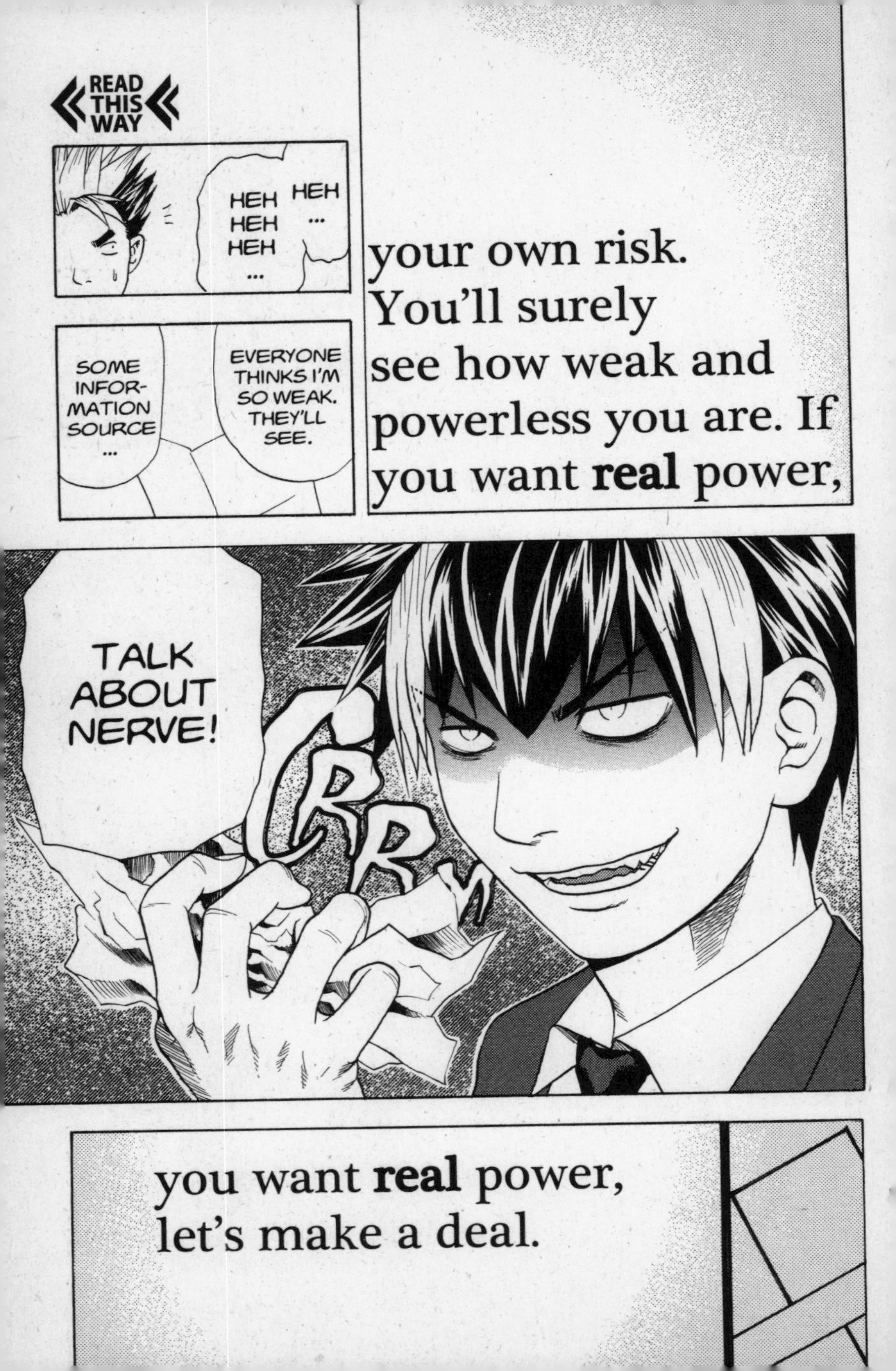
READ THIS WAY
your own risk. You'll surely see how weak and powerless you are. If you want **real** power,
HEH ...
HEH HEH HEH ...
EVERYONE THINKS I'M SO WEAK. THEY'LL SEE.
SOME INFOR-MATION SOURCE ...
TALK ABOUT NERVE!
you want **real** power, let's make a deal.

A DESIGN FOR THE
DARK LIEGE ARMY
UNIFORM THAT I
DREW BEFORE THE
MANGA STARTED.
IT'S SLIGHTLY
DIFFERENT NOW,
OBVIOUSLY.

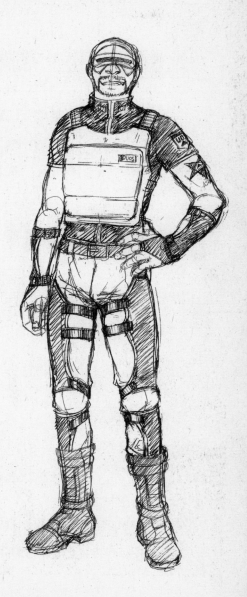

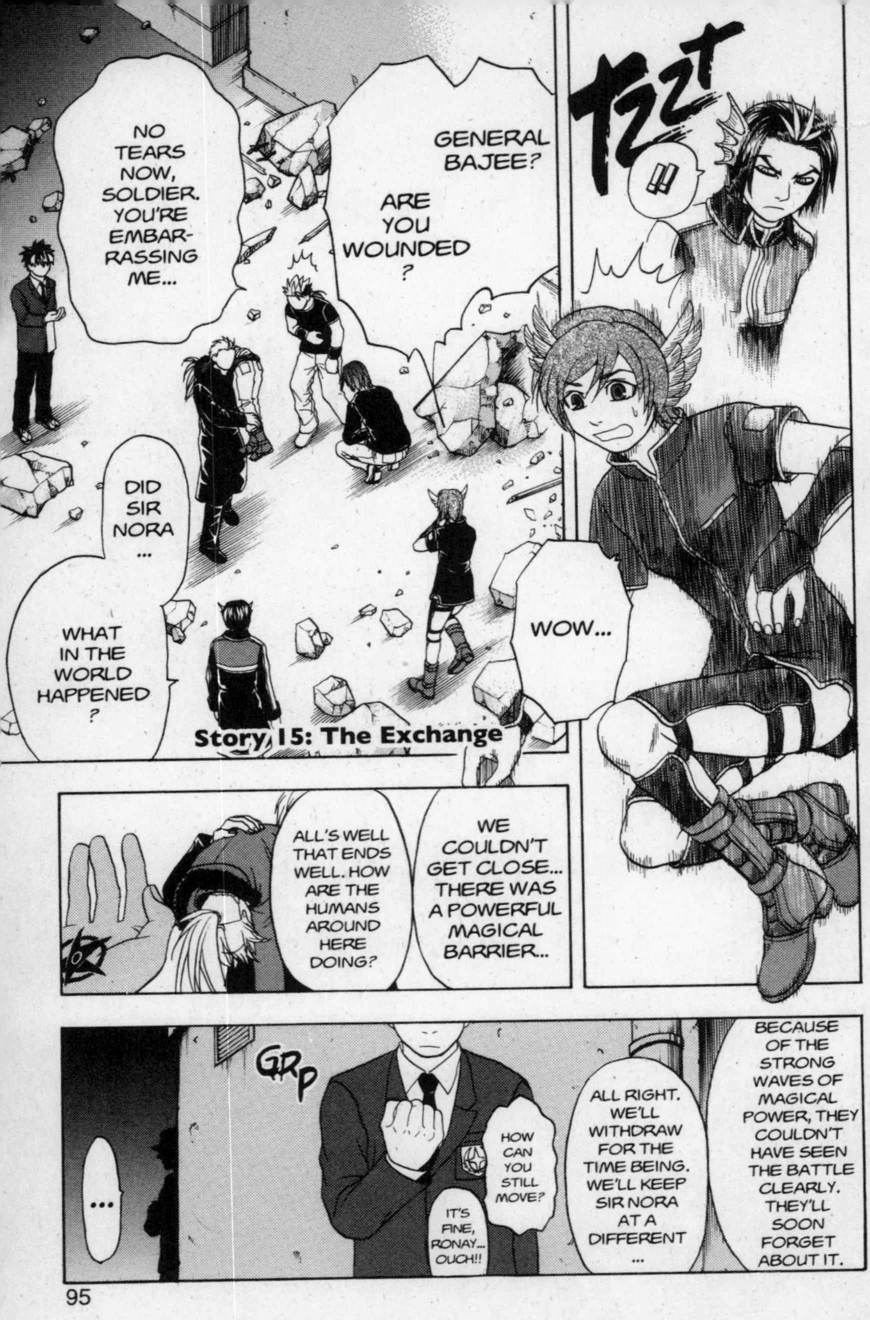
TZZT
!!
WOW...
GENERAL BAJEE? ARE YOU WOUNDED?
NO TEARS NOW, SOLDIER. YOU'RE EMBARRASSING ME...
DID SIR NORA...
WHAT IN THE WORLD HAPPENED?
Story 15: The Exchange
WE COULDN'T GET CLOSE... THERE WAS A POWERFUL MAGICAL BARRIER...
ALL'S WELL THAT ENDS WELL. HOW ARE THE HUMANS AROUND HERE DOING?
BECAUSE OF THE STRONG WAVES OF MAGICAL POWER, THEY COULDN'T HAVE SEEN THE BATTLE CLEARLY. THEY'LL SOON FORGET ABOUT IT.
ALL RIGHT. WE'LL WITHDRAW FOR THE TIME BEING. WE'LL KEEP SIR NORA AT A DIFFERENT...
HOW CAN YOU STILL MOVE?
IT'S FINE, RONAY... OUCH!!
GRP
...

Story 15: The Exchange

4,614 total votes!!
Thank you for your support!

1st Place: Nora, 902 Votes

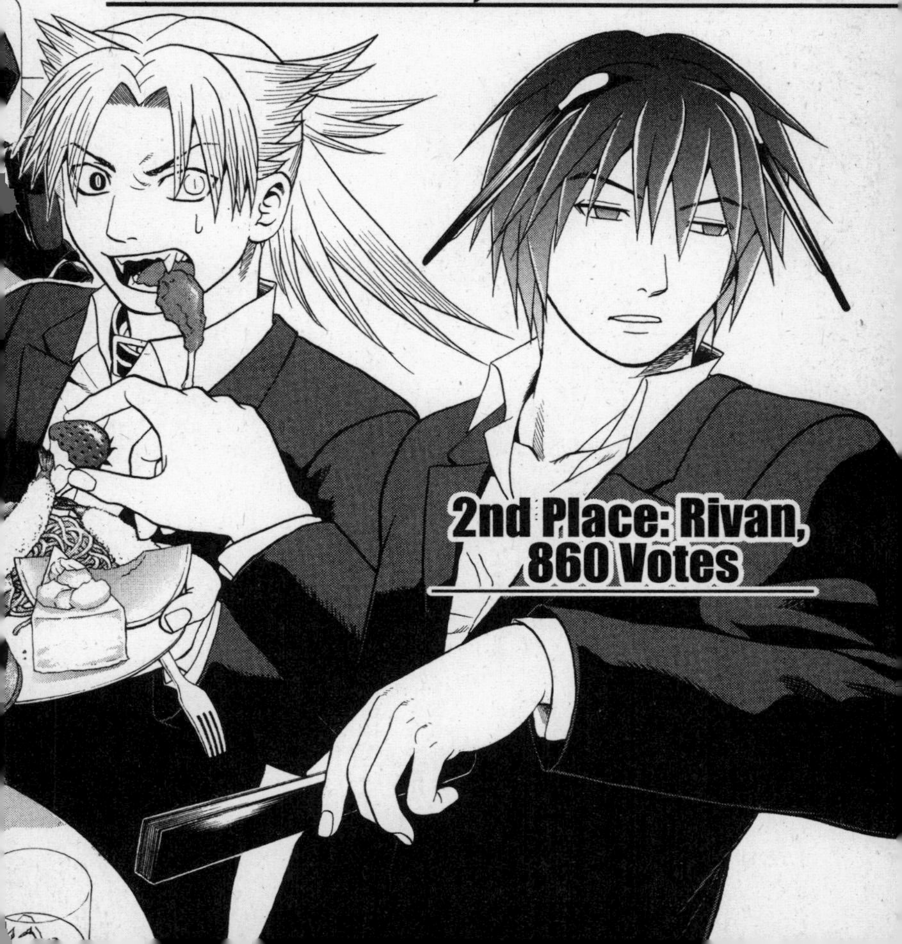
2nd Place: Rivan, 860 Votes

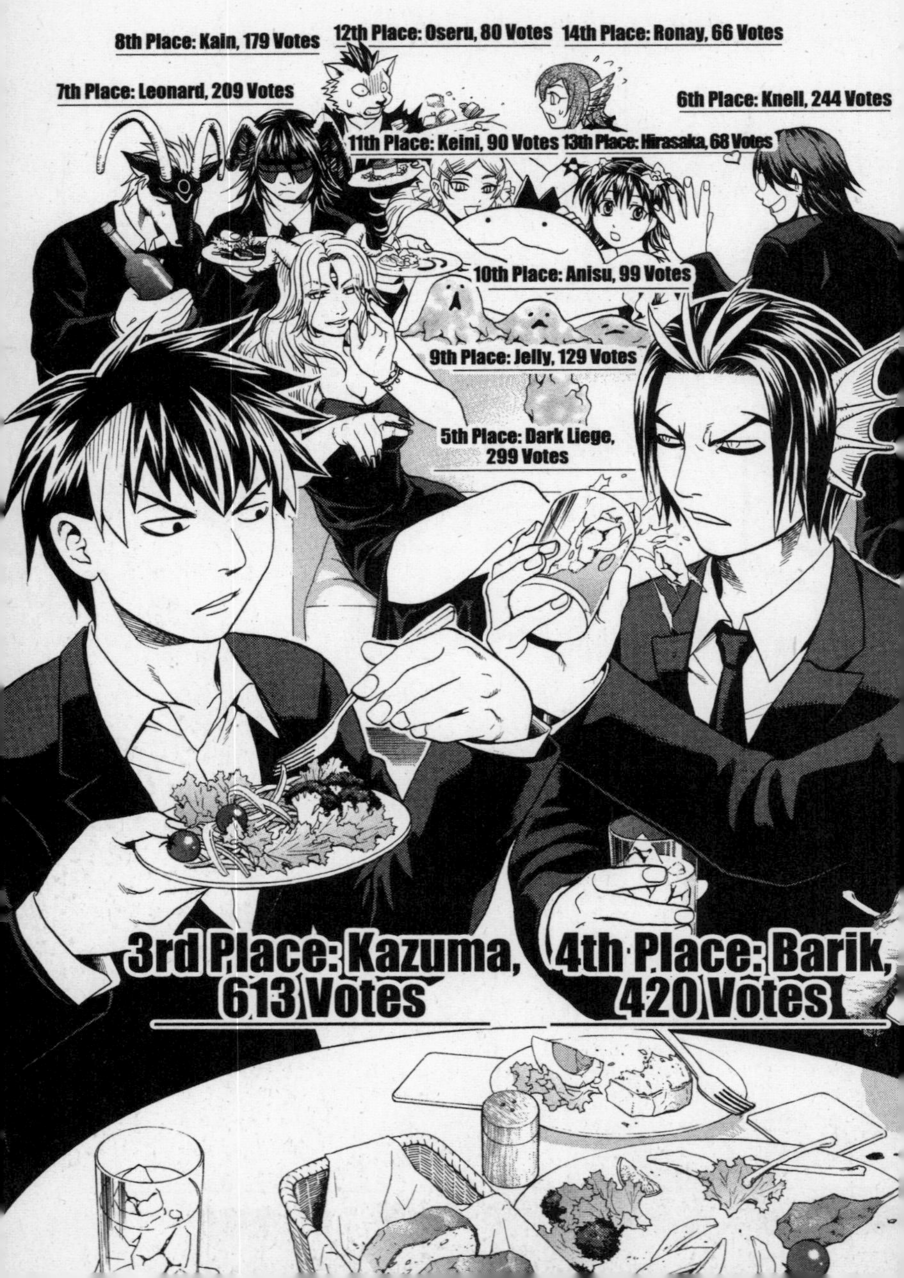

14th Place: Ronay, 66 Votes
12th Place: Oseru, 80 Votes
8th Place: Kain, 179 Votes
6th Place: Knell, 244 Votes
7th Place: Leonard, 209 Votes
13th Place: Hirasaka, 68 Votes
11th Place: Keini, 90 Votes
10th Place: Anisu, 99 Votes
9th Place: Jelly, 129 Votes
5th Place: Dark Liege, 299 Votes
4th Place: Barik, 420 Votes
3rd Place: Kazuma, 613 Votes

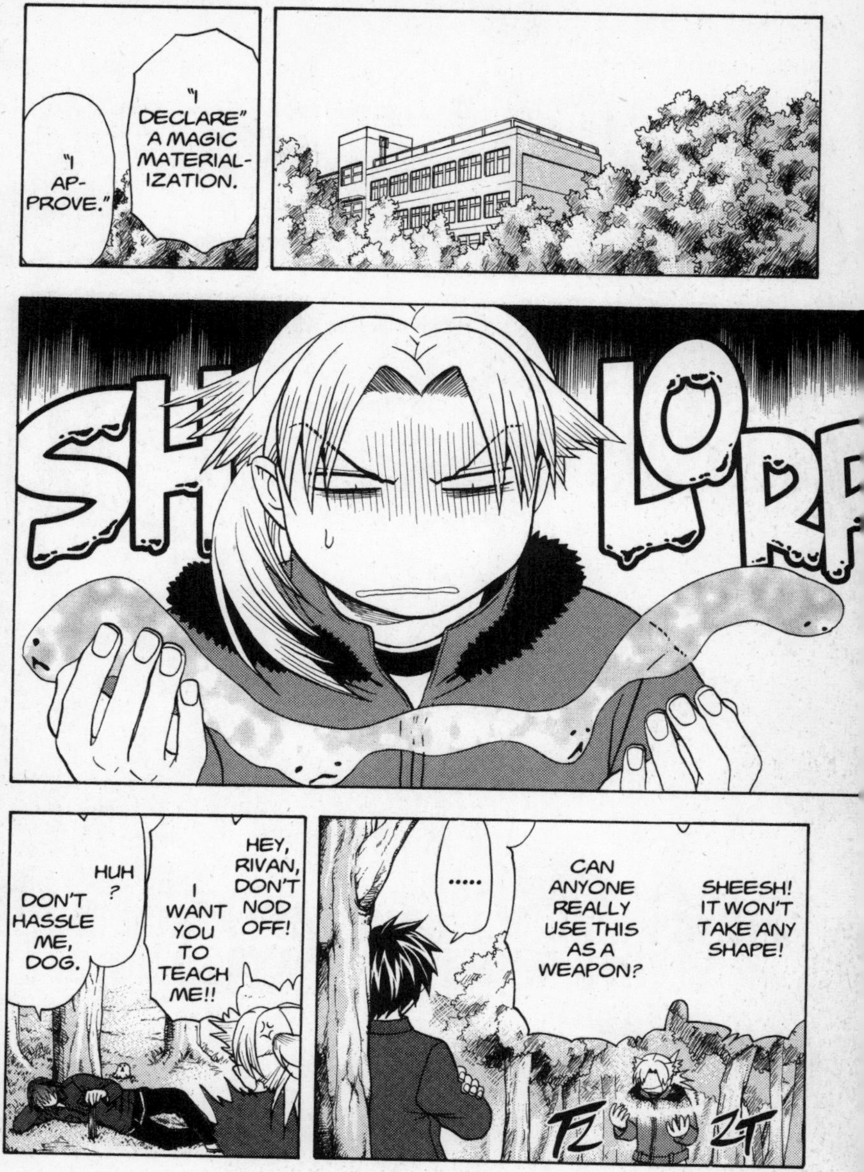
"I DECLARE" A MAGIC MATERIALIZATION.
"I APPROVE."
SH LORP
SHEESH! IT WON'T TAKE ANY SHAPE!
CAN ANYONE REALLY USE THIS AS A WEAPON?
......
TZ ZT
HEY, RIVAN, DON'T NOD OFF!
I WANT YOU TO TEACH ME!!
HUH?
DON'T HASSLE ME, DOG.

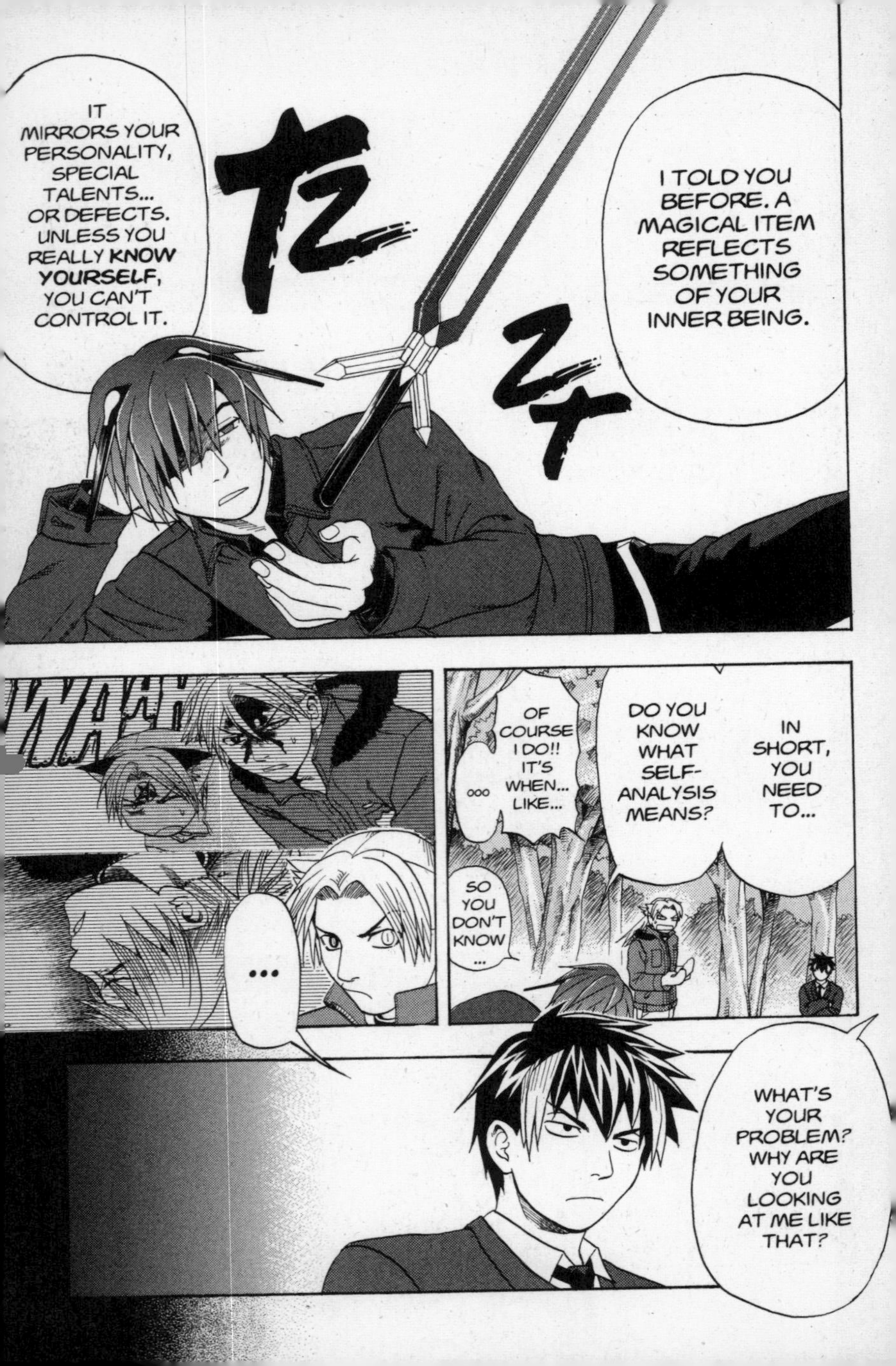
I TOLD YOU BEFORE. A MAGICAL ITEM REFLECTS SOMETHING OF YOUR INNER BEING.
IT MIRRORS YOUR PERSONALITY, SPECIAL TALENTS... OR DEFECTS. UNLESS YOU REALLY **KNOW YOURSELF**, YOU CAN'T CONTROL IT.
IN SHORT, YOU NEED TO...
DO YOU KNOW WHAT SELF-ANALYSIS MEANS?
OF COURSE I DO!! IT'S WHEN... LIKE...
ooo
SO YOU DON'T KNOW...
...
WHAT'S YOUR PROBLEM? WHY ARE YOU LOOKING AT ME LIKE THAT?

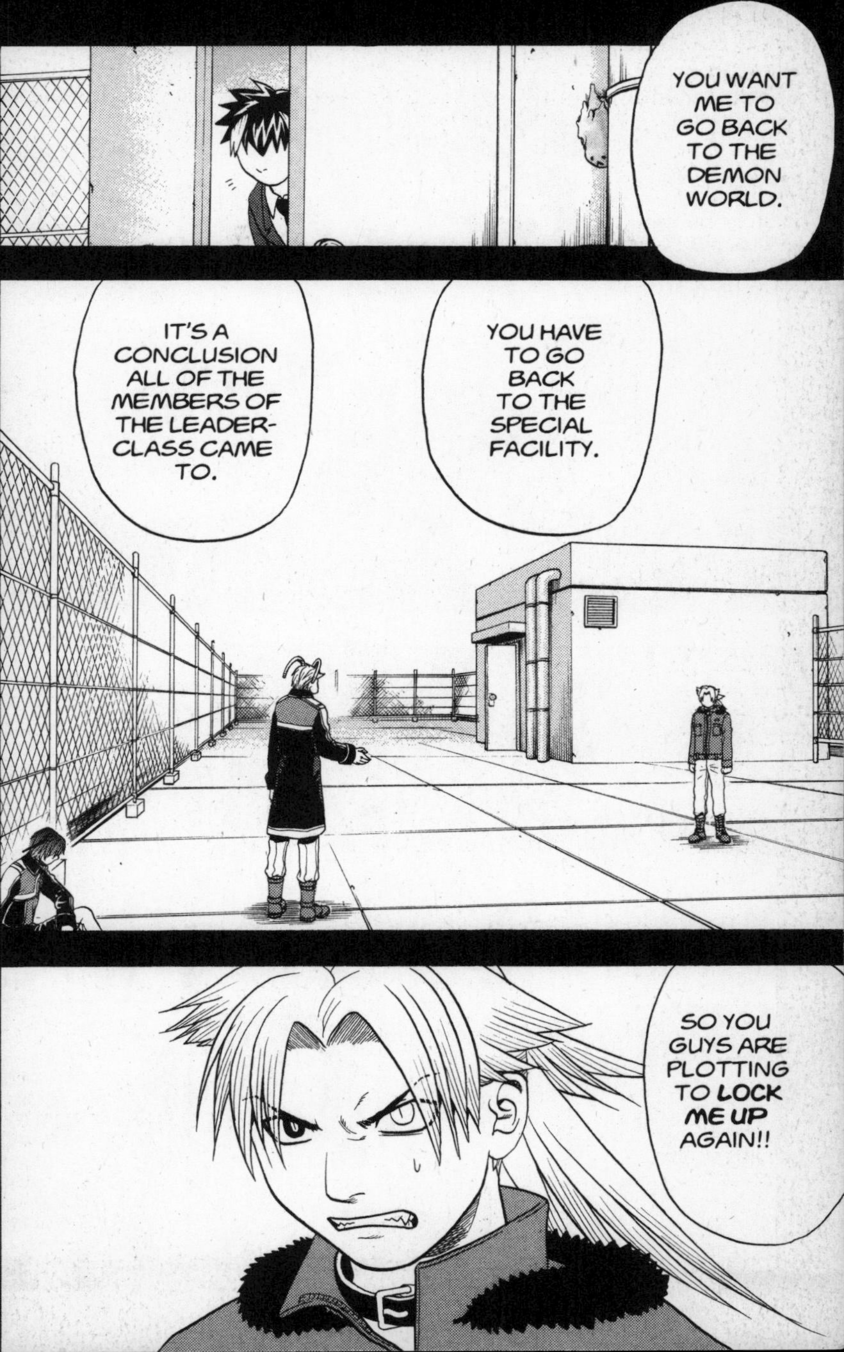
YOU WANT ME TO GO BACK TO THE DEMON WORLD.
YOU HAVE TO GO BACK TO THE SPECIAL FACILITY.
IT'S A CONCLUSION ALL OF THE MEMBERS OF THE LEADER-CLASS CAME TO.
SO YOU GUYS ARE PLOTTING TO **LOCK ME UP** AGAIN!!

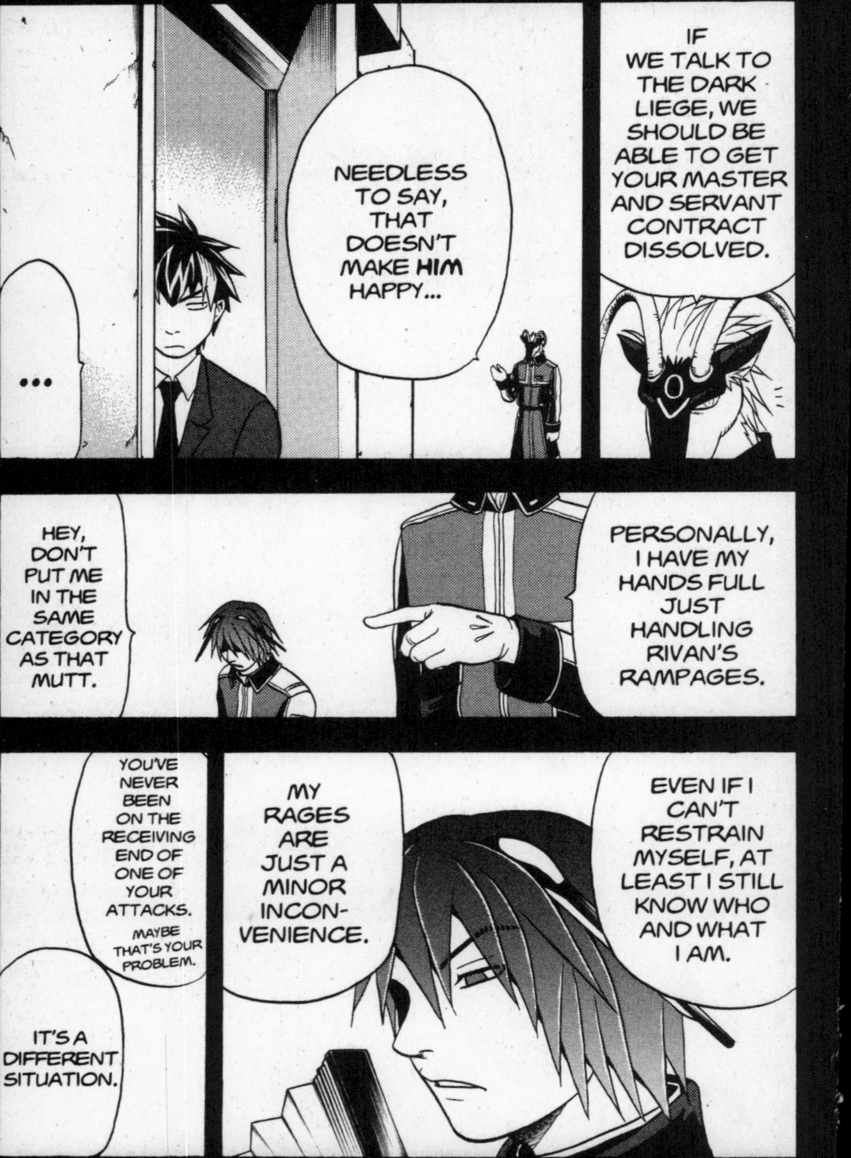
IF WE TALK TO THE DARK LIEGE, WE SHOULD BE ABLE TO GET YOUR MASTER AND SERVANT CONTRACT DISSOLVED.
NEEDLESS TO SAY, THAT DOESN'T MAKE **HIM** HAPPY...
...
PERSONALLY, I HAVE MY HANDS FULL JUST HANDLING RIVAN'S RAMPAGES.
HEY, DON'T PUT ME IN THE SAME CATEGORY AS THAT MUTT.
EVEN IF I CAN'T RESTRAIN MYSELF, AT LEAST I STILL KNOW WHO AND WHAT I AM.
MY RAGES ARE JUST A MINOR INCON-VENIENCE.
YOU'VE NEVER BEEN ON THE RECEIVING END OF ONE OF YOUR ATTACKS.
MAYBE THAT'S YOUR PROBLEM.
IT'S A DIFFERENT SITUATION.

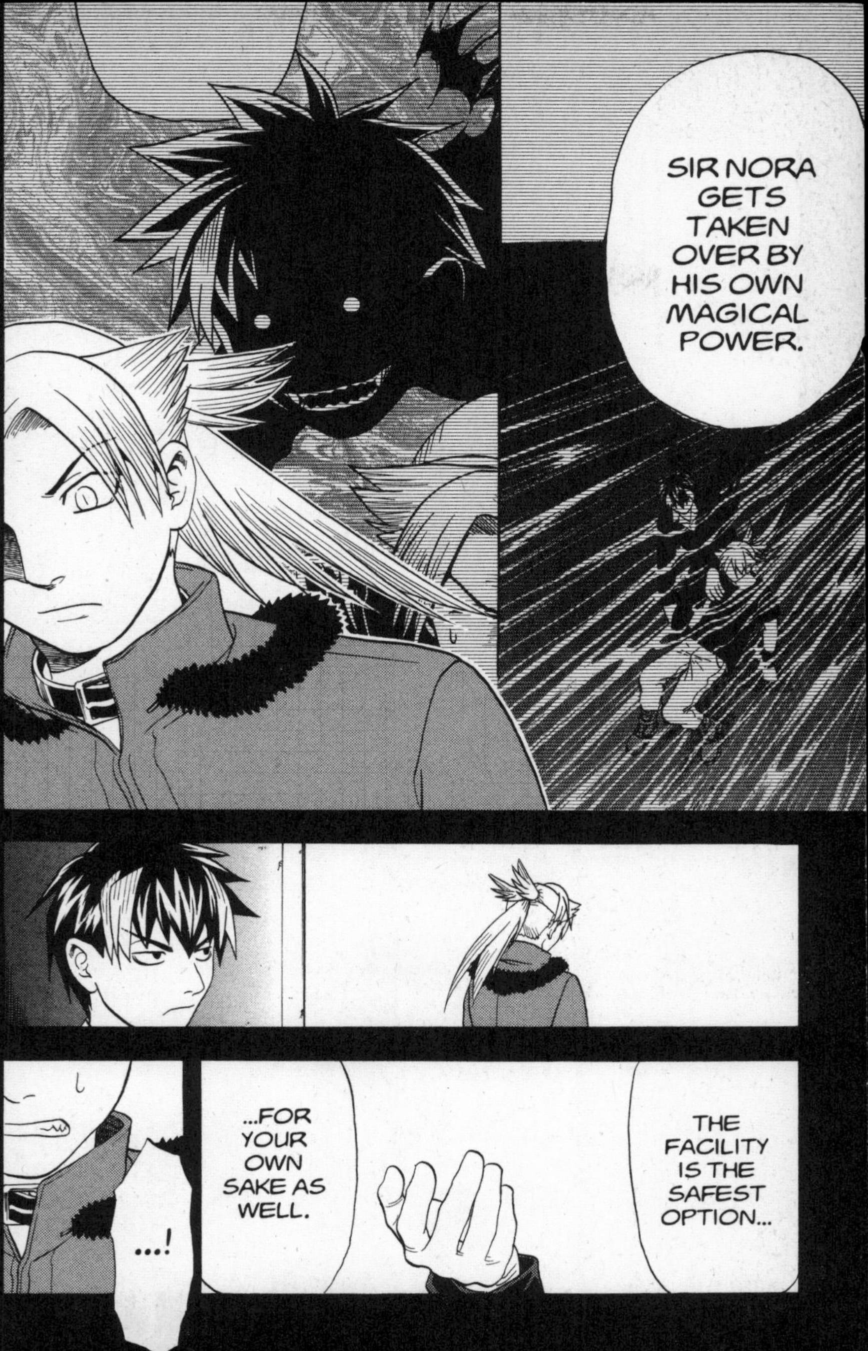
SIR NORA GETS TAKEN OVER BY HIS OWN MAGICAL POWER.
THE FACILITY IS THE SAFEST OPTION...
...FOR YOUR OWN SAKE AS WELL.
...!

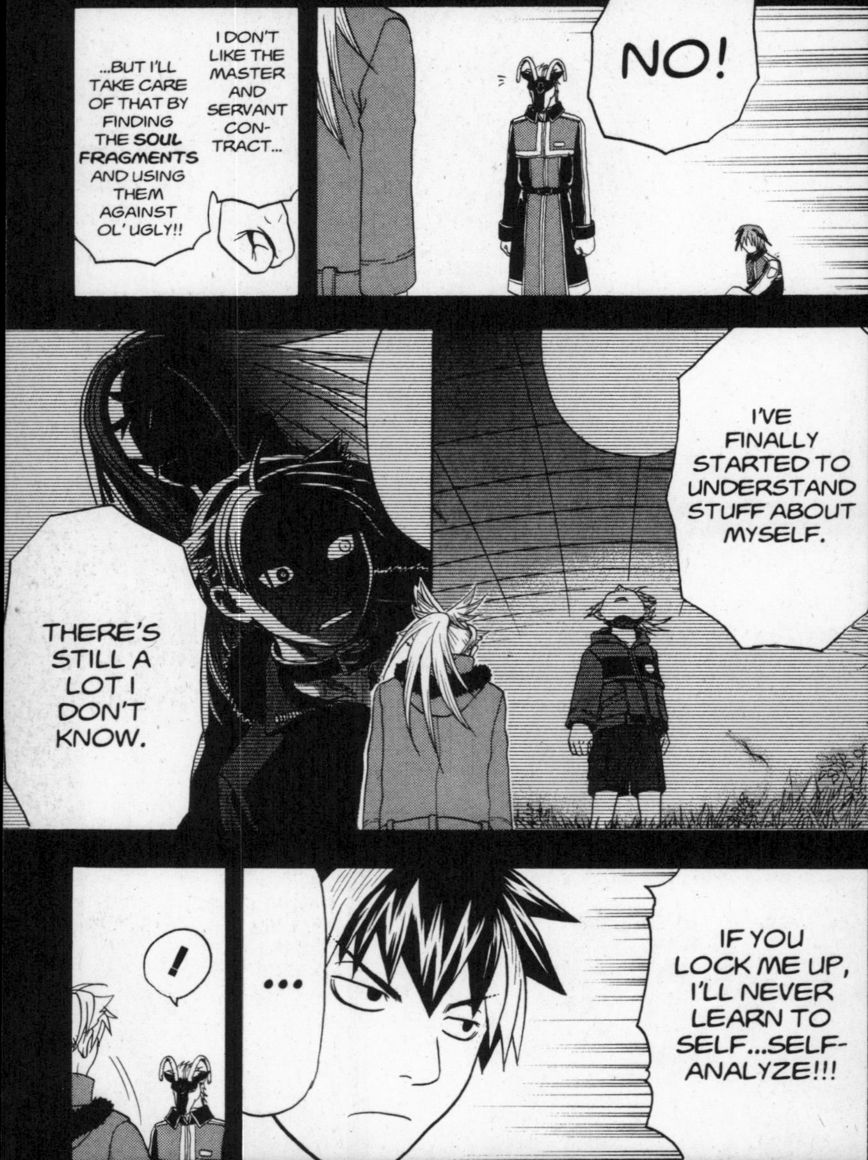
NO!
I DON'T LIKE THE MASTER AND SERVANT CONTRACT...
...BUT I'LL TAKE CARE OF THAT BY FINDING THE **SOUL FRAGMENTS** AND USING THEM AGAINST OL' UGLY!!
I'VE FINALLY STARTED TO UNDERSTAND STUFF ABOUT MYSELF.
THERE'S STILL A LOT I DON'T KNOW.
IF YOU LOCK ME UP, I'LL NEVER LEARN TO SELF...SELF-ANALYZE!!!
...
!

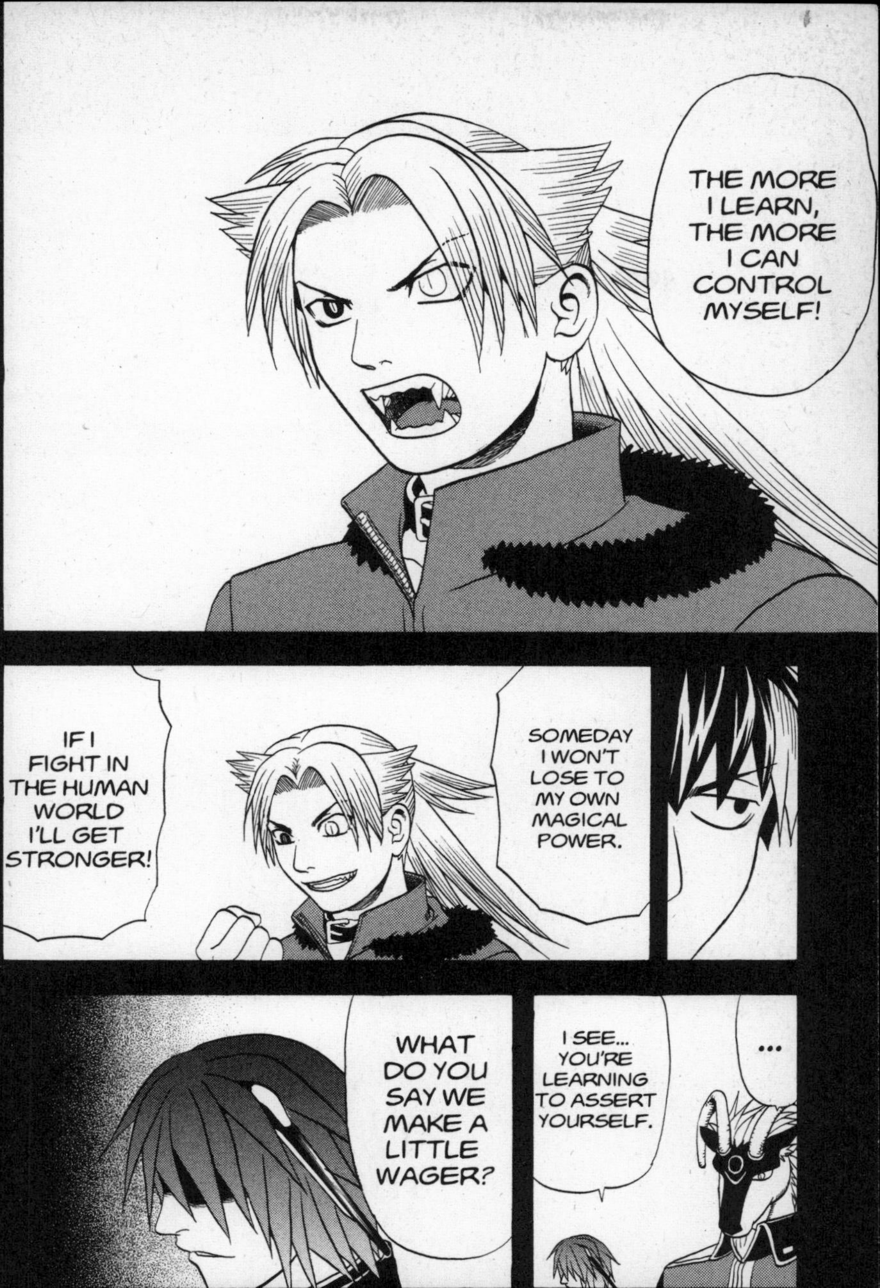
THE MORE I LEARN, THE MORE I CAN CONTROL MYSELF!
SOMEDAY I WON'T LOSE TO MY OWN MAGICAL POWER.
IF I FIGHT IN THE HUMAN WORLD I'LL GET STRONGER!
...
I SEE... YOU'RE LEARNING TO ASSERT YOURSELF.
WHAT DO YOU SAY WE MAKE A LITTLE WAGER?

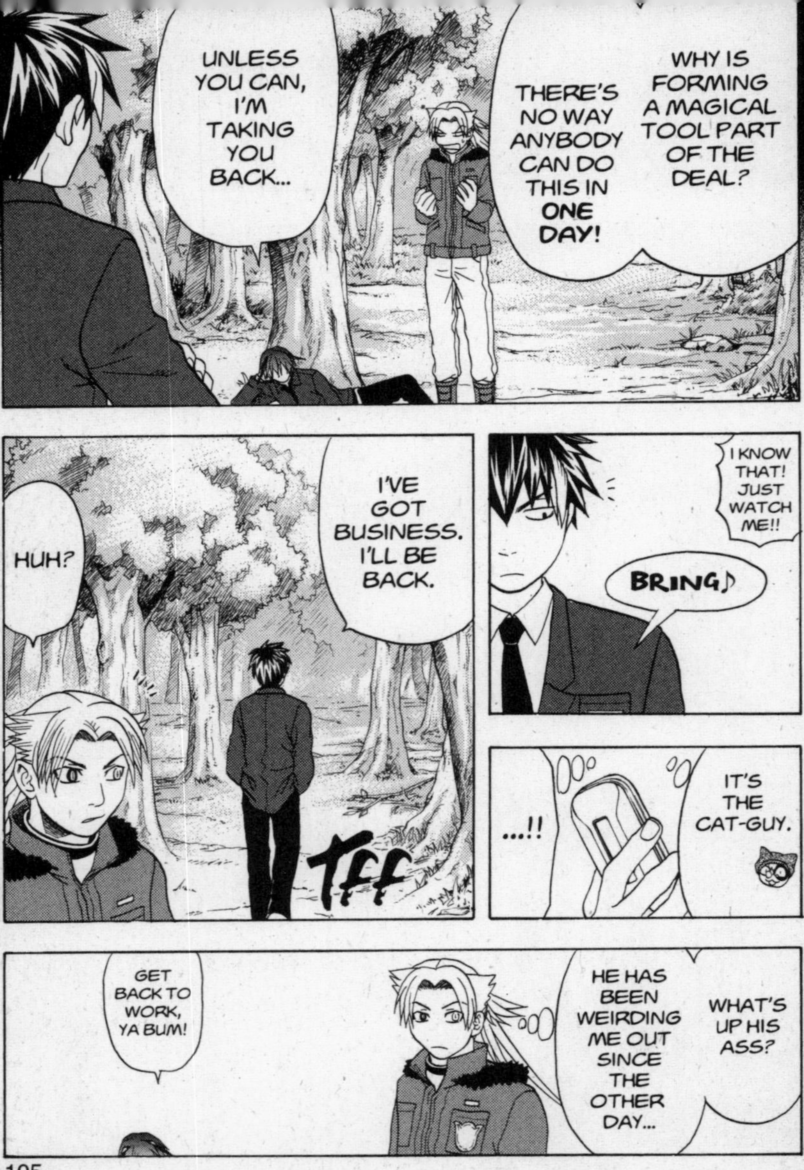

WHY IS FORMING A MAGICAL TOOL PART OF THE DEAL?
THERE'S NO WAY ANYBODY CAN DO THIS IN ONE DAY!
UNLESS YOU CAN, I'M TAKING YOU BACK...
I KNOW THAT! JUST WATCH ME!!
BRING♪
IT'S THE CAT-GUY.
...!!
I'VE GOT BUSINESS. I'LL BE BACK.
HUH?
TFF
WHAT'S UP HIS ASS?
HE HAS BEEN WEIRDING ME OUT SINCE THE OTHER DAY...
GET BACK TO WORK, YA BUM!

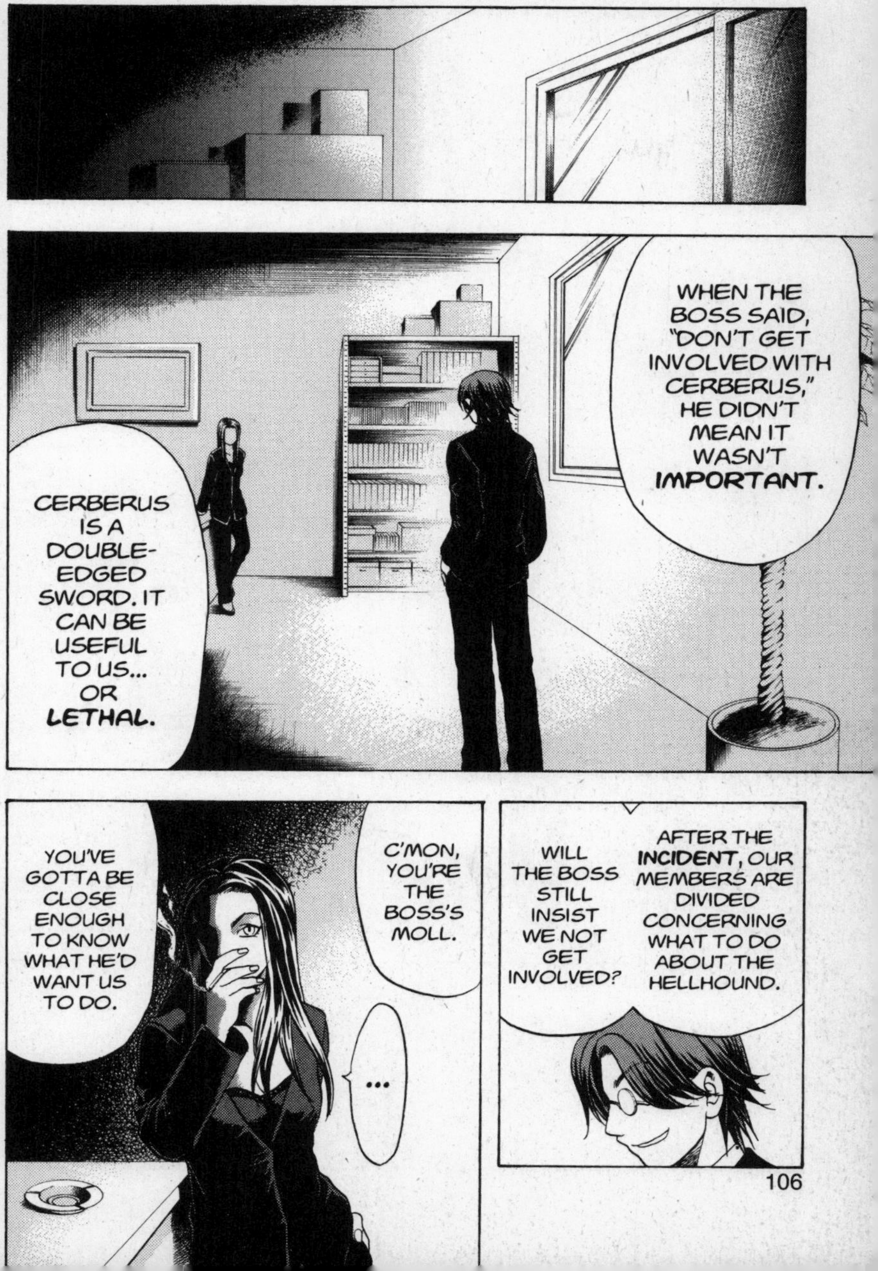
WHEN THE BOSS SAID, "DON'T GET INVOLVED WITH CERBERUS," HE DIDN'T MEAN IT WASN'T IMPORTANT.
CERBERUS IS A DOUBLE-EDGED SWORD. IT CAN BE USEFUL TO US... OR LETHAL.
AFTER THE INCIDENT, OUR MEMBERS ARE DIVIDED CONCERNING WHAT TO DO ABOUT THE HELLHOUND.
WILL THE BOSS STILL INSIST WE NOT GET INVOLVED?
C'MON, YOU'RE THE BOSS'S MOLL.
YOU'VE GOTTA BE CLOSE ENOUGH TO KNOW WHAT HE'D WANT US TO DO.
...

READ THIS WAY

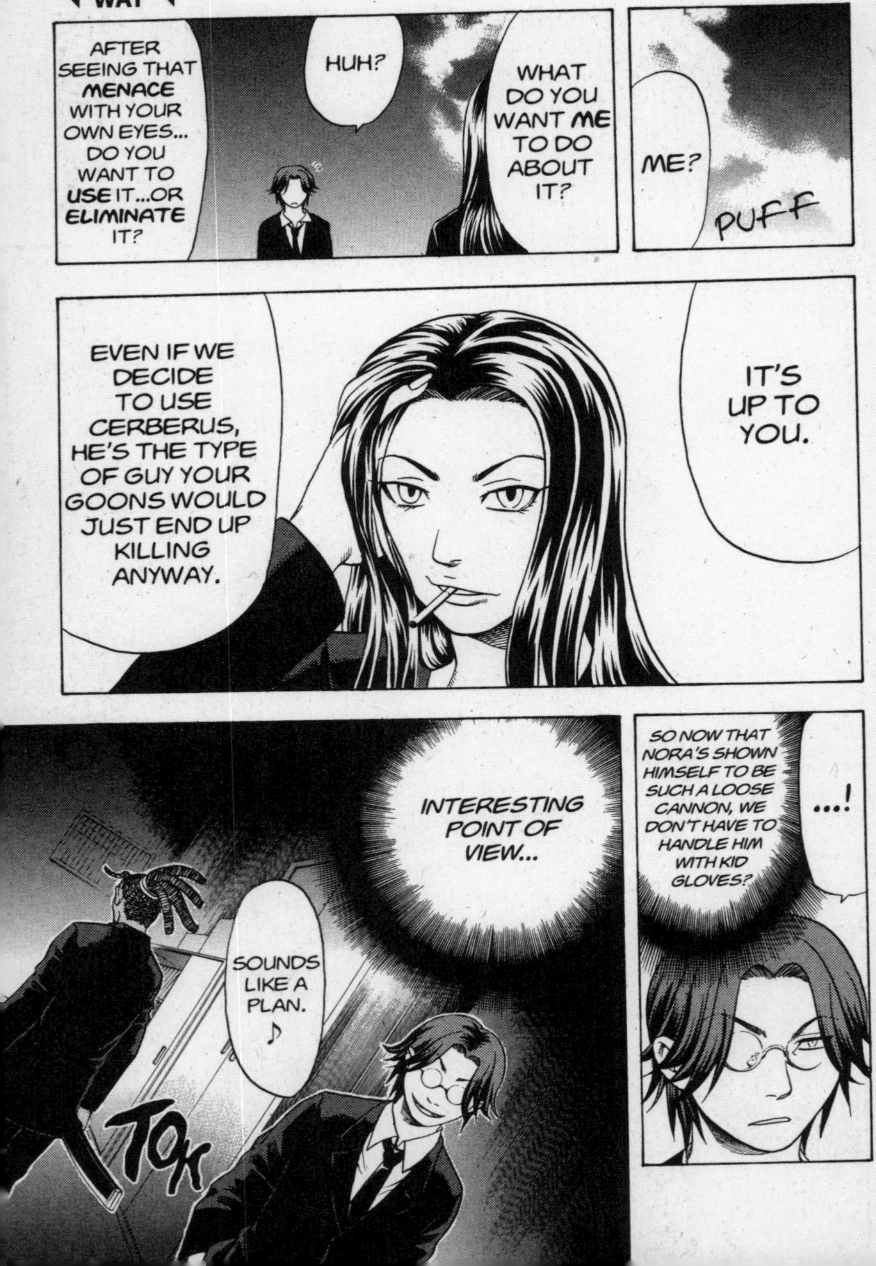
ME?
PUFF
WHAT DO YOU WANT ME TO DO ABOUT IT?
HUH?
AFTER SEEING THAT MENACE WITH YOUR OWN EYES... DO YOU WANT TO USE IT...OR ELIMINATE IT?
IT'S UP TO YOU.
EVEN IF WE DECIDE TO USE CERBERUS, HE'S THE TYPE OF GUY YOUR GOONS WOULD JUST END UP KILLING ANYWAY.
...!
SO NOW THAT NORA'S SHOWN HIMSELF TO BE SUCH A LOOSE CANNON, WE DON'T HAVE TO HANDLE HIM WITH KID GLOVES?
INTERESTING POINT OF VIEW...
SOUNDS LIKE A PLAN. ♪
TOK

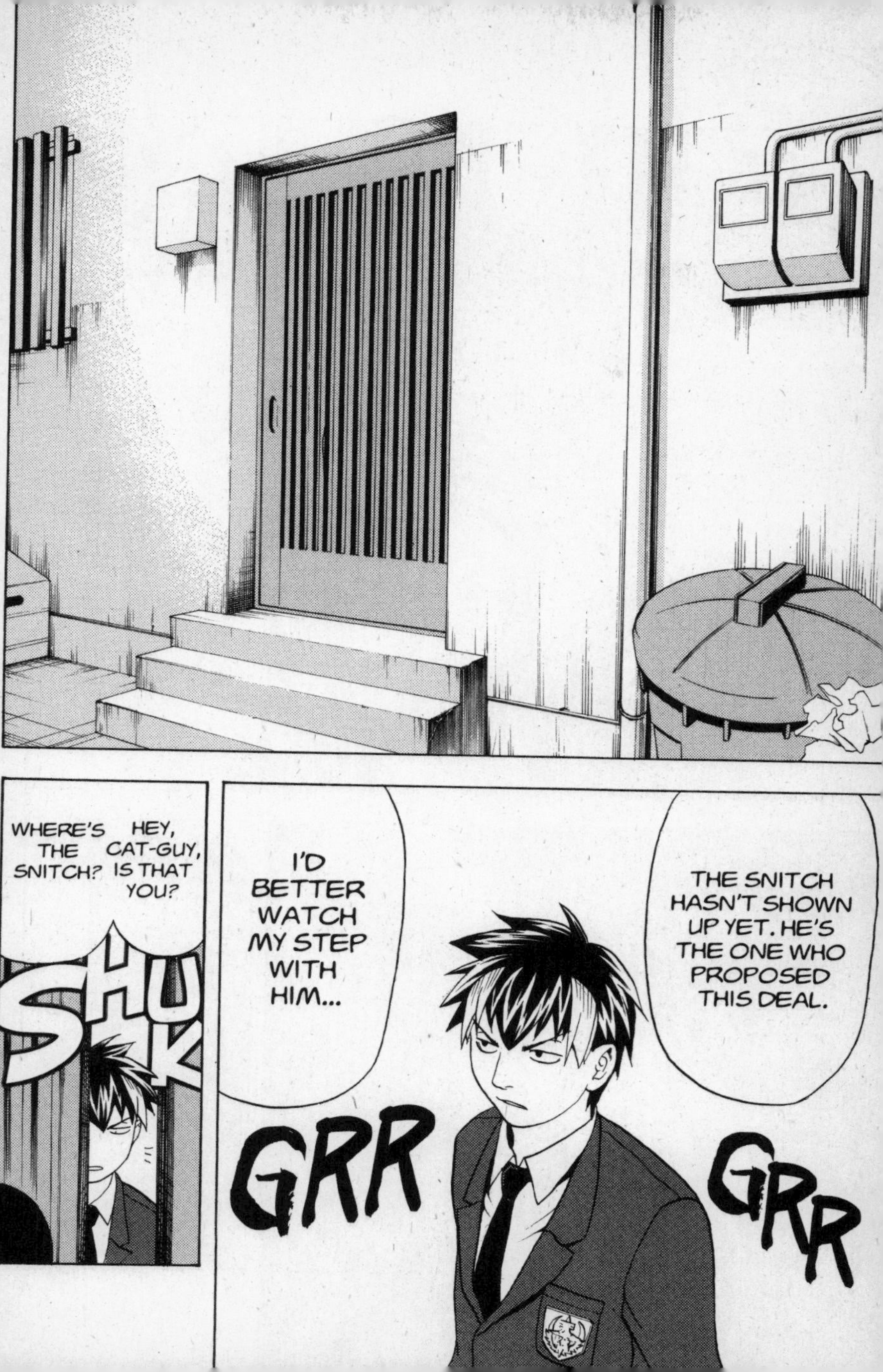
THE SNITCH HASN'T SHOWN UP YET. HE'S THE ONE WHO PROPOSED THIS DEAL.
I'D BETTER WATCH MY STEP WITH HIM...
GRR
GRR
HEY, CAT-GUY, IS THAT YOU?
WHERE'S THE SNITCH?
SHUK

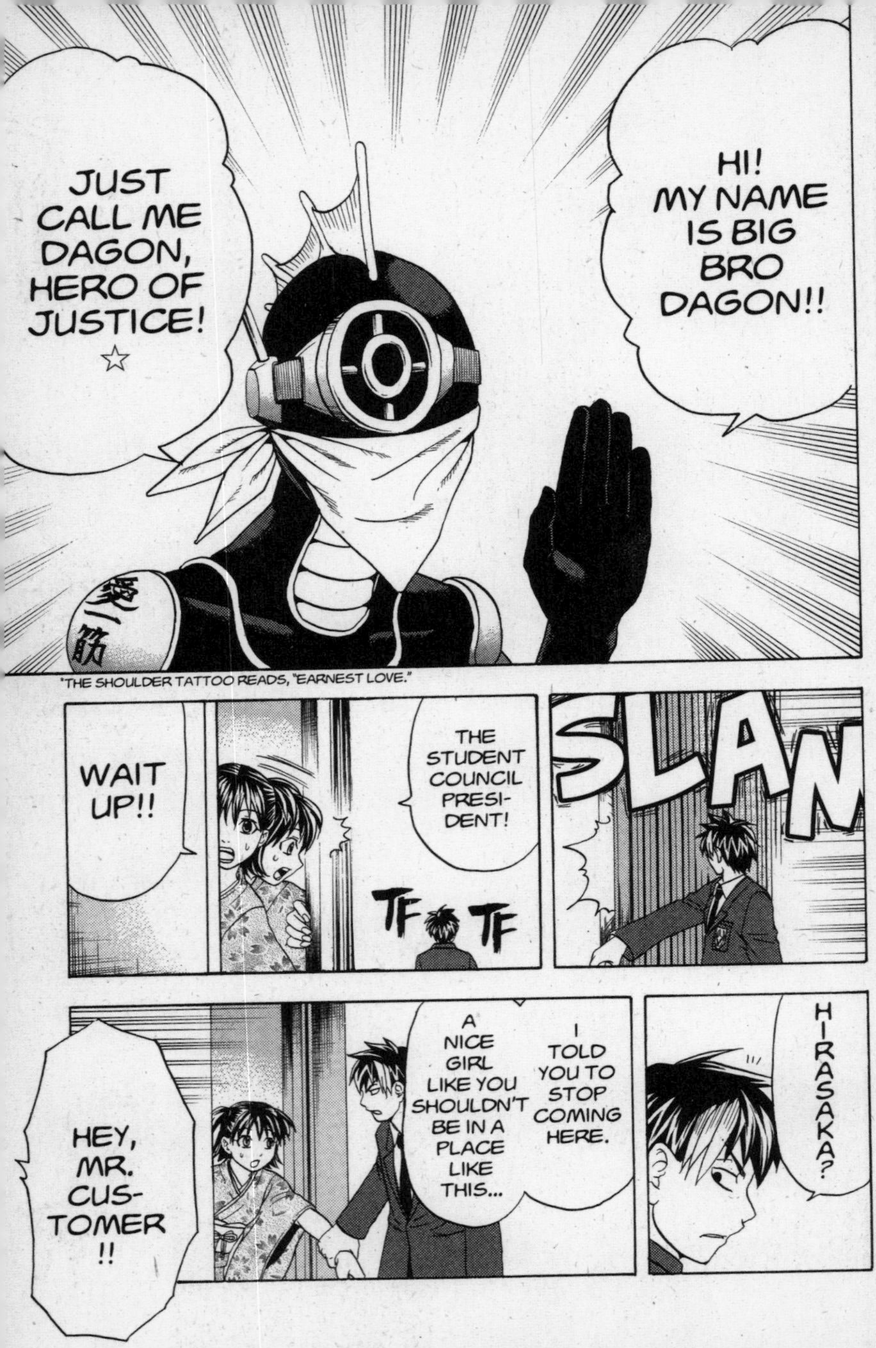
HI! MY NAME IS BIG BRO DAGON!!
JUST CALL ME DAGON, HERO OF JUSTICE! ☆
愛一筋
*THE SHOULDER TATTOO READS, "EARNEST LOVE."
SLAM
THE STUDENT COUNCIL PRESI- DENT!
TF TF
WAIT UP!!
HIRASAKA?
I TOLD YOU TO STOP COMING HERE.
A NICE GIRL LIKE YOU SHOULDN'T BE IN A PLACE LIKE THIS...
HEY, MR. CUS- TOMER!!

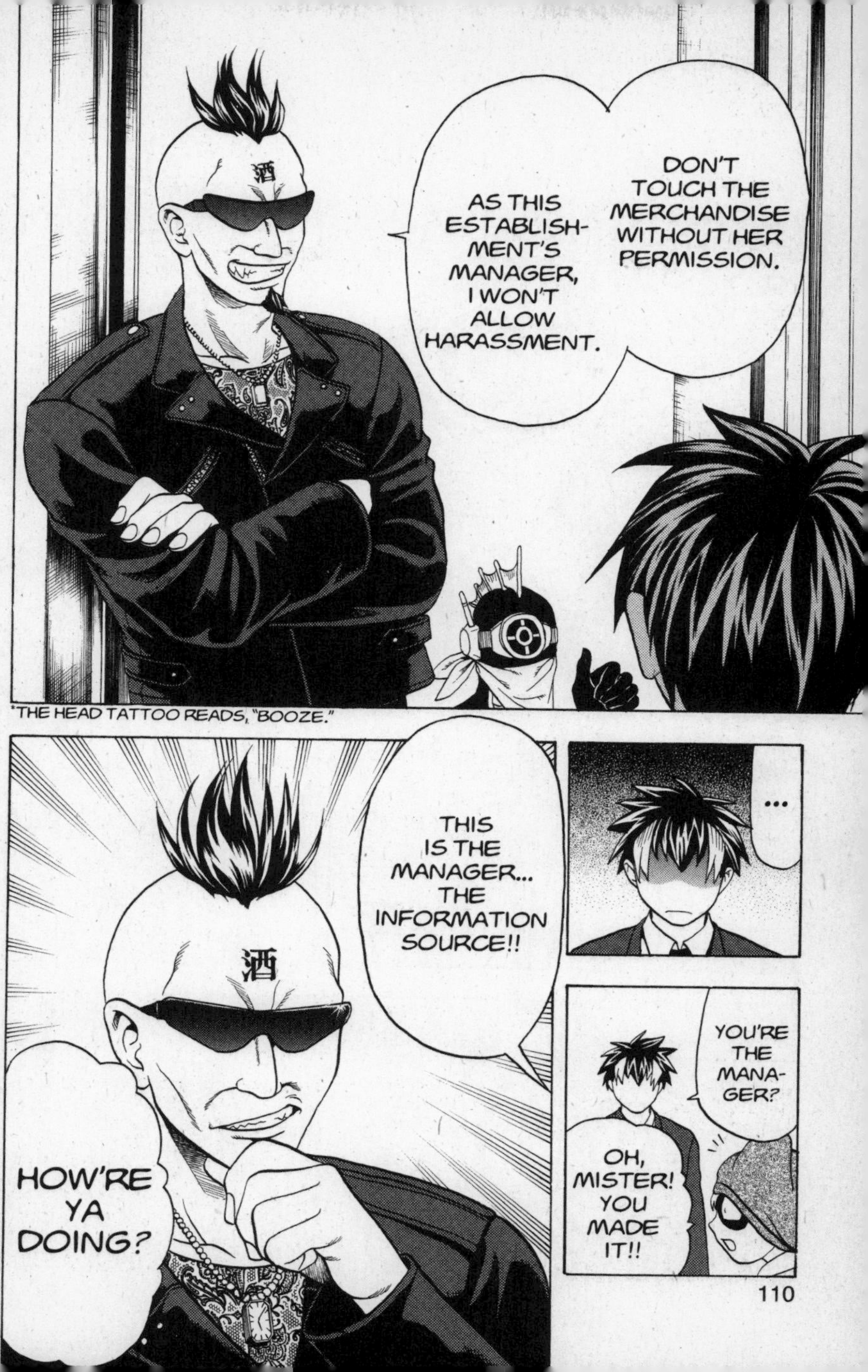
DON'T TOUCH THE MERCHANDISE WITHOUT HER PERMISSION.
AS THIS ESTABLISHMENT'S MANAGER, I WON'T ALLOW HARASSMENT.
酒
...
YOU'RE THE MANAGER?
OH, MISTER! YOU MADE IT!!
THIS IS THE MANAGER... THE INFORMATION SOURCE!!
酒
HOW'RE YA DOING?
*THE HEAD TATTOO READS, "BOOZE."

READ THIS WAY

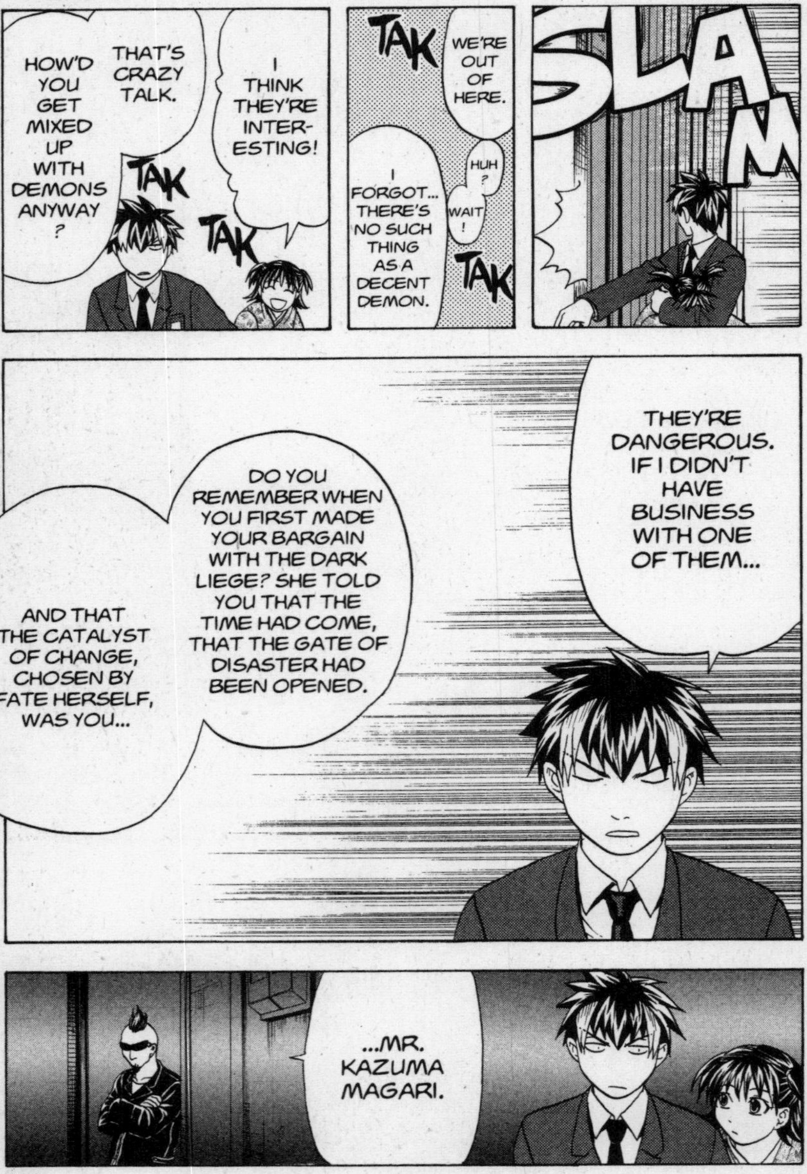

SLAM
WE'RE OUT OF HERE.
TAK
HUH?
WAIT!
I FORGOT... THERE'S NO SUCH THING AS A DECENT DEMON.
TAK
I THINK THEY'RE INTER-ESTING!
THAT'S CRAZY TALK.
HOW'D YOU GET MIXED UP WITH DEMONS ANYWAY?
TAK
TAK
THEY'RE DANGEROUS. IF I DIDN'T HAVE BUSINESS WITH ONE OF THEM...
DO YOU REMEMBER WHEN YOU FIRST MADE YOUR BARGAIN WITH THE DARK LIEGE? SHE TOLD YOU THAT THE TIME HAD COME, THAT THE GATE OF DISASTER HAD BEEN OPENED.
AND THAT THE CATALYST OF CHANGE, CHOSEN BY FATE HERSELF, WAS YOU...
...MR. KAZUMA MAGARI.

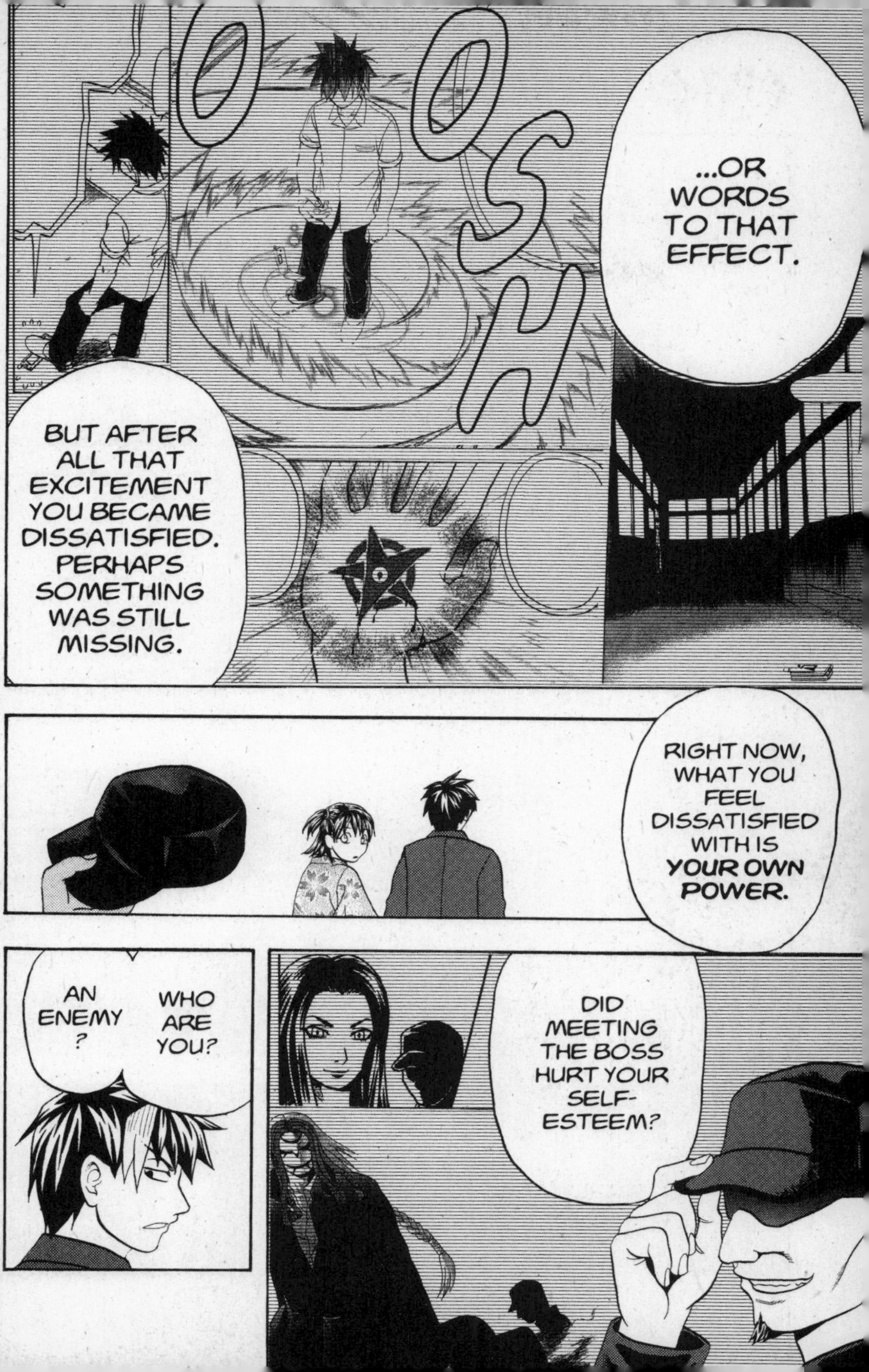

...OR WORDS TO THAT EFFECT.
OOSH
BUT AFTER ALL THAT EXCITEMENT YOU BECAME DISSATISFIED. PERHAPS SOMETHING WAS STILL MISSING.
RIGHT NOW, WHAT YOU FEEL DISSATISFIED WITH IS **YOUR OWN POWER.**
DID MEETING THE BOSS HURT YOUR SELF-ESTEEM?
WHO ARE YOU?
AN ENEMY?

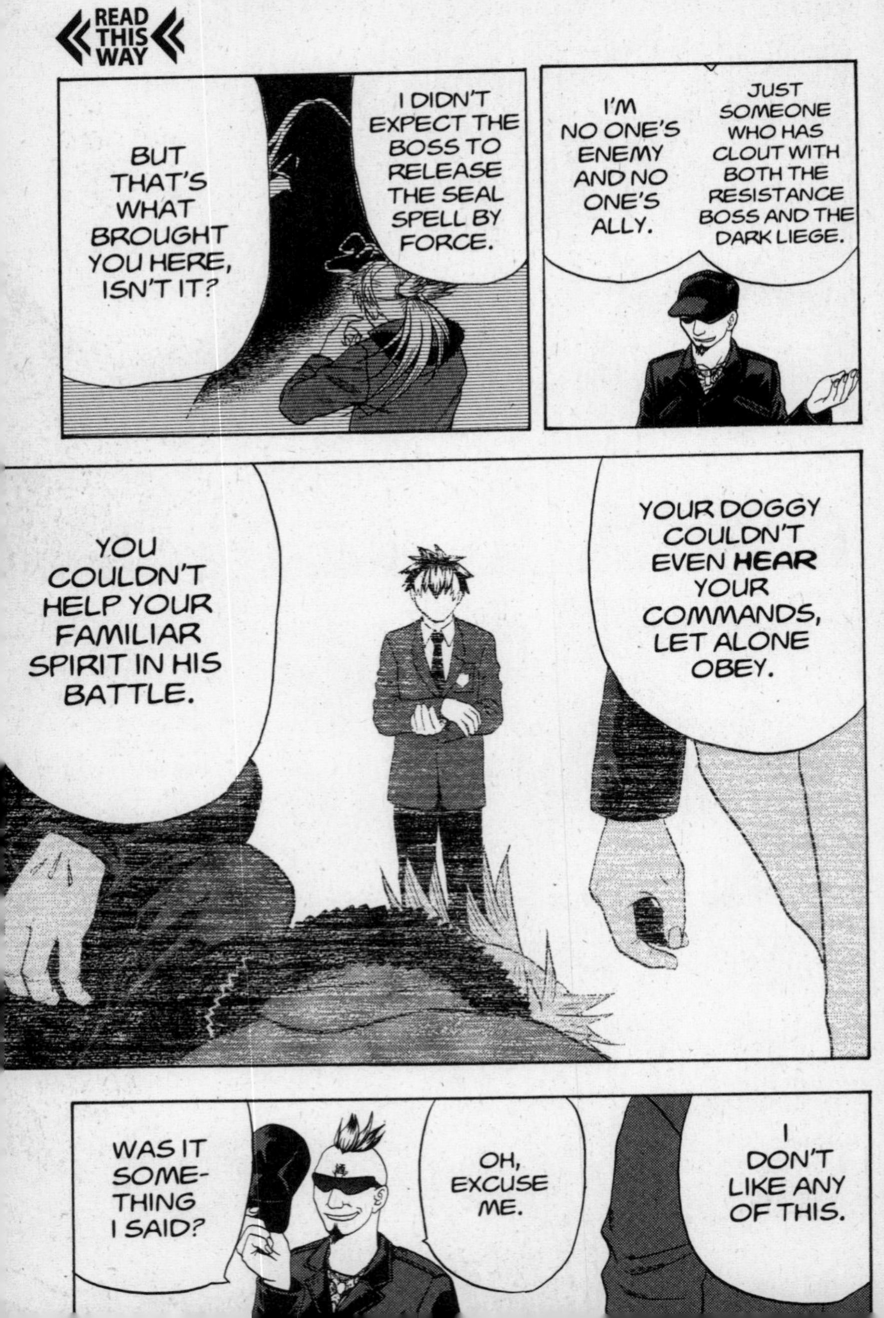
READ THIS WAY
JUST SOMEONE WHO HAS CLOUT WITH BOTH THE RESISTANCE BOSS AND THE DARK LIEGE.
I'M NO ONE'S ENEMY AND NO ONE'S ALLY.
I DIDN'T EXPECT THE BOSS TO RELEASE THE SEAL SPELL BY FORCE.
BUT THAT'S WHAT BROUGHT YOU HERE, ISN'T IT?
YOUR DOGGY COULDN'T EVEN **HEAR** YOUR COMMANDS, LET ALONE OBEY.
YOU COULDN'T HELP YOUR FAMILIAR SPIRIT IN HIS BATTLE.
I DON'T LIKE ANY OF THIS.
OH, EXCUSE ME.
WAS IT SOMETHING I SAID?

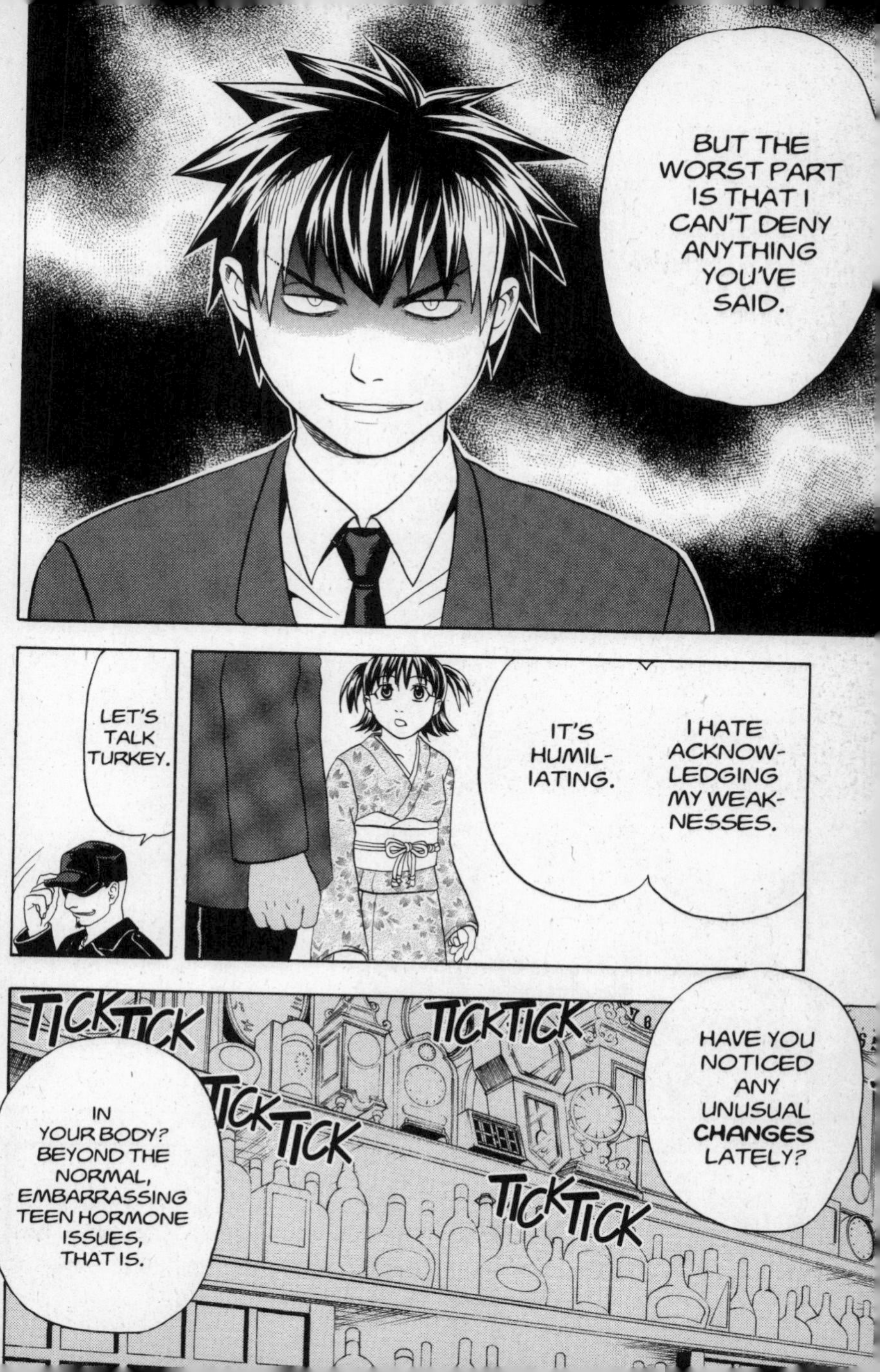
BUT THE WORST PART IS THAT I CAN'T DENY ANYTHING YOU'VE SAID.
I HATE ACKNOWLEDGING MY WEAKNESSES.
IT'S HUMILIATING.
LET'S TALK TURKEY.
HAVE YOU NOTICED ANY UNUSUAL **CHANGES** LATELY?
TICKTICK
TICKTICK
TICKTICK
TICKTICK
IN YOUR BODY? BEYOND THE NORMAL, EMBARRASSING TEEN HORMONE ISSUES, THAT IS.

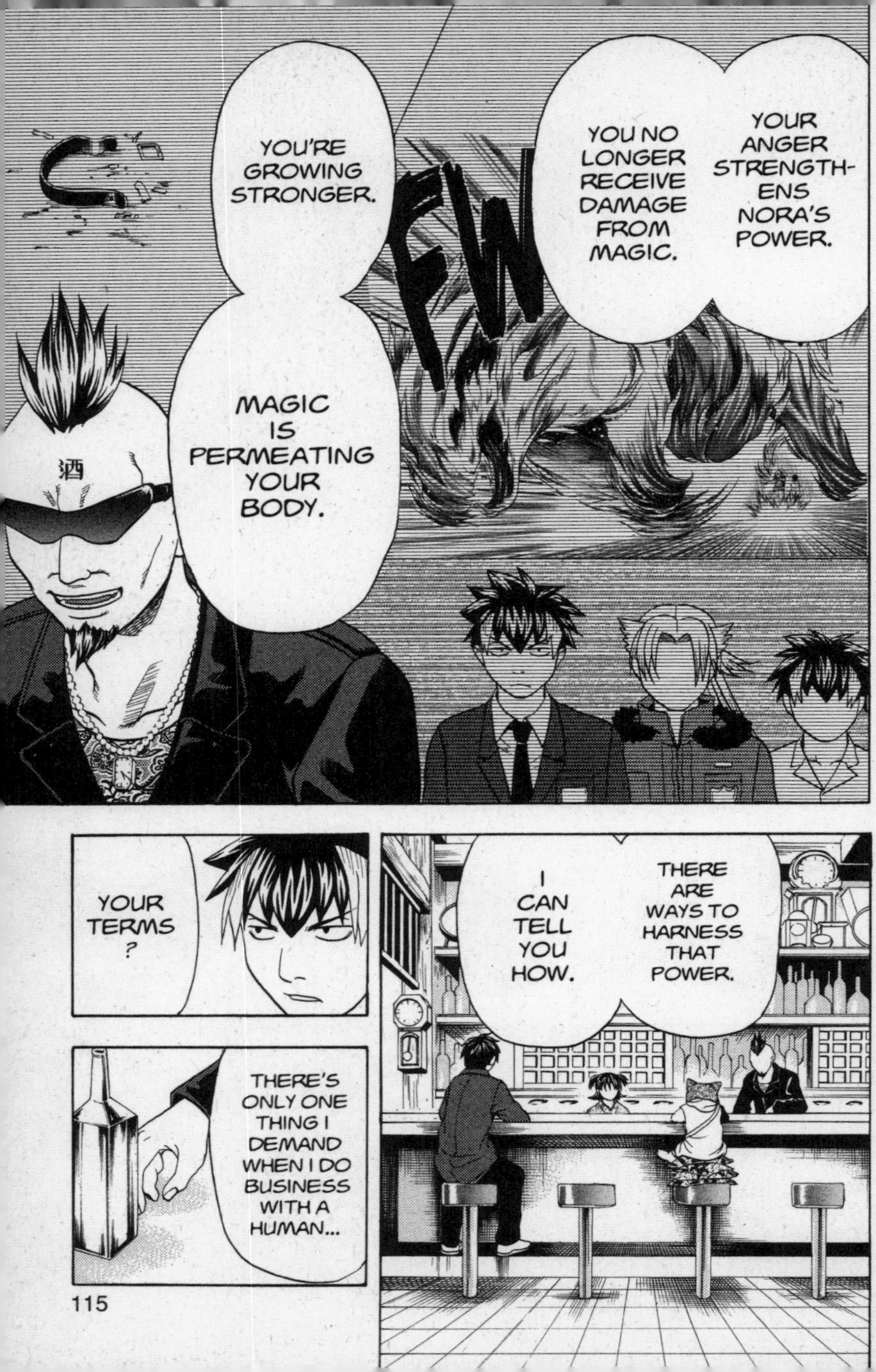
YOUR ANGER STRENGTH-ENS NORA'S POWER.
YOU NO LONGER RECEIVE DAMAGE FROM MAGIC.
FW
YOU'RE GROWING STRONGER.
MAGIC IS PERMEATING YOUR BODY.
酒
THERE ARE WAYS TO HARNESS THAT POWER.
I CAN TELL YOU HOW.
YOUR TERMS?
THERE'S ONLY ONE THING I DEMAND WHEN I DO BUSINESS WITH A HUMAN...

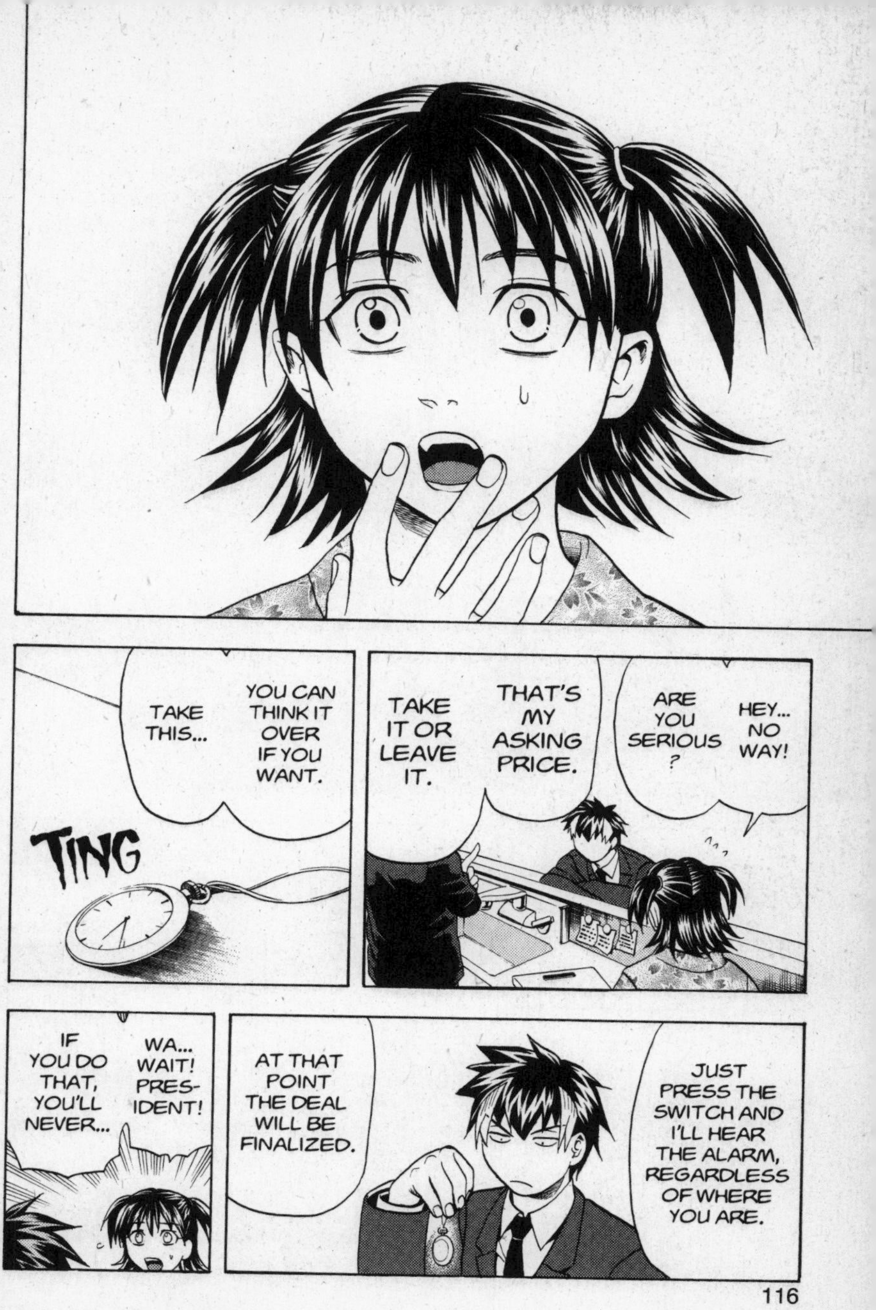
HEY... NO WAY!
ARE YOU SERIOUS?
THAT'S MY ASKING PRICE.
TAKE IT OR LEAVE IT.
YOU CAN THINK IT OVER IF YOU WANT.
TAKE THIS...
TING
JUST PRESS THE SWITCH AND I'LL HEAR THE ALARM, REGARDLESS OF WHERE YOU ARE.
AT THAT POINT THE DEAL WILL BE FINALIZED.
WA... WAIT! PRES-IDENT!
IF YOU DO THAT, YOU'LL NEVER...

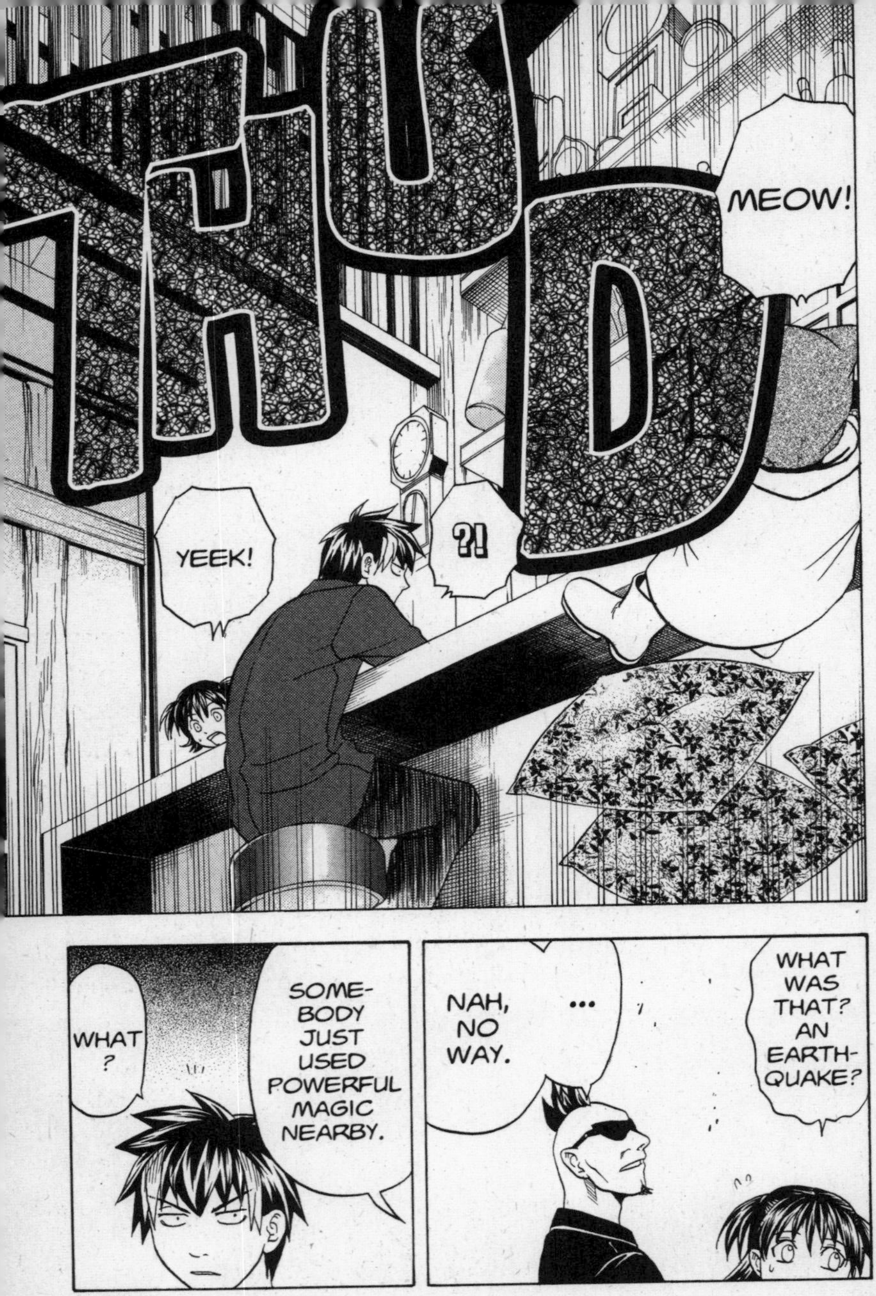
THUD
MEOW!
?!
YEEK!
WHAT WAS THAT? AN EARTH-QUAKE?
...
NAH, NO WAY.
SOME-BODY JUST USED POWERFUL MAGIC NEARBY.
WHAT?

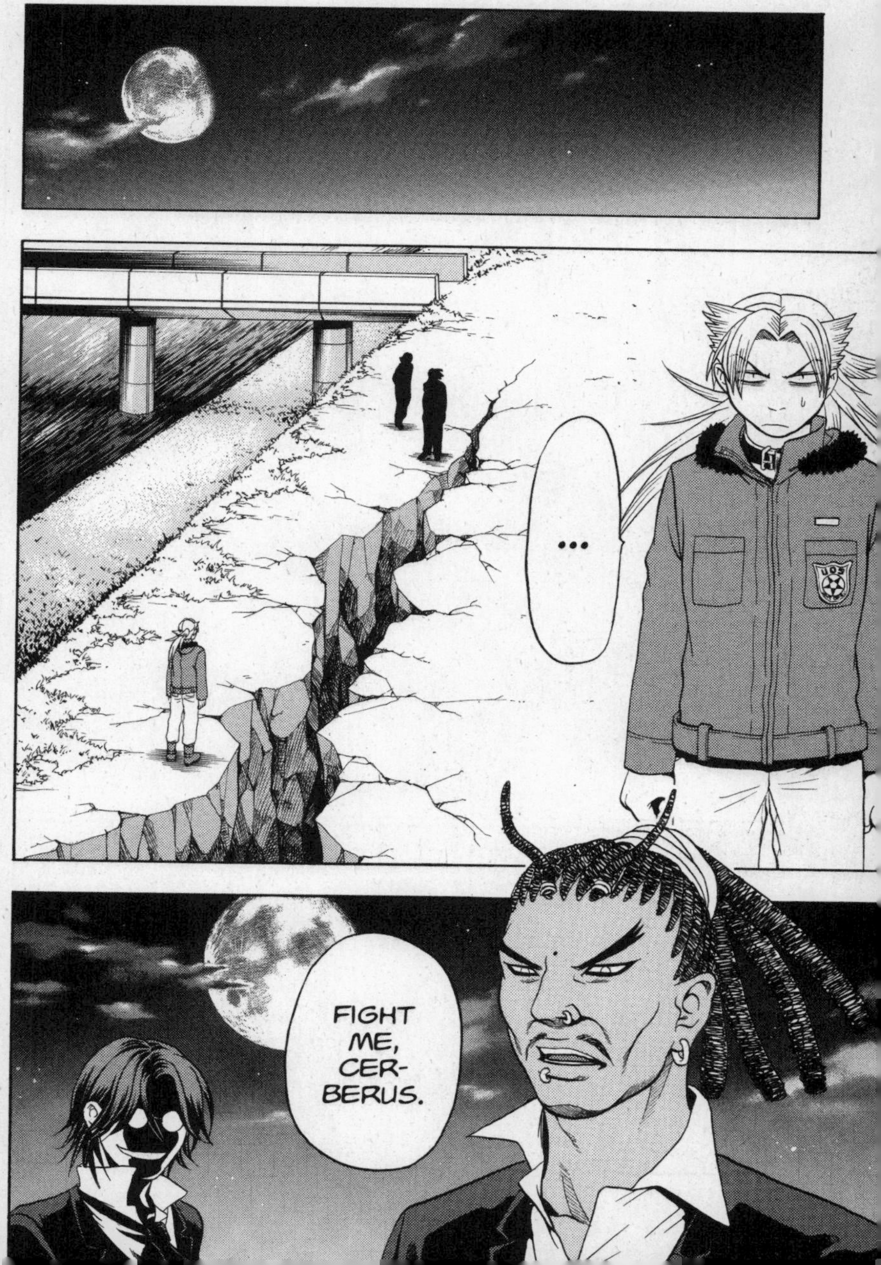
...
FIGHT ME, CER-BERUS.

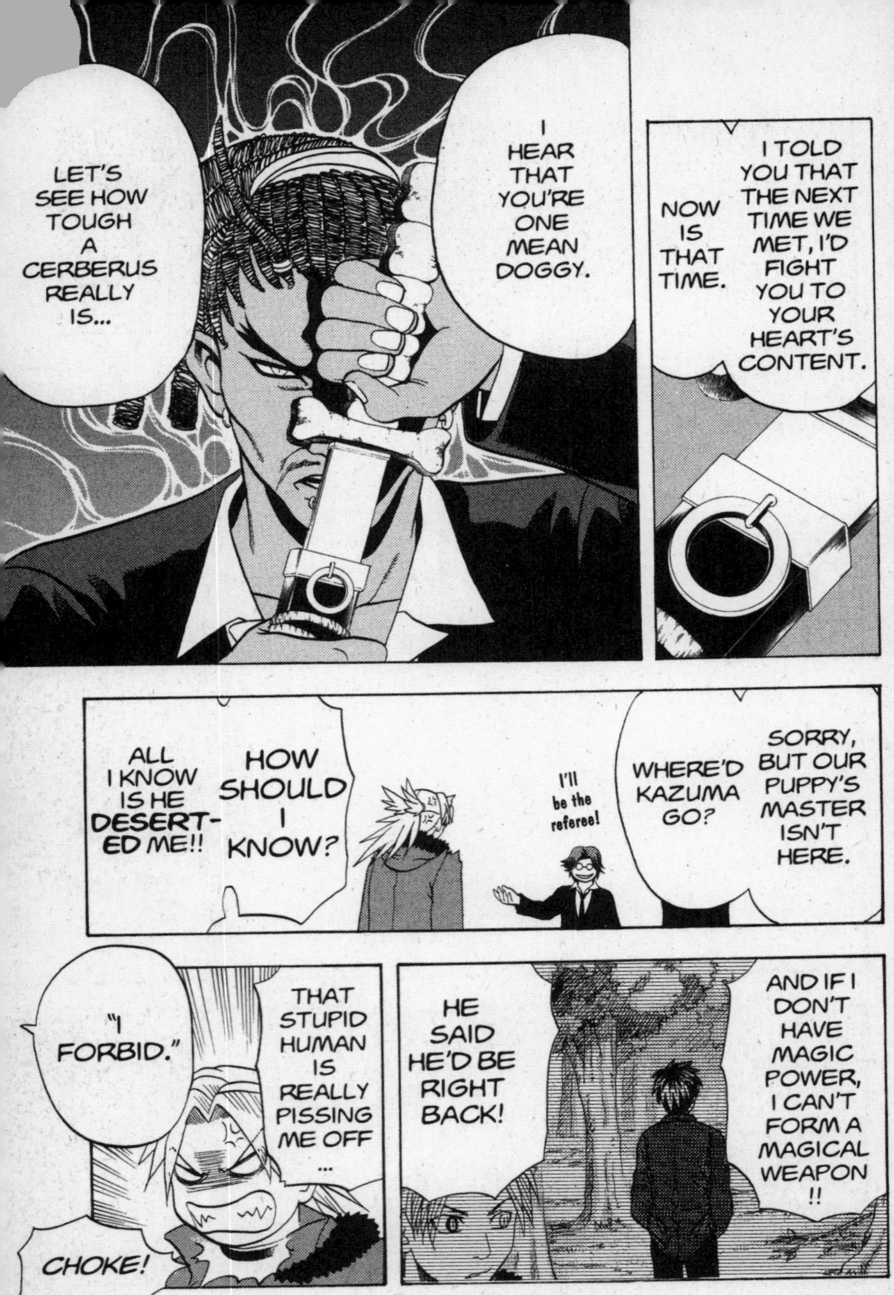
I TOLD YOU THAT THE NEXT TIME WE MET, I'D FIGHT YOU TO YOUR HEART'S CONTENT.
NOW IS THAT TIME.
I HEAR THAT YOU'RE ONE MEAN DOGGY.
LET'S SEE HOW TOUGH A CERBERUS REALLY IS...
SORRY, BUT OUR PUPPY'S MASTER ISN'T HERE.
WHERE'D KAZUMA GO?
I'll be the referee!
HOW SHOULD I KNOW?
ALL I KNOW IS HE DESERTED ME!!
AND IF I DON'T HAVE MAGIC POWER, I CAN'T FORM A MAGICAL WEAPON!!
HE SAID HE'D BE RIGHT BACK!
THAT STUPID HUMAN IS REALLY PISSING ME OFF...
"I FORBID."
CHOKE!

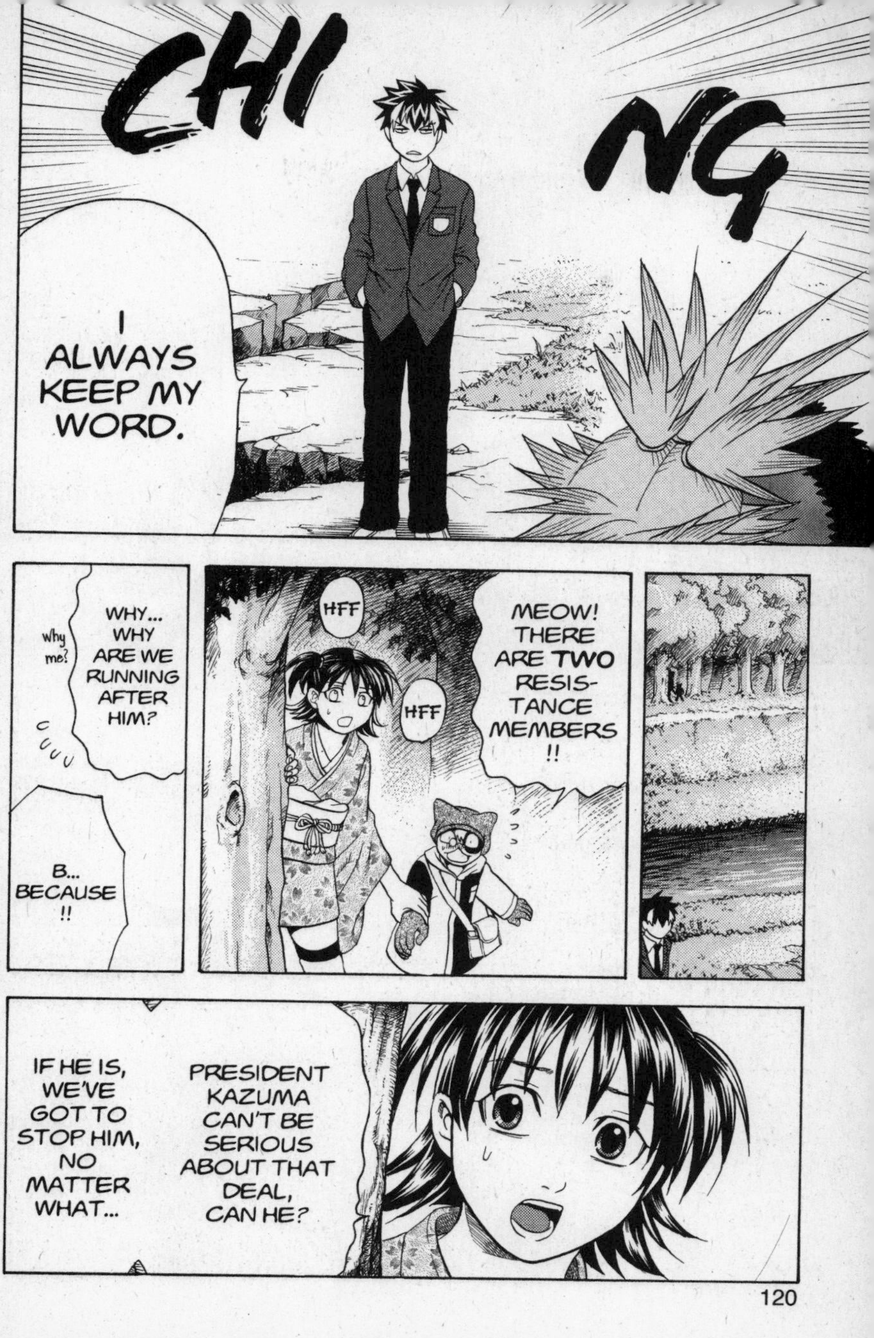
CHI NG
I ALWAYS KEEP MY WORD.
MEOW! THERE ARE TWO RESISTANCE MEMBERS !!
HFF
HFF
WHY... WHY ARE WE RUNNING AFTER HIM?
Why me?
B... BECAUSE !!
PRESIDENT KAZUMA CAN'T BE SERIOUS ABOUT THAT DEAL, CAN HE?
IF HE IS, WE'VE GOT TO STOP HIM, NO MATTER WHAT...

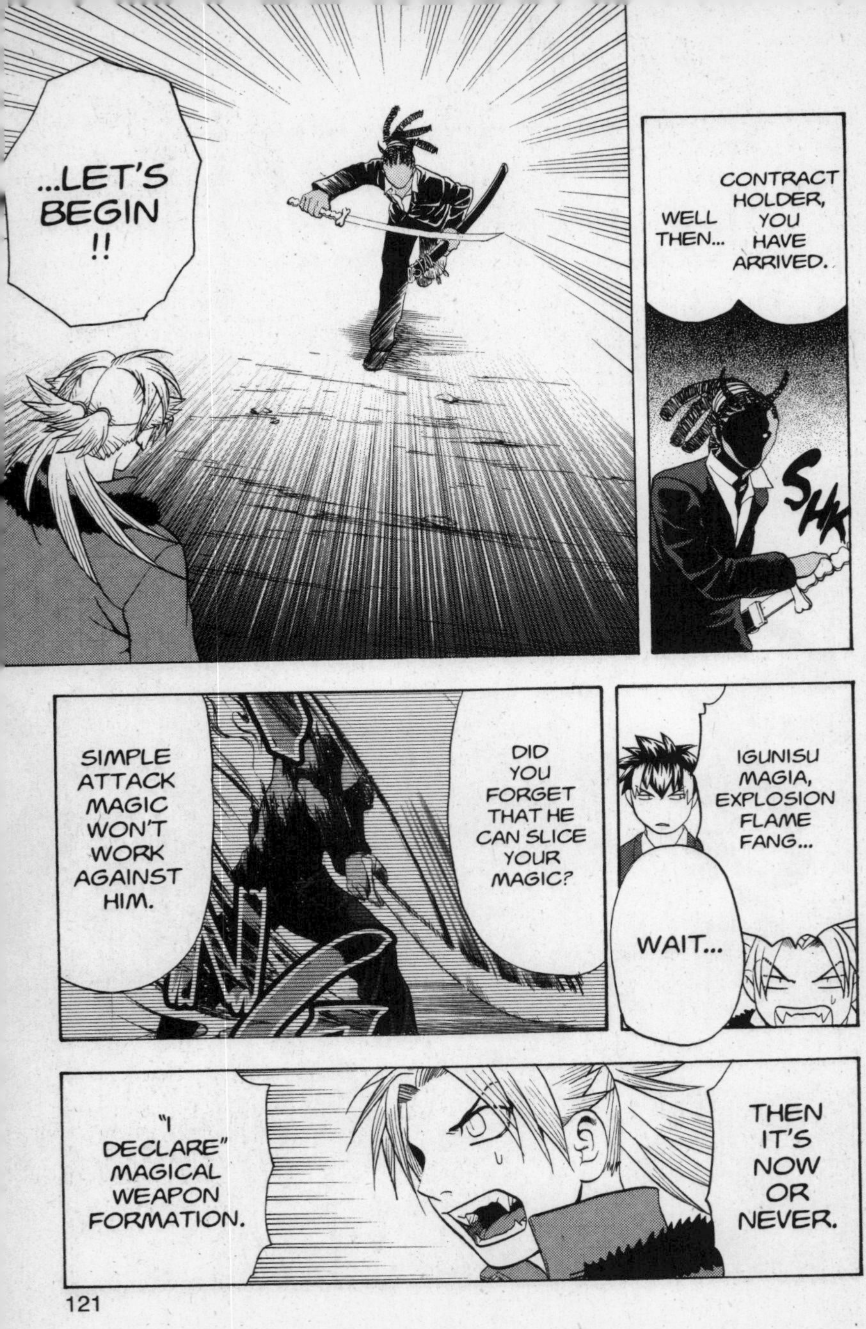
CONTRACT HOLDER, YOU HAVE ARRIVED.
WELL THEN...
SHK
...LET'S BEGIN !!
IGUNISU MAGIA, EXPLOSION FLAME FANG...
WAIT...
DID YOU FORGET THAT HE CAN SLICE YOUR MAGIC?
SIMPLE ATTACK MAGIC WON'T WORK AGAINST HIM.
THEN IT'S NOW OR NEVER.
"I DECLARE" MAGICAL WEAPON FORMATION.

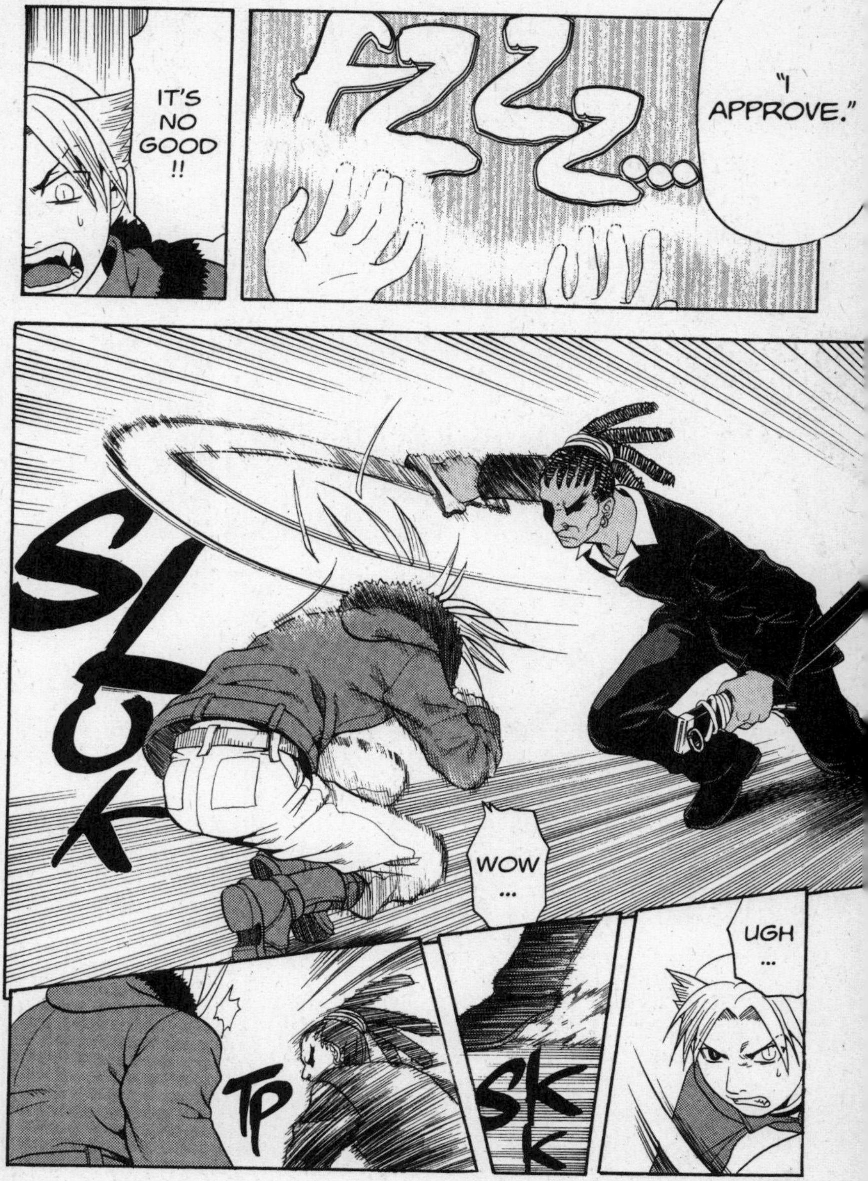
"I APPROVE."
FZZZ...
IT'S NO GOOD!!
SLICK
WOW...
UGH...
SKK
TP

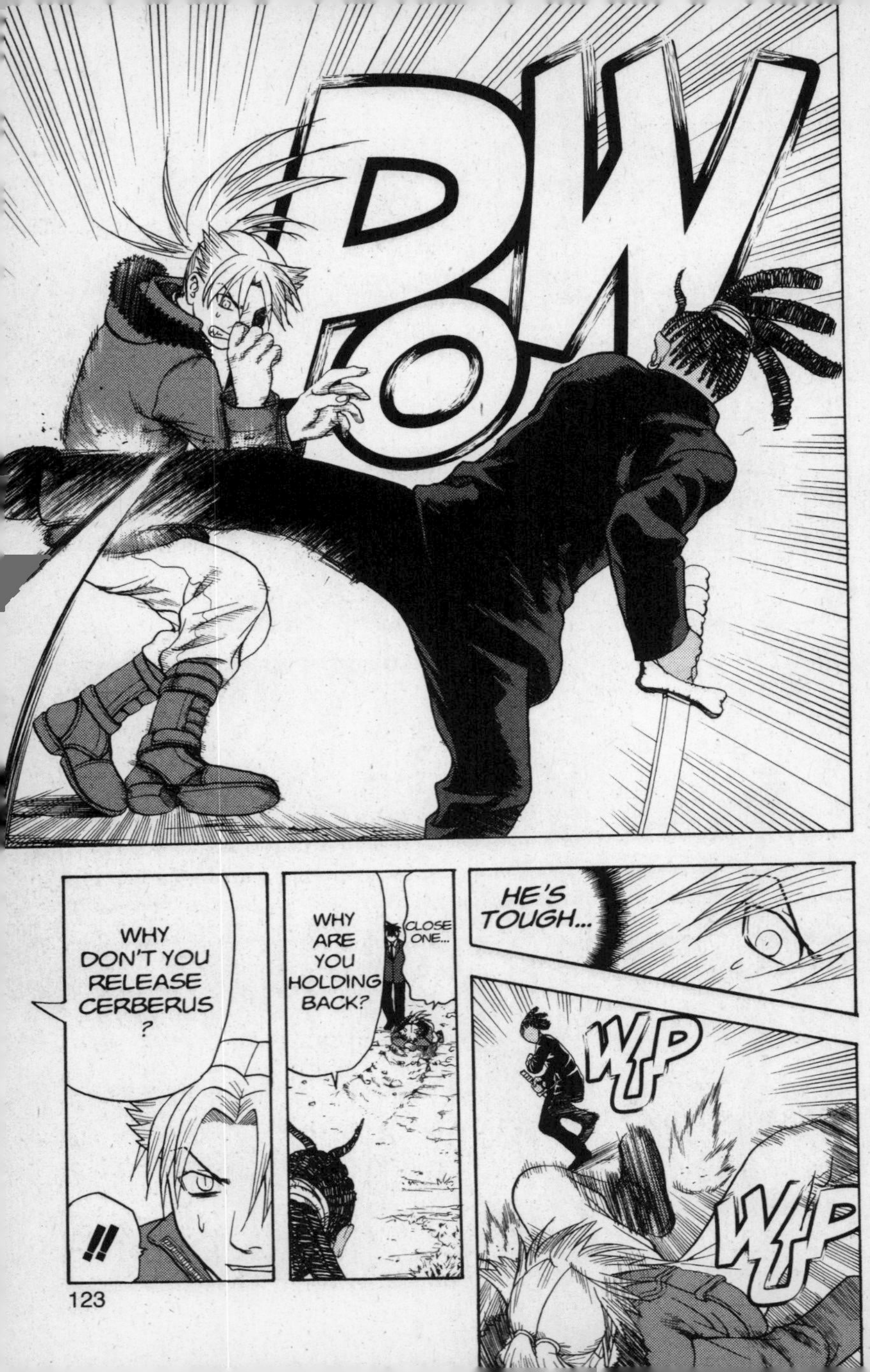
DWO
HE'S TOUGH...
WUP
WUP
CLOSE ONE...
WHY ARE YOU HOLDING BACK?
WHY DON'T YOU RELEASE CERBERUS?
!!

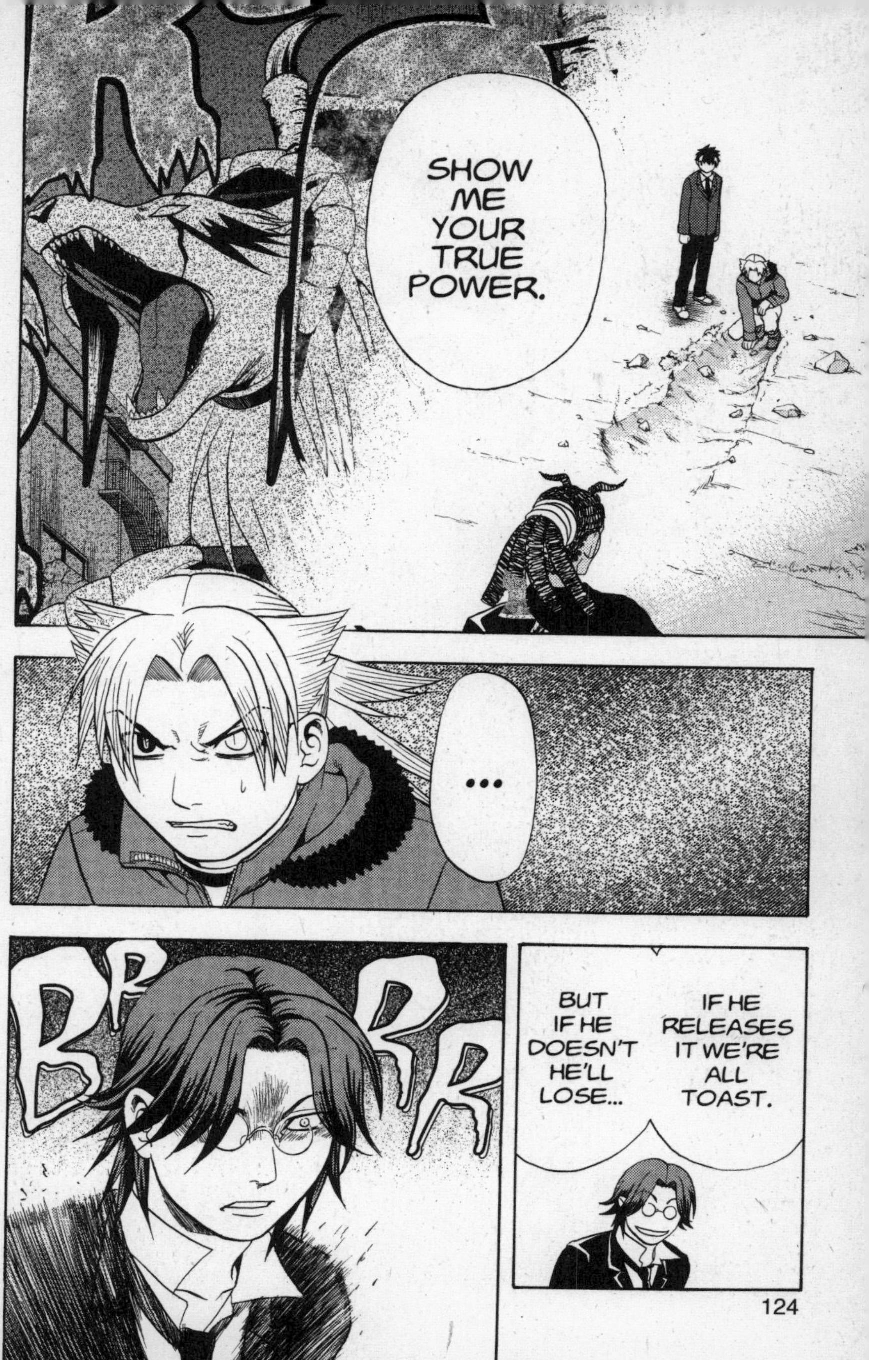
SHOW ME YOUR TRUE POWER.
...
IF HE RELEASES IT WE'RE ALL TOAST.
BUT IF HE DOESN'T HE'LL LOSE...
BRR

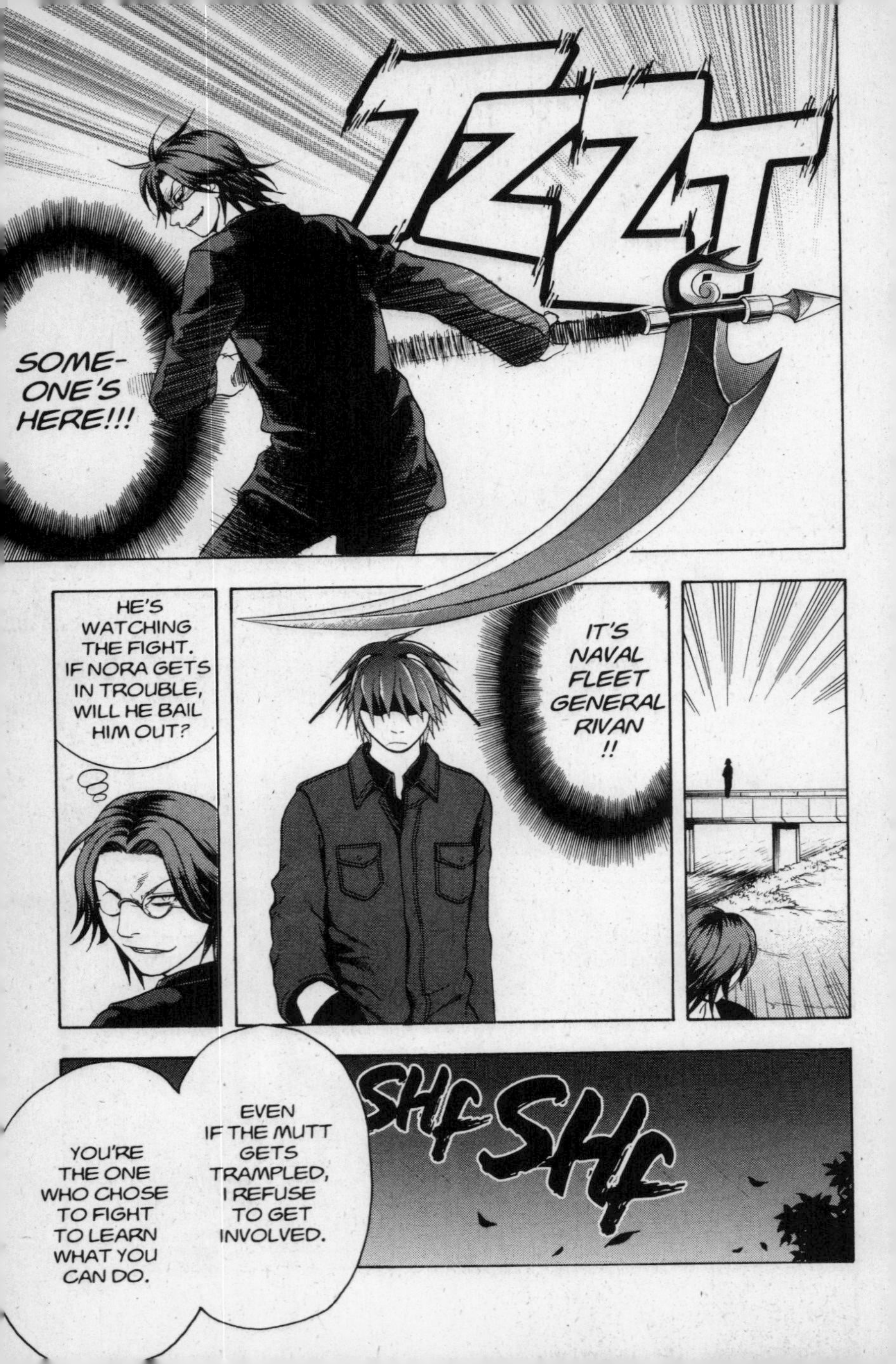
ZZT
SOME-ONE'S HERE!!!
IT'S NAVAL FLEET GENERAL RIVAN !!
HE'S WATCHING THE FIGHT. IF NORA GETS IN TROUBLE, WILL HE BAIL HIM OUT?
SHF SHF
EVEN IF THE MUTT GETS TRAMPLED, I REFUSE TO GET INVOLVED.
YOU'RE THE ONE WHO CHOSE TO FIGHT TO LEARN WHAT YOU CAN DO.

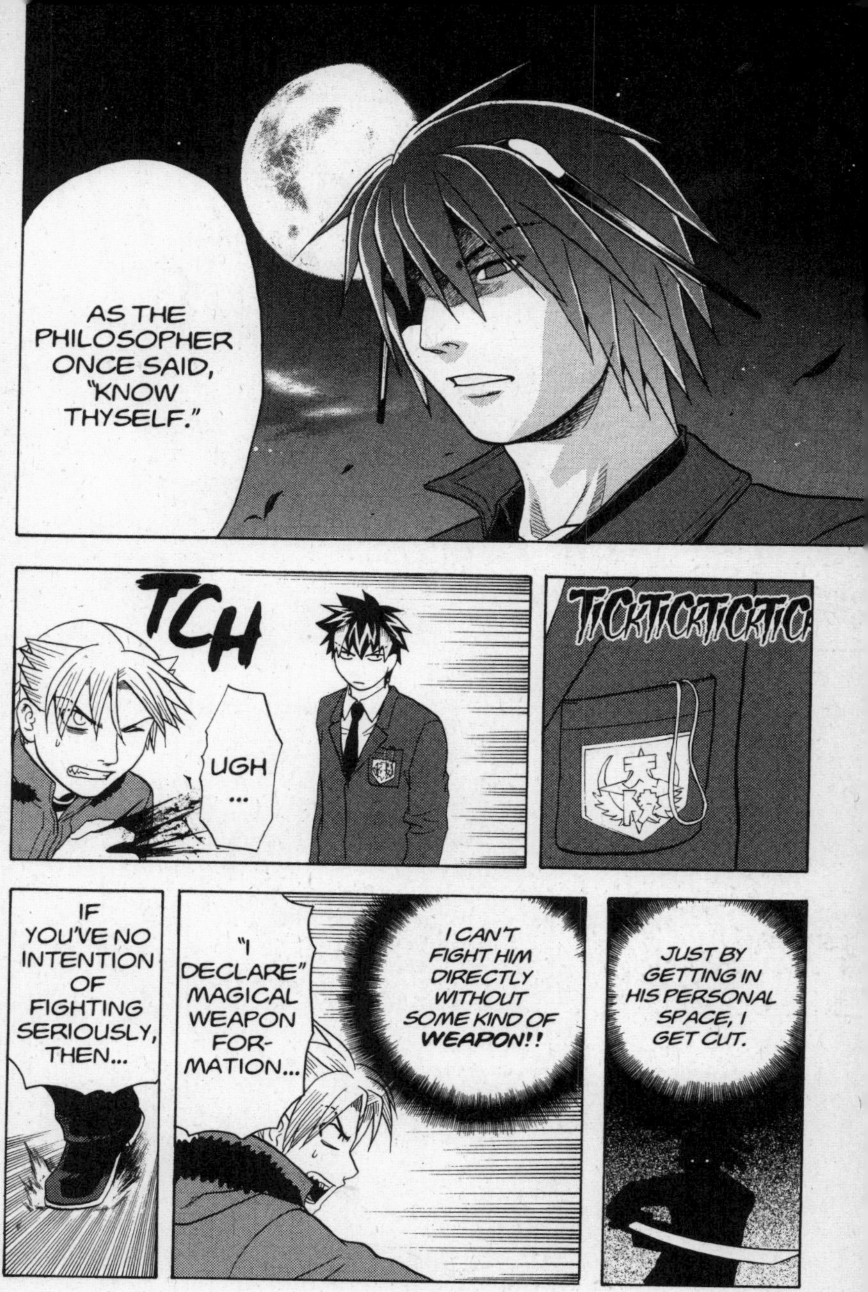
AS THE PHILOSOPHER ONCE SAID, "KNOW THYSELF."
TICKTICKTICKTICK
TCH
UGH ...
JUST BY GETTING IN HIS PERSONAL SPACE, I GET CUT.
I CAN'T FIGHT HIM DIRECTLY WITHOUT SOME KIND OF **WEAPON!!**
"I DECLARE" MAGICAL WEAPON FOR-MATION...
IF YOU'VE NO INTENTION OF FIGHTING SERIOUSLY, THEN...

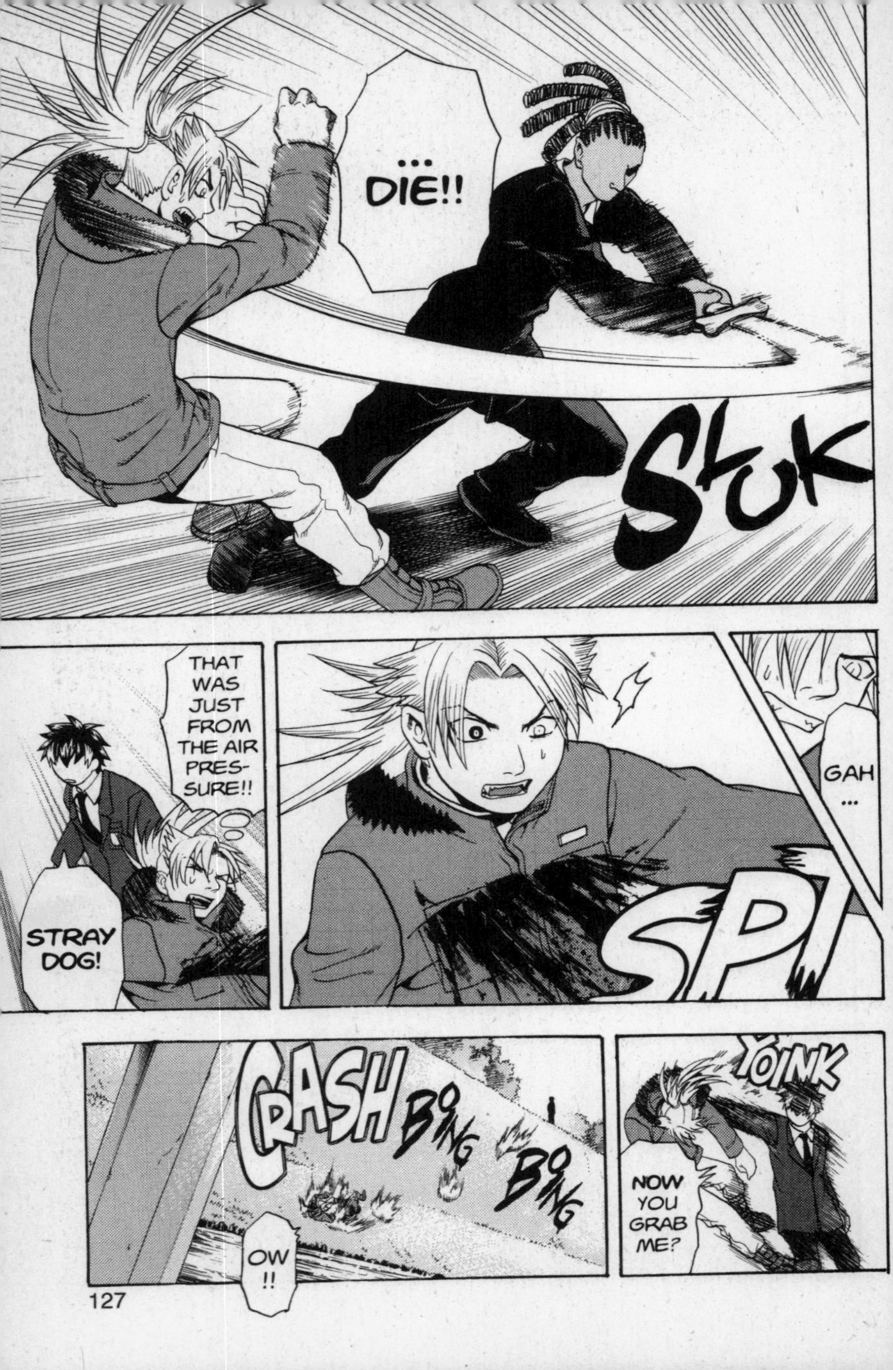

... DIE!!
SLUK
GAH ...
SP
THAT WAS JUST FROM THE AIR PRES-SURE!!
STRAY DOG!
YOINK
NOW YOU GRAB ME?
CRASH
BOING
BOING
OW !!

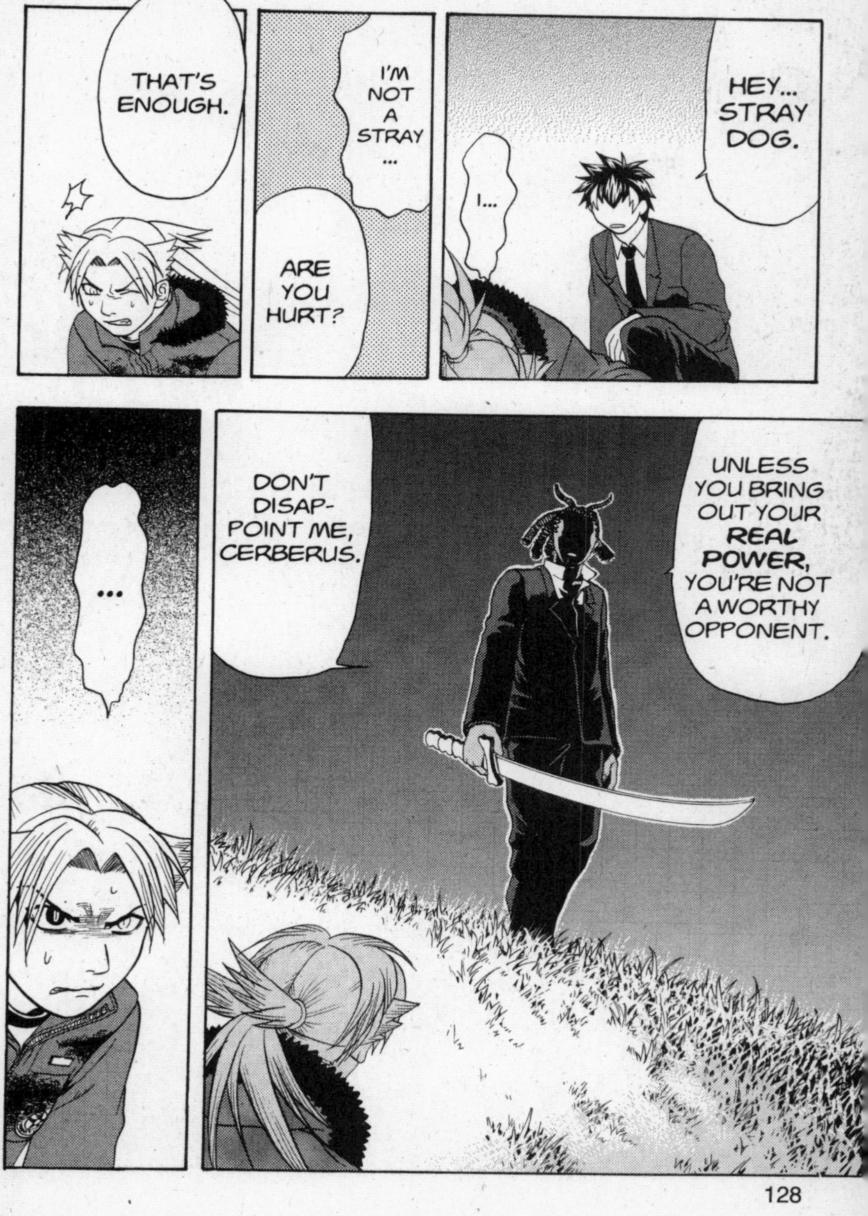
HEY... STRAY DOG.
I...
I'M NOT A STRAY ...
ARE YOU HURT?
THAT'S ENOUGH.
UNLESS YOU BRING OUT YOUR **REAL POWER,** YOU'RE NOT A WORTHY OPPONENT.
DON'T DISAP-POINT ME, CERBERUS.
...

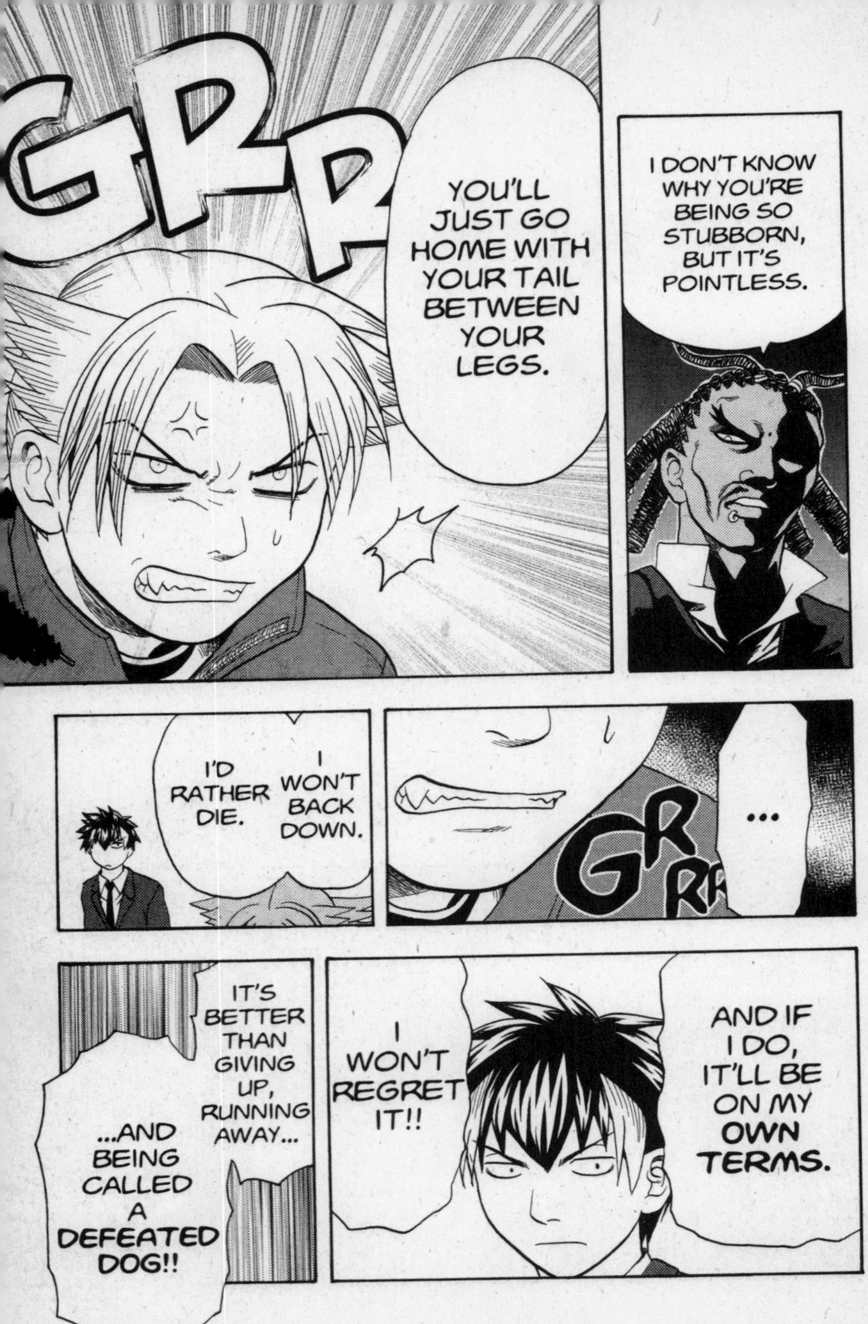
I DON'T KNOW WHY YOU'RE BEING SO STUBBORN, BUT IT'S POINTLESS.
YOU'LL JUST GO HOME WITH YOUR TAIL BETWEEN YOUR LEGS.
GRR
...
GRRR
I WON'T BACK DOWN.
I'D RATHER DIE.
AND IF I DO, IT'LL BE ON MY OWN TERMS.
I WON'T REGRET IT!!
IT'S BETTER THAN GIVING UP, RUNNING AWAY...
...AND BEING CALLED A DEFEATED DOG!!

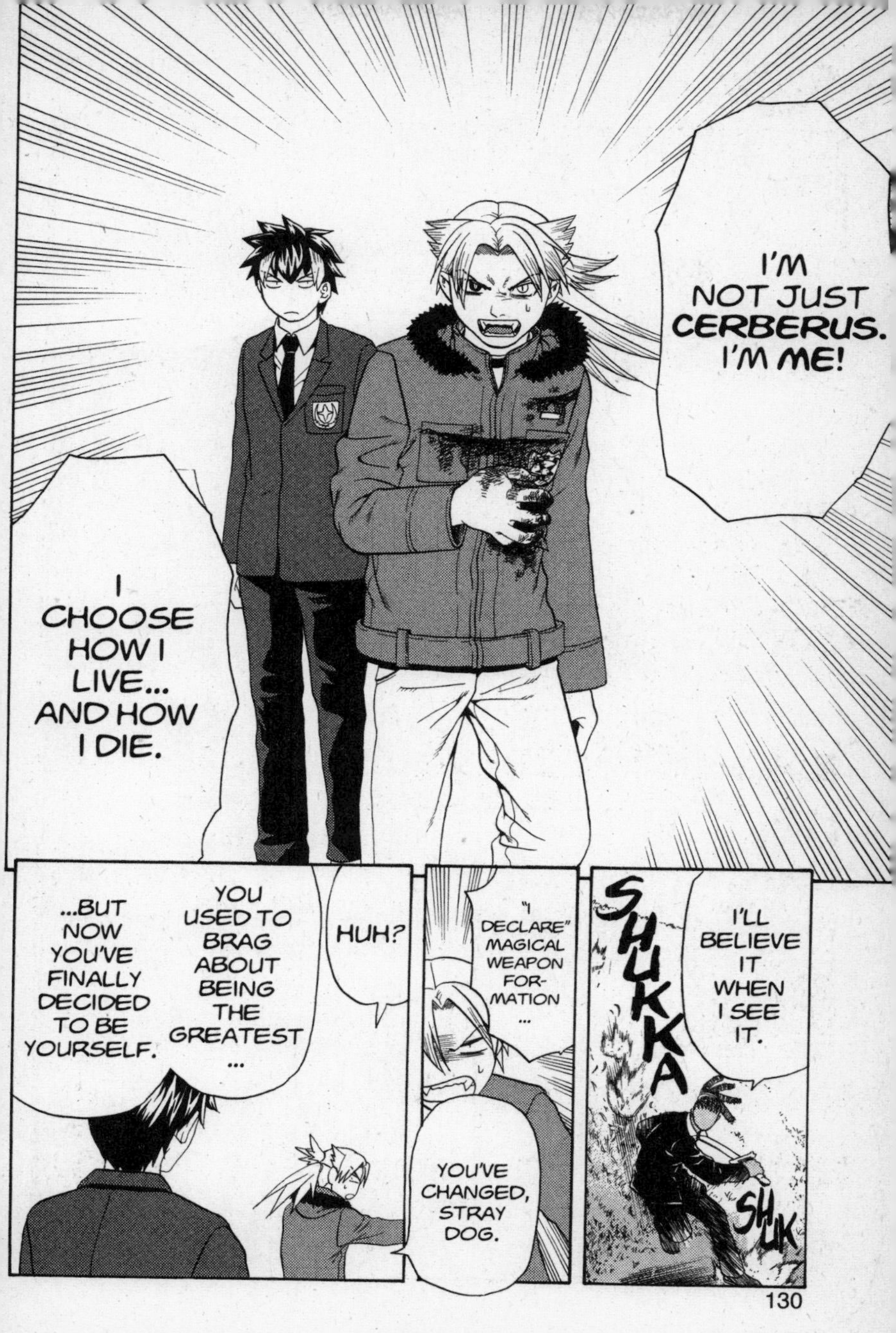
I'M NOT JUST CERBERUS. I'M ME!
I CHOOSE HOW I LIVE... AND HOW I DIE.
SHUKKA
I'LL BELIEVE IT WHEN I SEE IT.
SHUK
"I DECLARE" MAGICAL WEAPON FORMATION...
YOU'VE CHANGED, STRAY DOG.
HUH?
YOU USED TO BRAG ABOUT BEING THE GREATEST...
...BUT NOW YOU'VE FINALLY DECIDED TO BE YOURSELF.

READ THIS WAY

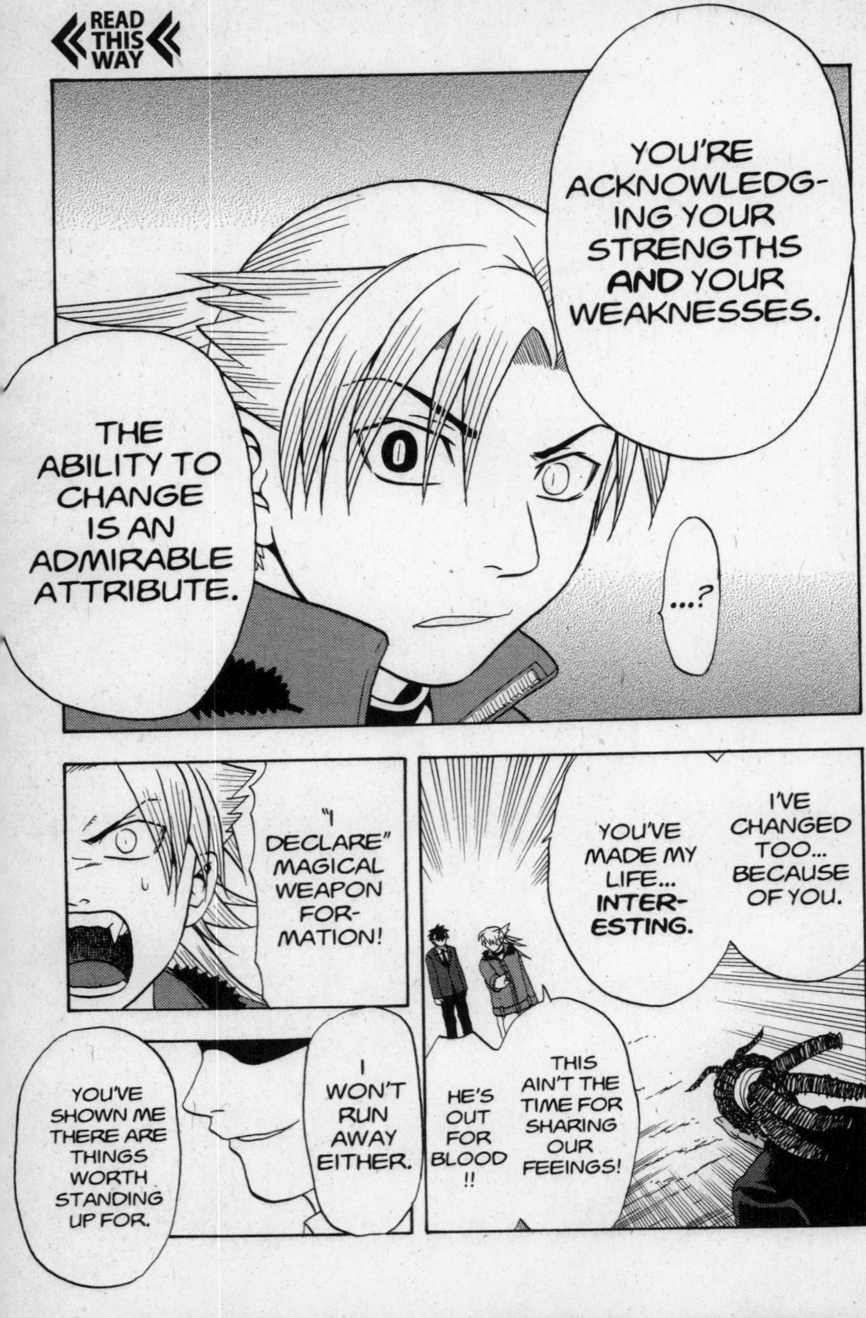

YOU'RE ACKNOWLEDG-ING YOUR STRENGTHS AND YOUR WEAKNESSES.
THE ABILITY TO CHANGE IS AN ADMIRABLE ATTRIBUTE.
...?
I'VE CHANGED TOO... BECAUSE OF YOU.
YOU'VE MADE MY LIFE... INTER-ESTING.
"I DECLARE" MAGICAL WEAPON FOR-MATION!
THIS AIN'T THE TIME FOR SHARING OUR FEEINGS!
HE'S OUT FOR BLOOD !!
I WON'T RUN AWAY EITHER.
YOU'VE SHOWN ME THERE ARE THINGS WORTH STANDING UP FOR.

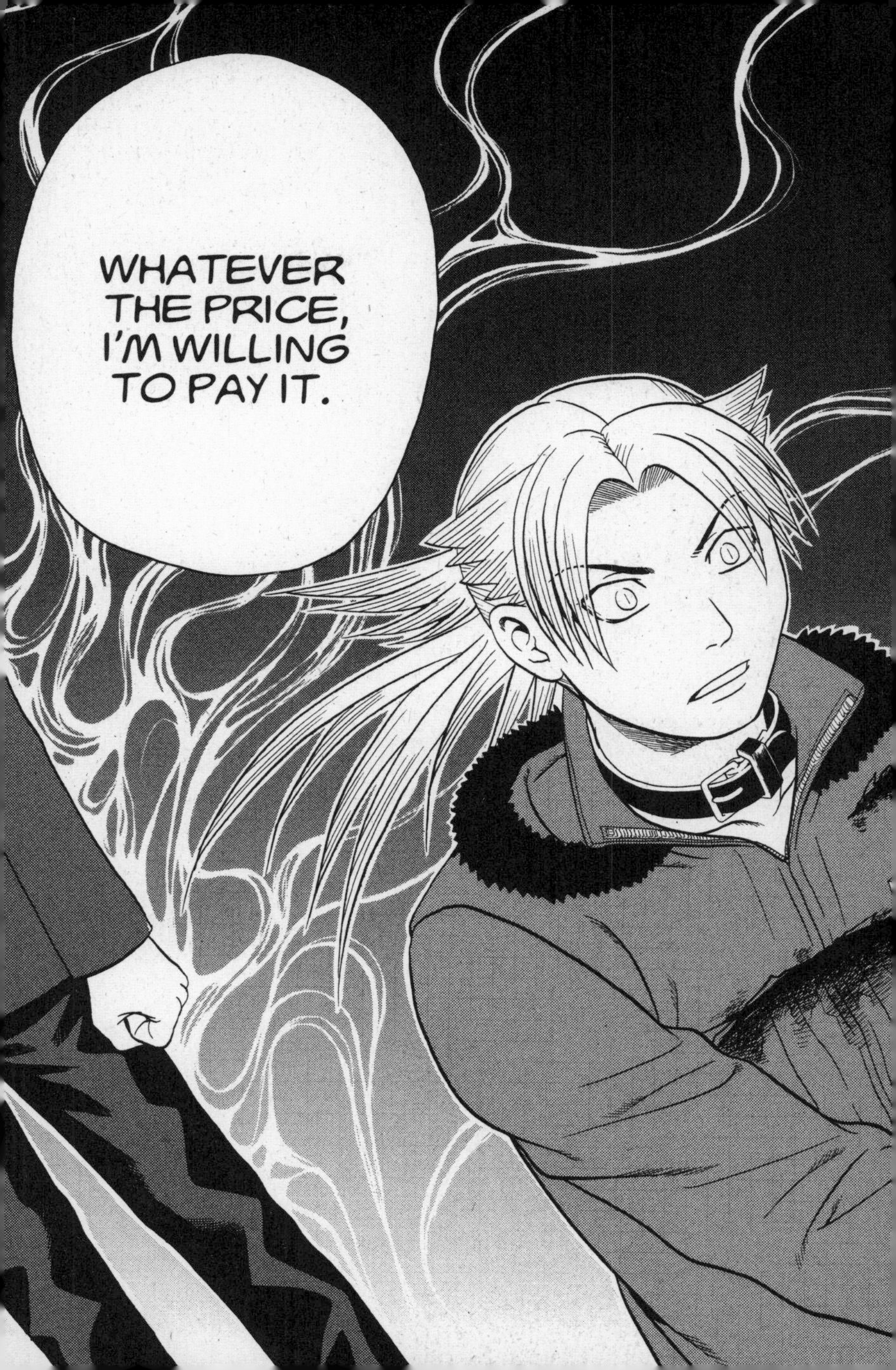
WHATEVER THE PRICE, I'M WILLING TO PAY IT.

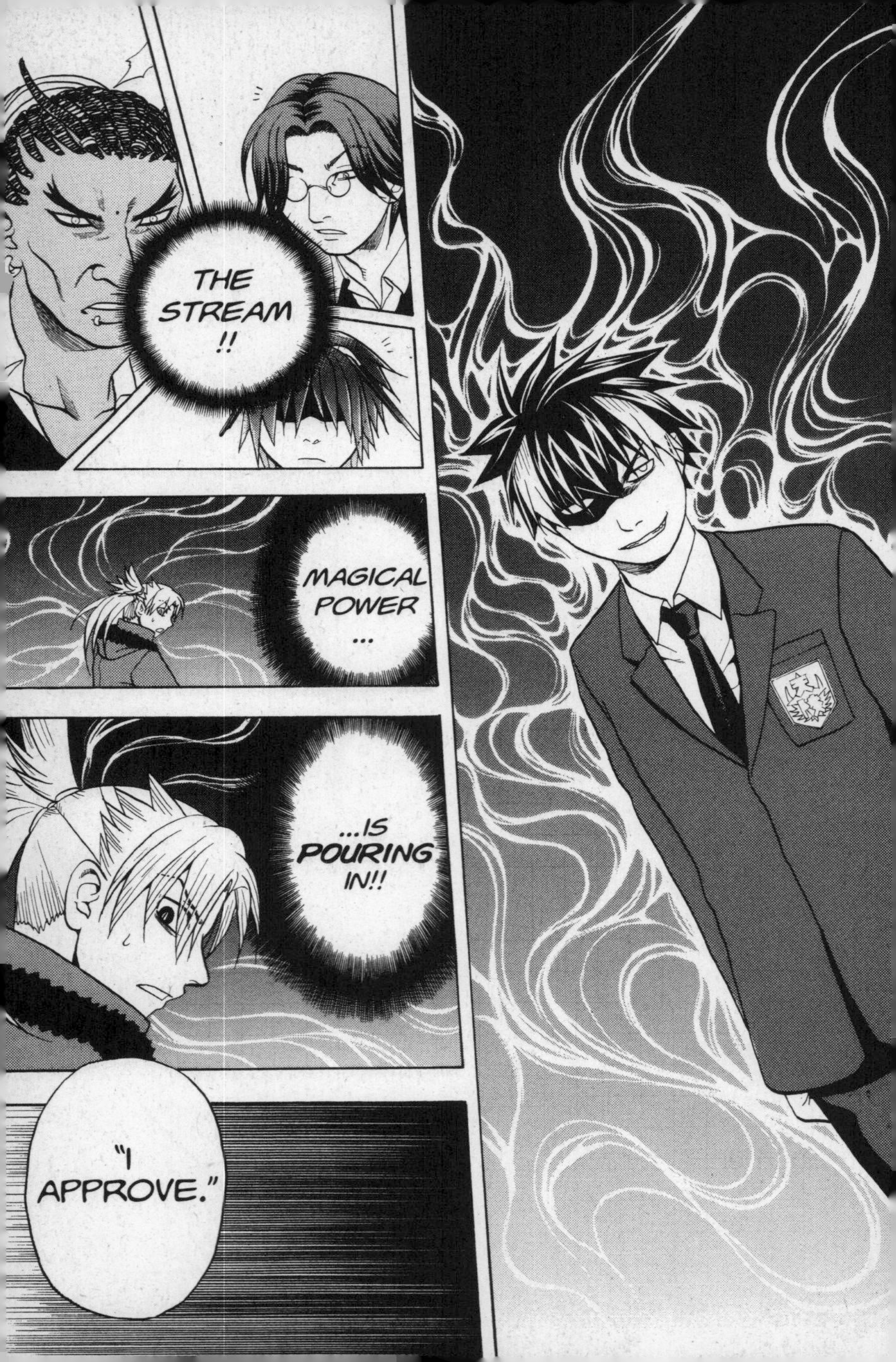
THE STREAM !!
MAGICAL POWER ...
...IS POURING IN!!
"I APPROVE."

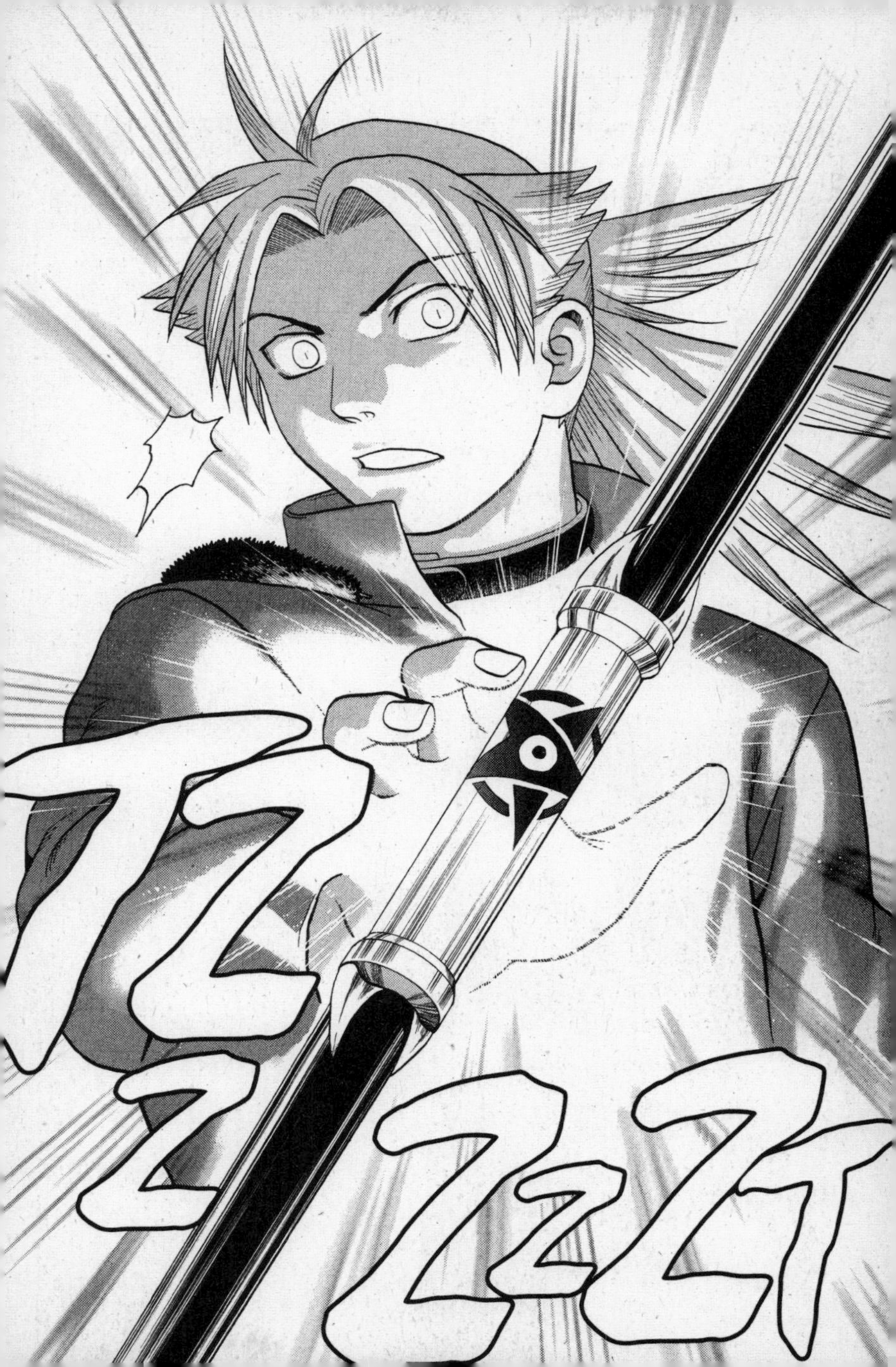
ZZZZzZT

READ THIS WAY

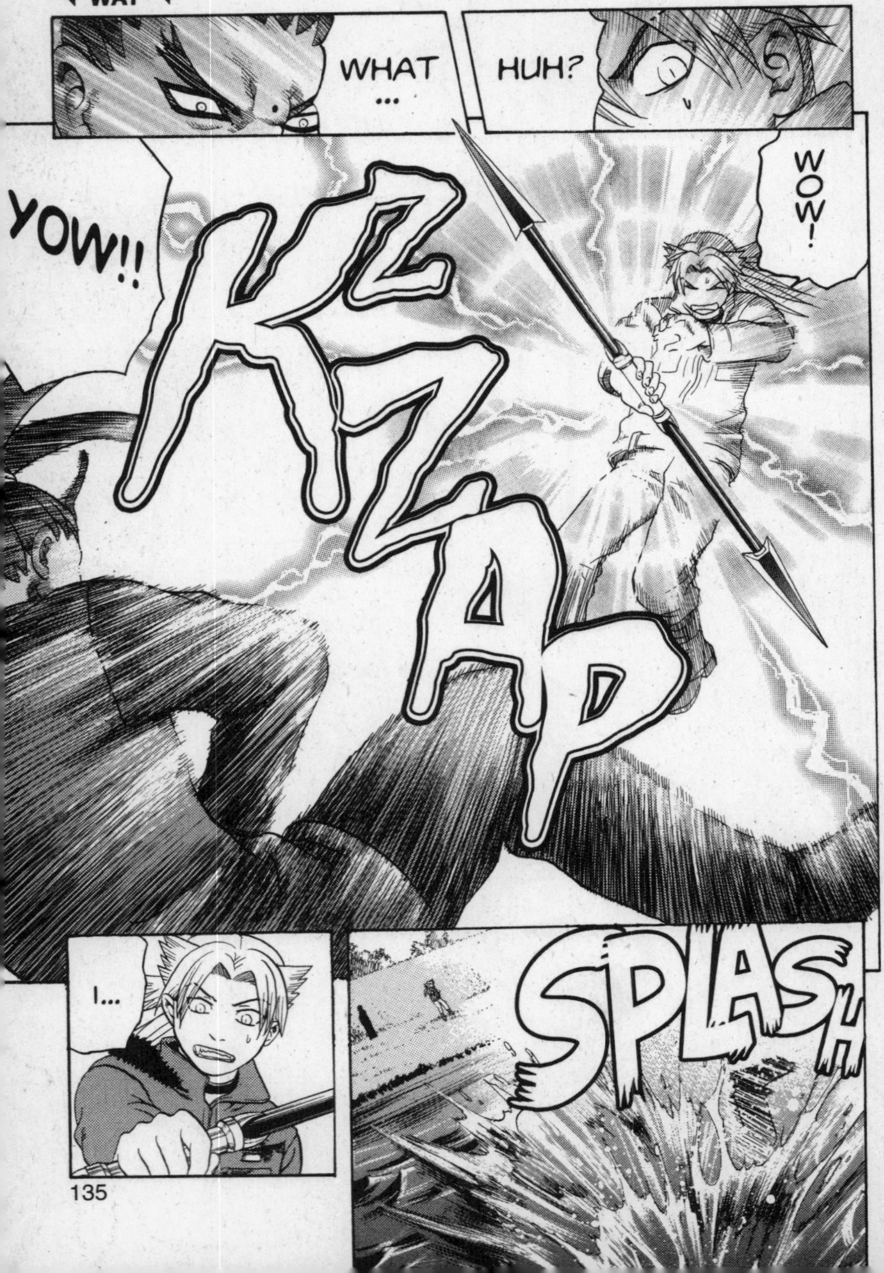
HUH?
WHAT ...
WOW!
KZZAP
YOW!!
SPLASH
I...

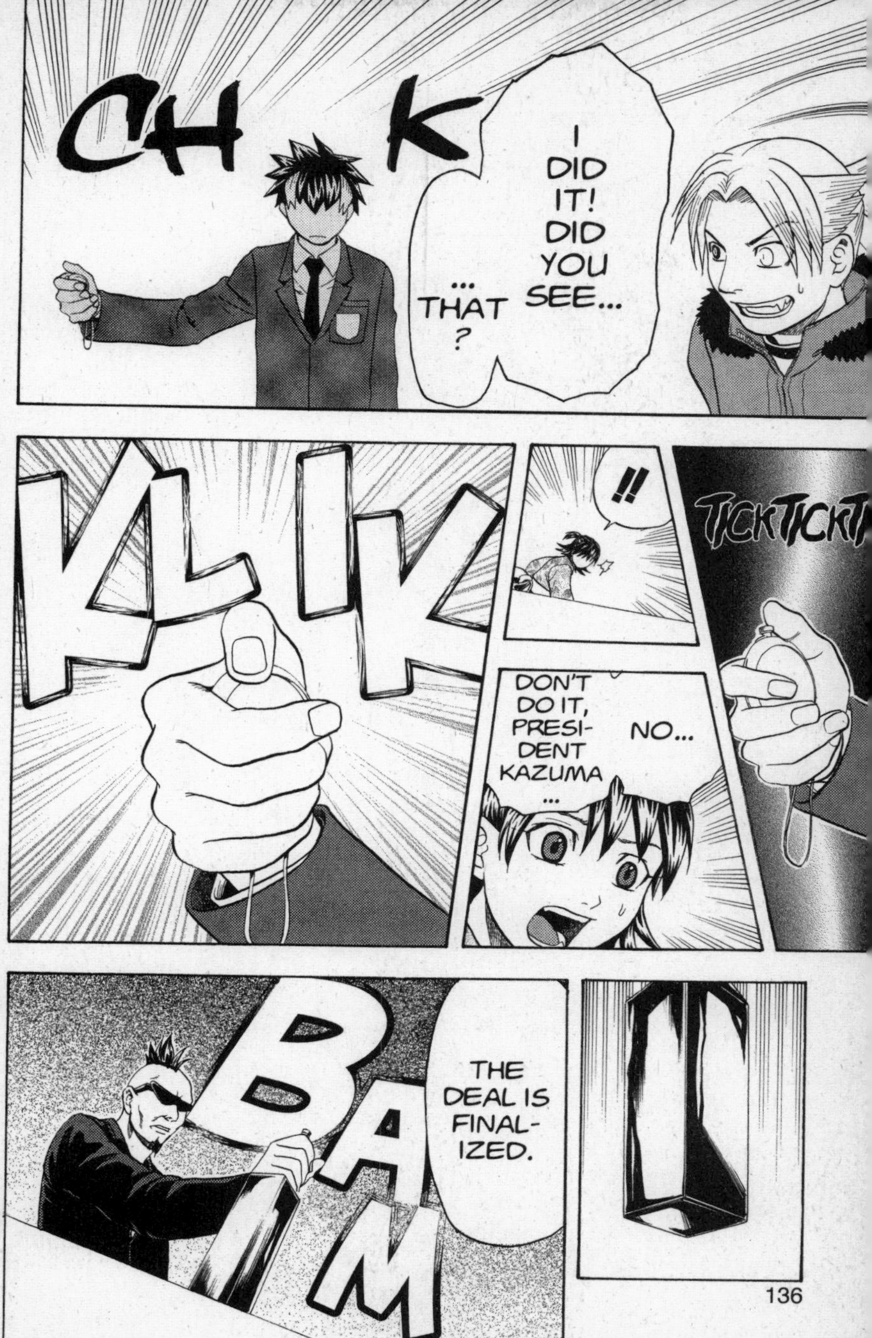
I DID IT! DID YOU SEE...
...THAT?
CHK
TICKTICKTI
!!
NO...
DON'T DO IT, PRESIDENT KAZUMA...
KLIK
THE DEAL IS FINALIZED.
BAM

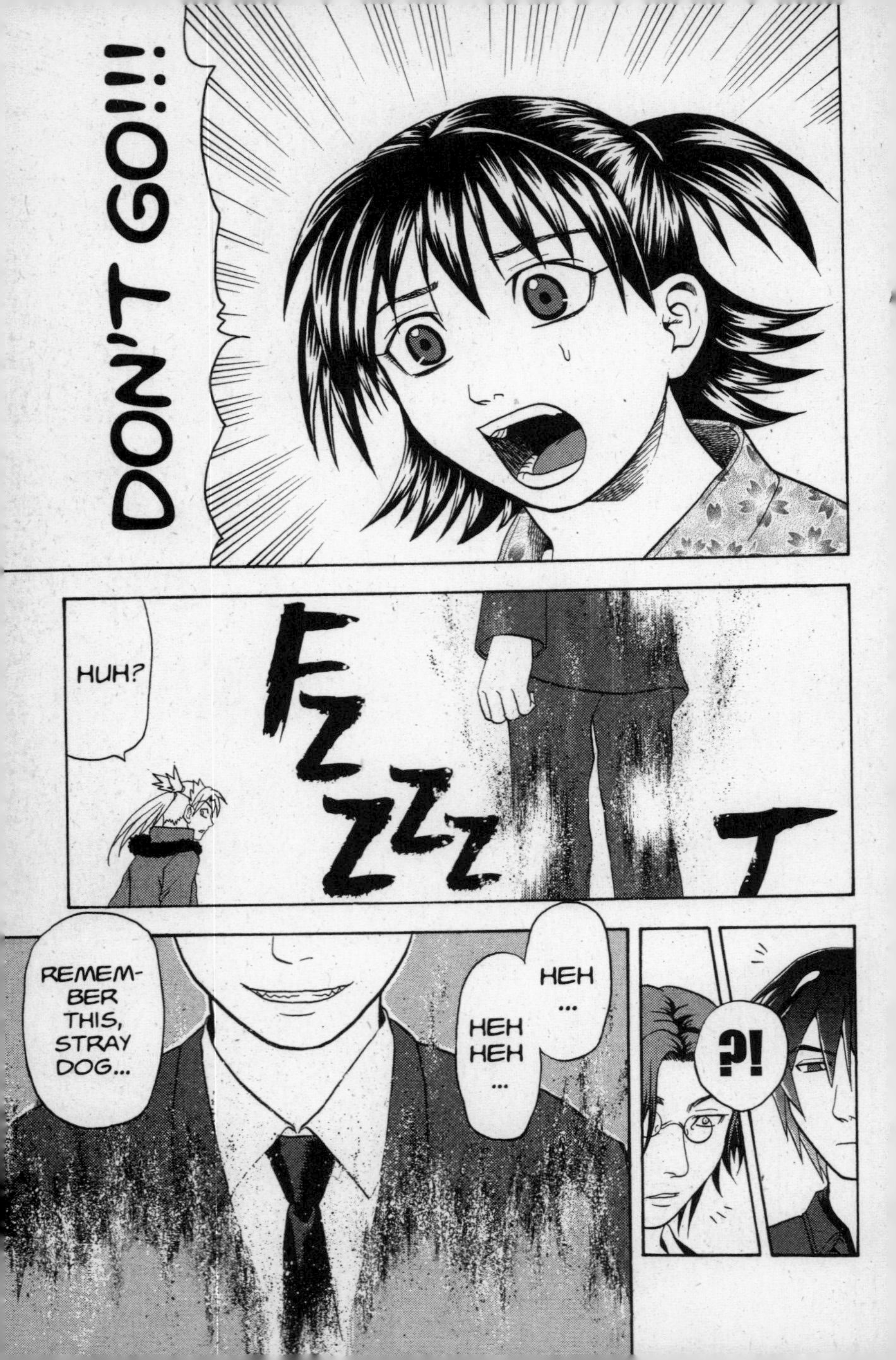
DON'T GO!!!
FZZZZT
HUH?
?!
HEH ... HEH HEH ...
REMEMBER THIS, STRAY DOG...

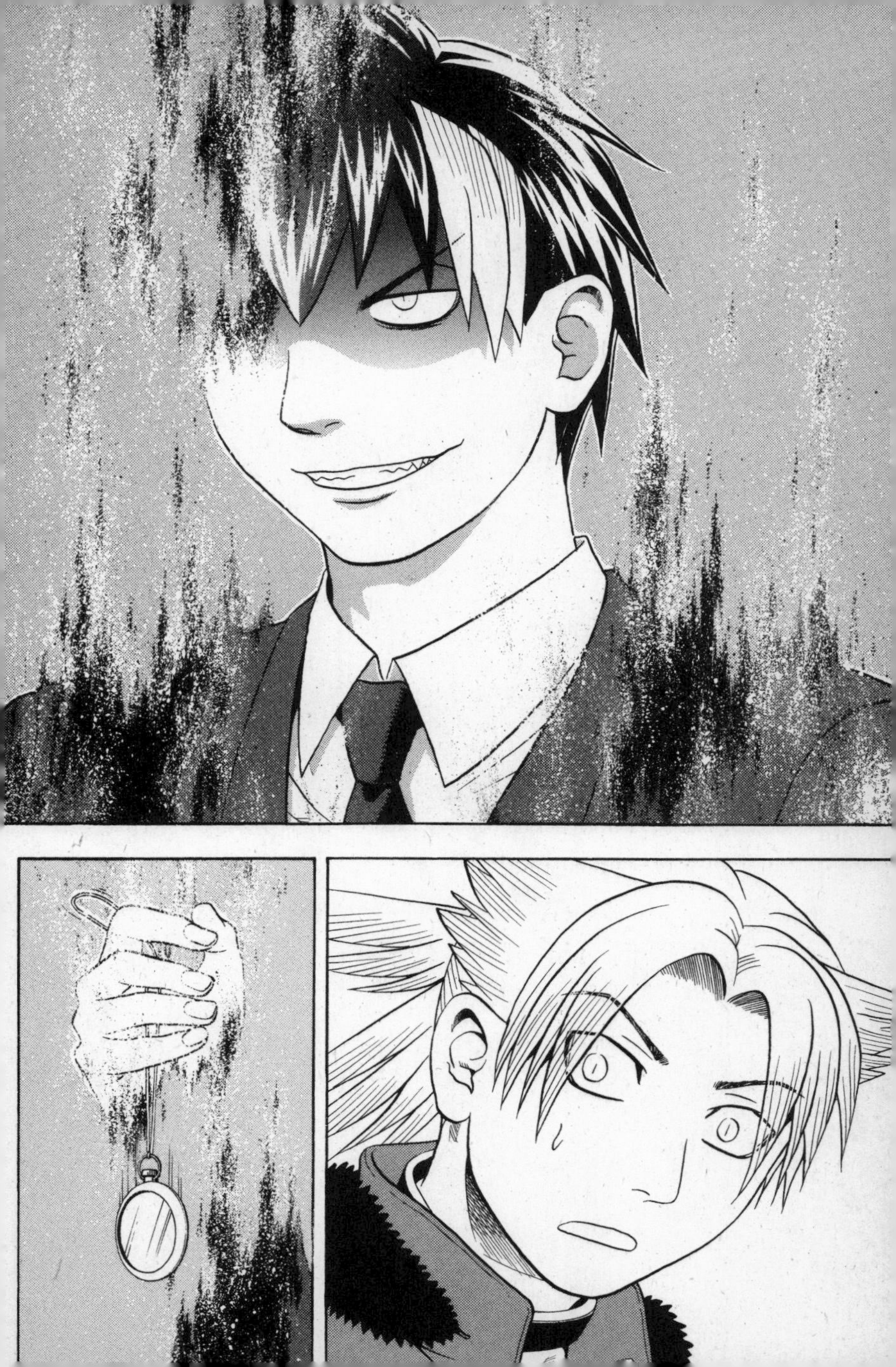

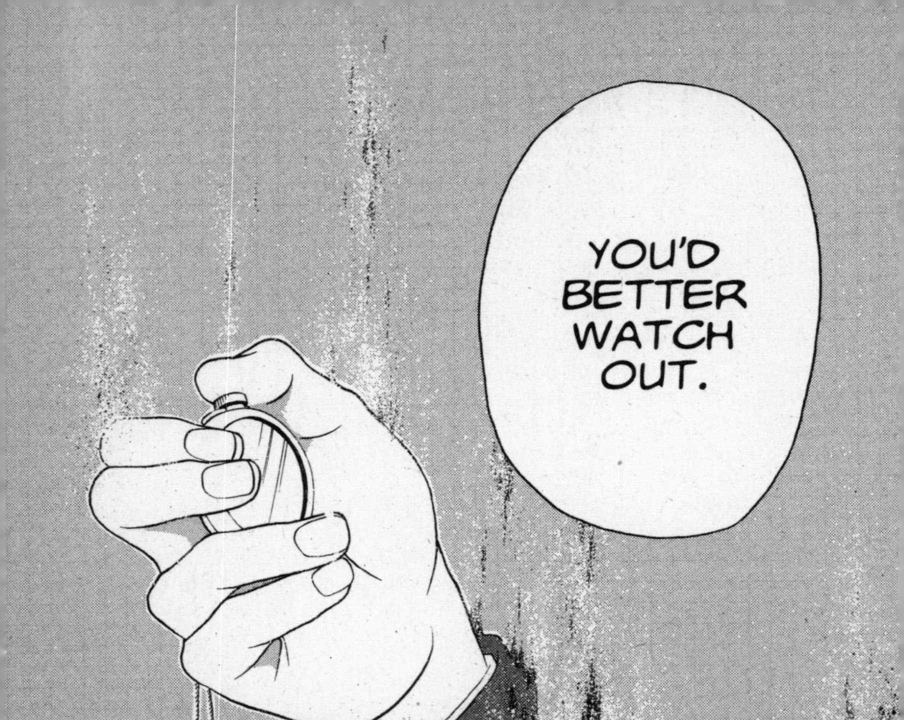
YOU'D BETTER WATCH OUT.
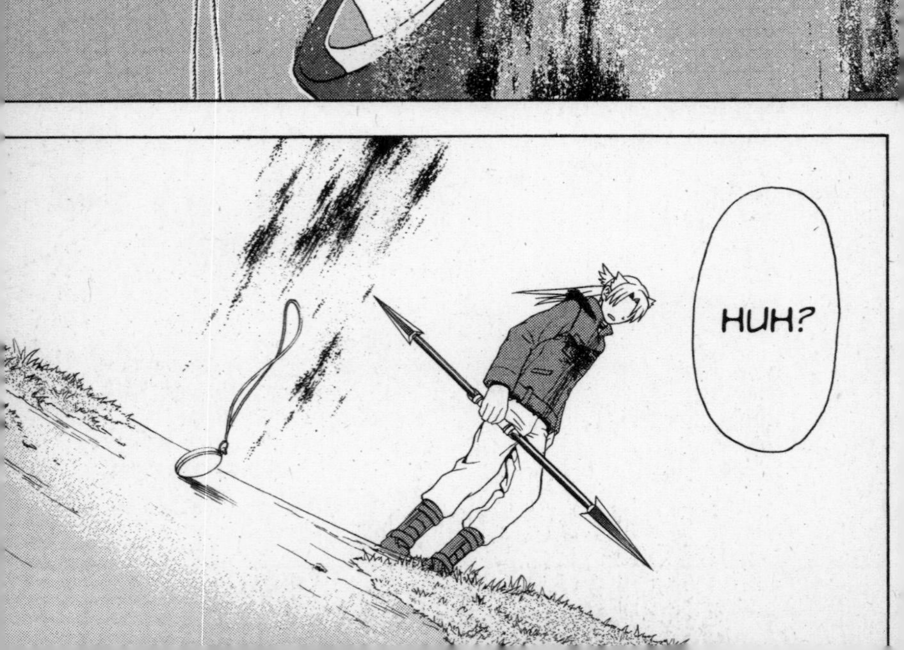
HUH?

THE INSIDE STORY OF THE POPULARITY POLL

WE RAN THE CHARACTER POPULARITY POLL AROUND THE TIME OF STORY 13, THE FIRST CHAPTER IN THIS VOLUME. I WAS SURPRISED BY RIVAN'S POPULARITY. ONLY NORA, THE MAIN CHARACTER, BEAT HIM!

KAZUMA, WHO'S THE OTHER MAIN CHARACTER BUT WASN'T TOO ACTIVE AT THE TIME, DID ALL RIGHT, AND SO DID BARIK. BUT THERE WAS A HUGE GAP IN POPULARITY BETWEEN RIVAN AND THE OTHER TWO. AND I WAS SHOCKED THAT RIVAN WAS POPULAR IN ALL DEMOGRAPHICS: YOUNG AND OLD, MALE AND FEMALE.

GOOD LUCK IN THE FUTURE, NORA AND KAZUMA!!

I'M SORRY I CAN'T SHARE THEM, BUT MANY PEOPLE SENT IN ILLUSTRATIONS AND MESSAGES ALONG WITH THE VOTES. I REALLY ENJOYED THEM. BY THE WAY, THE RESULTS FOR 15TH PLACE AND BELOW WERE:

* NICKS
* KETO-KETO
* SHINICHIRO MAGARI
* BAJEE
* KILLIE
* MYSTERIOUS GIRL
* POOSON
* TAMAO MAGARI
* KAZUNARI KAKEI
* JEEK
* HELL BUNS
* TYRON
* ASTO
* FUJIMOTO
* YANO
    ⋮
* THE BOSS
* KING JELLY
* GOMA
* BAD-ONE
  ...ETC.

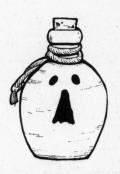

THANKS TO EVERYONE WHO VOTED FOR ME, THE AUTHOR!! AND I NEVER DREAMED THERE'D BE A COUPLE OF PEOPLE WHO'D VOTE FOR THE HELL BUNS...

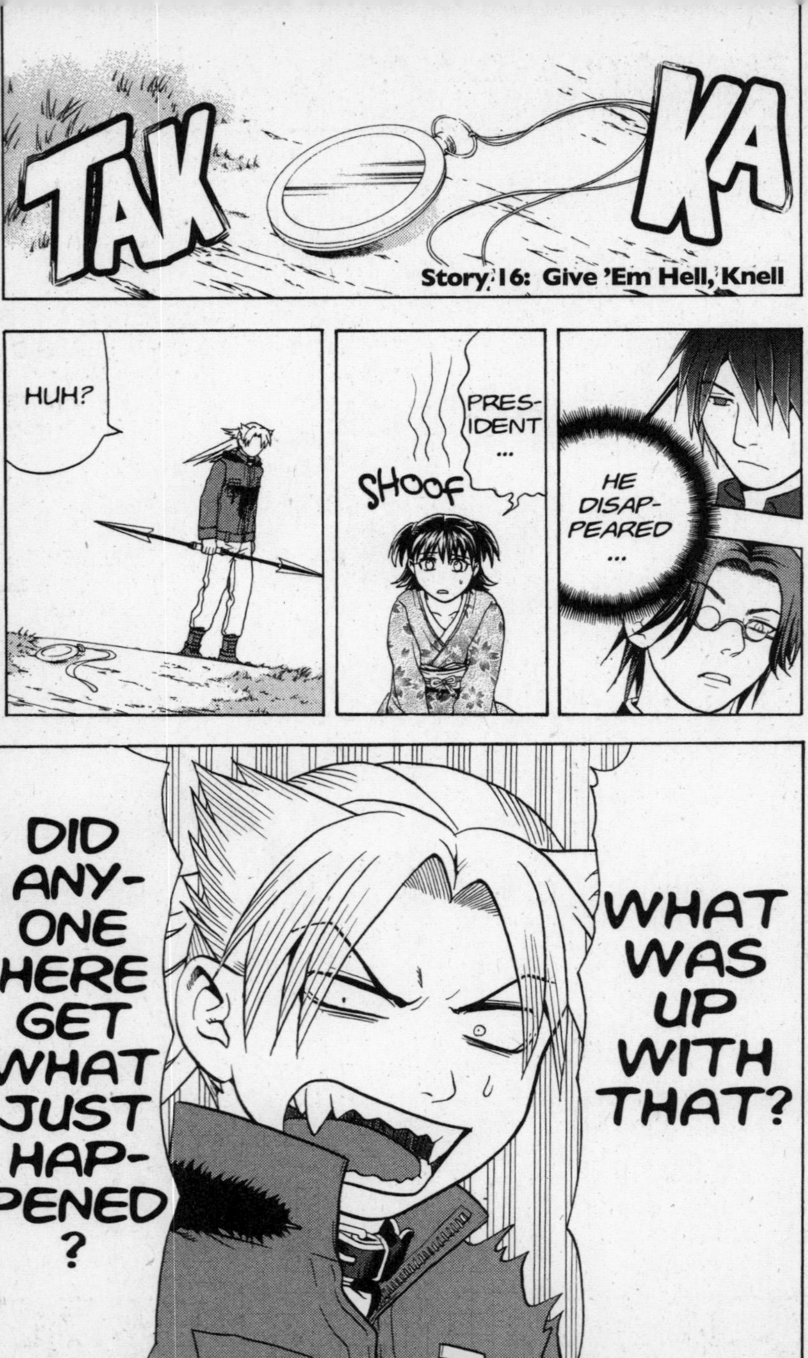
TAK
KA
Story 16: Give 'Em Hell, Knell
HE DISAPPEARED...
PRESIDENT...
SHOOF
HUH?
WHAT WAS UP WITH THAT?
DID ANYONE HERE GET WHAT JUST HAPPENED?

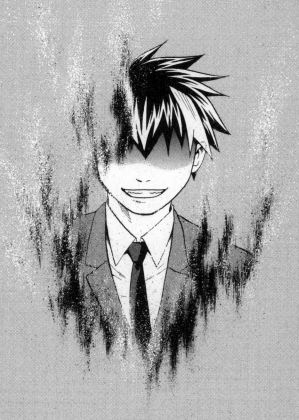

Story 16: Give 'Em Hell, Knell

READ THIS WAY

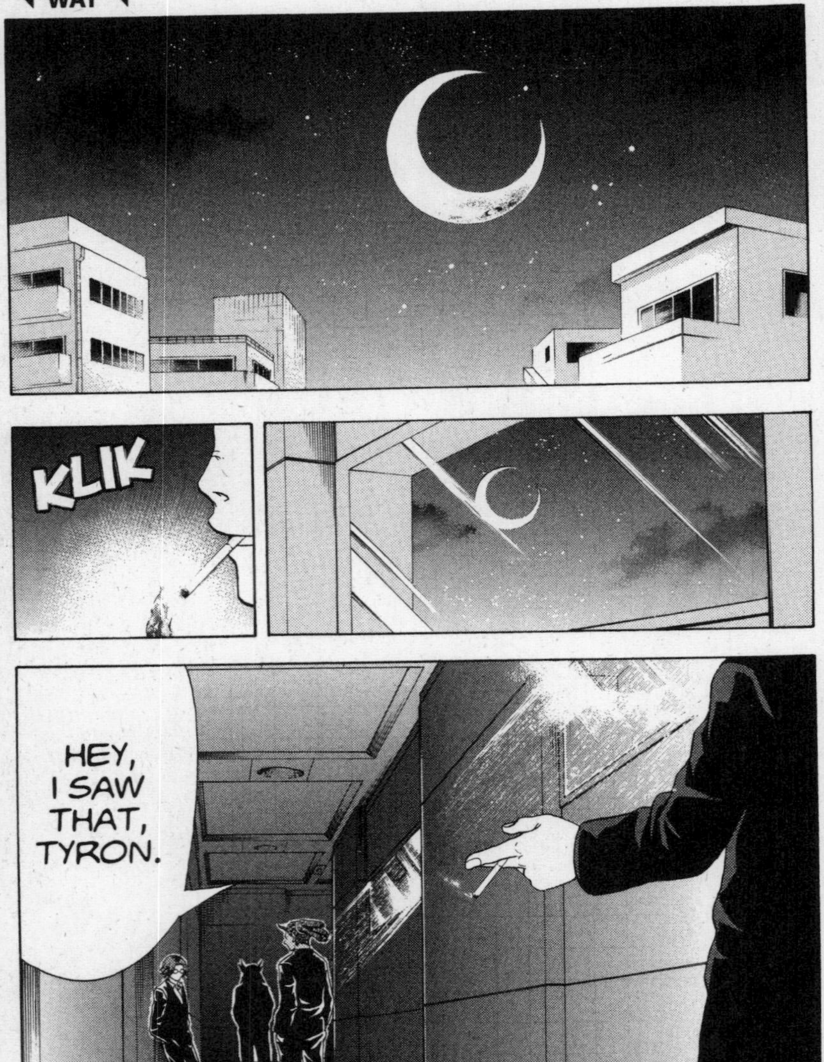
KLIK
HEY, I SAW THAT, TYRON.

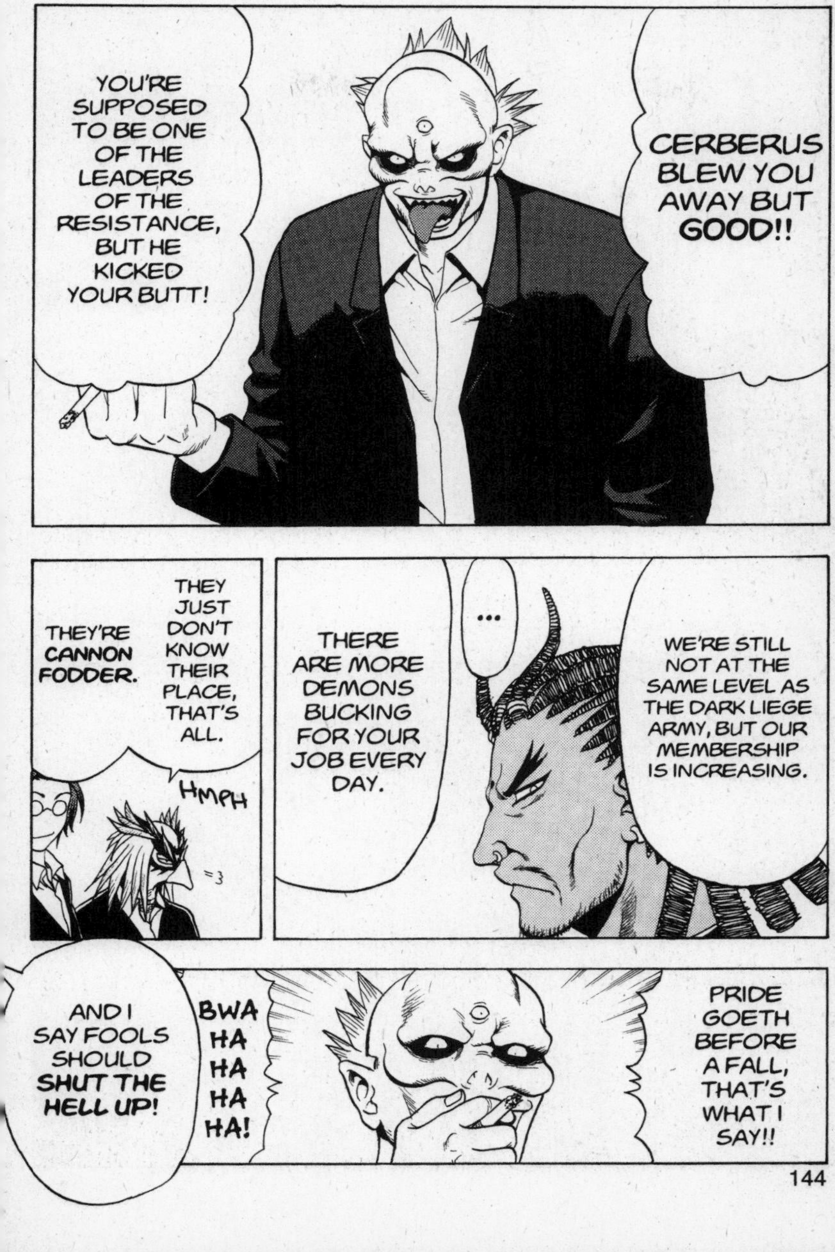
CERBERUS BLEW YOU AWAY BUT GOOD!!
YOU'RE SUPPOSED TO BE ONE OF THE LEADERS OF THE RESISTANCE, BUT HE KICKED YOUR BUTT!
WE'RE STILL NOT AT THE SAME LEVEL AS THE DARK LIEGE ARMY, BUT OUR MEMBERSHIP IS INCREASING.
...
THERE ARE MORE DEMONS BUCKING FOR YOUR JOB EVERY DAY.
THEY JUST DON'T KNOW THEIR PLACE, THAT'S ALL.
THEY'RE CANNON FODDER.
HMPH
PRIDE GOETH BEFORE A FALL, THAT'S WHAT I SAY!!
BWA HA HA HA HA!
AND I SAY FOOLS SHOULD SHUT THE HELL UP!

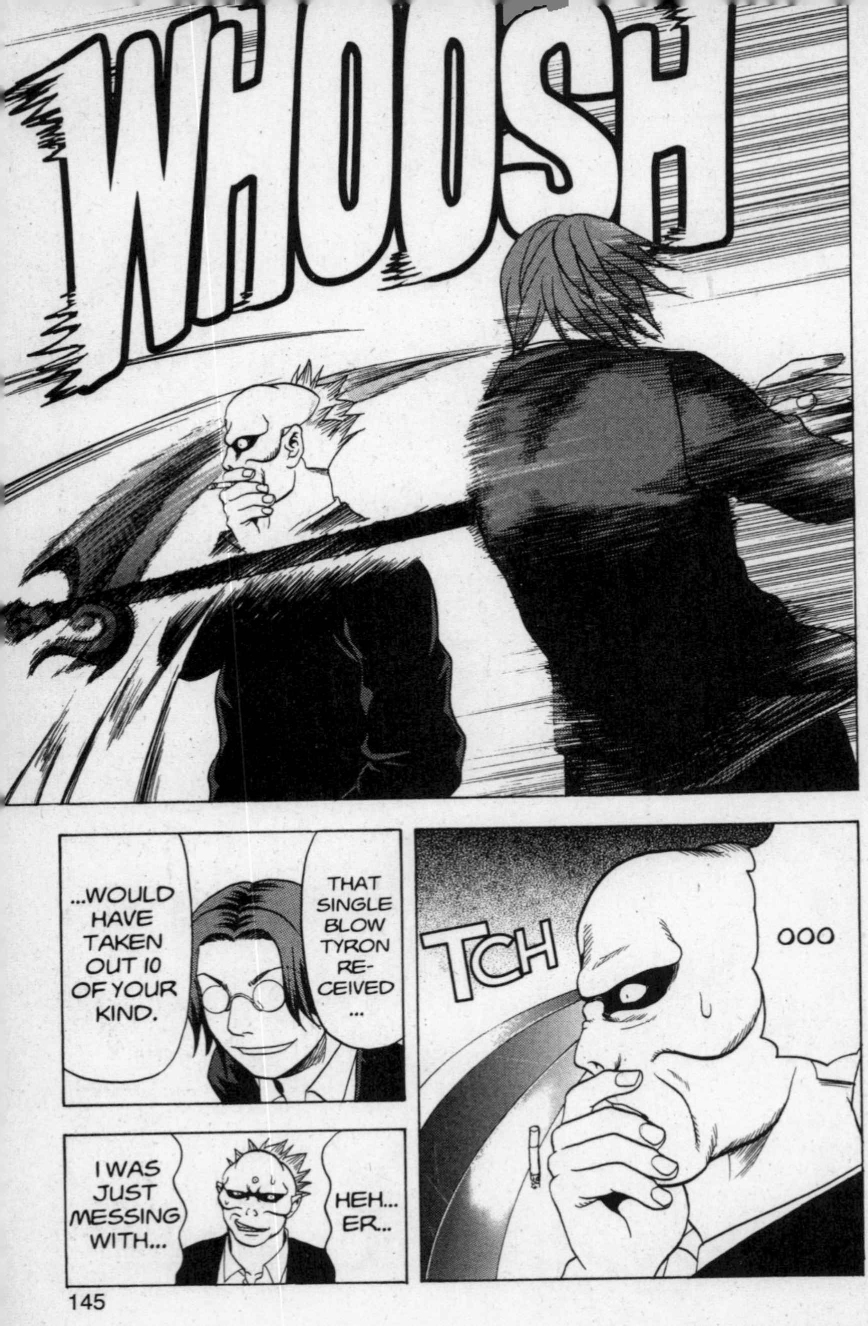
WHOOSH
OOO
TCH
THAT SINGLE BLOW TYRON RE-CEIVED ...
...WOULD HAVE TAKEN OUT 10 OF YOUR KIND.
HEH... ER...
I WAS JUST MESSING WITH...

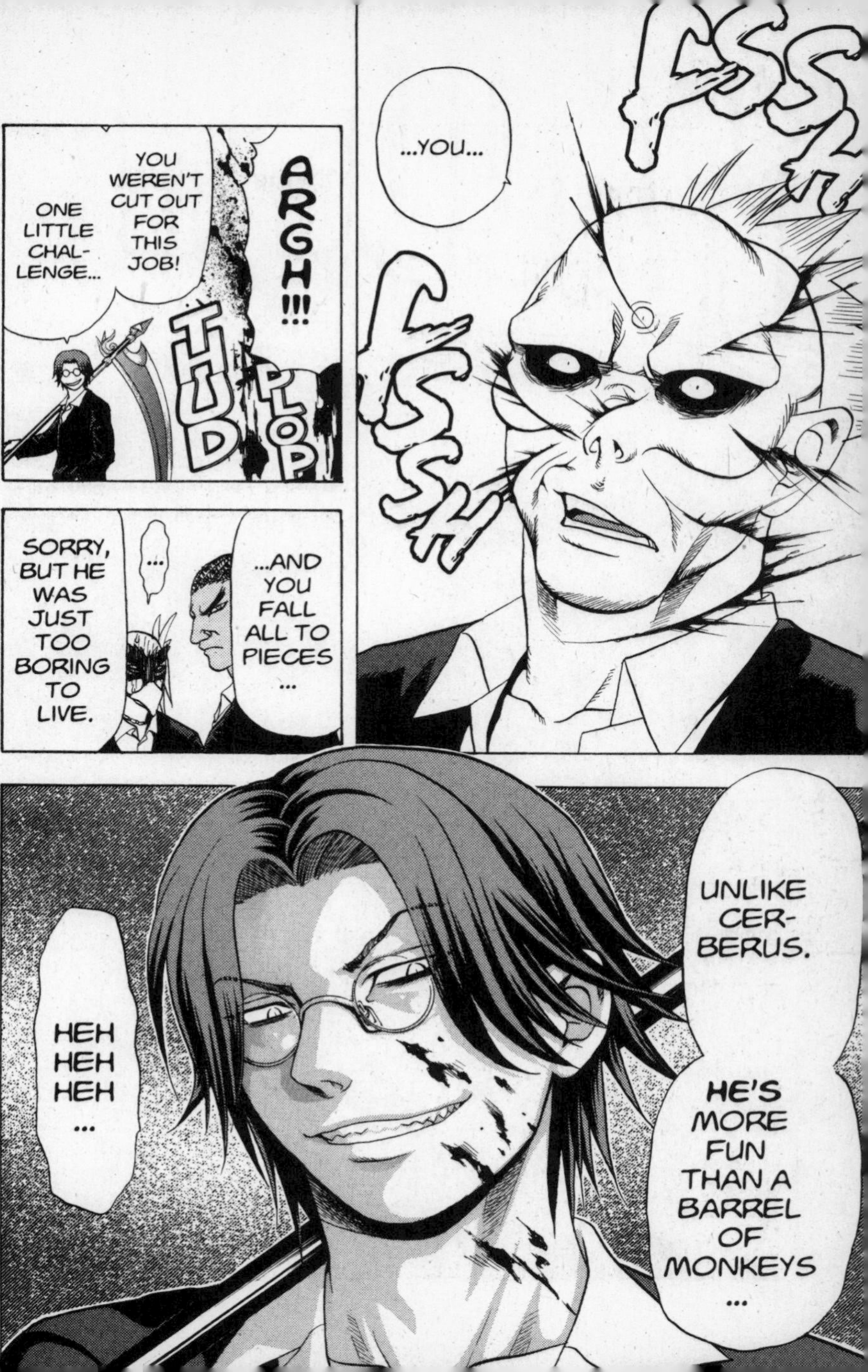
FSSH
...YOU...
FSSH
ARGH!!!
YOU WEREN'T CUT OUT FOR THIS JOB!
ONE LITTLE CHAL-LENGE...
PLOP
THUD
...AND YOU FALL ALL TO PIECES...
...
SORRY, BUT HE WAS JUST TOO BORING TO LIVE.
UNLIKE CER-BERUS.
HE'S MORE FUN THAN A BARREL OF MONKEYS...
HEH HEH HEH...

READ THIS WAY

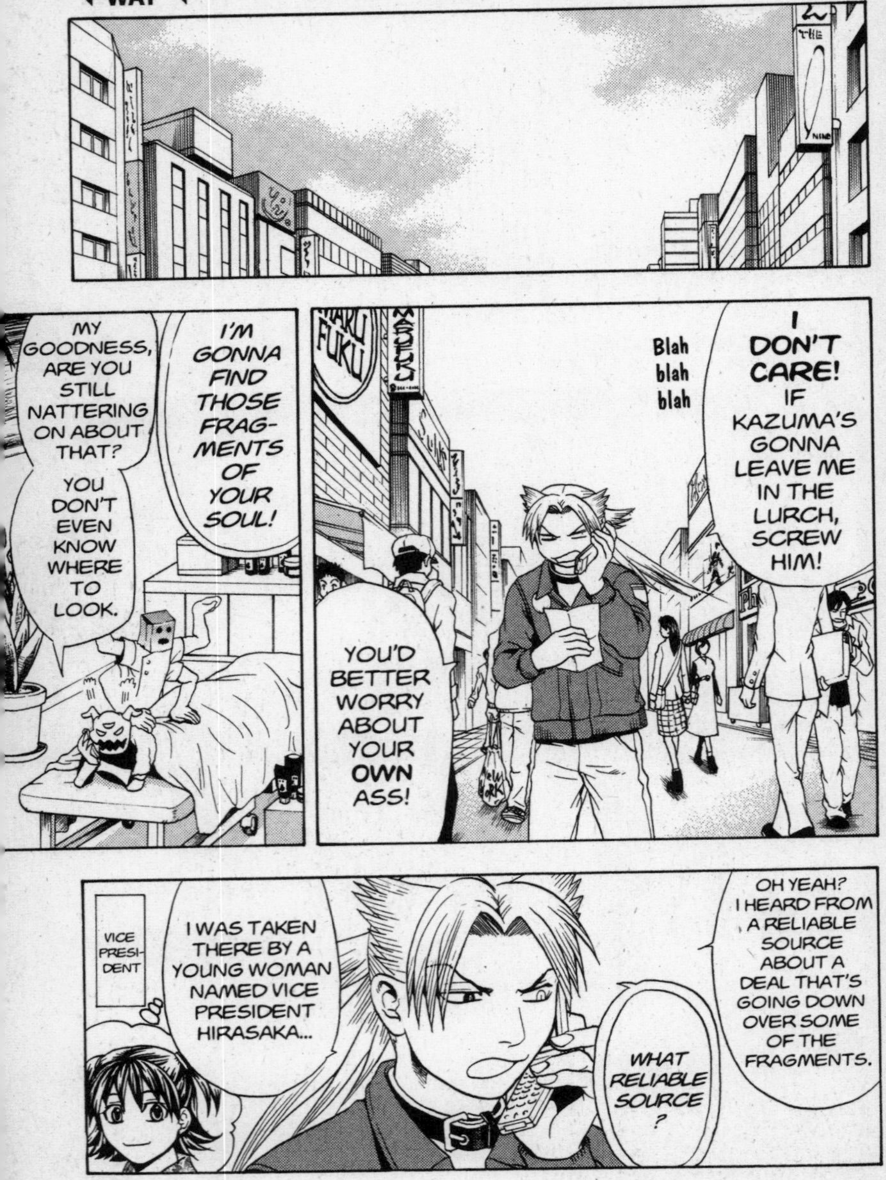

I DON'T CARE! IF KAZUMA'S GONNA LEAVE ME IN THE LURCH, SCREW HIM!
Blah blah blah
YOU'D BETTER WORRY ABOUT YOUR OWN ASS!
I'M GONNA FIND THOSE FRAG-MENTS OF YOUR SOUL!
MY GOODNESS, ARE YOU STILL NATTERING ON ABOUT THAT?
YOU DON'T EVEN KNOW WHERE TO LOOK.
OH YEAH? I HEARD FROM A RELIABLE SOURCE ABOUT A DEAL THAT'S GOING DOWN OVER SOME OF THE FRAGMENTS.
WHAT RELIABLE SOURCE?
I WAS TAKEN THERE BY A YOUNG WOMAN NAMED VICE PRESIDENT HIRASAKA...
VICE PRESI-DENT

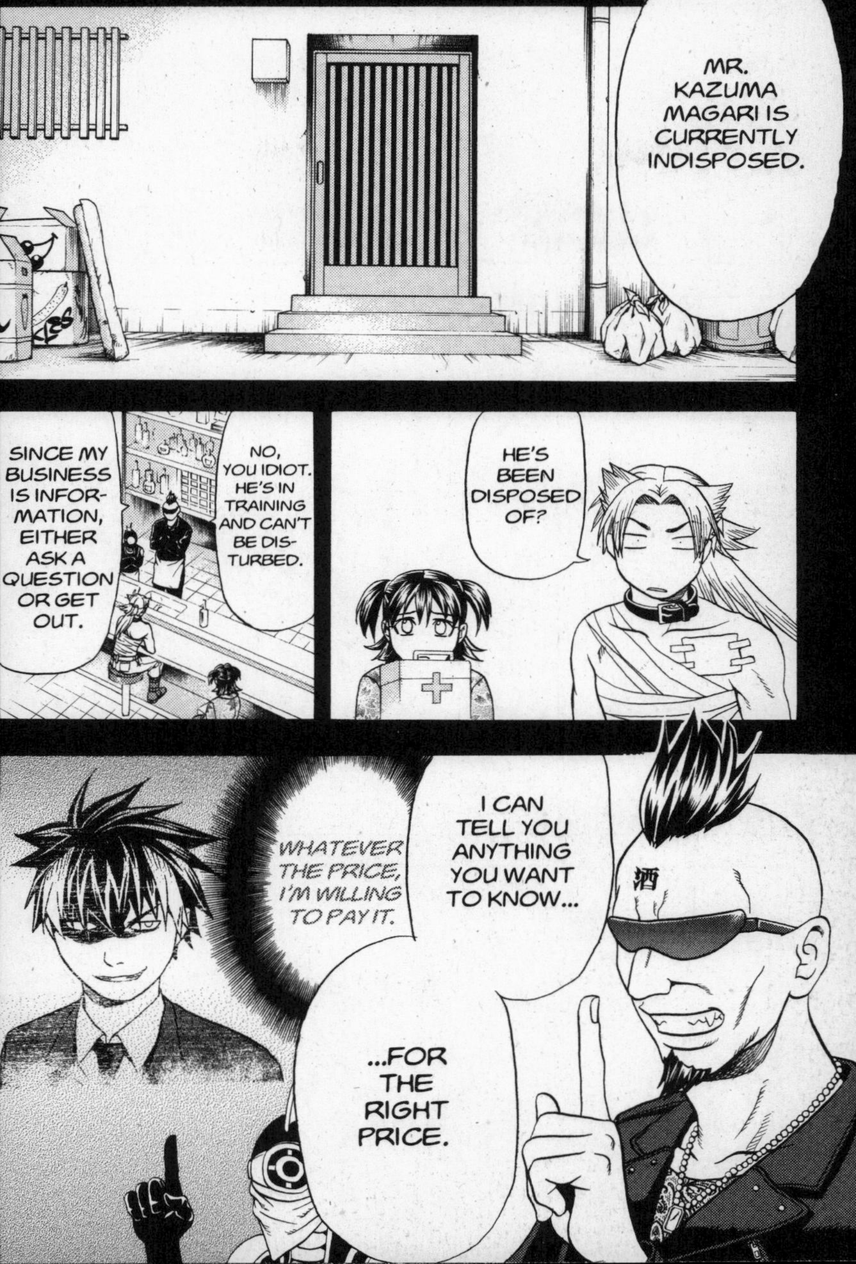
MR. KAZUMA MAGARI IS CURRENTLY INDISPOSED.
HE'S BEEN DISPOSED OF?
NO, YOU IDIOT. HE'S IN TRAINING AND CAN'T BE DISTURBED.
SINCE MY BUSINESS IS INFORMATION, EITHER ASK A QUESTION OR GET OUT.
I CAN TELL YOU ANYTHING YOU WANT TO KNOW...
酒
...FOR THE RIGHT PRICE.
WHATEVER THE PRICE, I'M WILLING TO PAY IT.

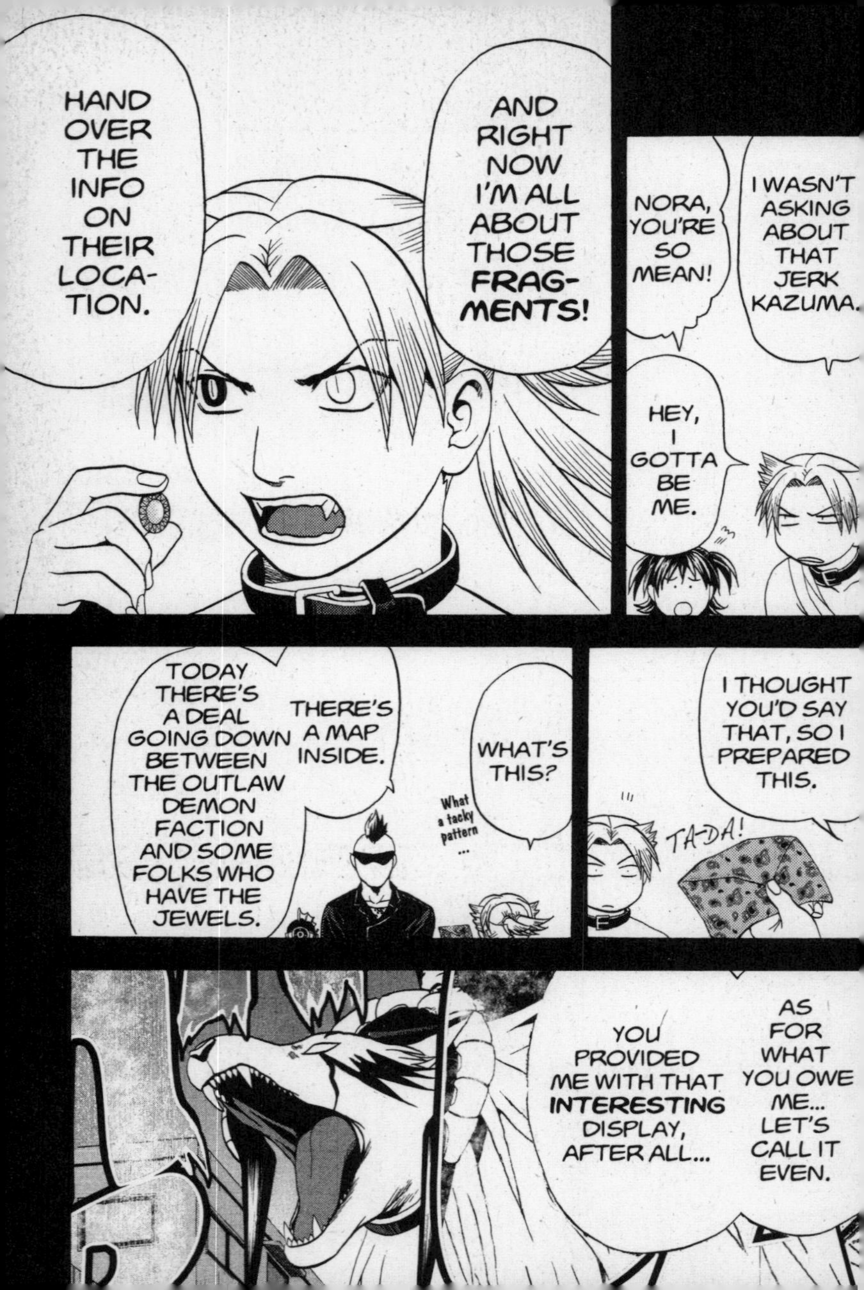
I WASN'T ASKING ABOUT THAT JERK KAZUMA.
NORA, YOU'RE SO MEAN!
HEY, I GOTTA BE ME.
AND RIGHT NOW I'M ALL ABOUT THOSE FRAGMENTS!
HAND OVER THE INFO ON THEIR LOCATION.
I THOUGHT YOU'D SAY THAT, SO I PREPARED THIS.
TA-DA!
WHAT'S THIS?
What a tacky pattern ...
THERE'S A MAP INSIDE.
TODAY THERE'S A DEAL GOING DOWN BETWEEN THE OUTLAW DEMON FACTION AND SOME FOLKS WHO HAVE THE JEWELS.
AS FOR WHAT YOU OWE ME... LET'S CALL IT EVEN.
YOU PROVIDED ME WITH THAT INTERESTING DISPLAY, AFTER ALL...

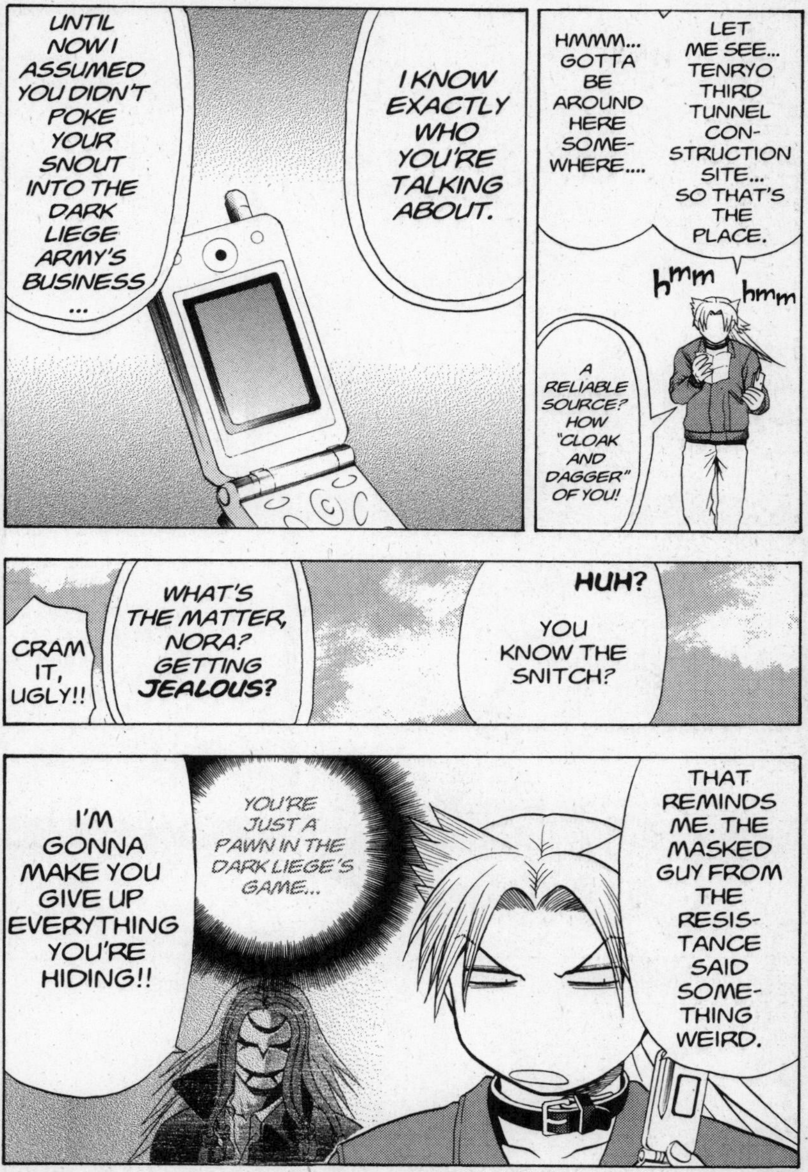
LET ME SEE... TENRYO THIRD TUNNEL CON-STRUCTION SITE... SO THAT'S THE PLACE.
HMMM... GOTTA BE AROUND HERE SOME-WHERE....
hmm hmm
A RELIABLE SOURCE? HOW "CLOAK AND DAGGER" OF YOU!
I KNOW EXACTLY WHO YOU'RE TALKING ABOUT.
UNTIL NOW I ASSUMED YOU DIDN'T POKE YOUR SNOUT INTO THE DARK LIEGE ARMY'S BUSINESS ...
HUH?
YOU KNOW THE SNITCH?
WHAT'S THE MATTER, NORA? GETTING JEALOUS?
CRAM IT, UGLY!!
THAT REMINDS ME. THE MASKED GUY FROM THE RESIS-TANCE SAID SOME-THING WEIRD.
YOU'RE JUST A PAWN IN THE DARK LIEGE'S GAME...
I'M GONNA MAKE YOU GIVE UP EVERYTHING YOU'RE HIDING!!

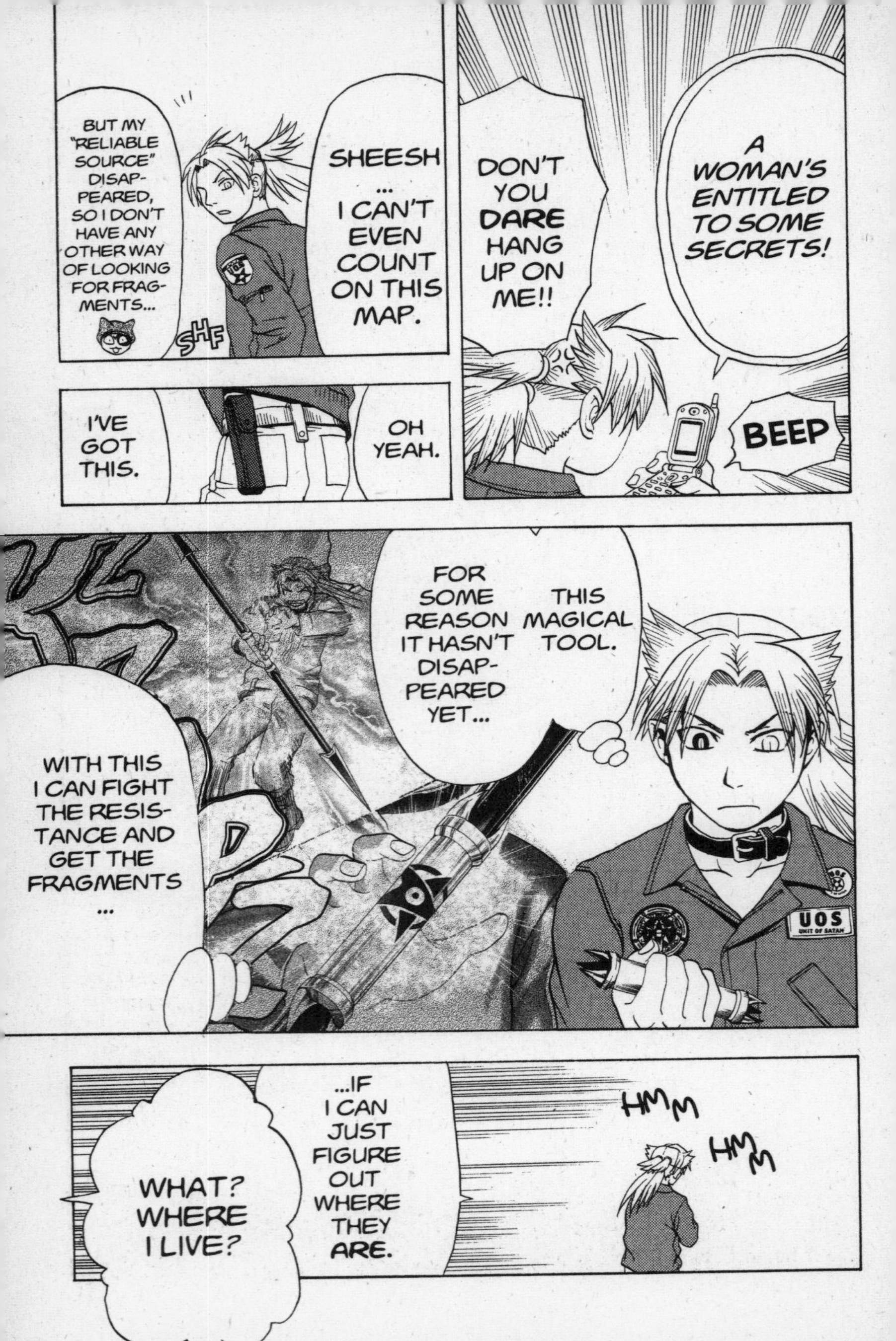
A WOMAN'S ENTITLED TO SOME SECRETS!
DON'T YOU DARE HANG UP ON ME!!
BEEP
SHEESH... I CAN'T EVEN COUNT ON THIS MAP.
BUT MY "RELIABLE SOURCE" DISAPPEARED, SO I DON'T HAVE ANY OTHER WAY OF LOOKING FOR FRAGMENTS...
SHF
OH YEAH.
I'VE GOT THIS.
THIS MAGICAL TOOL.
FOR SOME REASON IT HASN'T DISAPPEARED YET...
WITH THIS I CAN FIGHT THE RESISTANCE AND GET THE FRAGMENTS...
UOS
UNIT OF SATAN
HMM
HMM
...IF I CAN JUST FIGURE OUT WHERE THEY ARE.
WHAT? WHERE I LIVE?

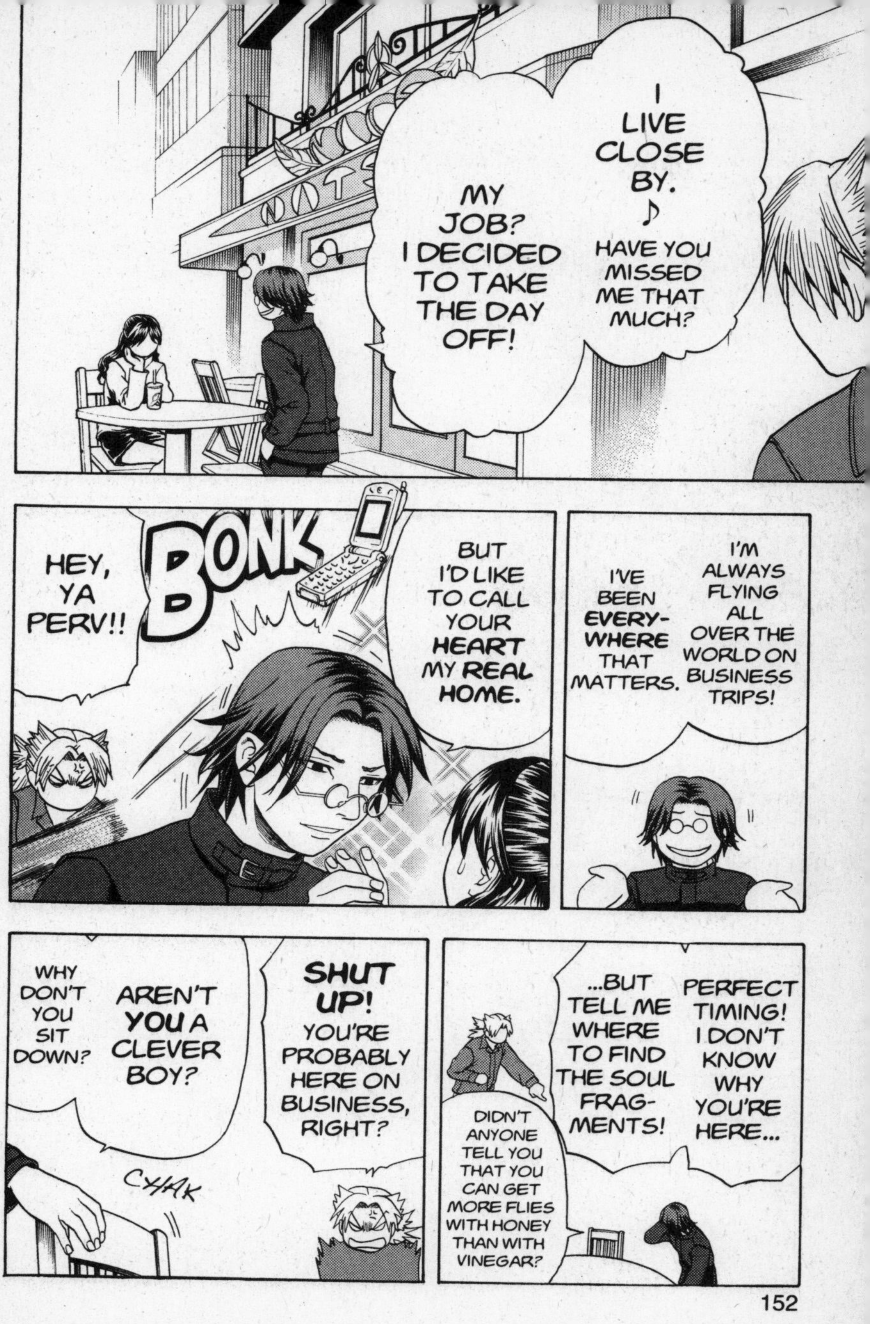
I LIVE CLOSE BY. ♪
HAVE YOU MISSED ME THAT MUCH?
MY JOB? I DECIDED TO TAKE THE DAY OFF!
I'M ALWAYS FLYING ALL OVER THE WORLD ON BUSINESS TRIPS!
I'VE BEEN EVERY-WHERE THAT MATTERS.
BUT I'D LIKE TO CALL YOUR HEART MY REAL HOME.
BONK
HEY, YA PERV!!
PERFECT TIMING! I DON'T KNOW WHY YOU'RE HERE...
...BUT TELL ME WHERE TO FIND THE SOUL FRAG-MENTS!
DIDN'T ANYONE TELL YOU THAT YOU CAN GET MORE FLIES WITH HONEY THAN WITH VINEGAR?
SHUT UP! YOU'RE PROBABLY HERE ON BUSINESS, RIGHT?
AREN'T YOU A CLEVER BOY?
WHY DON'T YOU SIT DOWN?
CHAK

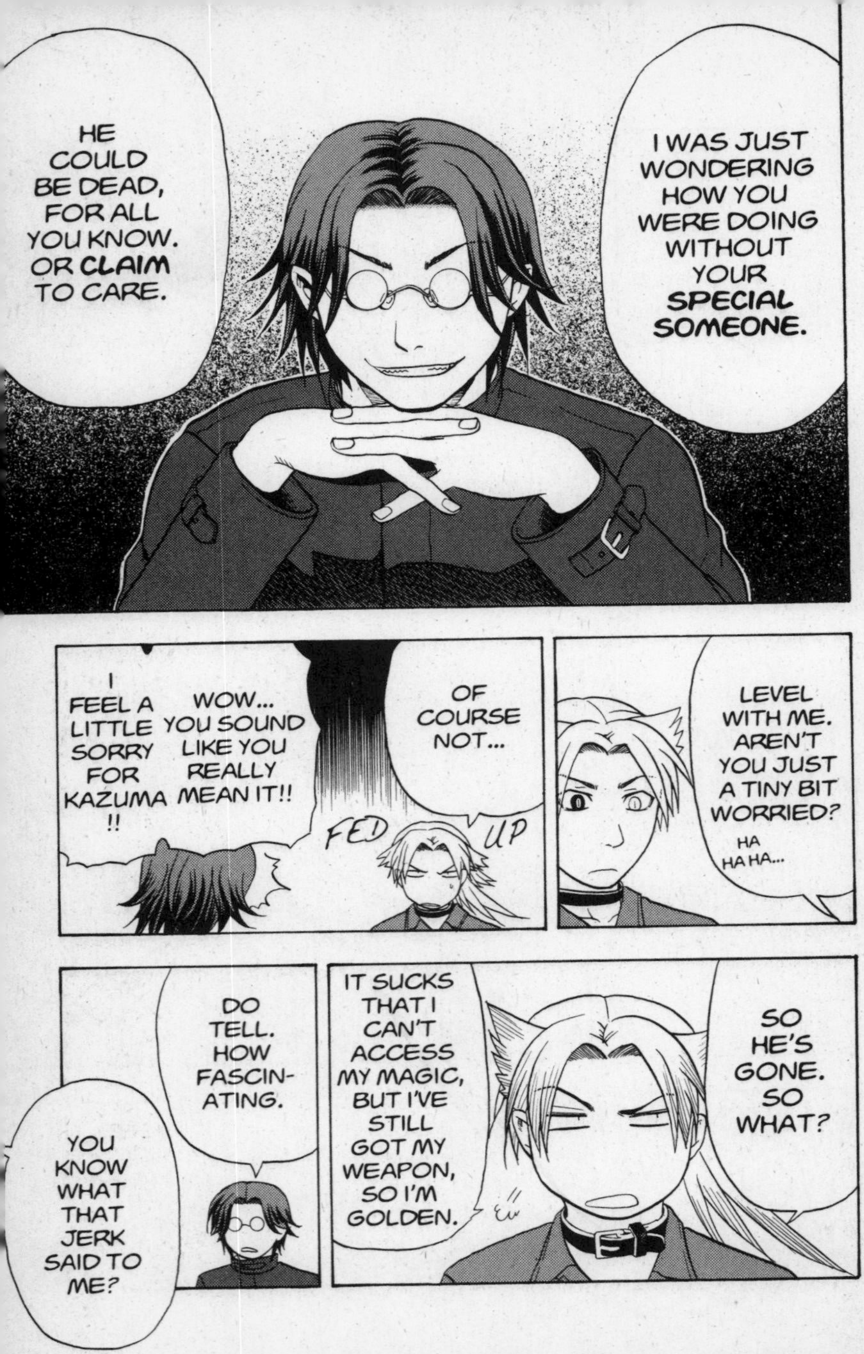
I WAS JUST WONDERING HOW YOU WERE DOING WITHOUT YOUR SPECIAL SOMEONE.
HE COULD BE DEAD, FOR ALL YOU KNOW. OR CLAIM TO CARE.
LEVEL WITH ME. AREN'T YOU JUST A TINY BIT WORRIED?
HA HA HA...
OF COURSE NOT...
FED UP
WOW... YOU SOUND LIKE YOU REALLY MEAN IT!!
I FEEL A LITTLE SORRY FOR KAZUMA!!
SO HE'S GONE. SO WHAT?
IT SUCKS THAT I CAN'T ACCESS MY MAGIC, BUT I'VE STILL GOT MY WEAPON, SO I'M GOLDEN.
DO TELL. HOW FASCIN-ATING.
YOU KNOW WHAT THAT JERK SAID TO ME?

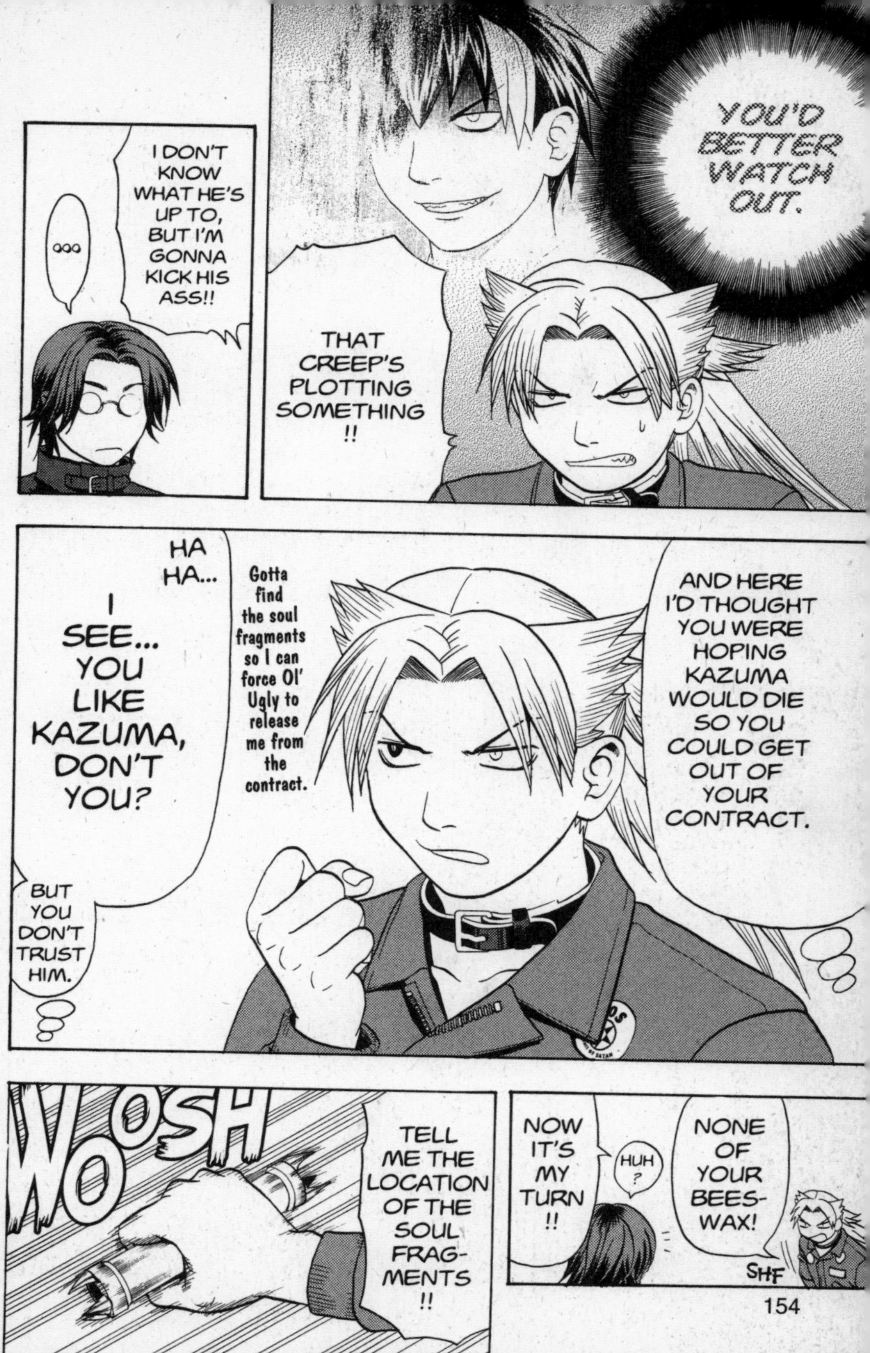
YOU'D BETTER WATCH OUT.
THAT CREEP'S PLOTTING SOMETHING !!
I DON'T KNOW WHAT HE'S UP TO, BUT I'M GONNA KICK HIS ASS!!
...
AND HERE I'D THOUGHT YOU WERE HOPING KAZUMA WOULD DIE SO YOU COULD GET OUT OF YOUR CONTRACT.
Gotta find the soul fragments so I can force Ol' Ugly to release me from the contract.
HA HA...
I SEE... YOU LIKE KAZUMA, DON'T YOU?
BUT YOU DON'T TRUST HIM.
NONE OF YOUR BEES-WAX!
SHF
HUH ?
NOW IT'S MY TURN !!
TELL ME THE LOCATION OF THE SOUL FRAG-MENTS !!
WOOSH

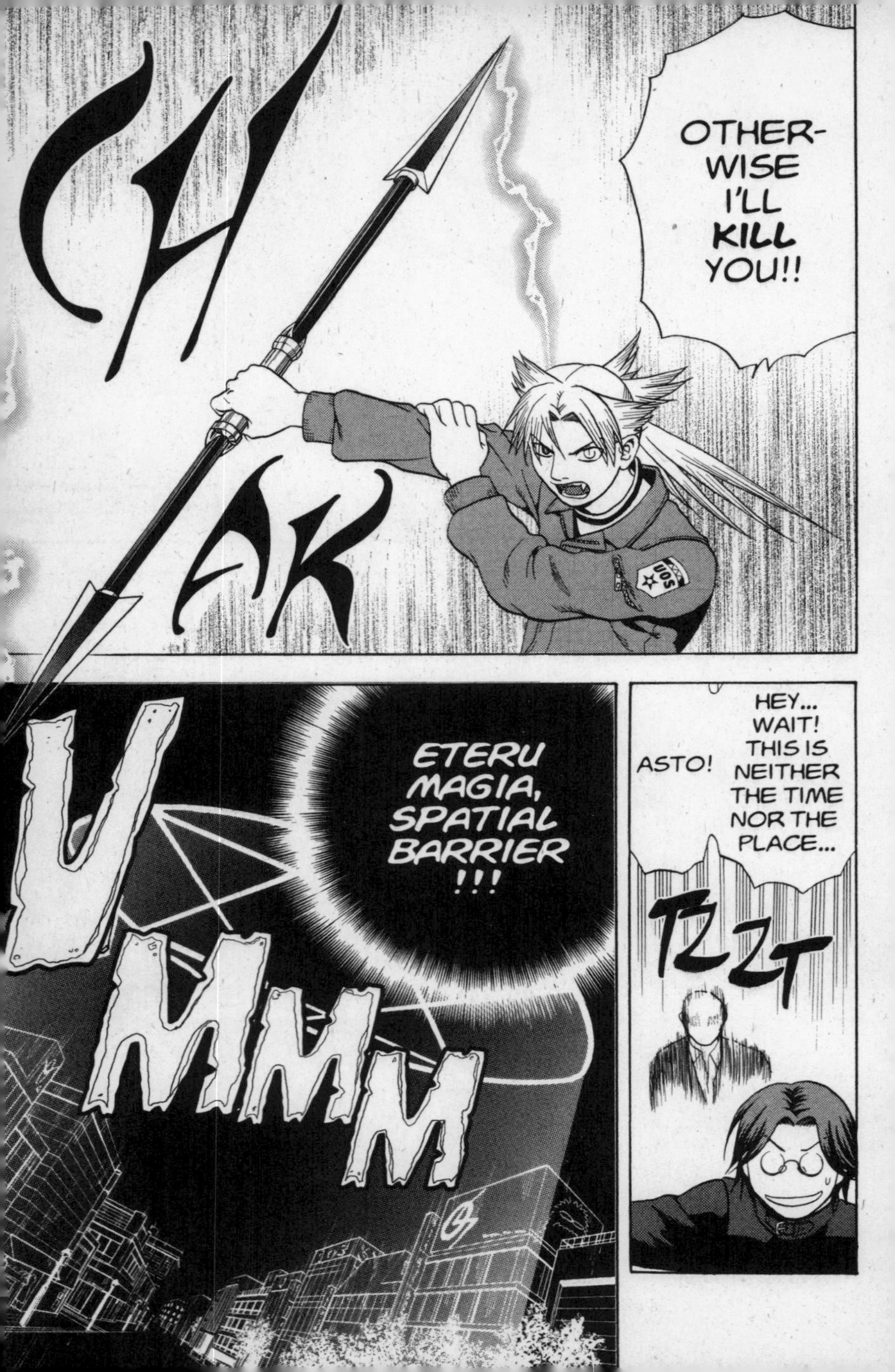
OTHER-WISE I'LL **KILL** YOU!!
CHAK
HEY... WAIT! THIS IS NEITHER THE TIME NOR THE PLACE...
ASTO!
TZZT
ETERU MAGIA, SPATIAL BARRIER!!!
VMMMM

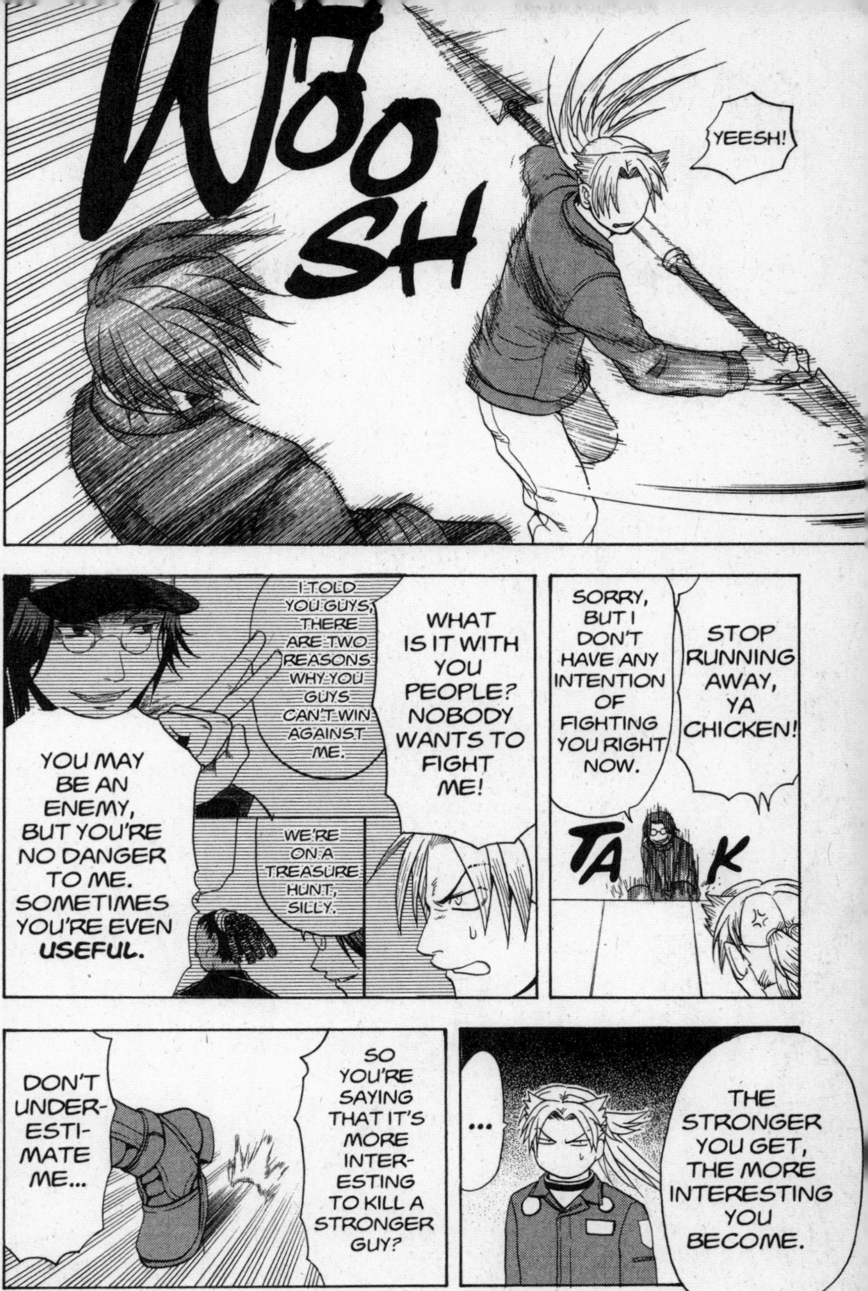
YEESH!
WOOSH
STOP RUNNING AWAY, YA CHICKEN!
SORRY, BUT I DON'T HAVE ANY INTENTION OF FIGHTING YOU RIGHT NOW.
TAK
WHAT IS IT WITH YOU PEOPLE? NOBODY WANTS TO FIGHT ME!
I TOLD YOU GUYS, THERE ARE TWO REASONS WHY YOU GUYS CAN'T WIN AGAINST ME.
WE'RE ON A TREASURE HUNT, SILLY.
YOU MAY BE AN ENEMY, BUT YOU'RE NO DANGER TO ME. SOMETIMES YOU'RE EVEN USEFUL.
THE STRONGER YOU GET, THE MORE INTERESTING YOU BECOME.
...
SO YOU'RE SAYING THAT IT'S MORE INTER-ESTING TO KILL A STRONGER GUY?
DON'T UNDER-ESTI-MATE ME...

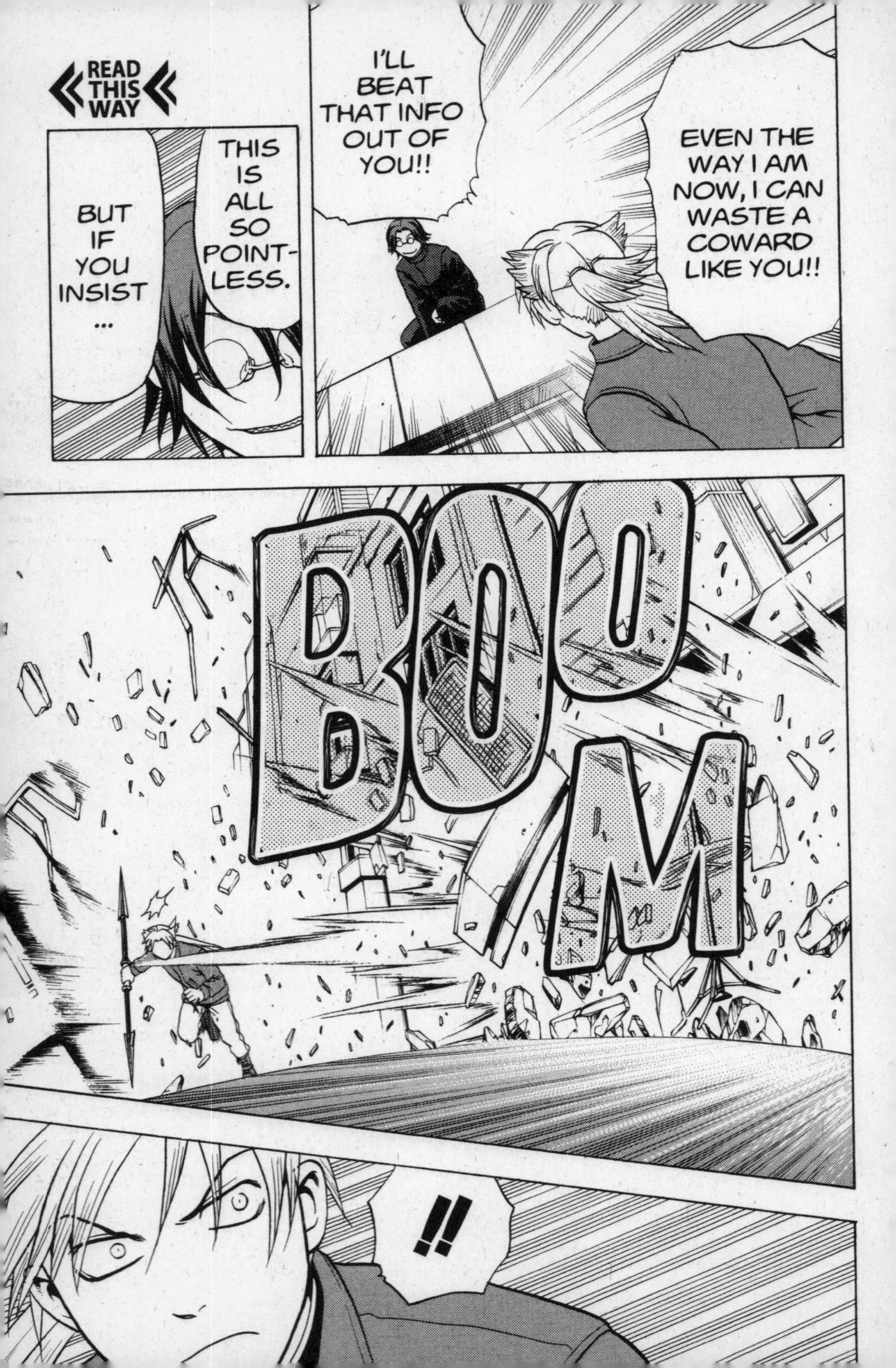
READ THIS WAY
EVEN THE WAY I AM NOW, I CAN WASTE A COWARD LIKE YOU!!
I'LL BEAT THAT INFO OUT OF YOU!!
THIS IS ALL SO POINTLESS.
BUT IF YOU INSIST ...
BOOOM
!!

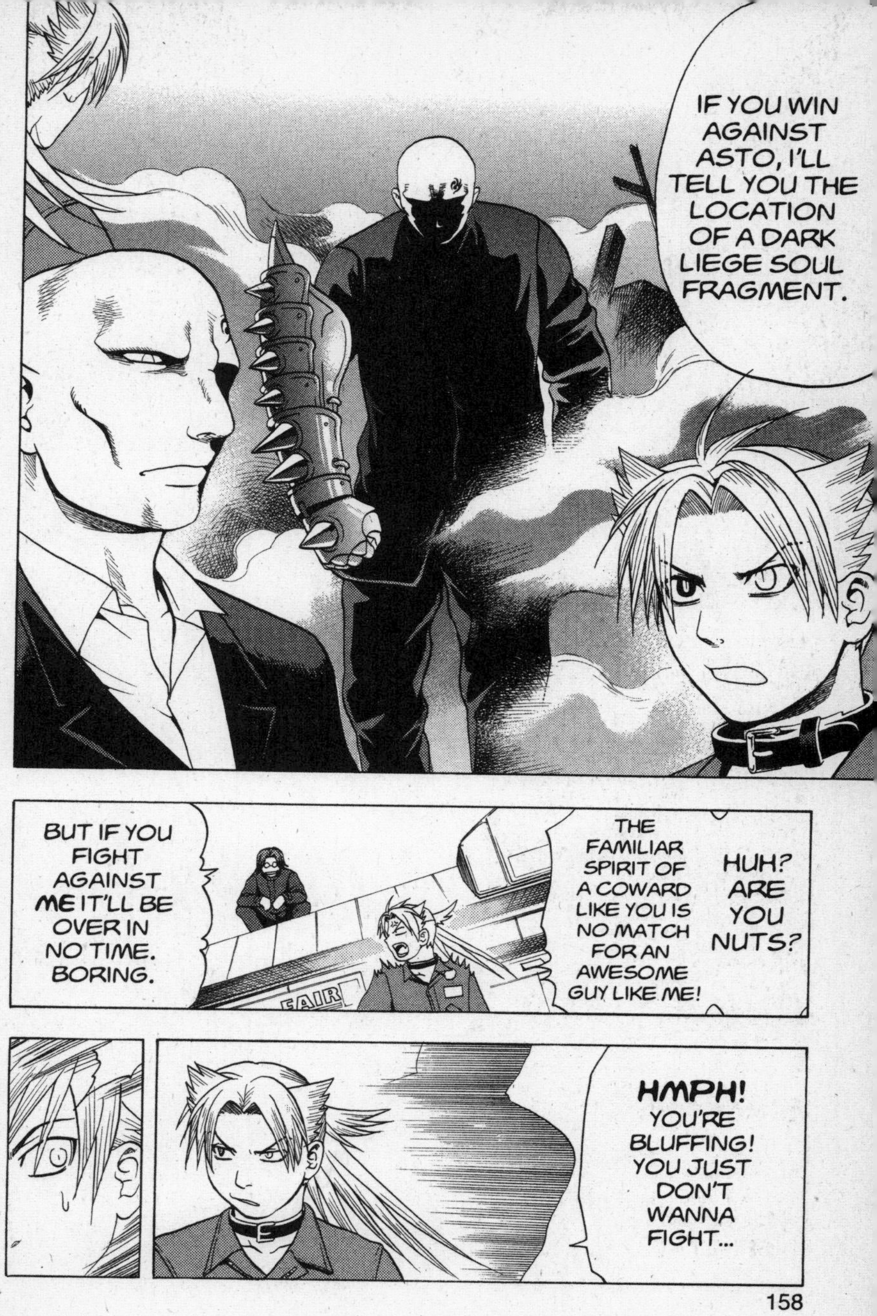
IF YOU WIN AGAINST ASTO, I'LL TELL YOU THE LOCATION OF A DARK LIEGE SOUL FRAGMENT.
HUH? ARE YOU NUTS?
THE FAMILIAR SPIRIT OF A COWARD LIKE YOU IS NO MATCH FOR AN AWESOME GUY LIKE ME!
BUT IF YOU FIGHT AGAINST ME IT'LL BE OVER IN NO TIME. BORING.
FAIR
HMPH! YOU'RE BLUFFING! YOU JUST DON'T WANNA FIGHT...

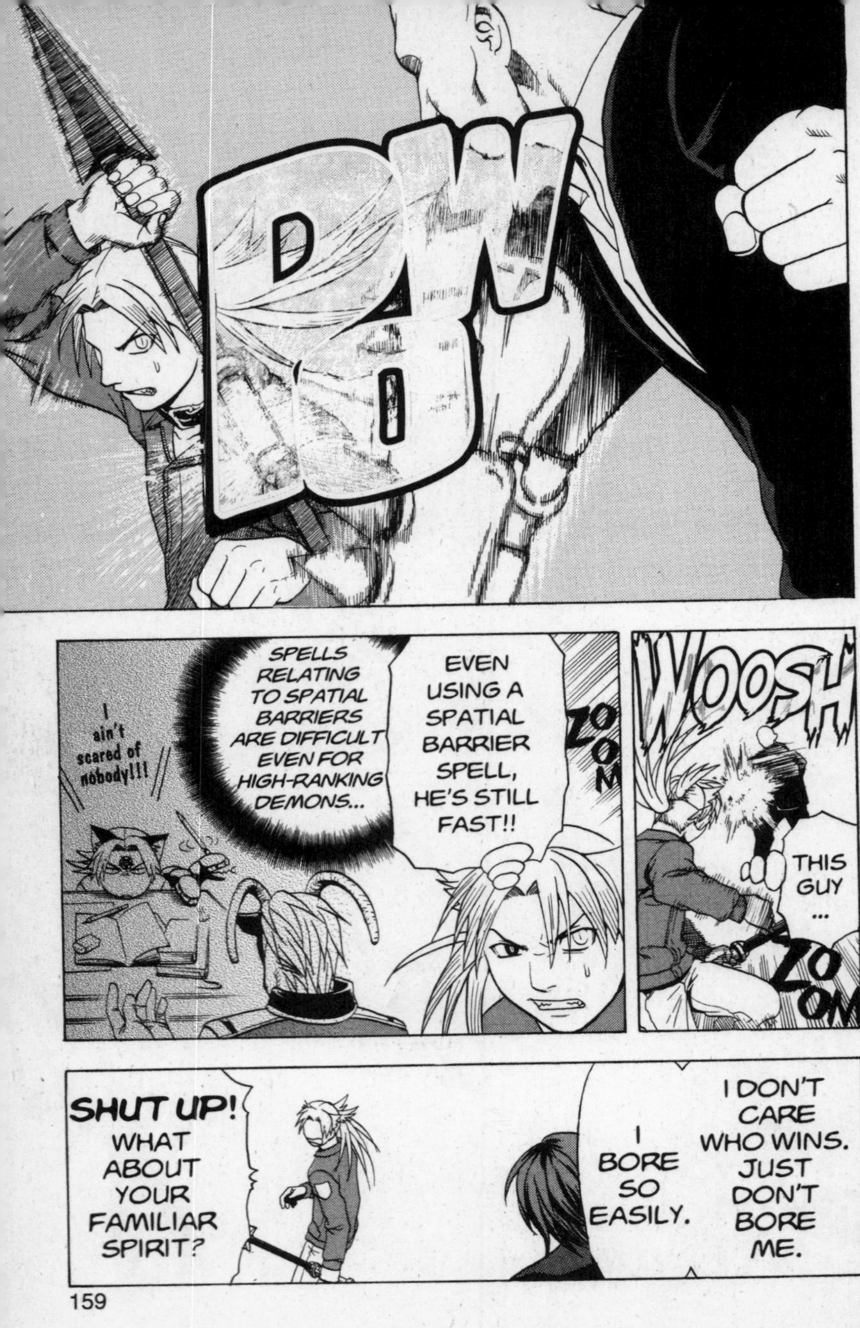
WOOSH
THIS GUY ...
ZOOM
ZOOM
EVEN USING A SPATIAL BARRIER SPELL, HE'S STILL FAST!!
SPELLS RELATING TO SPATIAL BARRIERS ARE DIFFICULT EVEN FOR HIGH-RANKING DEMONS...
I ain't scared of nobody!!!
I DON'T CARE WHO WINS. JUST DON'T BORE ME.
I BORE SO EASILY.
SHUT UP! WHAT ABOUT YOUR FAMILIAR SPIRIT?

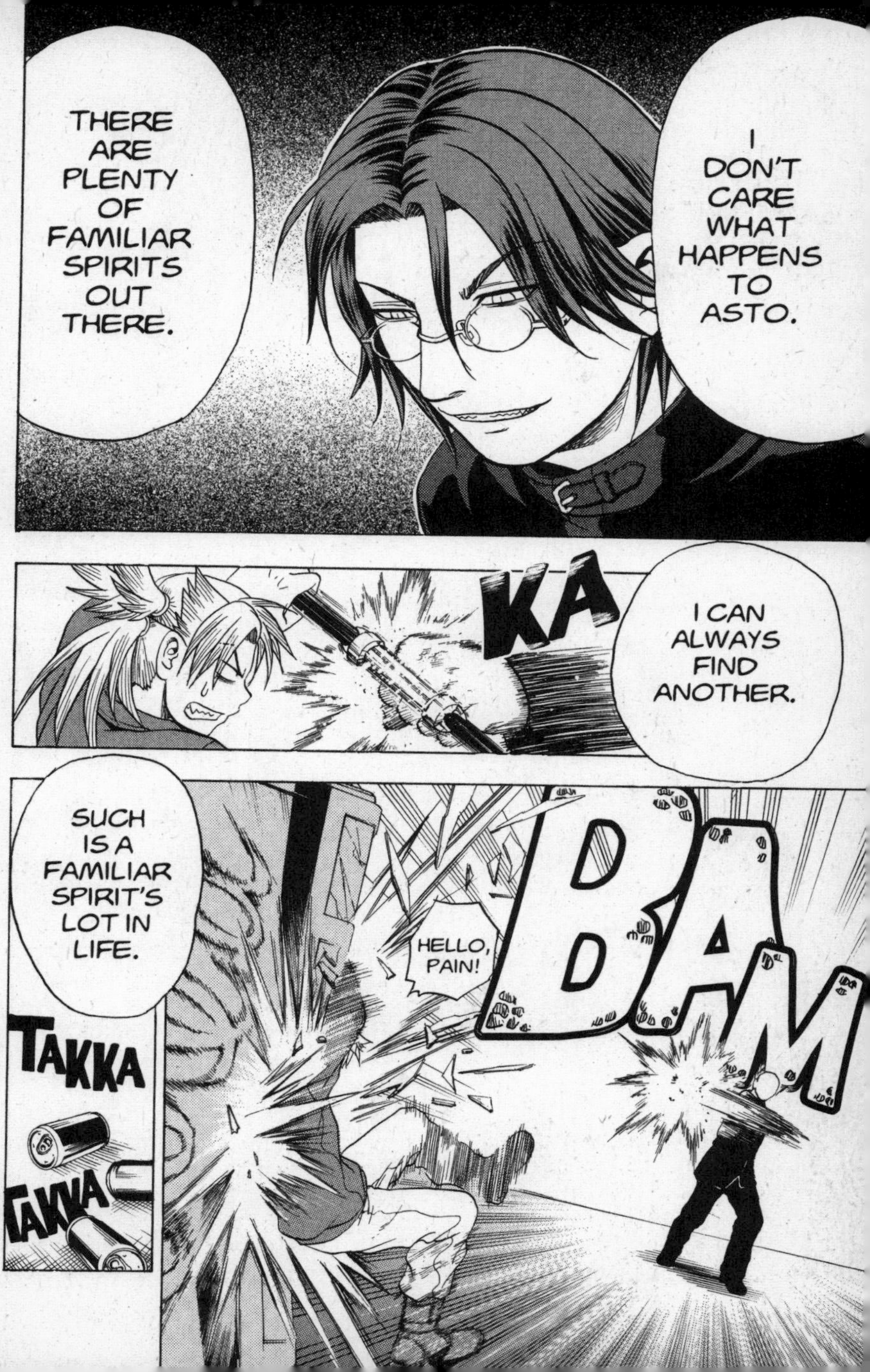
I DON'T CARE WHAT HAPPENS TO ASTO.
THERE ARE PLENTY OF FAMILIAR SPIRITS OUT THERE.
I CAN ALWAYS FIND ANOTHER.
KA
BAM
HELLO, PAIN!
SUCH IS A FAMILIAR SPIRIT'S LOT IN LIFE.
TAKKA
TAKKA

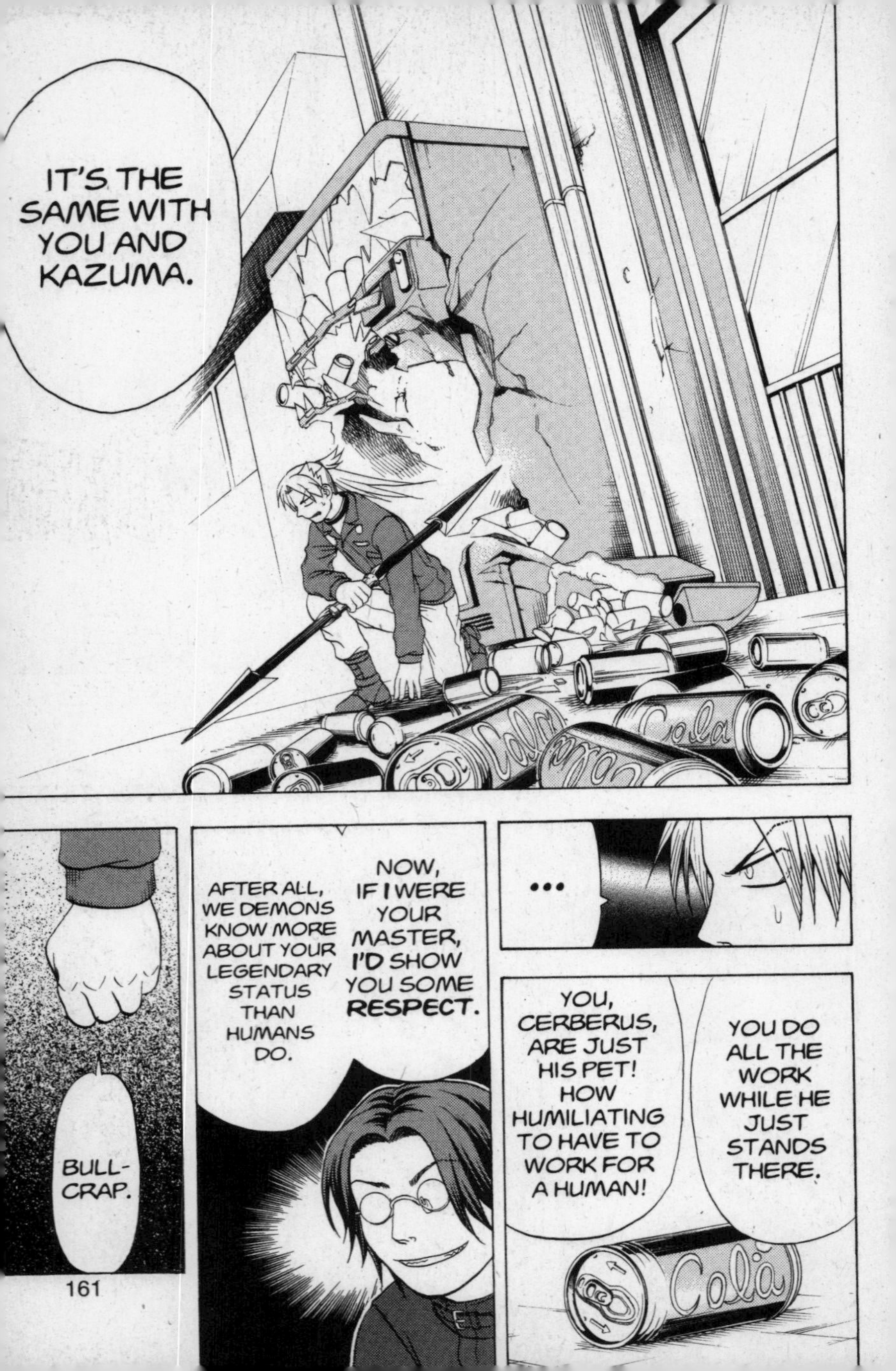
IT'S THE SAME WITH YOU AND KAZUMA.
...
YOU DO ALL THE WORK WHILE HE JUST STANDS THERE.
YOU, CERBERUS, ARE JUST HIS PET! HOW HUMILIATING TO HAVE TO WORK FOR A HUMAN!
NOW, IF I WERE YOUR MASTER, I'D SHOW YOU SOME **RESPECT**.
AFTER ALL, WE DEMONS KNOW MORE ABOUT YOUR LEGENDARY STATUS THAN HUMANS DO.
BULL-CRAP.

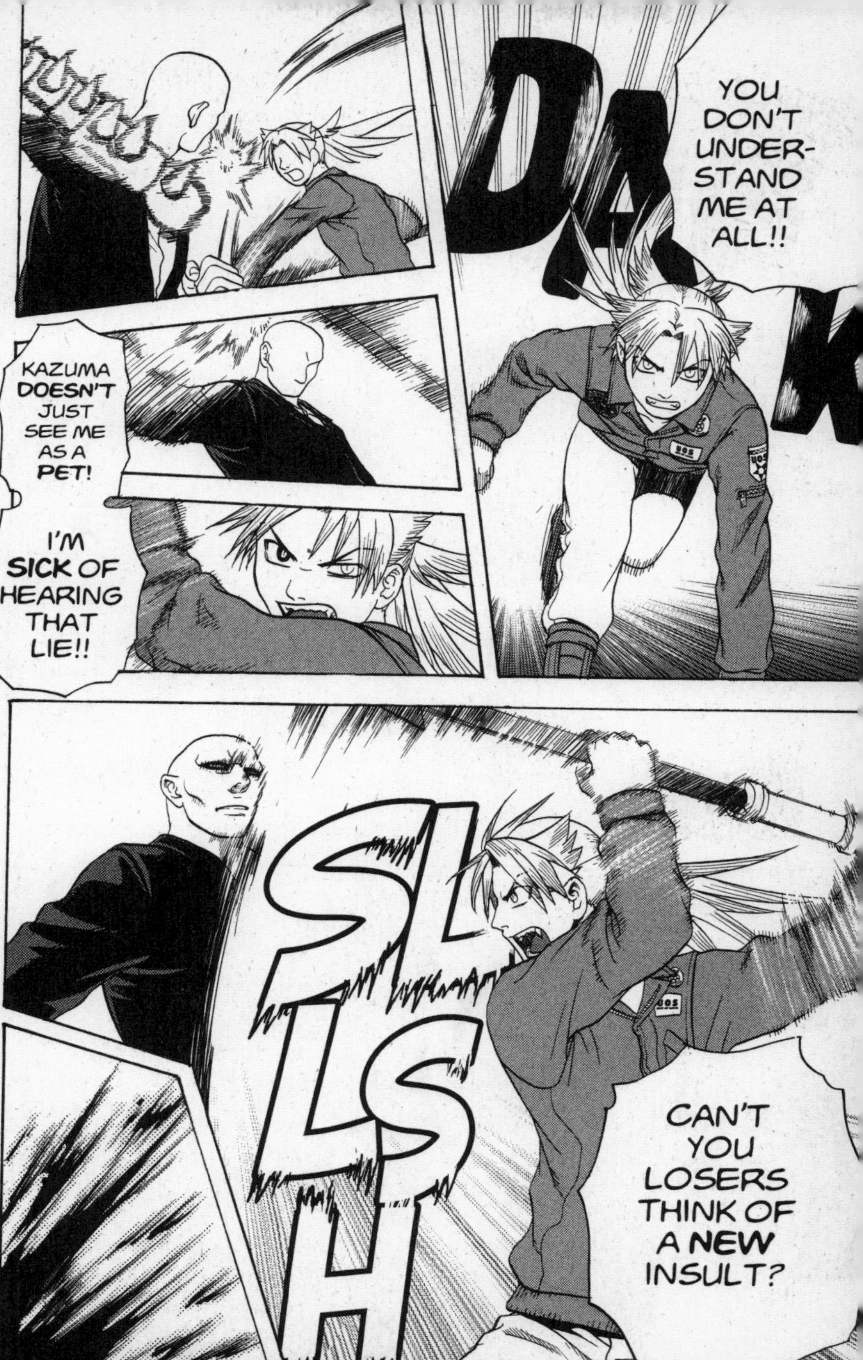

DAK
YOU DON'T UNDER-STAND ME AT ALL!!
KAZUMA **DOESN'T** JUST SEE ME AS A **PET**!
I'M **SICK** OF HEARING THAT LIE!!
SLLSH
CAN'T YOU LOSERS THINK OF A **NEW** INSULT?

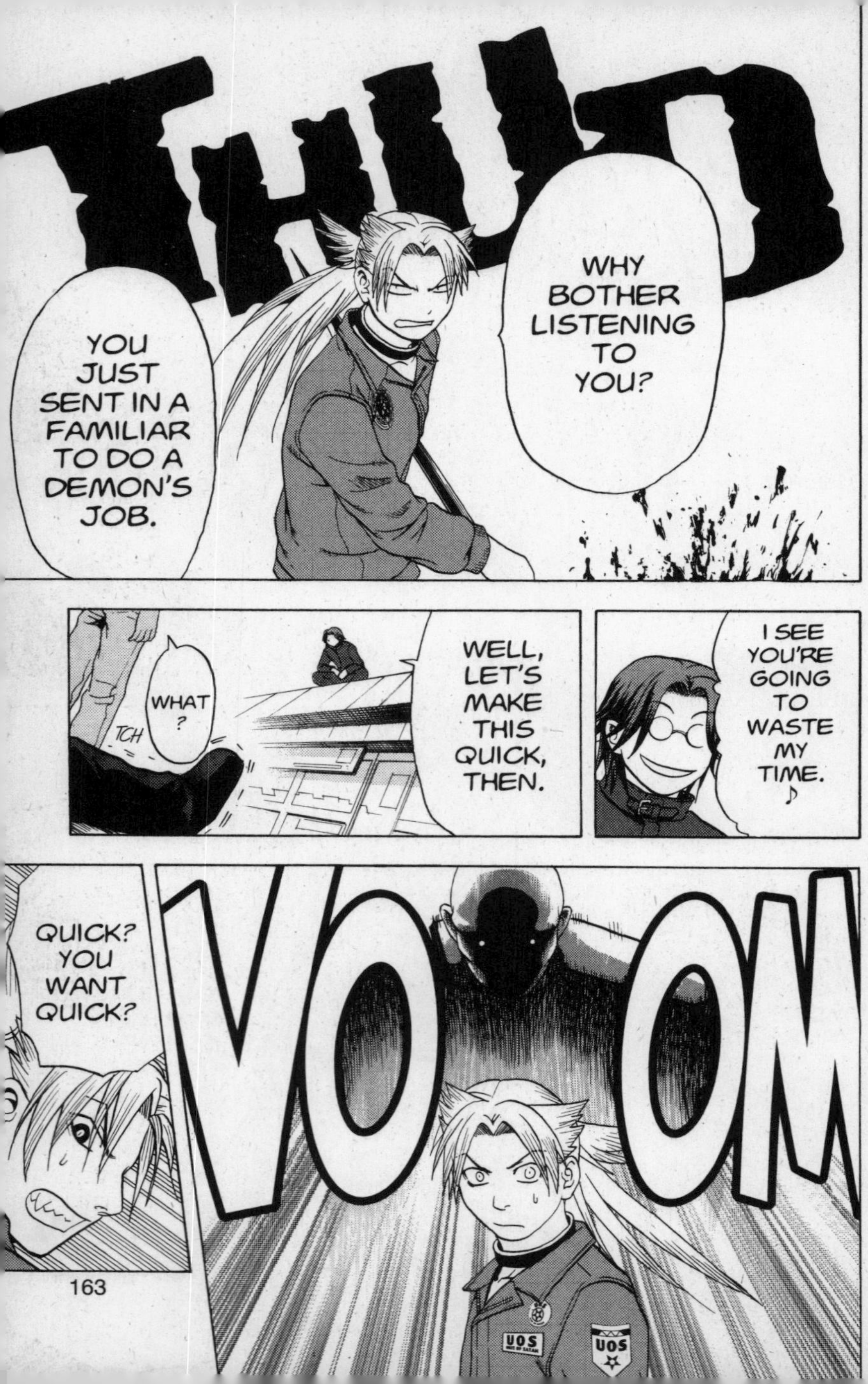
THUD
WHY BOTHER LISTENING TO YOU?
YOU JUST SENT IN A FAMILIAR TO DO A DEMON'S JOB.
I SEE YOU'RE GOING TO WASTE MY TIME. ♪
WELL, LET'S MAKE THIS QUICK, THEN.
WHAT?
TCH
VOOM
QUICK? YOU WANT QUICK?

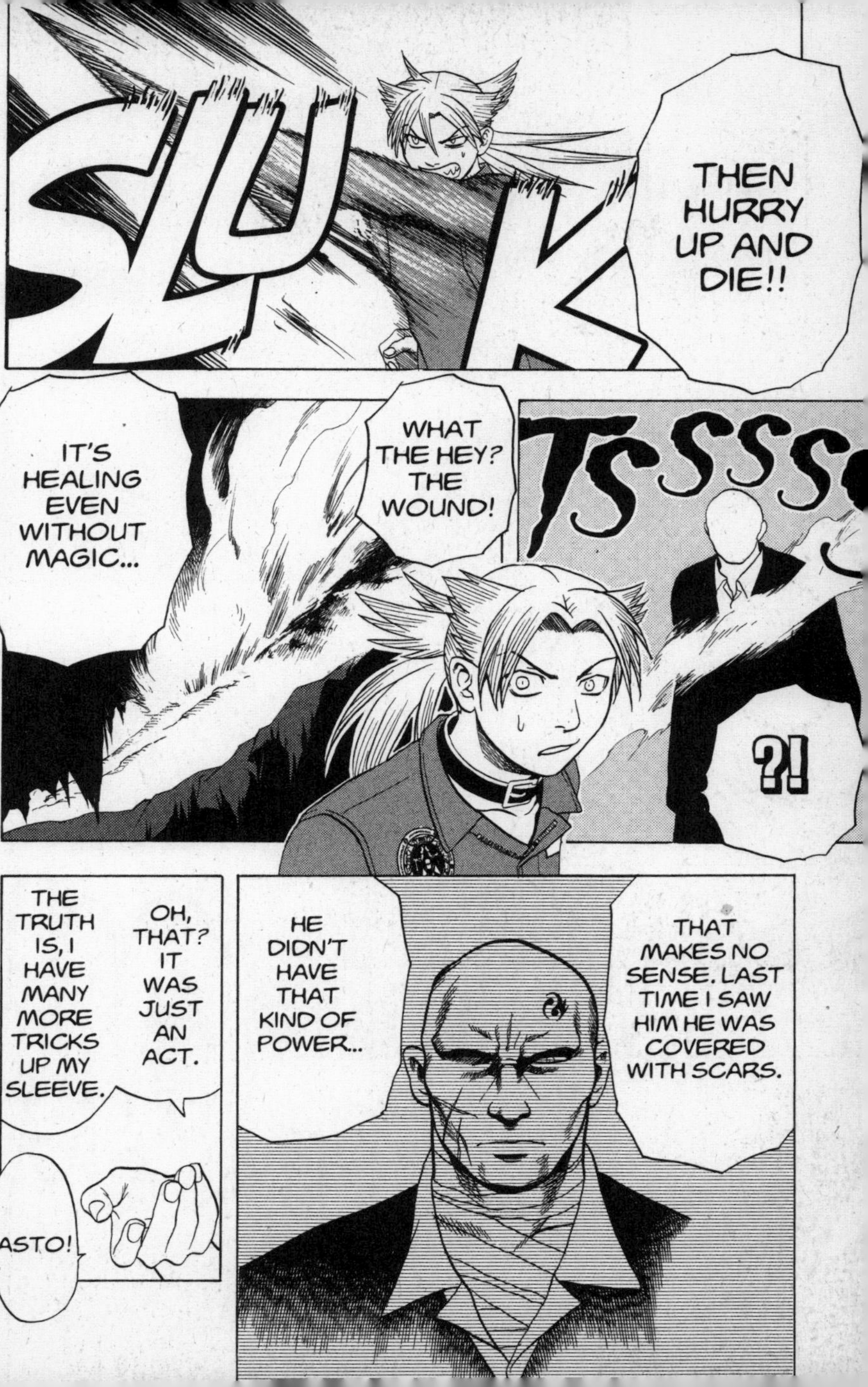
THEN HURRY UP AND DIE!!
SLUK
TSSSS
?!
WHAT THE HEY? THE WOUND!
IT'S HEALING EVEN WITHOUT MAGIC...
THAT MAKES NO SENSE. LAST TIME I SAW HIM HE WAS COVERED WITH SCARS.
HE DIDN'T HAVE THAT KIND OF POWER...
OH, THAT? IT WAS JUST AN ACT.
THE TRUTH IS, I HAVE MANY MORE TRICKS UP MY SLEEVE.
ASTO!

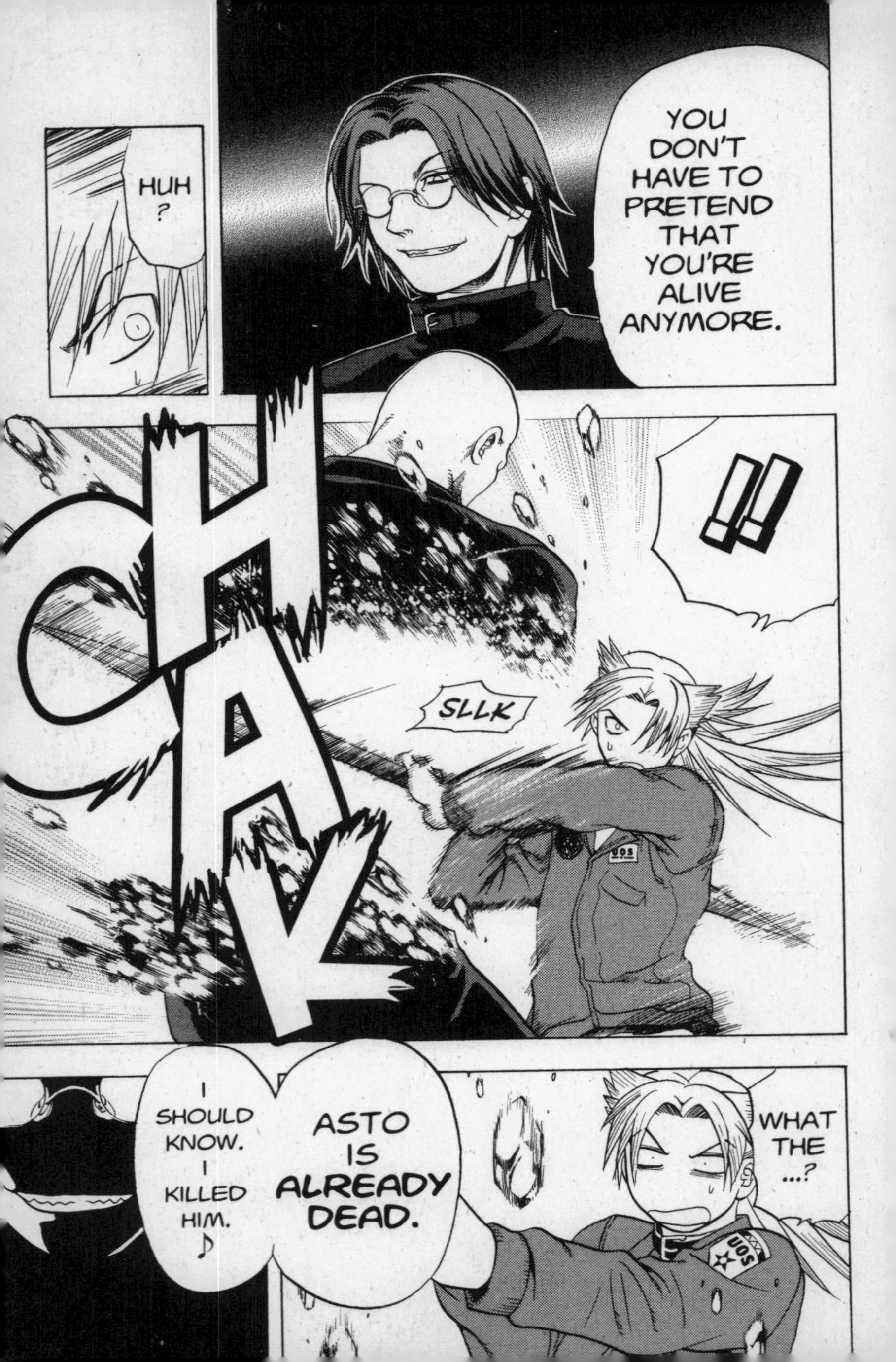
YOU DON'T HAVE TO PRETEND THAT YOU'RE ALIVE ANYMORE.
HUH?
!!
SLLK
CHAK
WHAT THE ...?
ASTO IS ALREADY DEAD.
I SHOULD KNOW. I KILLED HIM. ♪

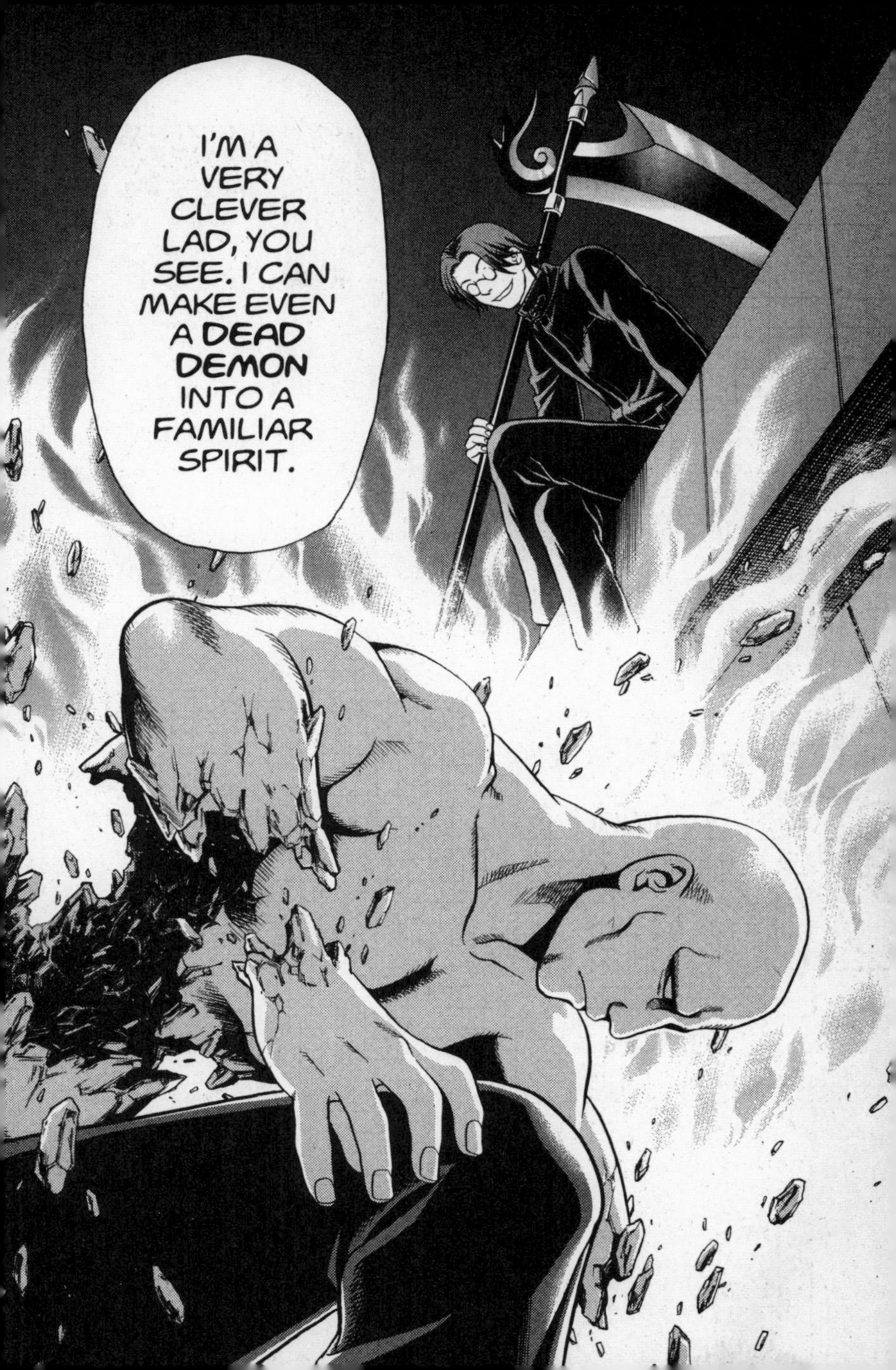
I'M A VERY CLEVER LAD, YOU SEE. I CAN MAKE EVEN A DEAD DEMON INTO A FAMILIAR SPIRIT.

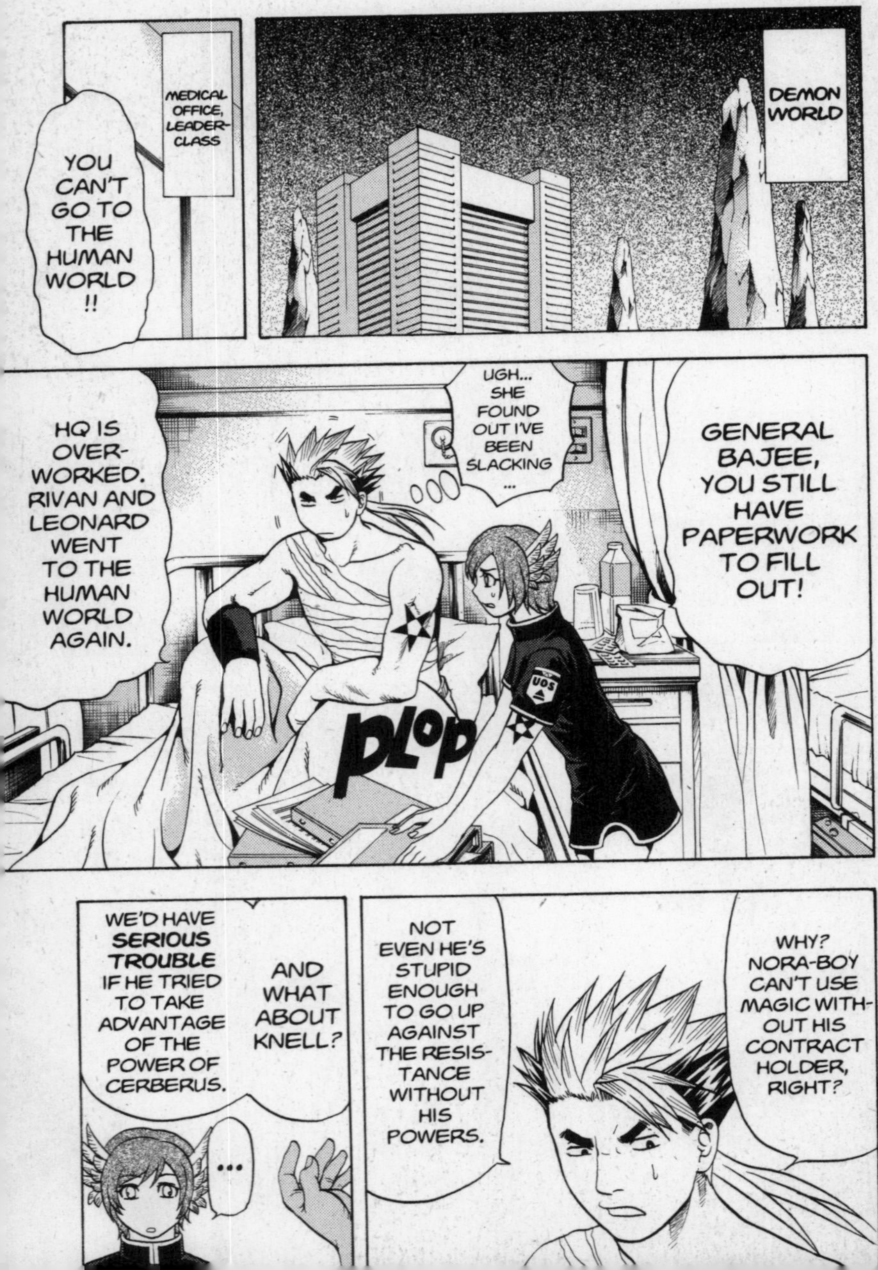
DEMON WORLD
MEDICAL OFFICE, LEADER-CLASS
YOU CAN'T GO TO THE HUMAN WORLD!!
GENERAL BAJEE, YOU STILL HAVE PAPERWORK TO FILL OUT!
UGH... SHE FOUND OUT I'VE BEEN SLACKING...
HQ IS OVERWORKED. RIVAN AND LEONARD WENT TO THE HUMAN WORLD AGAIN.
PLOP
WHY? NORA-BOY CAN'T USE MAGIC WITHOUT HIS CONTRACT HOLDER, RIGHT?
NOT EVEN HE'S STUPID ENOUGH TO GO UP AGAINST THE RESISTANCE WITHOUT HIS POWERS.
AND WHAT ABOUT KNELL?
WE'D HAVE **SERIOUS TROUBLE** IF HE TRIED TO TAKE ADVANTAGE OF THE POWER OF CERBERUS.
...

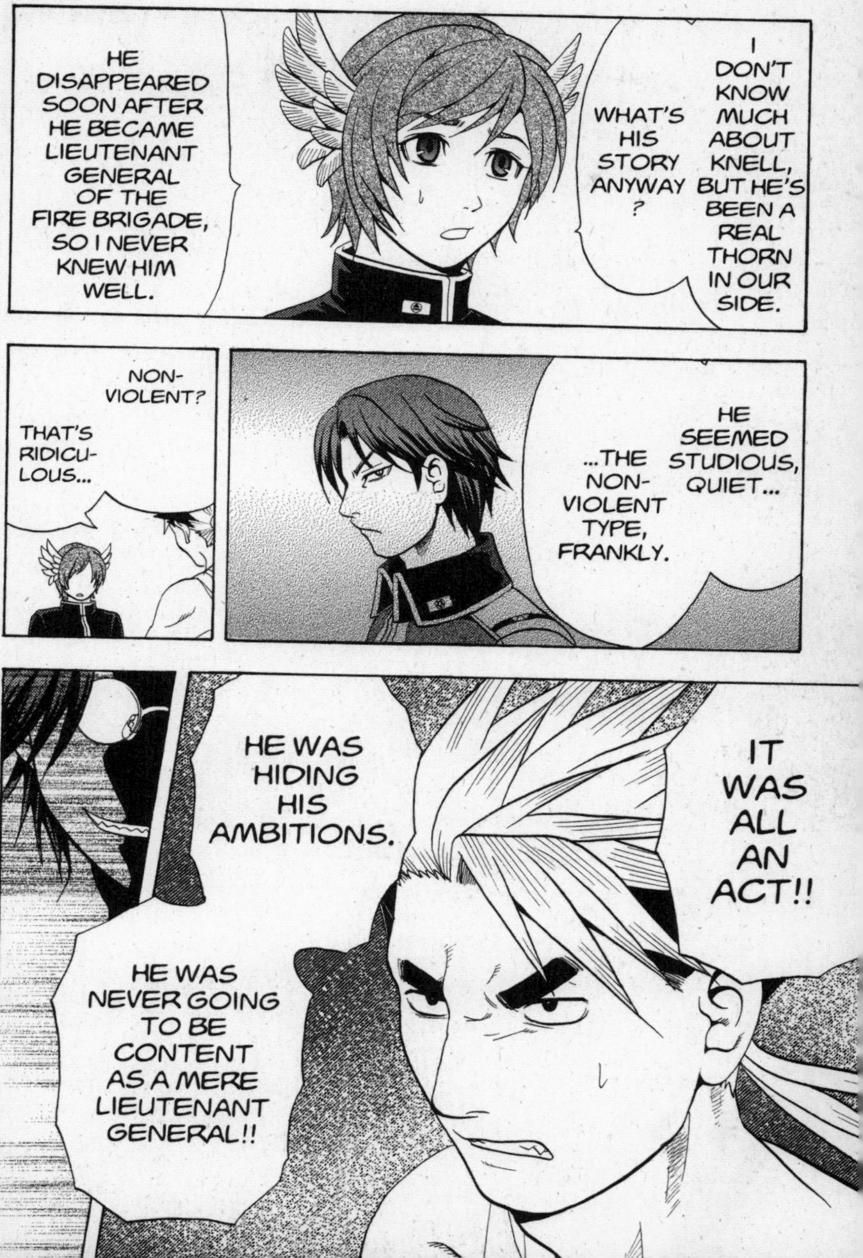
I DON'T KNOW MUCH ABOUT KNELL, BUT HE'S BEEN A REAL THORN IN OUR SIDE.
WHAT'S HIS STORY ANYWAY?
HE DISAPPEARED SOON AFTER HE BECAME LIEUTENANT GENERAL OF THE FIRE BRIGADE, SO I NEVER KNEW HIM WELL.
HE SEEMED STUDIOUS, QUIET...
...THE NON-VIOLENT TYPE, FRANKLY.
NON-VIOLENT?
THAT'S RIDICULOUS...
IT WAS ALL AN ACT!!
HE WAS HIDING HIS AMBITIONS.
HE WAS NEVER GOING TO BE CONTENT AS A MERE LIEUTENANT GENERAL!!

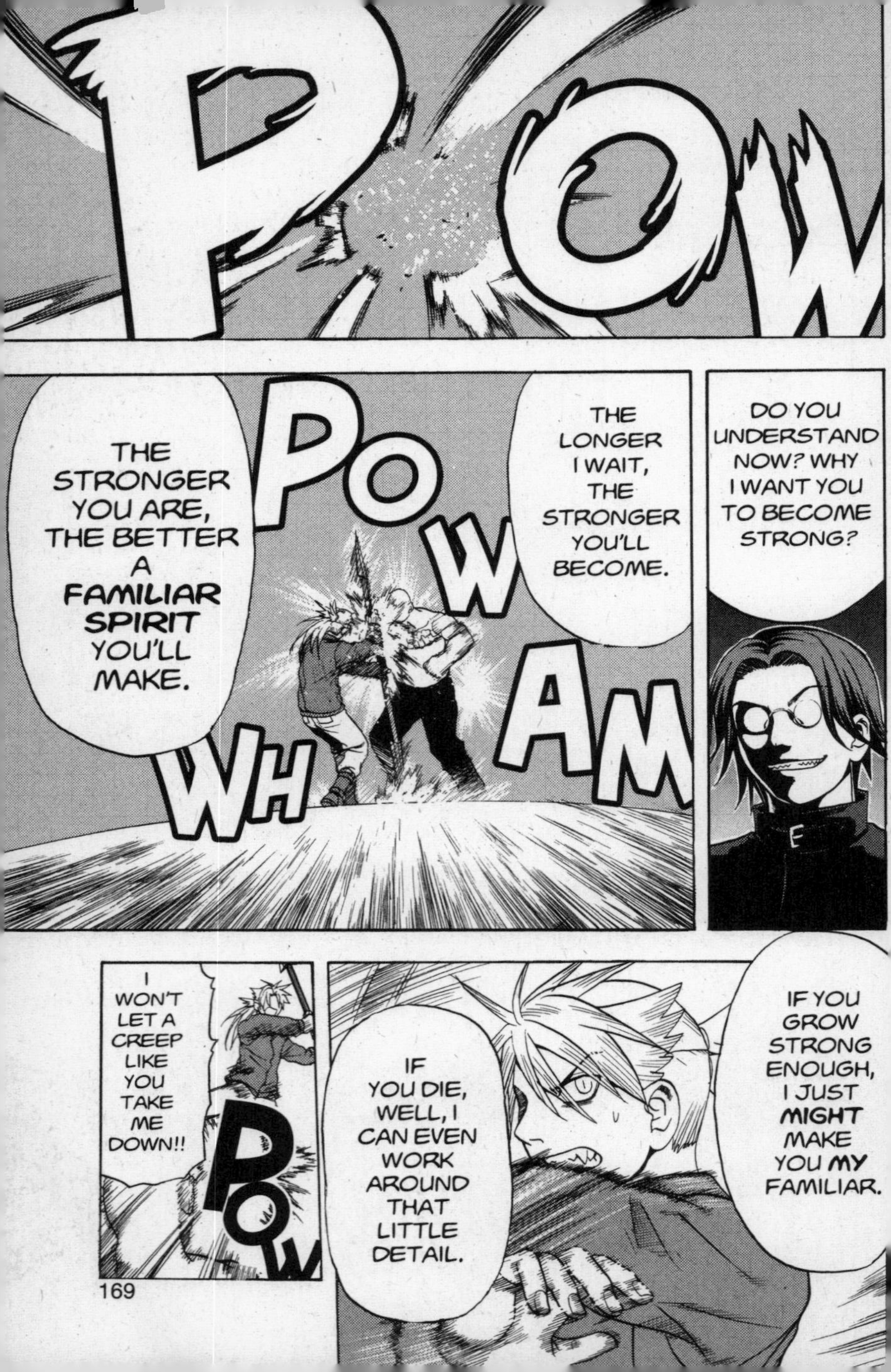
POW
DO YOU UNDERSTAND NOW? WHY I WANT YOU TO BECOME STRONG?
THE LONGER I WAIT, THE STRONGER YOU'LL BECOME.
THE STRONGER YOU ARE, THE BETTER A **FAMILIAR SPIRIT** YOU'LL MAKE.
POW
WHAM
IF YOU GROW STRONG ENOUGH, I JUST **MIGHT** MAKE YOU **MY** FAMILIAR.
IF YOU DIE, WELL, I CAN EVEN WORK AROUND THAT LITTLE DETAIL.
I WON'T LET A CREEP LIKE YOU TAKE ME DOWN!!
POW

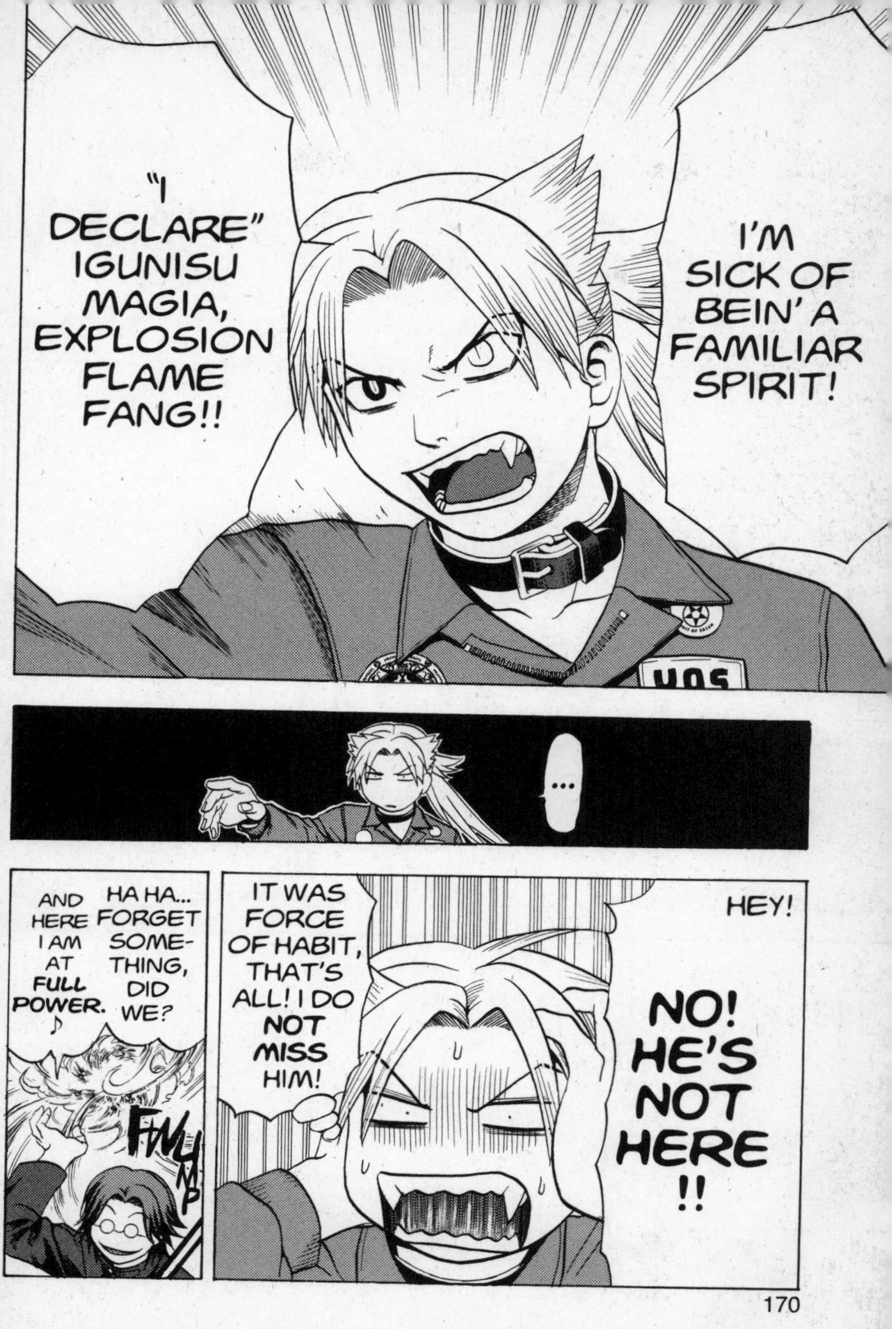
I'M SICK OF BEIN' A FAMILIAR SPIRIT!
"I DECLARE" IGUNISU MAGIA, EXPLOSION FLAME FANG!!
UOS
...
HEY!
NO! HE'S NOT HERE!!
IT WAS FORCE OF HABIT, THAT'S ALL! I DO NOT MISS HIM!
HA HA... FORGET SOME-THING, DID WE?
AND HERE I AM AT FULL POWER. ♪
FWUMP

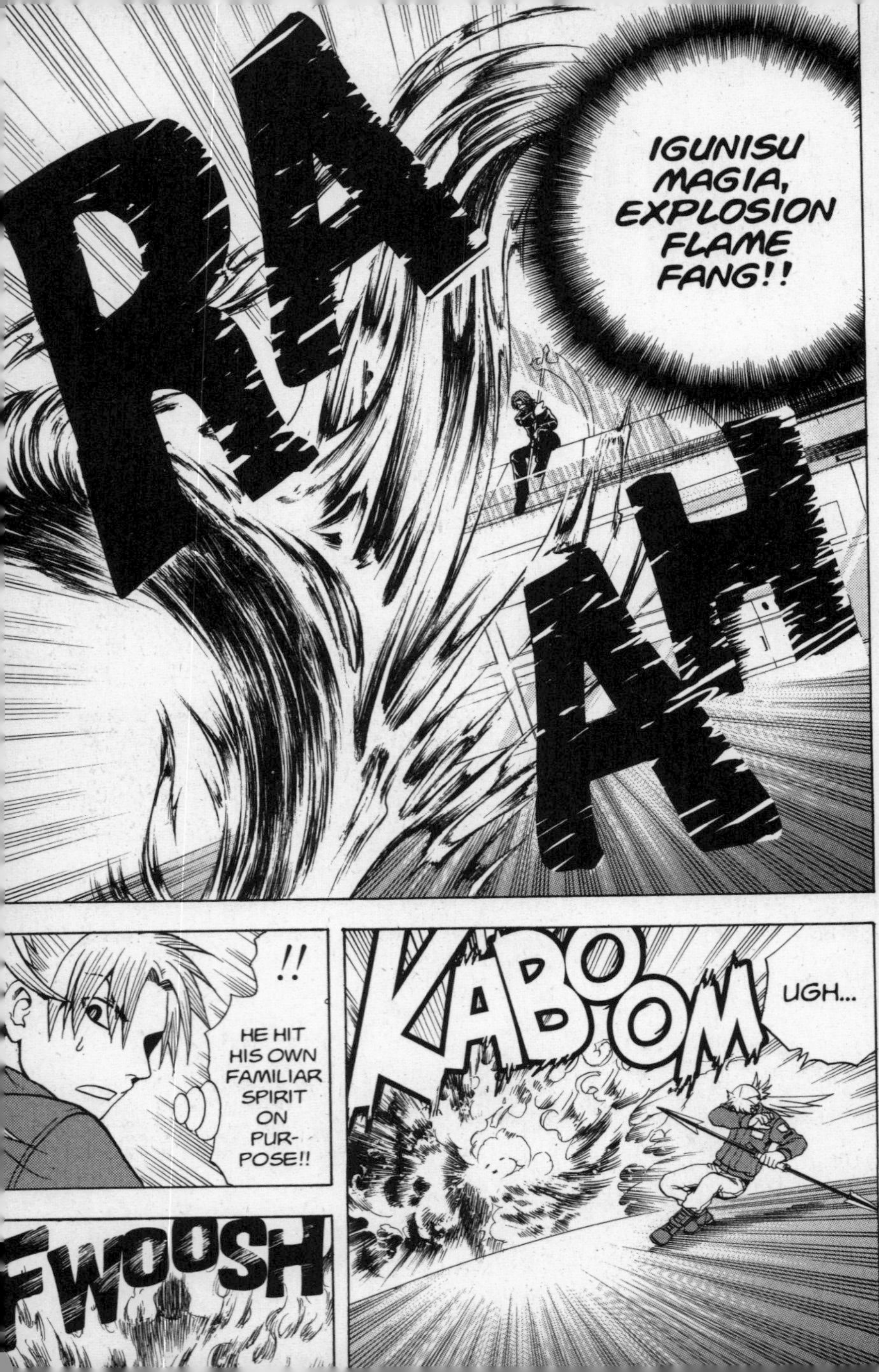
IGUNISU MAGIA, EXPLOSION FLAME FANG!!
RAAH
KABOOM
UGH...
!!
HE HIT HIS OWN FAMILIAR SPIRIT ON PUR-POSE!!
FWOOSH

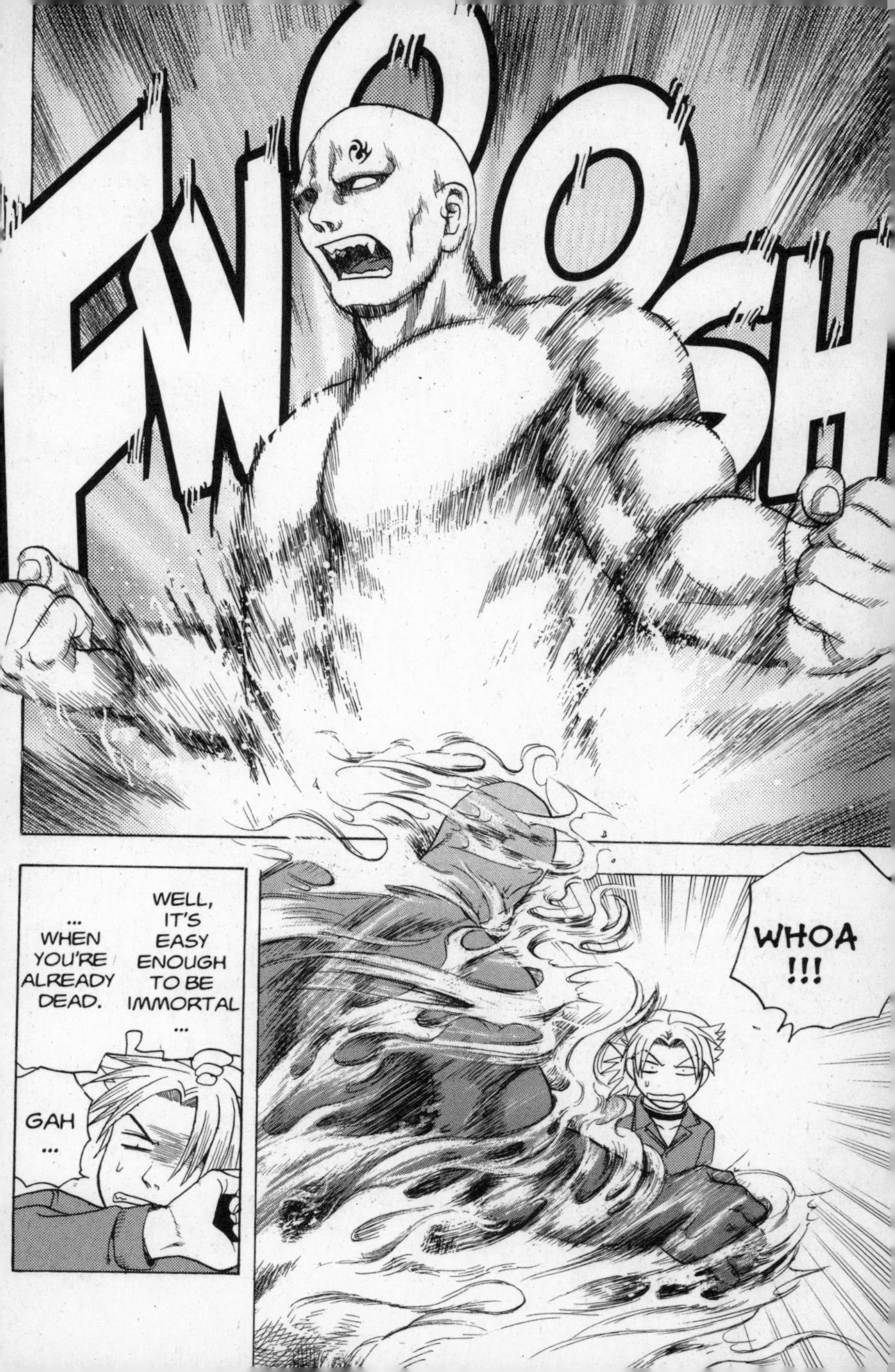
FWOOSH
WHOA !!!
WELL, IT'S EASY ENOUGH TO BE IMMORTAL ...
... WHEN YOU'RE ALREADY DEAD.
GAH ...

« READ THIS WAY «

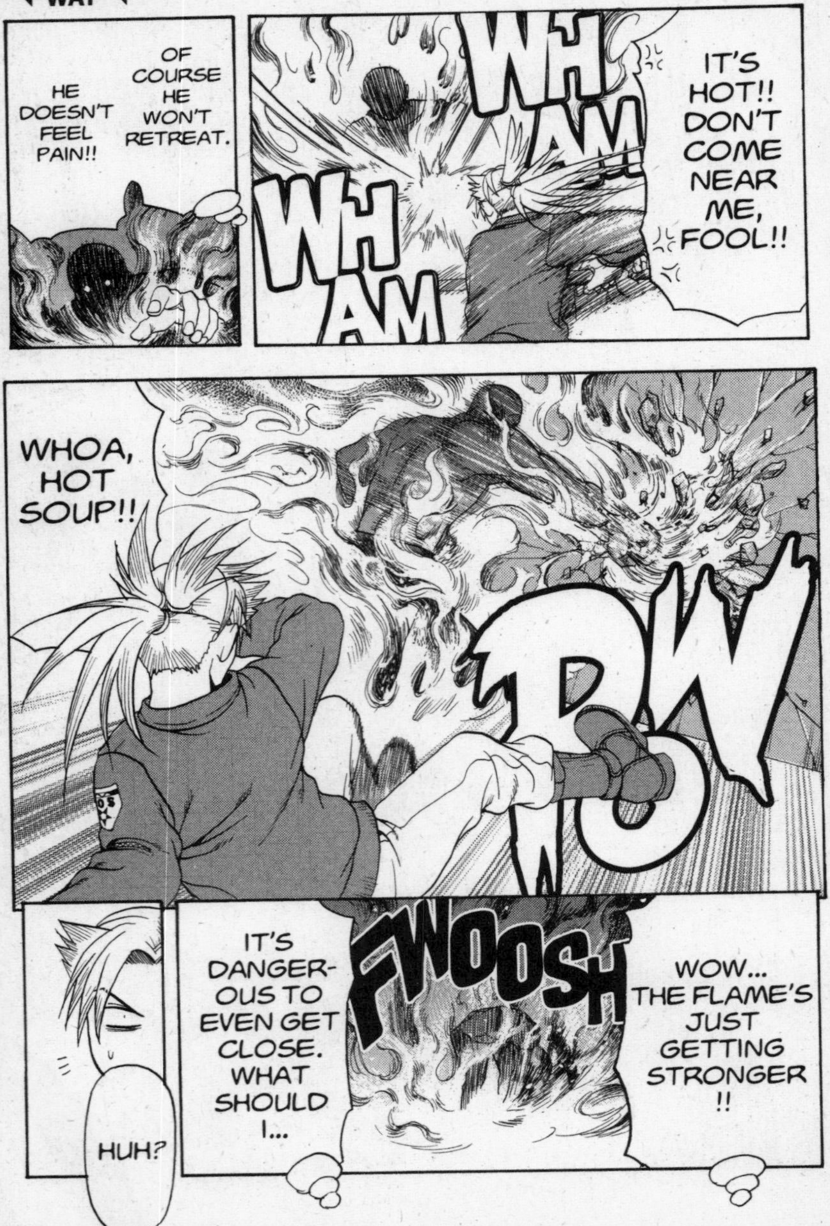
WHAM
WHAM
IT'S HOT!! DON'T COME NEAR ME, FOOL!!
OF COURSE HE WON'T RETREAT.
HE DOESN'T FEEL PAIN!!
WHOA, HOT SOUP!!
WOW... THE FLAME'S JUST GETTING STRONGER!!
FWOOSH
IT'S DANGER-OUS TO EVEN GET CLOSE. WHAT SHOULD I...
HUH?

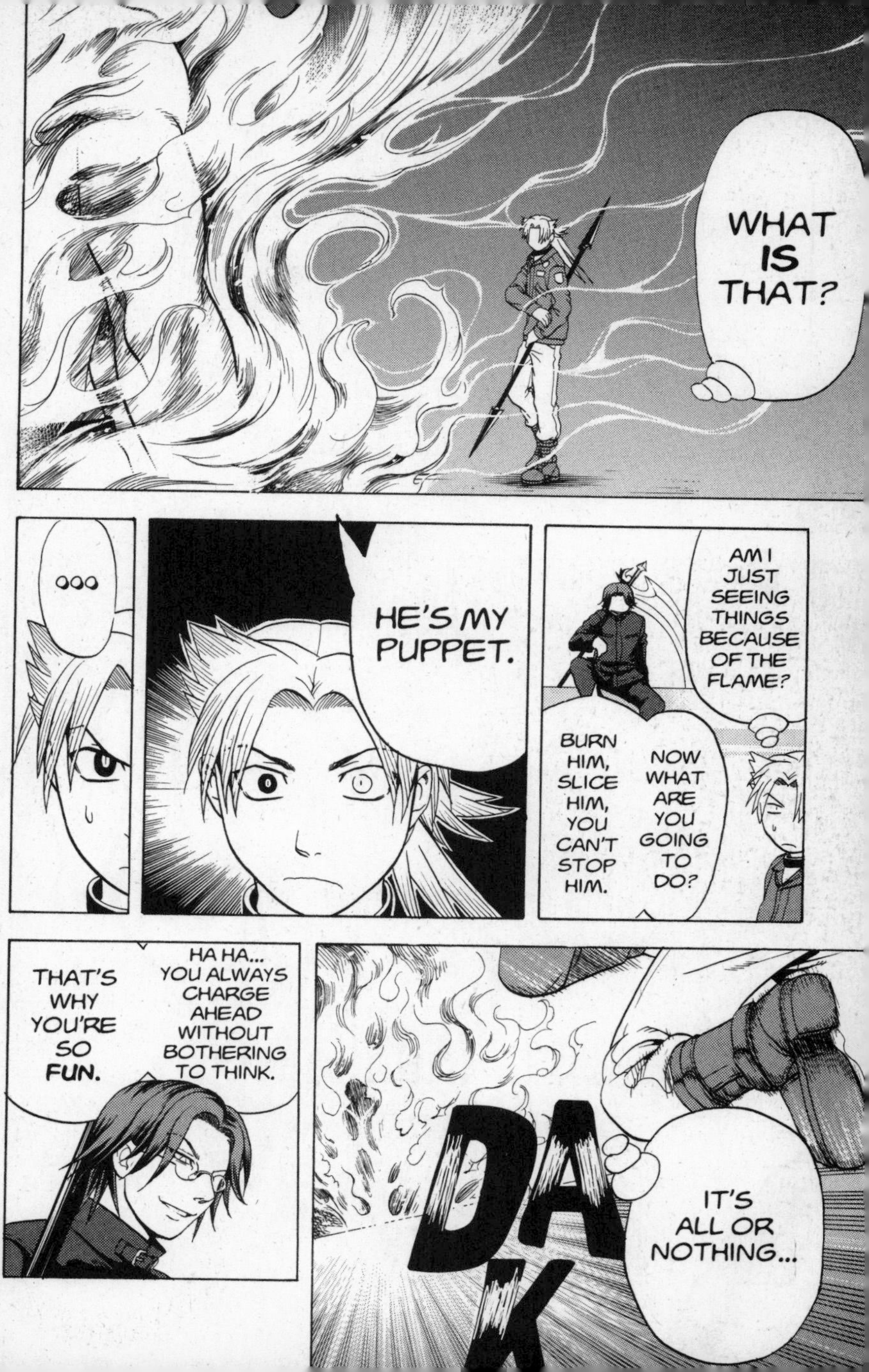
WHAT **IS** THAT?
AM I JUST SEEING THINGS BECAUSE OF THE FLAME?
NOW WHAT ARE YOU GOING TO DO?
BURN HIM, SLICE HIM, YOU CAN'T STOP HIM.
HE'S MY PUPPET.
...
DAK
IT'S ALL OR NOTHING...
HA HA... YOU ALWAYS CHARGE AHEAD WITHOUT BOTHERING TO THINK.
THAT'S WHY YOU'RE SO **FUN**.

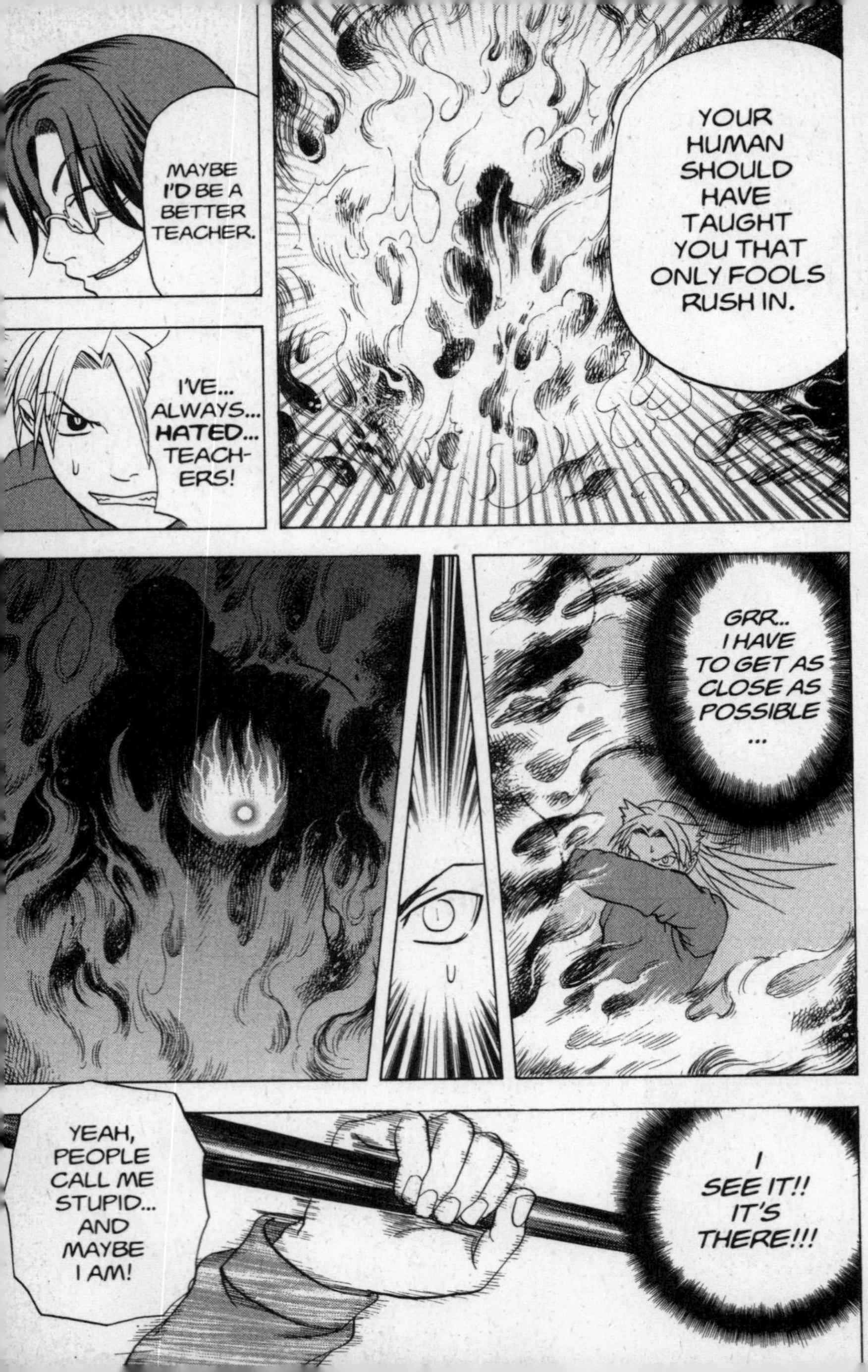
YOUR HUMAN SHOULD HAVE TAUGHT YOU THAT ONLY FOOLS RUSH IN.
MAYBE I'D BE A BETTER TEACHER.
I'VE... ALWAYS... HATED... TEACHERS!
GRR.. I HAVE TO GET AS CLOSE AS POSSIBLE ...
I SEE IT!! IT'S THERE!!!
YEAH, PEOPLE CALL ME STUPID... AND MAYBE I AM!

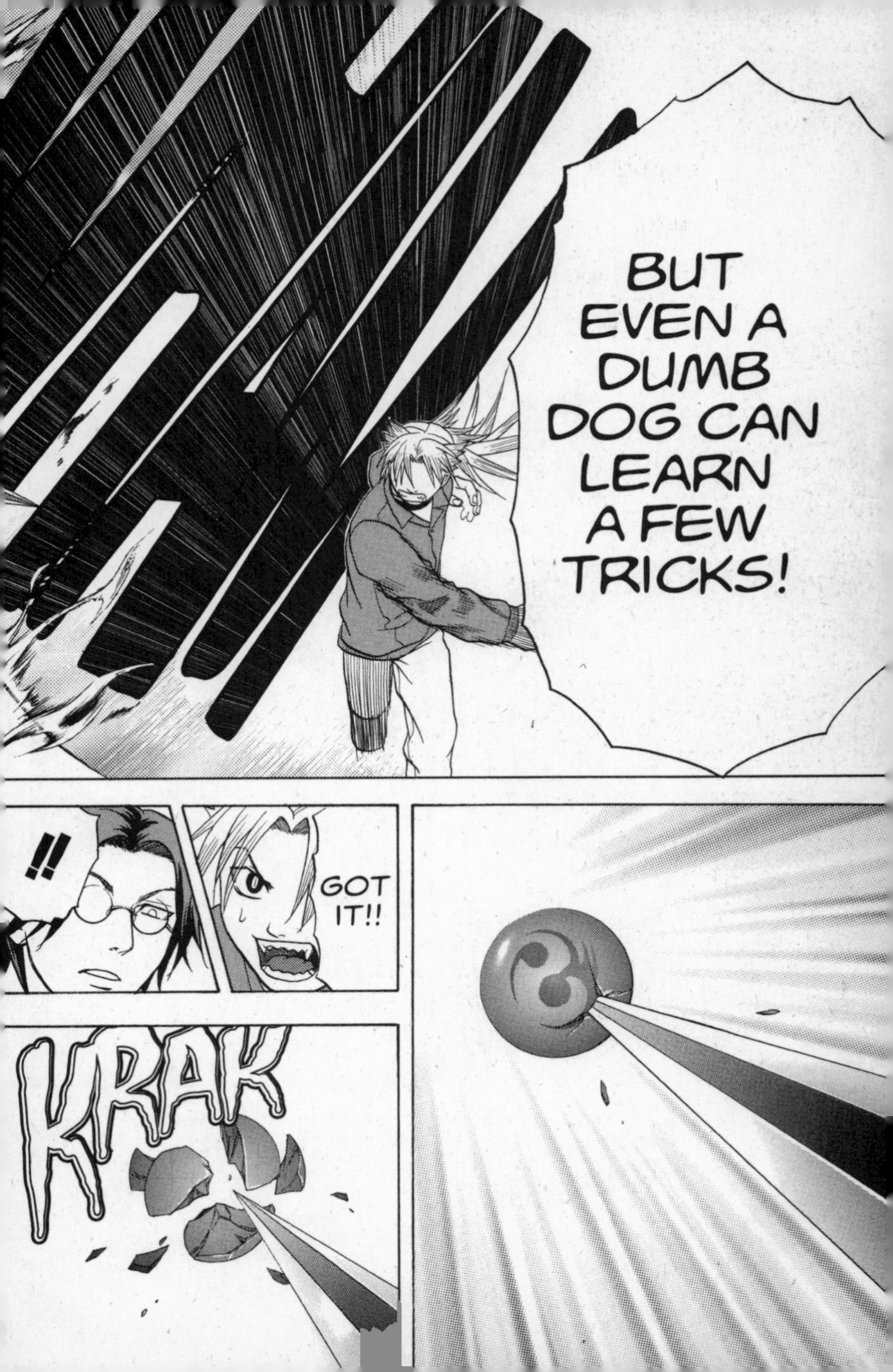
BUT EVEN A DUMB DOG CAN LEARN A FEW TRICKS!
GOT IT!!
!!
KRAK

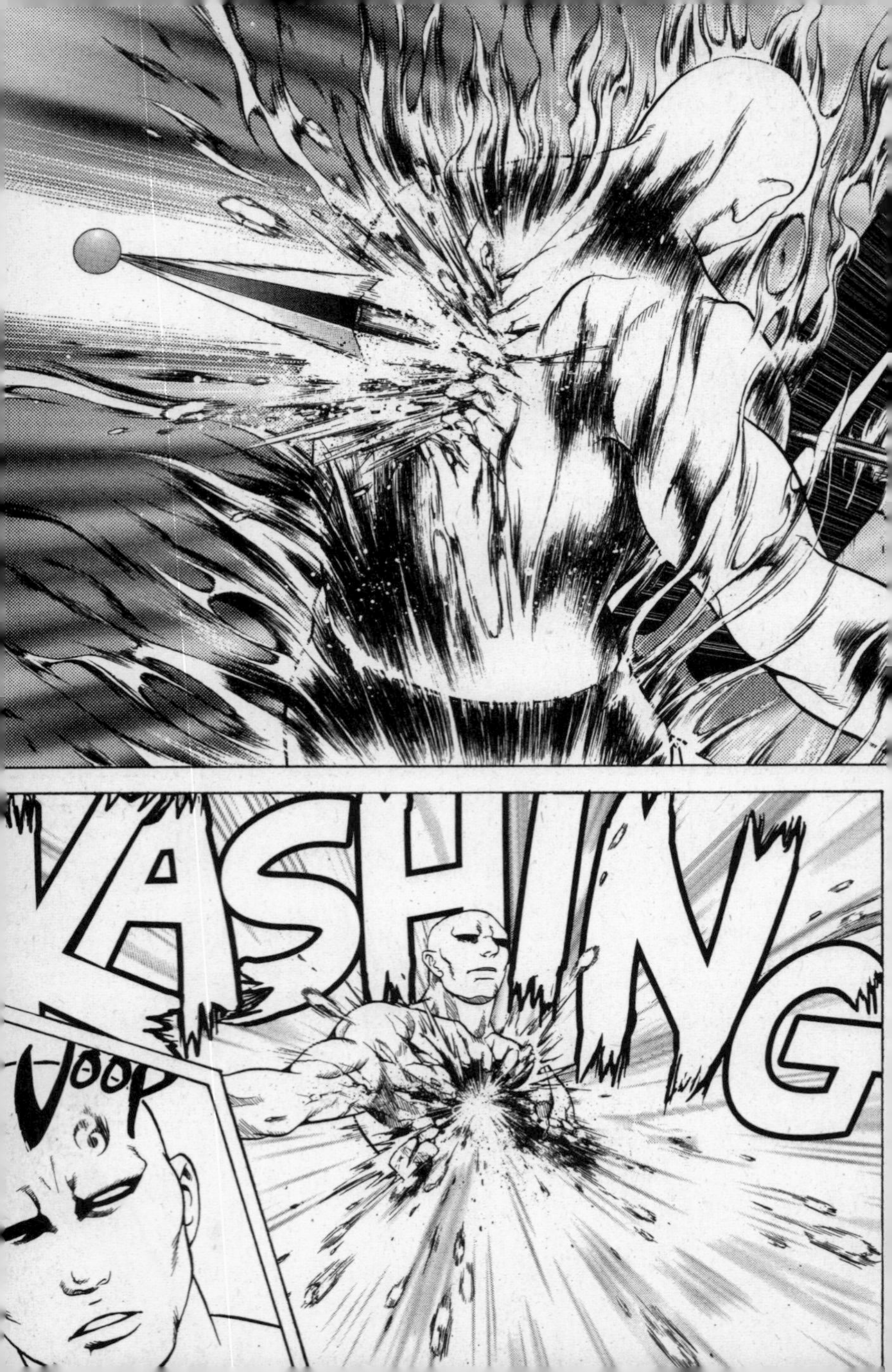
VASHING
JOOP

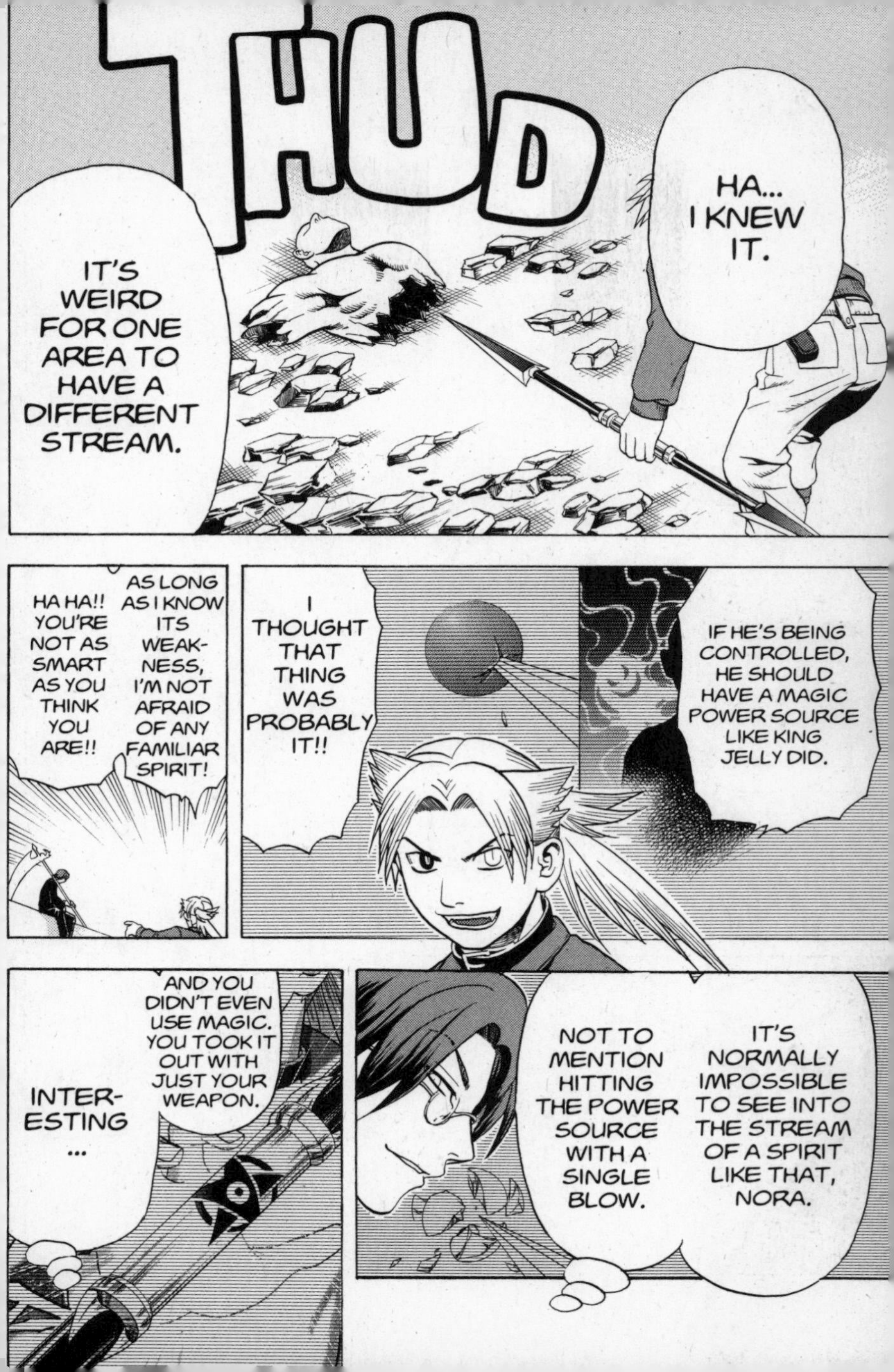
THUD
HA... I KNEW IT.
IT'S WEIRD FOR ONE AREA TO HAVE A DIFFERENT STREAM.
IF HE'S BEING CONTROLLED, HE SHOULD HAVE A MAGIC POWER SOURCE LIKE KING JELLY DID.
I THOUGHT THAT THING WAS PROBABLY IT!!
AS LONG AS I KNOW ITS WEAK-NESS, I'M NOT AFRAID OF ANY FAMILIAR SPIRIT!
HA HA!! YOU'RE NOT AS SMART AS YOU THINK YOU ARE!!
IT'S NORMALLY IMPOSSIBLE TO SEE INTO THE STREAM OF A SPIRIT LIKE THAT, NORA.
NOT TO MENTION HITTING THE POWER SOURCE WITH A SINGLE BLOW.
AND YOU DIDN'T EVEN USE MAGIC. YOU TOOK IT OUT WITH JUST YOUR WEAPON.
INTER-ESTING ...

READ THIS WAY

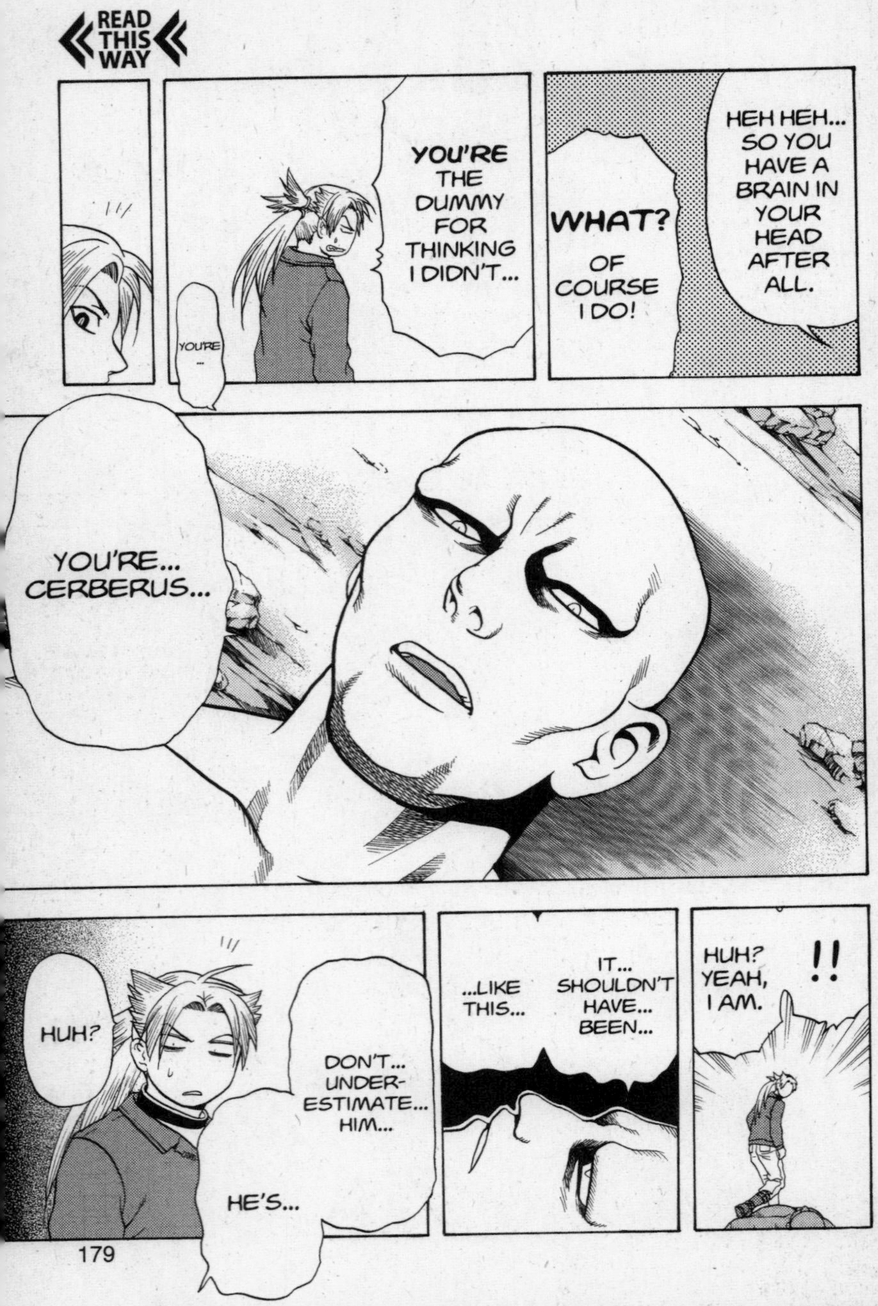

HEH HEH... SO YOU HAVE A BRAIN IN YOUR HEAD AFTER ALL.
WHAT? OF COURSE I DO!
YOU'RE THE DUMMY FOR THINKING I DIDN'T...
YOU'RE ...
YOU'RE... CERBERUS...
!!
HUH? YEAH, I AM.
IT... SHOULDN'T HAVE... BEEN...
...LIKE THIS...
DON'T... UNDER-ESTIMATE... HIM...
HUH?
HE'S...

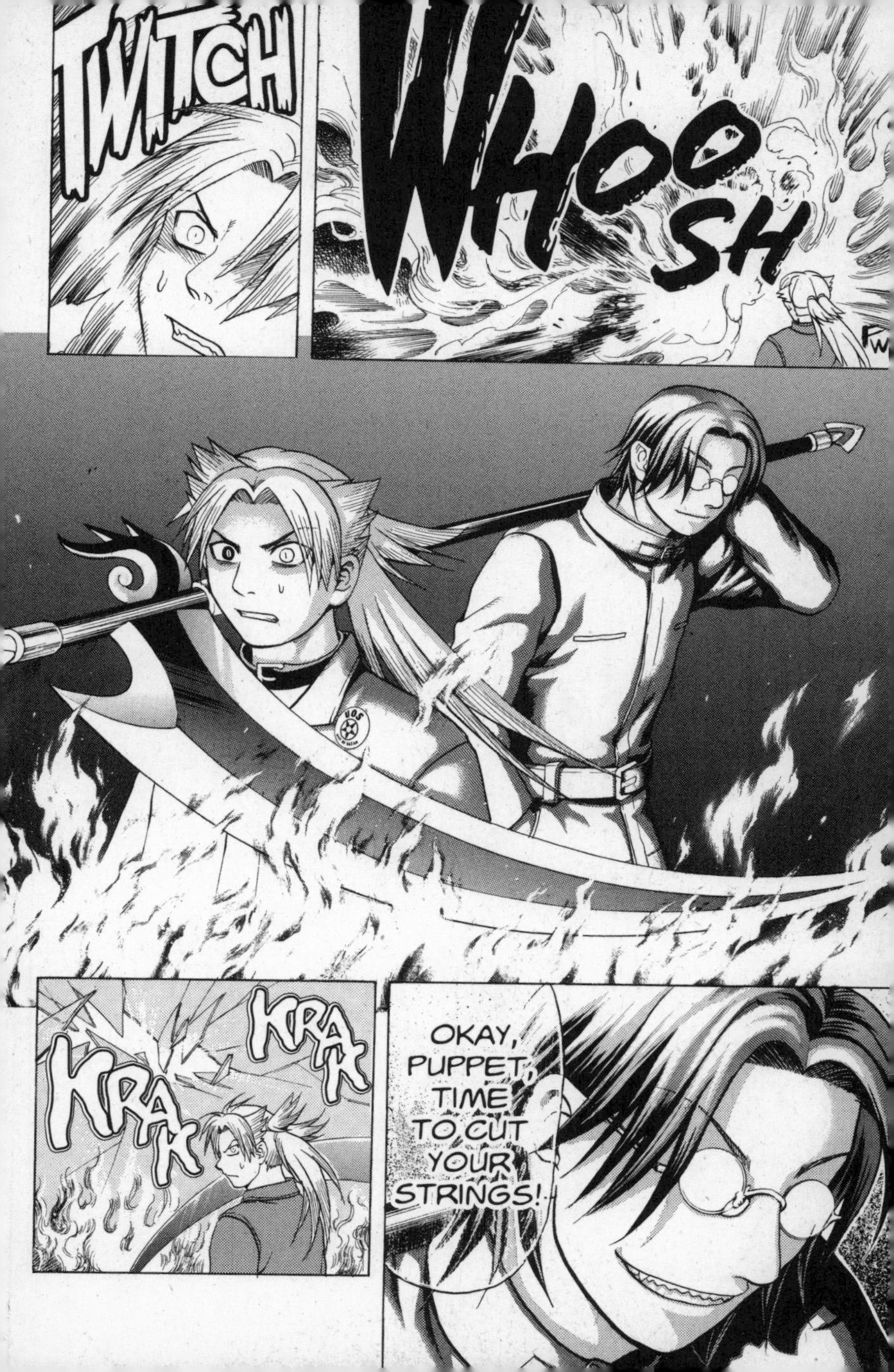
WHOOSH
FW
TWITCH
OKAY, PUPPET, TIME TO CUT YOUR STRINGS!
KRAK
KRAK

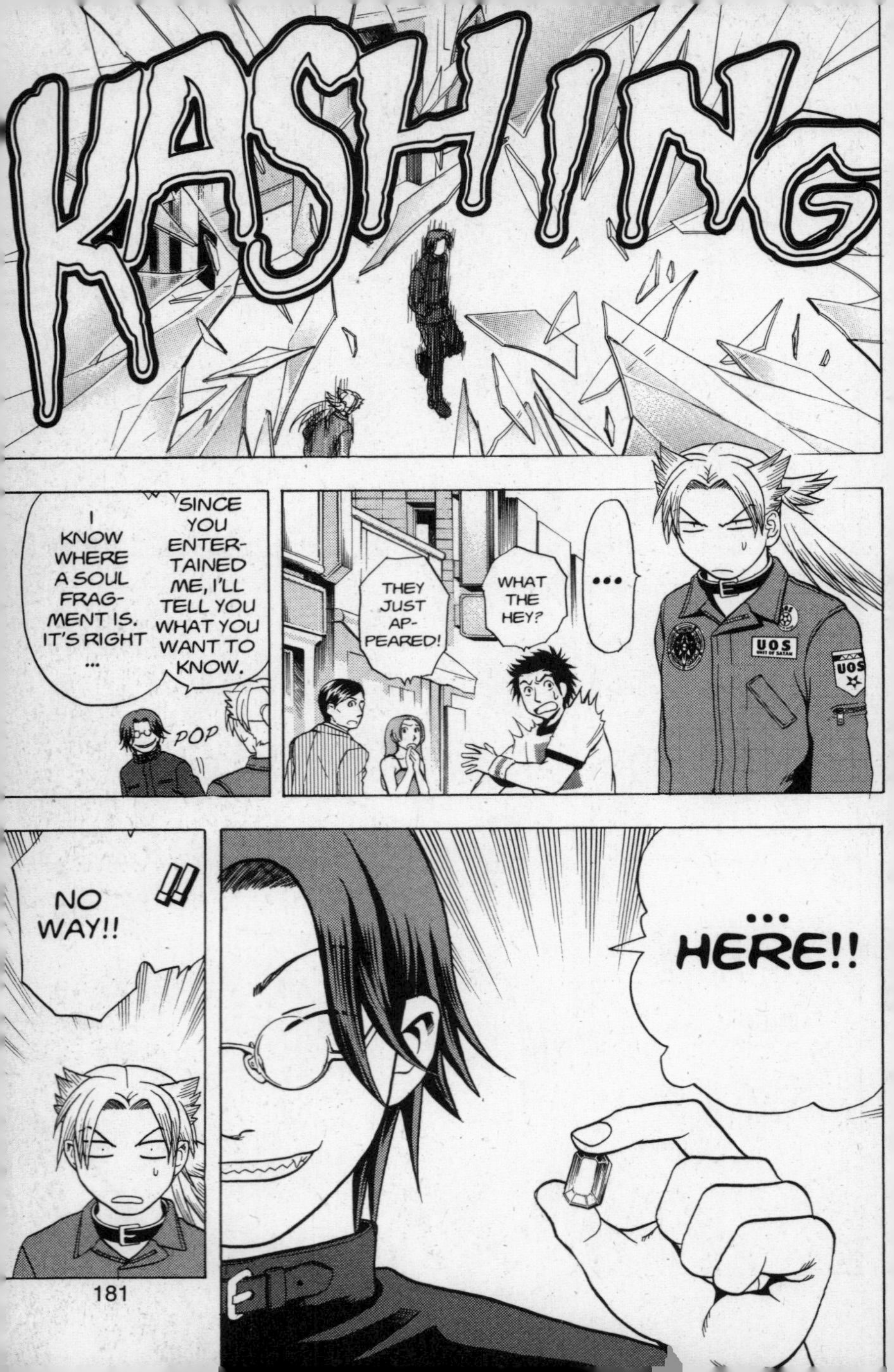
KASHING
...
WHAT THE HEY?
THEY JUST APPEARED!
SINCE YOU ENTERTAINED ME, I'LL TELL YOU WHAT YOU WANT TO KNOW.
I KNOW WHERE A SOUL FRAGMENT IS. IT'S RIGHT ...
POP
... HERE!!
!!
NO WAY!!

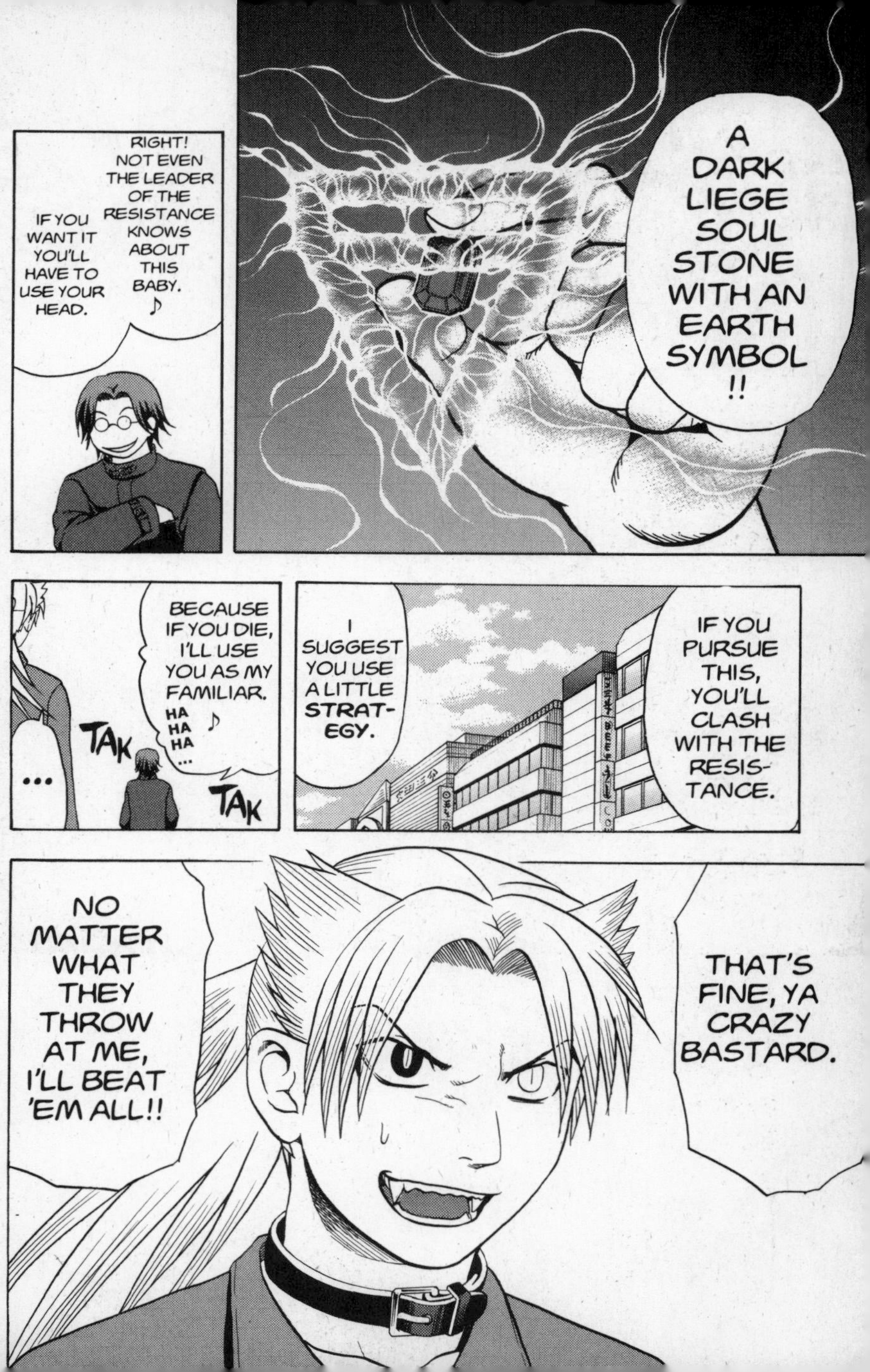
A DARK LIEGE SOUL STONE WITH AN EARTH SYMBOL!!
RIGHT! NOT EVEN THE LEADER OF THE RESISTANCE KNOWS ABOUT THIS BABY. ♪
IF YOU WANT IT YOU'LL HAVE TO USE YOUR HEAD.
IF YOU PURSUE THIS, YOU'LL CLASH WITH THE RESISTANCE.
I SUGGEST YOU USE A LITTLE STRATEGY.
BECAUSE IF YOU DIE, I'LL USE YOU AS MY FAMILIAR.
HA HA HA... ♪
TAK
TAK
...
THAT'S FINE, YA CRAZY BASTARD.
NO MATTER WHAT THEY THROW AT ME, I'LL BEAT 'EM ALL!!

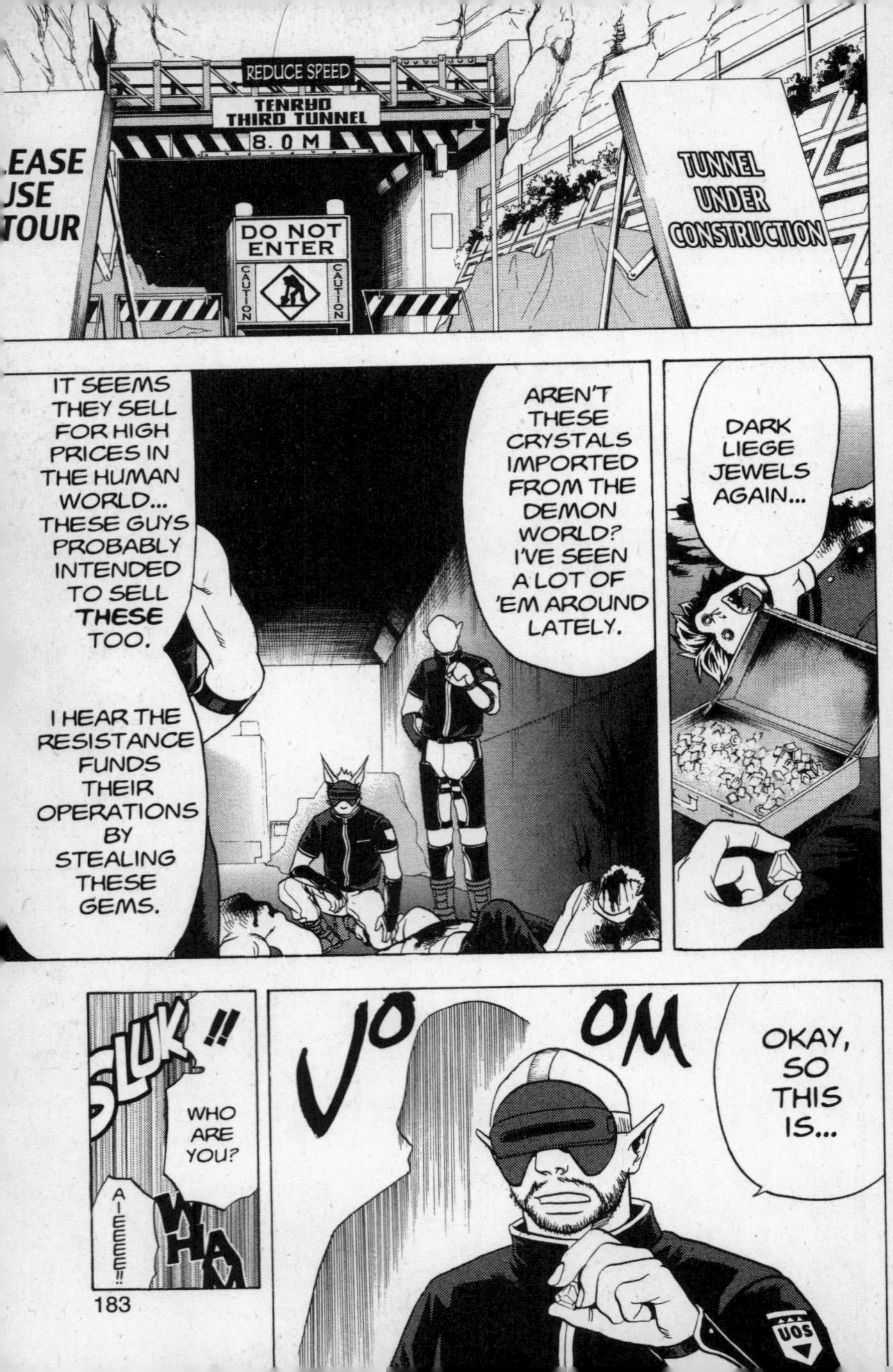
REDUCE SPEED
TENRYO THIRD TUNNEL
8.0 M
TUNNEL UNDER CONSTRUCTION
DO NOT ENTER
CAUTION
CAUTION
EASE
SE
TOUR
DARK LIEGE JEWELS AGAIN...
AREN'T THESE CRYSTALS IMPORTED FROM THE DEMON WORLD? I'VE SEEN A LOT OF 'EM AROUND LATELY.
IT SEEMS THEY SELL FOR HIGH PRICES IN THE HUMAN WORLD... THESE GUYS PROBABLY INTENDED TO SELL **THESE** TOO.
I HEAR THE RESISTANCE FUNDS THEIR OPERATIONS BY STEALING THESE GEMS.
VOOM
OKAY, SO THIS IS...
UOS
SLUK!!
WHO ARE YOU?
WHA
A-IEEEE!!

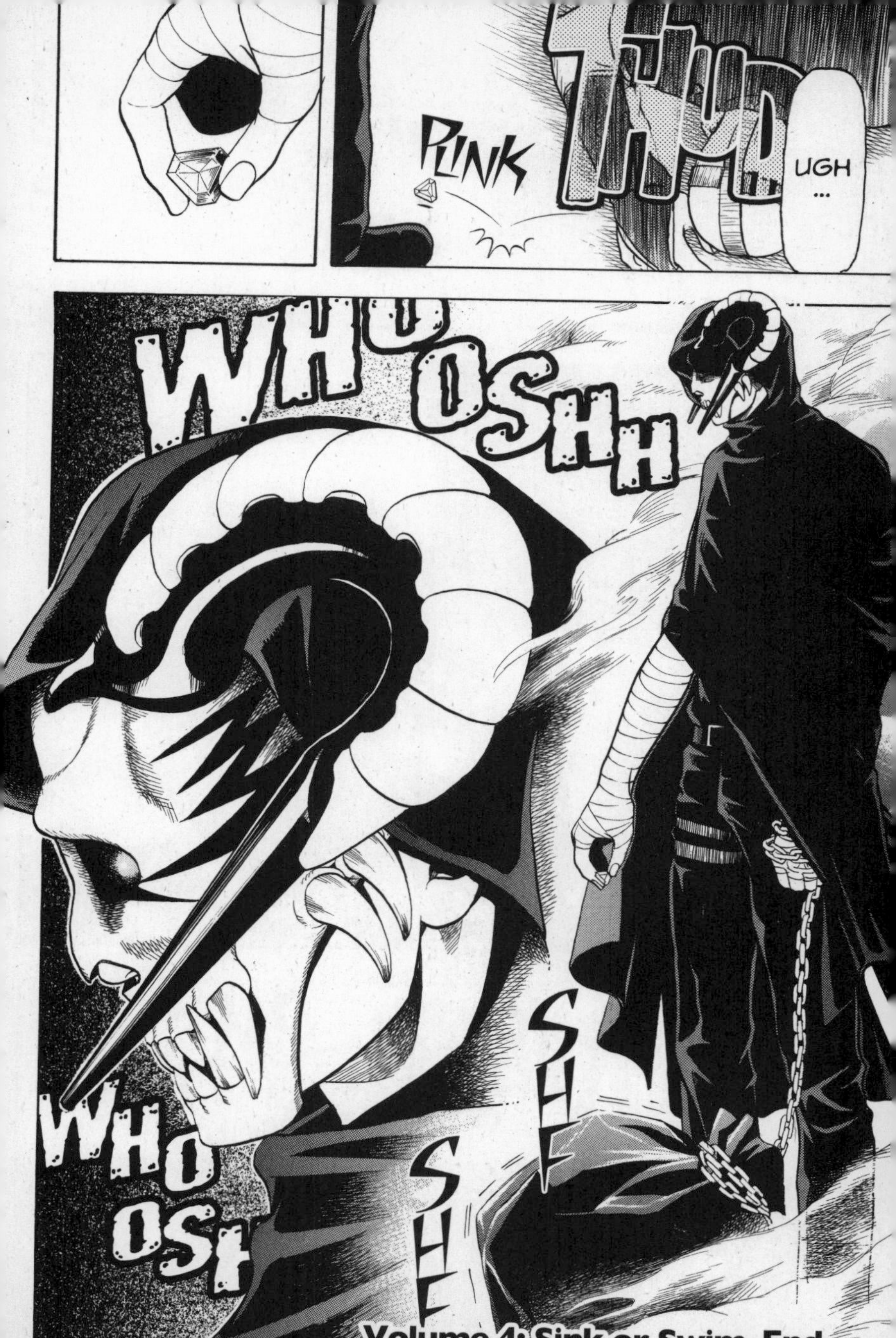
THUD
UGH ...
PLINK
WHOOSHH
SHF
SHF
WHOOS

Volume 4: Sink or Swim-End

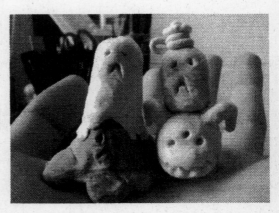

CREATED BY YOSHINON & DR. KOBAYASHI
(MADE FROM MODELING CLAY)

OLD HABITS DIE HARD

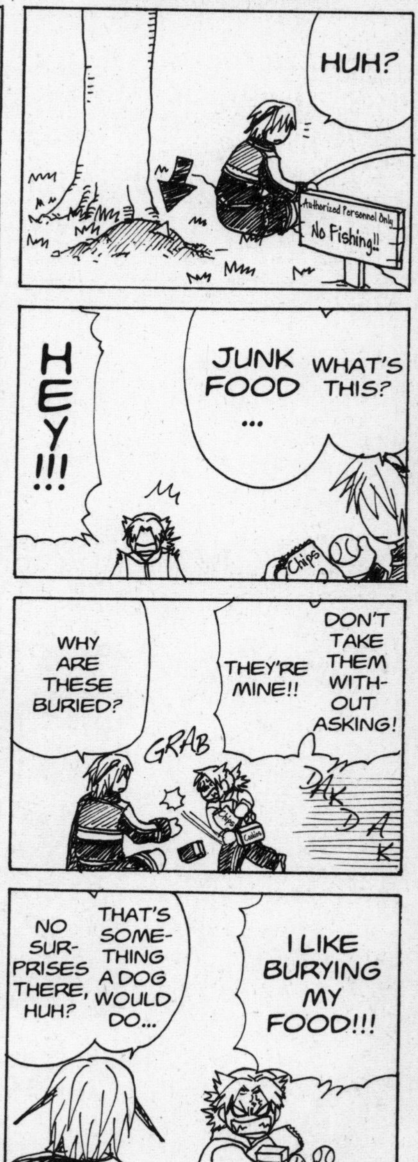
HUH?
Authorized Personnel Only
No Fishing!!
WHAT'S THIS?
JUNK FOOD ...
HEY!!!
Chips
DON'T TAKE THEM WITH-OUT ASKING!
THEY'RE MINE!!
WHY ARE THESE BURIED?
GRAB
DAK DAK
Chips
Cookies
I LIKE BURYING MY FOOD!!!
THAT'S SOME-THING A DOG WOULD DO...
NO SUR-PRISES THERE, HUH?

A MAGIC CALLED EXPERIENCE

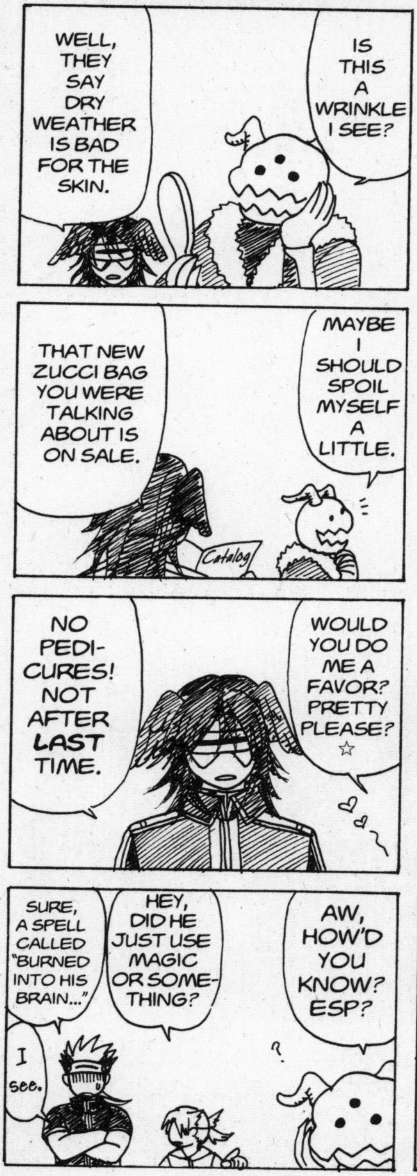
IS THIS A WRINKLE I SEE?
WELL, THEY SAY DRY WEATHER IS BAD FOR THE SKIN.
MAYBE I SHOULD SPOIL MYSELF A LITTLE.
THAT NEW ZUCCI BAG YOU WERE TALKING ABOUT IS ON SALE.
Catalog
WOULD YOU DO ME A FAVOR? PRETTY PLEASE? ☆
NO PEDI-CURES! NOT AFTER LAST TIME.
AW, HOW'D YOU KNOW? ESP?
HEY, DID HE JUST USE MAGIC OR SOME-THING?
SURE, A SPELL CALLED "BURNED INTO HIS BRAIN..."
I see.

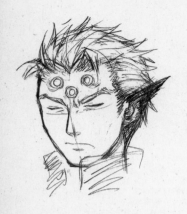

← LEONARD WITH A SEAL SPELL ON. THIS IS ONE OF THE DESIGN SKETCHES DONE BEFORE *NORA* WAS SERIALIZED. THE EXTENT OF THE SEAL SPELL IS DIFFERENT NOW. (HE APPEARS LIKE THIS ON THE TITLE PAGE FOR STORY 1). INITIALLY I PICTURED HIM AS MORE HIGH-STRUNG THAN HE TURNED OUT TO BE.

BAJEE'S CHANGED SINCE THE → EARLY DAYS. I ORIGINALLY IMAGINED HIM TO BE MORE AGGRESSIVE AND MORE LIKE A BIG-CITY TOKYO GUY. HE WAS SKINNIER TOO. THE MUSCLES CAME LATER.

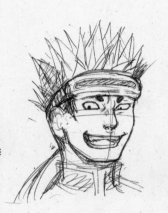

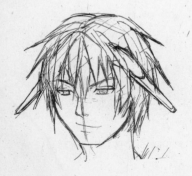

←I INITIALLY SAW RIVAN AS A VILLAINOUS CHARACTER, BUT THAT CHANGED.

BY THE WAY, STORY 5 (THE FIRST APPEARANCE OF THE DARK LIEGE ARMY) WAS GOING TO FEATURE RIVAN AND LEONARD, BUT IT DIDN'T QUITE WORK OUT.

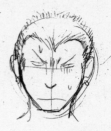

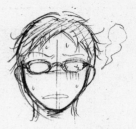

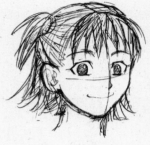

CHARACTER DESIGNS FOR THE STUDENT COUNCIL MEMBERS. REALLY, THEIR APPEARANCES AND CHARACTERS HAVEN'T CHANGED THAT MUCH.

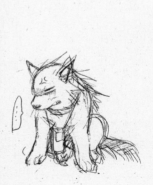

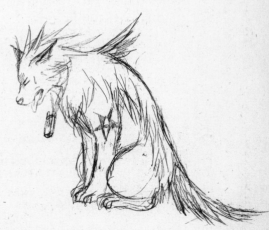

I INITIALLY WANTED NORA TO LOOK MORE DOG-LIKE, BUT I CHANGED MY MIND.

NORA MAILBAG

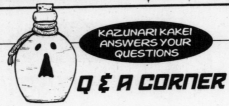

KAZUNARI KAKEI ANSWERS YOUR QUESTIONS

Q & A CORNER

Q : HOW MANY DIFFERENT TYPES OF MAGIC ARE THERE? ARE LOWER-LEVEL DEMONS ONLY ABLE TO USE ONE TYPE OF MAGIC? (MR. KEN ISHII, HOKKAIDO)

A : THERE ARE FIVE ELEMENTS OF MAGIC: FIRE, WATER, WIND, EARTH AND SOUL. A DEMON'S CLASS DOESN'T USUALLY AFFECT HIS OR HER ABILITIES. ALSO, NOT ALL DEMONS CAN USE MAGIC.

Q : BARIK HAS A GIRLFRIEND? TELL US MORE! (K AND FRIENDS, KANAGAWA PREFECTURE)

A : I WAS SURPRISED BY HOW MANY PEOPLE HAVE ASKED ME ABOUT HER...

* HER NAME IS LUCY.
* SHE'S A GOOD COOK.
* SHE'S SOMEWHAT FRAIL.
* SHE'S LOVELY. SHE'S ABOUT THE LUCKIEST THING THAT'S EVER HAPPENED TO HIM.
* ALTHOUGH I THINK IT'S A BIT MUSHY, PEOPLE SEEM TO LIKE THE IDEA OF BARIK HAVING A GIRLFRIEND.

Q : THERE SEEM TO BE TWO GENERALS IN THE FIRE BRIGADE... (NATSUMI KINEBUCHI AND OTHERS, NIIGATA PREFECTURE)

A : THERE'S A REASON FOR THAT. I MAY GET TO IT IN FUTURE VOLUMES OF NORA.

←CONTINUED ON THE NEXT PAGE...

NORA MAILBAG

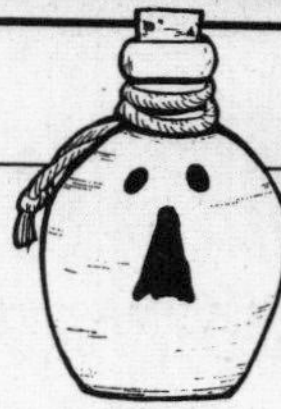

KAZUNARI KAKEI
ANSWERS YOUR
QUESTIONS

Q & A CORNER

Q : HOW OLD IS THE CAST OF NORA ANYWAY?
(RYU AND FRIENDS, HYOGO PREFECTURE,)

A : IN HUMAN YEARS...

RIVAN: 27
BAJEE: 31
LEONARD: 32
OSERU: 25
BARIK: 25
KILLIE: 24
ANISU: 26
RONAY: 24

NORA: 16
KAZUMA: 14 (AS OF VOLUME 4)
DARK LIEGE: FOREVER YOUNG
KAIN: ?
KNELL: 23
KEINI: 16
NICKS: 29
TYRON: 41

I'LL REVEAL OTHER CHARACTERS' AGES SOME OTHER TIME!

●●●●●● MORE LETTERS IN VOLUME 5 (PROBABLY).

SEND MAIL TO:
NORA EDITOR
VIZ MEDIA, LLC
P.O. BOX 77010
SAN FRANCISCO, CA 94107

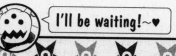

I'll be waiting!~♥

Staff Page

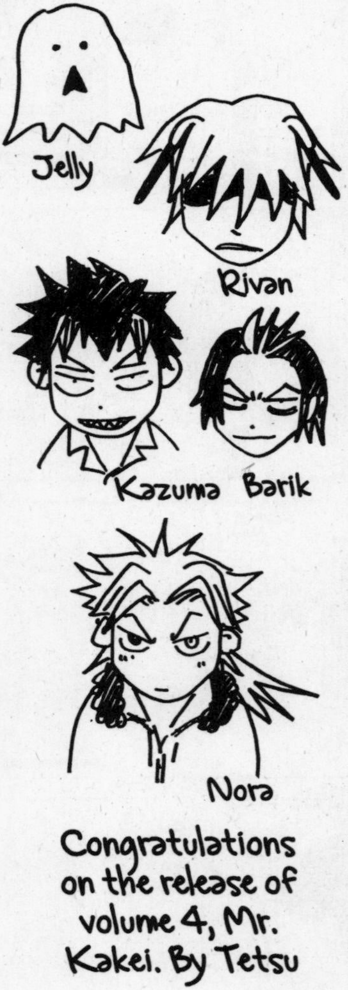
Jelly
Rivan
Kazuma
Barik
Nora
Congratulations on the release of volume 4, Mr. Kakei. By Tetsu

DRAWN BY HIRAKAWA, THE OVERSTRESSED ONE, WHO DREW THIS WHILE GROUSING, "I DON'T HAVE TIME FOR THIS!"

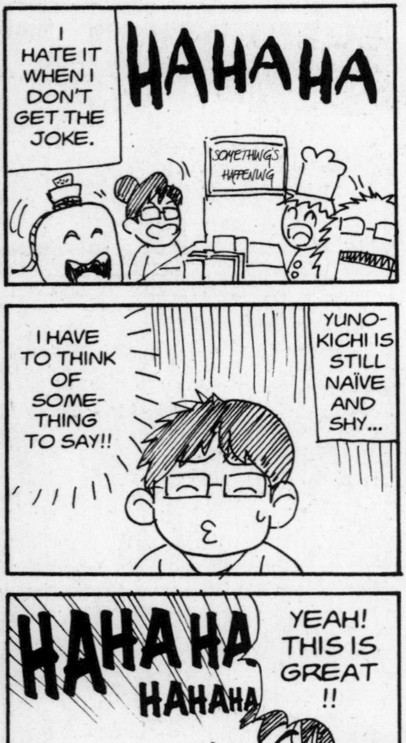
HAHAHA
I HATE IT WHEN I DON'T GET THE JOKE.
SOMETHING'S HAPPENING
YUNOKICHI IS STILL NAÏVE AND SHY...
I HAVE TO THINK OF SOMETHING TO SAY!!
YEAH! THIS IS GREAT!!
HAHAHA
HAHAHA
UH, YEAH, GREAT!!
WHY DON'T I EVER FIT IN?
YUNOKICHI, THE ORIGINAL SQUARE PEG IN THE ROUND HOLE.

DRAWN BY YUNOKICHI, THE OTHERWISE NICE GUY WHO ALWAYS MANAGES TO PUT HIS FOOT IN HIS MOUTH.

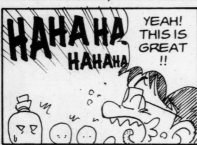

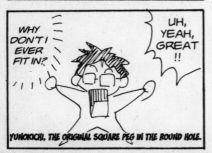

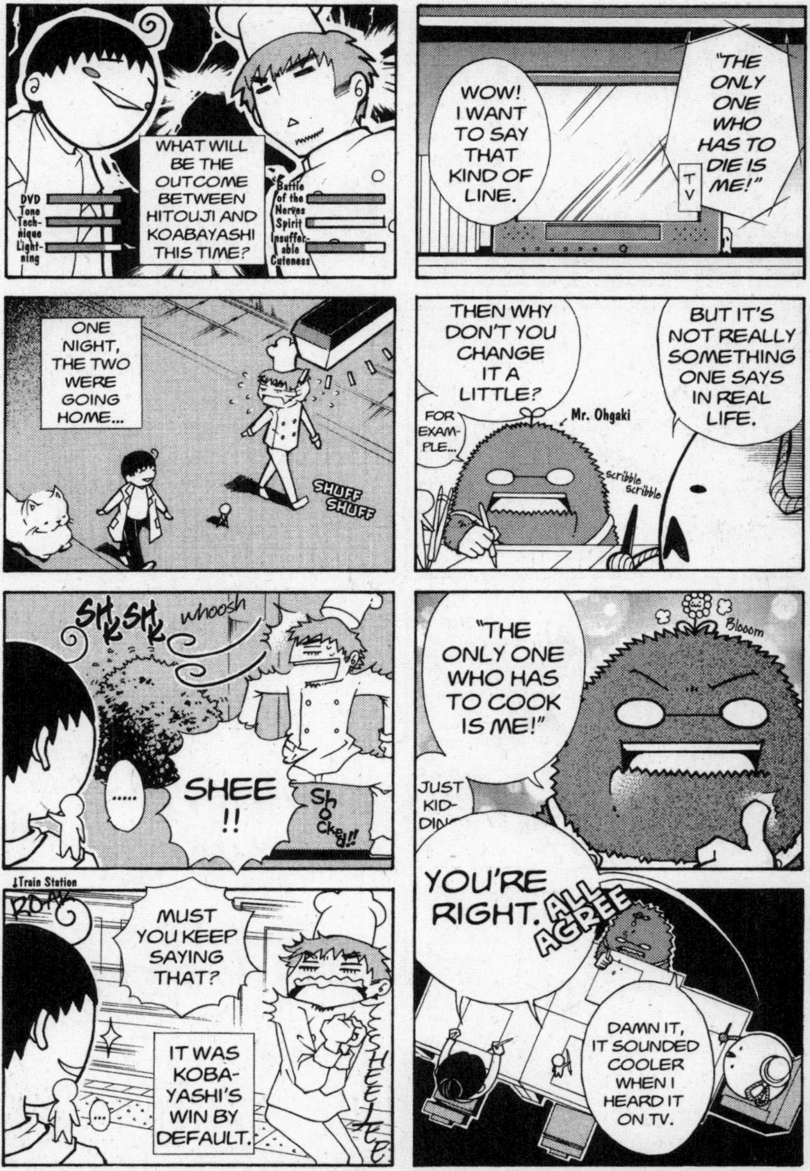
"THE ONLY ONE WHO HAS TO DIE IS ME!"
TV
WOW! I WANT TO SAY THAT KIND OF LINE.
BUT IT'S NOT REALLY SOMETHING ONE SAYS IN REAL LIFE.
THEN WHY DON'T YOU CHANGE IT A LITTLE?
Mr. Ohgaki
FOR EXAMPLE...
scribble scribble
Blooom
"THE ONLY ONE WHO HAS TO COOK IS ME!"
JUST KIDDING
YOU'RE RIGHT.
ALL AGREE
DAMN IT, IT SOUNDED COOLER WHEN I HEARD IT ON TV.
WHAT WILL BE THE OUTCOME BETWEEN HITOUJI AND KOABAYASHI THIS TIME?
Battle of the Nerves
Spirit
Insufferable Cuteness
DVD
Tone Technique
Lightning
ONE NIGHT, THE TWO WERE GOING HOME...
SHUFF SHUFF
SHK SHK
whoosh
SHEE !!
Shocked!!
......
↓Train Station
ROAR
MUST YOU KEEP SAYING THAT?
IT WAS KOBAYASHI'S WIN BY DEFAULT.
SHEEHEE
...

DRAWN BY SHIBAYAN, OUR WONDERFUL THUMBELINA WHO HAS STARTED MAKING DESSERTS FOR US AFTER SEEING ON TV THAT AGAR IS BETTER FOR YOU THAN SUGAR.

LANGUAGE BARRIER

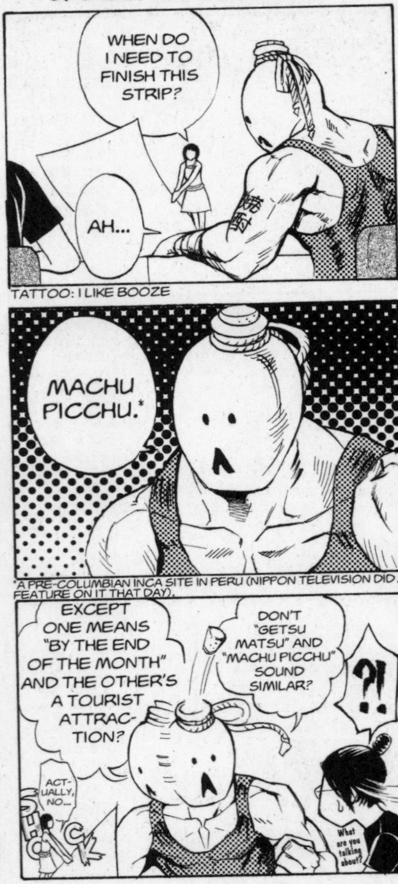
WHEN DO I NEED TO FINISH THIS STRIP?
AH...
TATTOO: I LIKE BOOZE
MACHU PICCHU.*
*A PRE-COLUMBIAN INCA SITE IN PERU (NIPPON TELEVISION DID A FEATURE ON IT THAT DAY).
?!
DON'T "GETSU MATSU" AND "MACHU PICCHU" SOUND SIMILAR?
What are you talking about?
EXCEPT ONE MEANS "BY THE END OF THE MONTH" AND THE OTHER'S A TOURIST ATTRACTION?
ACTUALLY, NO...
SHOCK
IGNORE HIM!!
"MACHU PICCHU," "GETSU MATSU."
C'MON, THEY SOUND ALIKE!
IGNORE HIM, SHIBAYAN!!
CRUSH
IF ONLY I COULD...!

THE GREAT OUTDOORS

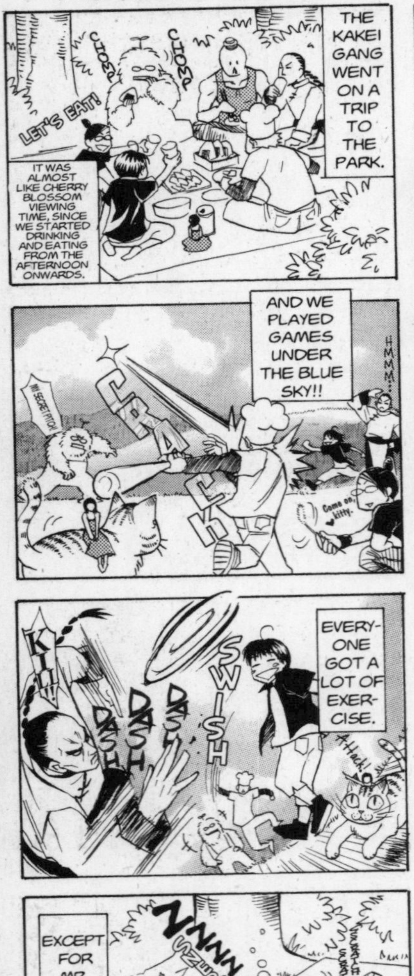
THE KAKEI GANG WENT ON A TRIP TO THE PARK.
CHOMP
CHOMP
LET'S EAT!
IT WAS ALMOST LIKE CHERRY BLOSSOM VIEWING TIME, SINCE WE STARTED DRINKING AND EATING FROM THE AFTERNOON ONWARDS.
AND WE PLAYED GAMES UNDER THE BLUE SKY!!
HMMM...
MY SECRET PITCH!
CRACK
Come on, kitty.
EVERYONE GOT A LOT OF EXERCISE.
SWISH
Attack!
DASH DASH DASH
KILL!!
EXCEPT FOR MR. KAKEI.
NNNN
SCRATCH SCRATCH
Got it!

DRAWN BY: YOSHINON, THE BEAUTY QUEEN WITH THE VICIOUS TONGUE FOR EVERYONE BUT MACHO GUYS AND MADMEN (BECAUSE THEY'RE HER TYPE).

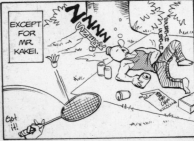

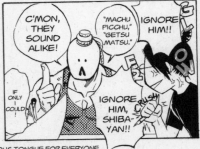

THANKS, EVERYONE!

SEE THE PREVIOUS PAGE.

BECAUSE I WAS SAYING I WANTED TO BECOME MORE MACHO, YOSHINON DREW ME TO LOOK LIKE A HE-MAN.

It's the exact opposite of me in many ways.

HELLO TO EVERYBODY WHO BOUGHT VOLUME 4. THIS IS YOUR PUNY CREATOR, KAZUNARI KAKEI.

IT WAS THE START OF A NEW PHASE FOR ME AS WELL BECAUSE MY EDITOR IN CHIEF AND MANGA EDITOR CHANGED AT THE SAME TIME.

Thank you for helping me.

About Nora's past and Kazuma's decision.

THIS VOLUME MARKS NORA'S SECOND YEAR OF SERIALIZATION AND THE STORY REACHES A TURNING POINT...

I ESPECIALLY WANT TO THANK THOSE FANS WHO HAVE SENT ME LETTERS AND EVEN PRESENTS.

Although it's not possible to write a reply to everybody, I'll do my best.

I'M REALLY THANKFUL FOR THE PEOPLE WHO HAVE CHEERED ME ON.

ALTHOUGH I STILL LACK EXPERIENCE, I WANT TO CONTINUE WORKING HARD SO THAT THE STORY AND I CAN GROW TOGETHER.

Thank you very much!

NORA IS MY FIRST MANGA AND ALSO A RECORD OF MY GROWTH AS A CREATOR.

覚一成
2005/07
Kazunari Kakei 07/2005

BALANCED DIET

I CAN'T DO ANYTHING ABOUT THE FIRST THREE...

THE CAUSE MIGHT BE FATIGUE, LACK OF SLEEP, STRESS... OR EVEN DIET.

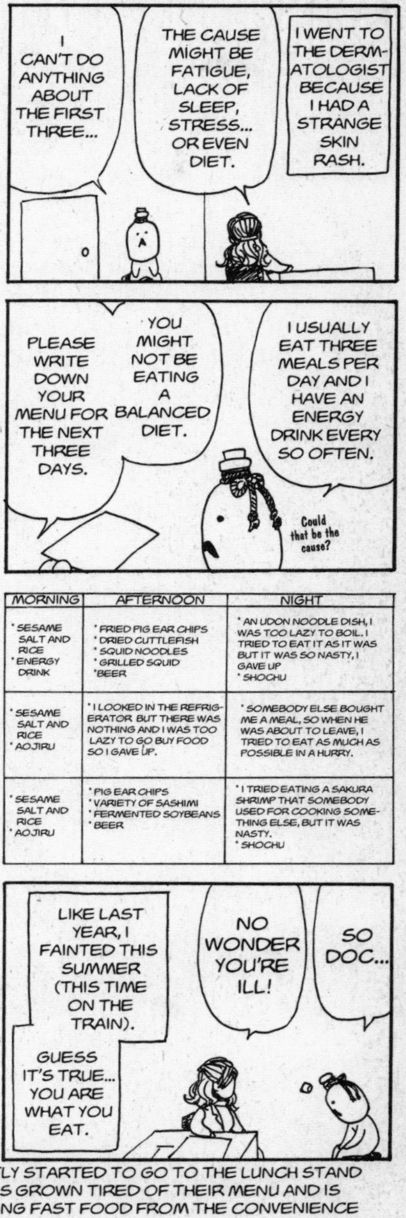

I WENT TO THE DERMATOLOGIST BECAUSE I HAD A STRANGE SKIN RASH.

PLEASE WRITE DOWN YOUR MENU FOR THE NEXT THREE DAYS.

YOU MIGHT NOT BE EATING A BALANCED DIET.

I USUALLY EAT THREE MEALS PER DAY AND I HAVE AN ENERGY DRINK EVERY SO OFTEN.

Could that be the cause?

MORNING	AFTERNOON	NIGHT
* SESAME SALT AND RICE * ENERGY DRINK	* FRIED PIG EAR CHIPS * DRIED CUTTLEFISH * SQUID NOODLES * GRILLED SQUID * BEER	* AN UDON NOODLE DISH, I WAS TOO LAZY TO BOIL. I TRIED TO EAT IT AS IT WAS BUT IT WAS SO NASTY, I GAVE UP * SHOCHU
* SESAME SALT AND RICE * AOJIRU	* I LOOKED IN THE REFRIGERATOR BUT THERE WAS NOTHING AND I WAS TOO LAZY TO GO BUY FOOD SO I GAVE UP.	* SOMEBODY ELSE BOUGHT ME A MEAL, SO WHEN HE WAS ABOUT TO LEAVE, I TRIED TO EAT AS MUCH AS POSSIBLE IN A HURRY.
* SESAME SALT AND RICE * AOJIRU	* PIG EAR CHIPS * VARIETY OF SASHIMI * FERMENTED SOYBEANS * BEER	* I TRIED EATING A SAKURA SHRIMP THAT SOMEBODY USED FOR COOKING SOMETHING ELSE, BUT IT WAS NASTY. * SHOCHU

LIKE LAST YEAR, I FAINTED THIS SUMMER (THIS TIME ON THE TRAIN).

GUESS IT'S TRUE... YOU ARE WHAT YOU EAT.

NO WONDER YOU'RE ILL!

SO DOC...

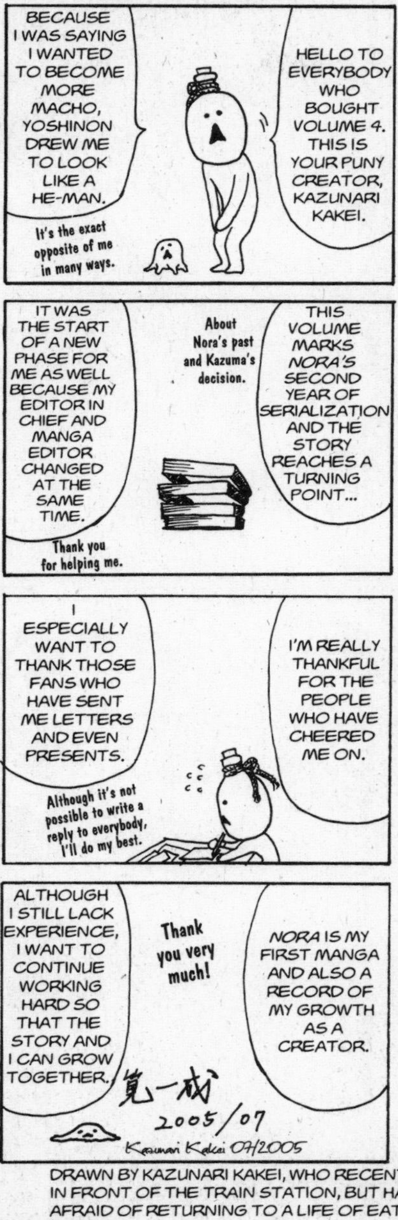

DRAWN BY KAZUNARI KAKEI, WHO RECENTLY STARTED TO GO TO THE LUNCH STAND IN FRONT OF THE TRAIN STATION, BUT HAS GROWN TIRED OF THEIR MENU AND IS AFRAID OF RETURNING TO A LIFE OF EATING FAST FOOD FROM THE CONVENIENCE STORE.

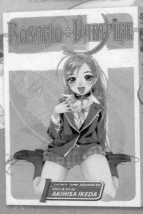

ROSARIO + VAMPIRE

TSUKUNE'S GOT SOME MONSTROUS GIRL PROBLEMS!

MANGA SERIES ON SALE NOW

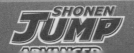

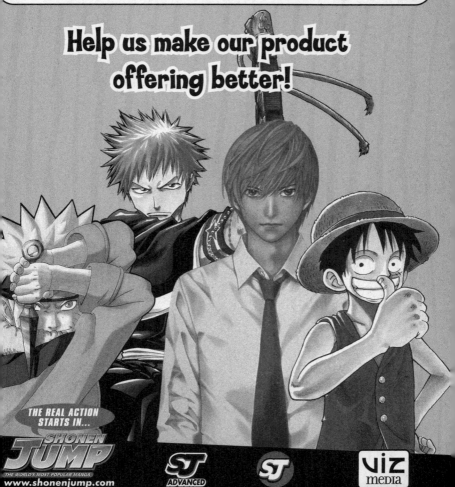

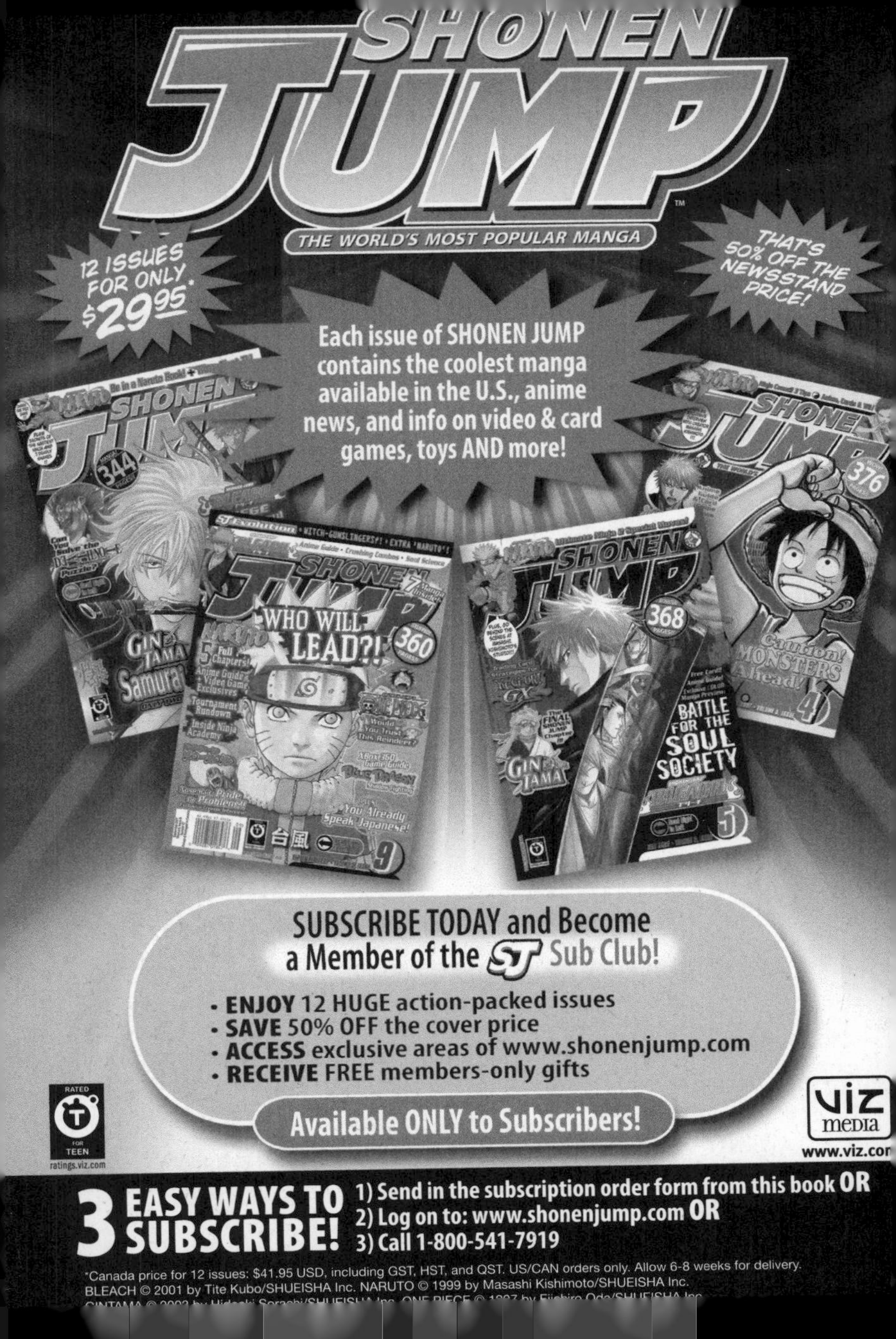

SHONEN JUMP™
THE WORLD'S MOST POPULAR MANGA
12 ISSUES FOR ONLY $29.95*
THAT'S 50% OFF THE NEWSSTAND PRICE!
Each issue of SHONEN JUMP contains the coolest manga available in the U.S., anime news, and info on video & card games, toys AND more!
SUBSCRIBE TODAY and Become a Member of the SJ Sub Club!
• ENJOY 12 HUGE action-packed issues
• SAVE 50% OFF the cover price
• ACCESS exclusive areas of www.shonenjump.com
• RECEIVE FREE members-only gifts
Available ONLY to Subscribers!
RATED T FOR TEEN
ratings.viz.com
VIZ media
www.viz.com
3 EASY WAYS TO SUBSCRIBE!
1) Send in the subscription order form from this book OR
2) Log on to: www.shonenjump.com OR
3) Call 1-800-541-7919
*Canada price for 12 issues: $41.95 USD, including GST, HST, and QST. US/CAN orders only. Allow 6-8 weeks for delivery.
BLEACH © 2001 by Tite Kubo/SHUEISHA Inc. NARUTO © 1999 by Masashi Kishimoto/SHUEISHA Inc.

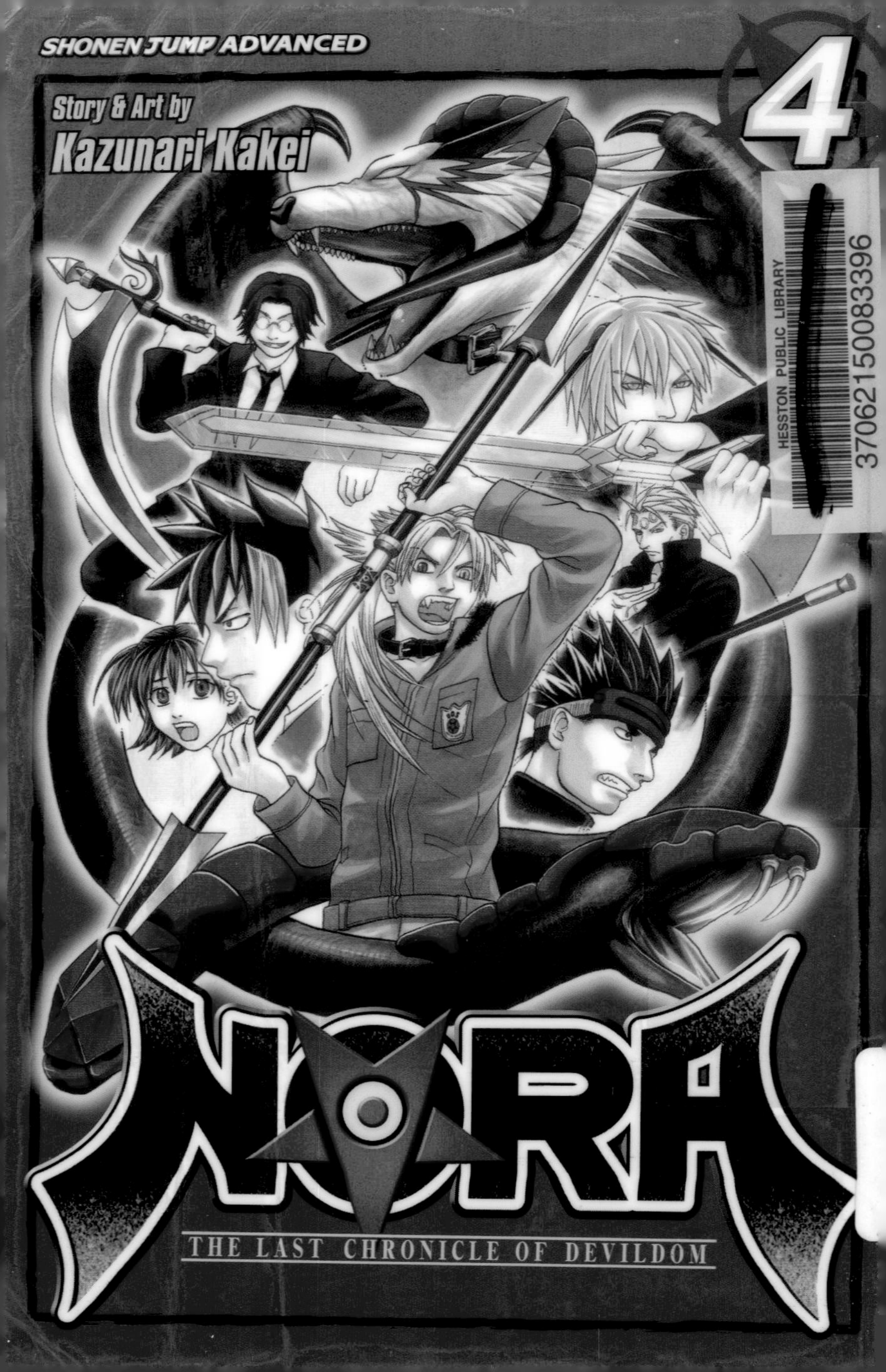
SHONEN JUMP ADVANCED
Story & Art by
Kazunari Kakei
4
NORA
THE LAST CHRONICLE OF DEVILDOM

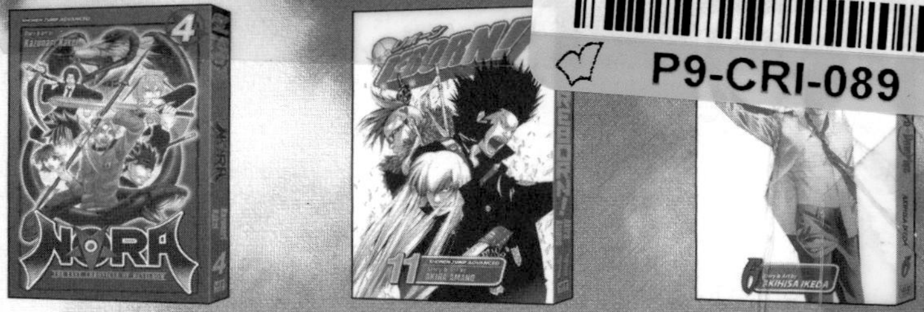

NORA
THE LAST CHRONICLE OF DEVILDOM
4
SHONEN JUMP ADVANCED
11
AKIRA AMANO
AKIHISA IKEDA

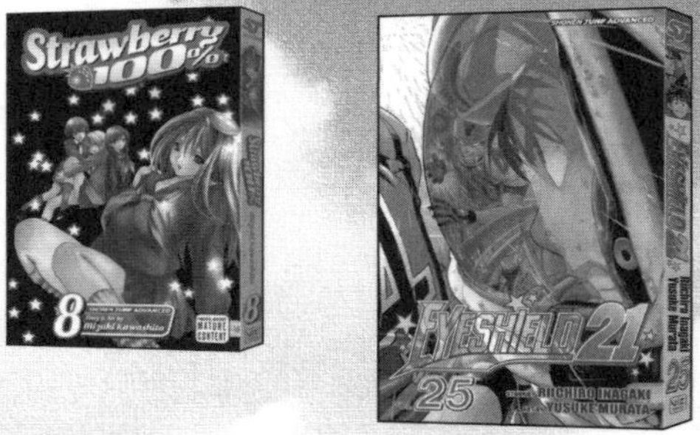

Strawberry 100%
8
SHONEN JUMP ADVANCED
Mizuki Kawashita
MATURE CONTENT
EYESHIELD 21
25
RIICHIRO INAGAKI
YUSUKE MURATA

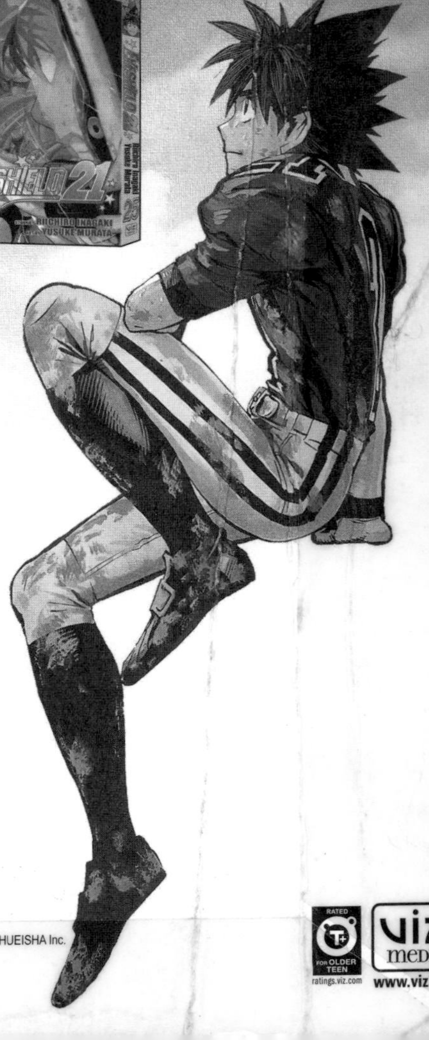

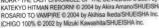